Marcus Tullius Cicero (106–43 BCE) introduced Romans to the major schools of Greek philosophy, forging a Latin conceptual vocabulary that was entirely new. But for all the sophistication of his thinking, it is perhaps for his political and oratorical career that Cicero is best remembered. He was the nemesis of Catiline, whose plot to overthrow the Republic he famously denounced to the Senate. He was the selfless politician who turned down the opportunity to join Julius Caesar and Pompey in their ruling triumvirate with Crassus. He was briefly Rome's leading man after Caesar's assassination in 44 BCE. And he was the great political orator whose bitter conflict with Mark Antony led to his own violent death in 43 BCE.

In her authoritative survey, Gesine Manuwald evokes the many faces of Cicero as well as his complexities and seeming contradictions. She focuses on his major works, allowing the great writer to speak for himself. Cicero's rich legacy is seen to endure in the works of Quintilian and the Church Fathers as well as in the speeches of Harry S. Truman and Barack Obama.

GESINE MANUWALD is Professor of Latin at University College London. She is the author of *Cicero, Philippics 3–9* (2007), *Roman Drama: A Reader* (2010) and *Roman Republican Theatre* (2011).

This zesty introduction is a welcome addition to the enormous bibliography on Cicero. Presenting the material thematically, rather than chronologically, Gesine Manuwald takes a fresh look at the life and career of the great Roman statesman and author. Her aim is to reach the 'real' Cicero, and in this she succeeds brilliantly. Manuwald begins her study with a discussion of Cicero's last years; in subsequent chapters she skilfully develops our understanding of 'Who was Cicero?' by presenting the themes of his life – oratory, philosophy, politics, literature, and so on – in a lively and engaging manner. Cicero's own words are the basis for her discussion in every chapter; she has chosen them well and explicated them clearly. The book concludes with an excellent chapter on the reception of Cicero from the time of his death to the present. A full and informative glossary, a useful bibliography and index are valuable additions. *Cicero* is a real pleasure to read, authoritative and charming at the same time, and I for one feel that I know Cicero better than ever for having read it. Students, scholars and the general public will too.

—Jane Crawford, Professor of Classics,
University of Virginia

UNDERSTANDING CLASSICS

EDITOR: RICHARD STONEMAN (UNIVERSITY OF EXETER)

When the great Roman poets of the Augustan Age – Ovid, Virgil and Horace – composed their odes, love poetry and lyrical verse, could they have imagined that their works would one day form a cornerstone of Western civilization, or serve as the basis of study for generations of schoolchildren learning Latin? Could Aeschylus or Euripides have envisaged the remarkable popularity of contemporary stagings of their tragedies? The legacy and continuing resonance of Homer's *Iliad* and *Odyssey* – Greek poetical epics written many millennia ago – again testify to the capacity of the classics to cross the divide of thousands of years and speak powerfully and relevantly to audiences quite different from those to which they were originally addressed.

Understanding Classics is a specially commissioned series which aims to introduce the outstanding authors and thinkers of antiquity to a wide audience of appreciative modern readers, whether undergraduate students of classics, literature, philosophy and ancient history or generalists interested in the classical world. Each volume – written by leading figures internationally – will examine the historical significance of the writer or writers in question; their social, political and cultural contexts; their use of language, literature and mythology; extracts from their major works; and their reception in later European literature, art, music and culture. *Understanding Classics* will build a library of readable, authoritative introductions offering fresh and elegant surveys of the greatest literatures, philosophies and poetries of the ancient world.

UNDERSTANDING CLASSICS

CICERO

Gesine Manuwald

UNDERSTANDING CLASSICS SERIES EDITOR:
RICHARD STONEMAN

Published in 2015 by I.B.Tauris & Co Ltd
6 Salem Road, London W2 4BU
175 Fifth Avenue, New York NY 10010
www.ibtauris.com

Distributed in the United States and Canada Exclusively by Palgrave Macmillan
175 Fifth Avenue, New York NY 10010

ISBN: 978 1 78076 401 6 (HB)
          978 1 78076 402 3 (PB)
eISBN: 978 0 85773 515 7

A full CIP record for this book is available from the British Library
A full CIP record is available from the Library of Congress

Library of Congress Catalog Card Number: available

Text design, typesetting and eBook versions by Tetragon, London

Printed and bound in Great Britain by T.J. International, Padstow, Cornwall

CONTENTS

ILLUSTRATIONS

PREFACE

Miss Blimber, too, although a slim and graceful maid, did no soft violence to the gravity of the house. There was no light nonsense about Miss Blimber. She kept her hair short and crisp, and wore spectacles. She was dry and sandy with working in the graves of deceased languages. None of your live languages for Miss Blimber. They must be dead – stone dead – and then Miss Blimber dug them up like a Ghoul.

Mrs Blimber, her mama, was not learned herself, but she pretended to be, and that did quite as well. She said at evening parties, that if she could have known Cicero, she thought she could have died contented. [...]

'But really,' pursued Mrs Blimber, 'I think if I could have known Cicero, and been his friend, and talked with him in his retirement at Tusculum (beautiful Tusculum!), I could have died contented.'

THIS EXTRACT FROM *Dombey and Son* (1848) by Charles Dickens (1812–70)[1] shows that the name of 'Cicero', because it is so widely known, may appear in unexpected circumstances, even in a novel, and may carry a lot of baggage, symbolizing learning (with or without justification). Part of the problem of getting a more precise idea of Cicero as a person and as a writer and of going beyond name-dropping is that the language he wrote in is indeed 'dead', and it will remain Mrs Blimber's dream to meet him at his favourite retreat outside Rome and talk to him. While this book cannot bring Cicero (and his language) back to life or enable readers to enter into a proper conversation with him, it aims to present a vivid portrait of the key aspects of the life and works of Marcus Tullius Cicero (106–43 BCE); this is why it gives ample room to his own words (in English), so that there is at least a basis for a kind of 'dialogue'.

Since there is so much evidence about Cicero, inevitably every treatment is selective, presenting a particular point of view. This book tries to introduce Cicero's life and works by focusing on themes rather than chronology, by providing paradigmatic examples instead of a comprehensive overview and by including a brief summary of the changing reception of him and his writings from antiquity until the present day. There will be less emphasis on historical facts and the technical aspects of rhetoric and philosophy and more of a focus on the question of how the different facets of his life and activities combine to create the interesting individual known as 'Cicero'.

Several friends and colleagues took the time to read through a draft of this book or parts of it, particularly Bernard Danson and Kathryn Tempest. The volume has benefited enormously from their helpful comments, and I would like to thank them all for their advice and assistance. However, they should not be held responsible for any faults that remain.

In addition, I am especially grateful to Richard Stoneman and Alex Wright at I.B.Tauris for encouraging me to write this book and for their support throughout, as well as to the production and copy-editing team for their expert help in seeing the book through the final stages of the publication process.

G.M., LONDON, JANUARY 2014

INTRODUCTION: WHO IS CICERO?

MARCUS TULLIUS CICERO (106–43 BCE) continues to be one of the most famous figures from classical antiquity: many people are familiar with his name and have vague ideas about or specific views on his personality and his writings. Therefore, few ask the question 'Who is Cicero?' and pursue in greater detail the questions of what his life and works were like. On the contrary, assessments of him as a 'stylish writer of Latin', a 'deft politician', an 'egotist and weak person', a 'gifted orator', a 'great philosopher' or an 'imitator of the Greeks' are handed down without being checked.

This book will consider aspects of the question of how these perceptions came about and try to contribute to a balanced understanding of Cicero by looking at his life and writings from a variety of angles, giving due prominence to primary sources. On this basis it may be possible to establish a (relatively) nuanced portrait, owing to the exceptionally large amount of available evidence about him and his time (which consists mainly of his own writings).

Cicero produced items in different literary genres, often working on several pieces simultaneously, though the various types of writings are not spread evenly across his career since they also respond to the changing contemporary situation. He was actively involved in political developments as a magistrate as well as a forensic and political orator, during a period of Roman history when the continuation of the Roman Republican system of government was at risk. His speeches, a number of which were written up and circulated after the event, not only demonstrate their political importance, but also convey a portrait of Cicero as a politician and orator. Moreover, he was a great letter writer, and a collection of his letters was published later. But his publications are not limited to topical issues: Cicero was also concerned with rhetorical and philosophical questions, which he discussed in theoretical treatises. In addition, he wrote poetry. Since many of Cicero's writings survive in complete or fragmentary form, a lot can be said about his life and works; correspondingly there is a wide range of scholarly and popular publications.

For obvious reasons, many comprehensive treatments of Cicero follow a biographical, linear–chronological approach and/or focus on his output, discussing it according to genres and/or periods of his life. This book attempts to offer a different perspective on Cicero; it starts with a look at the figure of Cicero as a coherent whole: since many of his characteristic thoughts and modes of behaviour can be seen particularly clearly at the end of his life, this volume begins with a description of his political and literary activities during his final years. It then goes on to sketch the developments that led to his standing in Rome with respect to his career as a politician and writer, to present his political philosophy, to survey his interventions as an orator and his views on rhetoric, to consider his attitude to philosophical issues and to look at his thoughts on literature and his literary style. Cicero's activities and ideas in all these fields are closely linked, but for reasons of presentation they are discussed over separate chapters, complemented by a section offering a tentative look at his personality. Once a portrait of Cicero in his own time has been sketched, the penultimate chapter can set this against views of him that have developed over subsequent centuries, from his death until the present day, highlighting telling examples of engagement with his life and works. On this basis the final chapter tries to answer the question raised at the start of this introductory section: 'Who is Cicero?'

Cicero's lifetime during the first century BCE, the last decades of the

Roman Republic, is one of the most eventful and best-documented phases of Roman history. A significant part of the evidence for this period comes from Cicero's own writings. Hence there is the risk of circular argument and of being taken in by one individual's views. More importantly, Cicero's writings were not intended to give a factual account of current circumstances, but were composed in particular situations, pursuing specific aims, be it persuading the Senate or the popular assembly of the adoption of a policy or a jury of the innocence of the accused in speeches, promoting tenets of philosophy in treatises or arguing with individuals in letters. In all cases Cicero is likely to have considered ways of creating a portrayal of himself. Accordingly, from a historical point of view, not everything Cicero says can be taken at face value. Still, since Cicero was speaking to contemporaries, it is unlikely that he changed facts completely, but he will have presented them in his own selection and interpretation (consciously or unconsciously). Cicero's understanding and presentation of matters can be illuminating, but it must be distinguished from establishing historical 'facts'.

Further evidence about Cicero and the intellectual and literary culture of his time can be gained from reactions of contemporaries, many of whom were acquainted with him. Reflections of their views can be found in Cicero's comments on standpoints of others in all his writings as well as in his epistolary, which contains almost 100 letters from others to Cicero; beyond that, of particular relevance are learned treatises by the polymath M. Terentius Varro, one of Cicero's friends (116–27 BCE); the love poems and political poetry of Catullus (c.86–56 BCE), who addresses one of his poems (49) to Cicero; the biographical sketches of famous Greek and Roman men, for instance of Cicero's friend Atticus, by Cornelius Nepos (c.100–24 BCE); the didactic poem on Epicurean philosophy by Lucretius (c.96–55 BCE), a pioneer of Roman philosophical writing like Cicero, and the report on the Gallic and the subsequent civil wars by C. Iulius Caesar (100–44 BCE), whose appointment as dictator for life and subsequent assassination triggered the change from Republic to principate.

The historical events during Cicero's lifetime were later treated by C. Sallustius Crispus (86–34 BCE) in his work on the Catilinarian

Conspiracy of 63 BCE, and more comprehensively by Appian of Alexandreia (*c.*90/95–165 CE), Cassius Dio Cocceianus (*c.*164–235 CE) and Plutarch (*c.*45–125 CE; *Life of Cicero* and biographies of contemporary figures) in their historiographical and biographical works (in Greek); some details also appear in the Epitome (*c.* fourth century CE) of T. Livius' history of Rome (59 BCE–17 CE) and in the works of the Greek Nicolaus of Damascus (b. *c.*60 BCE; *Life of Augustus*) as well as of Velleius Paterculus (20/19 BCE– after 30 CE) and Florus (first/second century CE). These writers were not eyewitnesses to the events and were active at (sometimes significantly) later dates; therefore they may have been influenced by Cicero's writings and the Ciceronian tradition developed from them and do not necessarily present a more reliable account.

In this book the primary sources provided will mainly be Cicero's texts, but they will be interpreted with due caution and hence be used as a means of showing Cicero's views. Thereby readers will get a taste of most of Cicero's works and be in a position to judge Cicero for themselves. To make the text more readable, all quotations from Cicero's works are given in English translation only (except for one intended to illustrate Cicero's style as well as Latin keywords throughout); the passages are clearly identified, and information on editions of the Latin texts and on commentaries is given in the select bibliography at the end of this volume. The bibliography also lists a selection of modern works of secondary literature, to which no specific references will be made (see also 'Note on Sources and Abbreviations').

Key dates of Cicero's biography and the titles and dates of his works have been collated in tabular form in a section at the end of this volume; a brief narrative biography can be found in Chapter II. Since the book focuses on the figure of Cicero, discussions of the situation in the late Republic have been kept to a minimum and have only been included where relevant to a better understanding of details of Cicero's life. A glossary at the end of the volume presents brief explanations of historical figures and technical terms connected with the Roman Republic; it offers information on important concepts and their relationship to Cicero's life and works.

I

CULMINATION OF
A LIFE IN POLITICS
AND WRITING

BORN IN 106 BCE, Cicero became one of the two consuls for 63 BCE, the highest elected magistrates of the Roman Republic. Afterwards he was politically sidelined for long periods, particularly during his exile in 58–57 BCE and later during the civil war in 49–45 BCE. Yet Cicero made an impressive return to the stage of Republican Rome for a final appearance in the last two years of his life (44–43 BCE): after the assassination of the dictator (C. Iulius) Caesar (100–44 BCE) on the Ides of March (15 March) 44 BCE, until his own assassination on 7 December 43 BCE, he led a political and rhetorical campaign in response to the claims to power by the young Octavian (63 BCE–14 CE; the future emperor Augustus; fig. 1.1) and Mark Antony (82–30 BCE; the remaining consul of 44 BCE; fig. 1.2).

Cicero was aware that these activities might cause his death,[1] but he was happy to take the risk, making an attempt at freeing and saving the Republic, as he maintained he had done as consul.[2] Although he was often uncertain and afraid, as, in particular, his letters to Atticus reveal, being involved in

1.1   Gold coin (*aureus*) of Octavian (Roman,
28 BCE, probably minted in Asia Minor).

SIDE A: head of Octavian; Latin legend: IMP CAESAR DIVI F COS VI
('Emperor Caesar, son of the divine [i.e. Iulius Caesar], consul for the sixth time').

SIDE B: Octavian seated in a toga, holding out a scroll; Latin legend:
LEGES ET IVRA P[OPVLO] R[OMANO] RESTITVIT ('he
has restored the laws and rights to the Roman People').

political life at the highest level was what he always aimed for. Since the
position of an influential ex-consul had been denied to him for many years,
he relished the opportunity to take centre stage in 44–43 BCE and to try
to preserve what he regarded as the traditional and ideal political system
of the Roman Republic.

Politically speaking, after Caesar's assassination, in which Cicero was
not involved, but of which he approved, there was a kind of power vacuum.
Since of the two consuls of that year only Caesar had been killed, Cicero
believed that the job had only been half-done: the praetors (the magistrates
just below the consuls) and leading conspirators, M. Iunius Brutus and
C. Cassius Longinus, could not take decisive action while Mark Antony,
the surviving consul, tried to exploit the situation and the young Octavian
laid claim to the legacy of his adoptive father, C. Iulius Caesar.[3]

Cicero was unhappy with this unclear and potentially dangerous situation and at first was unsure about the best course of action: he did not
know whom to side with.[4] Eventually, he decided to enter into a temporary

coalition with Octavian, since he thought him to be the lesser evil, to fight against and eliminate Mark Antony, which would allow a return to the traditional Republican structure. Some of Cicero's friends were sceptical about Octavian from the outset,[5] but Cicero admitted only at the very end that he had misjudged Octavian.[6]

Due to the uncertain political situation, Cicero initially left Rome after Caesar's death; he then became all the more active after his return in autumn 44 BCE.[7] At this point Cicero was a senior ex-consul, whose views would be sought at an early stage in a Senate debate, but he did not hold a political office with executive power and did not command a military force. Therefore the only way to have an effect on political developments was to persuade audiences (especially the Senate) by his oratory, thereby prompting them to agree initiatives he regarded as necessary and appropriate. Cicero was conscious of the uneven nature of the fight and knew that he was fighting with 'words against weapons' (*Fam.* 12.22.1). Yet as consul he had rejoiced in being 'a single civilian – myself – as [...] leader and commander' (*Cat.* 2.28; 3.23), that is, sorting out political unrest without military confrontations, and he was still one of the foremost orators in Rome. So fighting in this way was familiar territory (as Cicero did not get tired of pointing out), and there was at least a chance of success.

1.2   Red jasper intaglio of Mark Antony (Roman, *c.*40–30 BCE).

Cicero's public interventions in this period are documented by a group of orations called *Philippics*, which have survived and were presumably selected for dissemination from a larger number of speeches made by him during those months. As his letters reveal,[8] the title was selected by Cicero himself and was not chosen factually, but rather ideologically, to indicate a connection with the cycle of *Philippics* delivered by the Greek orator Demosthenes (384–322 BCE) in a conflict with Philip, king of Macedon, in the mid fourth century BCE. Demosthenes was not only a paradigmatic orator for Romans of Cicero's time, mentioned with praise in Cicero's rhetorical treatises,[9] but, as Cicero says with respect to his own consular speeches, he also provided an example of an orator having 'turned away from this argumentative, forensic type of oratory to appear in the more elevated role of statesman' (*Att.* 2.1.3). Presumably this is how Cicero too wanted to appear on the basis of his consular speeches and later of his *Philippics*. The published versions of these speeches spread Cicero's political views and proposed strategy to a wider audience, beyond those who had listened to the oral versions.

Cicero's *Philippics* are now a group of 14 speeches, while Demosthenes' *Philippics* in a broader sense (not just the speeches entitled 'Against Philip', but all the pieces composed in this context) seem to have been a group of 12 in ancient editions. It is therefore likely that *Philippics* 3–14 are meant to be Cicero's *Philippics* in the strict sense: these speeches were delivered after Antony had left Rome and argue for a clear, single purpose. *Philippics* 1–2, given under slightly different circumstances, were presumably added to the collection later because of the similarity of context.

Cicero's awareness of the precariousness of his situation and his determination to speak up in the interest of the Republic are highlighted already at the end of *Philippic* 1, the speech given on 2 September 44 BCE at the start of the open campaign against Mark Antony, just after Cicero's return to Rome. While the oration is certainly intended to rouse the senators, the underlying feeling that this is a decisive moment seems genuine (*Phil.* 1.38):

> Members of the Senate, I am well rewarded for my return [i.e. to Rome] inasmuch as whatever chance may now befall, my words will stand as a witness to my steadfast purpose; and you have given me a courteous

and attentive hearing. If I have the opportunity to address you more frequently without danger to you or myself, I shall take advantage of it. If not, I shall, to the best of my ability, preserve my life, not so much for myself as for the Republic. For myself, I have lived pretty well long enough, whether in years or in glory. If more is to come, it will come not so much for me as for you and for the Republic.

Since oratory was Cicero's only weapon, and he had considerable experience of using it, he was able to deploy it drawing on all aspects of the art. Over this period Cicero made speeches in the Senate to provoke his fellow senators into passing particular decrees; with the Senate effectively the executive, this was the most promising way of pushing through the intended measures. In addition, Cicero appeared before the popular assembly to report on senatorial decrees and to create a supportive atmosphere for his policies. So, after the first Senate decree backing his policy on 20 December 44 BCE, Cicero conveyed this as a great success to the popular assembly later in the day, opening the speech as follows (*Phil.* 4.1–3):

> Your extraordinary numbers, Men of Rome, and the size of this meeting, larger than any I can remember, fills me with a lively eagerness to defend the Republic and with hope of regaining it. [...] For today, Men of Rome, in case you think we have been transacting some business of minor importance, the groundwork has been laid for future operations. For Antonius has been pronounced a public enemy by the senate – in actuality, though not yet in words. [2] Now it much emboldens me, this loud and unanimous agreement from you that he *is* a public enemy. And after all, Men of Rome, there is no way out of it: either those who have raised armies against a consul are traitors, or he against whom arms have rightfully been taken up is an enemy. This doubt, therefore, the senate has today eliminated – not that any doubt existed, but in case there could be any. Gaius Caesar [i.e. Octavian], who has protected and is protecting the Republic and your freedom with his zeal, judgment, even his patrimony, has been honored by the senate's highest commendations. [3] I commend, I commend you, Men of Rome, for saluting

> in heartfelt gratitude the name of an illustrious young man, or rather
> boy; for his deeds belong to immortality, the name is a matter of age.

Cicero tells the audience that Antony has effectively, although not formally, been declared a public enemy. Having Antony declared a public enemy (*hostis*) was Cicero's long-term goal, but he knew that it would not be possible at this stage to talk the senators into doing so (it was only decreed about four months later). Therefore, in the Senate meeting preceding this speech to the People Cicero moved that the unauthorized military actions of Decimus Brutus and Octavian be acknowledged and that they and their legions be commended.[10] Indirectly, this amounts to a condemnation of Antony's deeds, but in the motion (and thus in the subsequent Senate decree) nothing is said about Antony; interpreting this statement as a declaration of Antony as a public enemy is therefore a strong inference. Cicero cleverly uses the speech to the People to promote this interpretation of the first step as decisive; he will then be able to build on this in subsequent speeches.

Although this excerpt comes from a speech, by the arrangement of his comments Cicero has it appear as if there were reactions from the audience and that they showed approval and agreement with what he had just said or was about to say. This technique, which makes full use of the performance situation in the Roman Forum, creates a strong bond between speaker and audience, triggers feelings of unity and unanimity and establishes the notion that a spokesman voices what the members of the group have been thinking all along, rather than that a view is imposed upon them. Irrespective of what the atmosphere in the Roman Forum on that day was actually like, this (written) version of the speech disseminated after the event conveys to a wider audience the impression of general agreement with Cicero's assessment of the protagonists in the fight and of the appropriate measures to be taken; in addition, it creates the sense of a momentous occasion in the history of Rome as evidenced by the great interest among citizens.

While Cicero seems to have believed that he was pursuing the most promising course in the interest of the Republic, his private letters from that period (in contrast to his speeches) show that he was not so sure of the validity of the arguments he used in public to achieve the desired effect on the audience: for instance, at his first mention in the *Philippics* the young Octavian is praised excessively as an almost divine being,[11] while in roughly contemporary letters Cicero expresses doubts as to whether Octavian can be trusted as a true Republican (given his connections to Caesar) and will have military success.[12] In public, such reservations had to be ignored, so as not to invalidate the policy promoted: once Cicero had decided to work with Octavian against Mark Antony, only the latter was presented in a negative light.

Like earlier political struggles, Cicero describes this confrontation as a fight between the entire populace and a single, completely unacceptable individual; this person, Mark Antony, is isolated, and the whole matter is sketched with black-and-white contrasts. The underlying assumption is that, if this one troublesome and disreputable character is eliminated, a return to the traditional structure will be possible. Although Cicero knew that the men he opposed had followers, he did not address these conflicts as a contrast between different groups, nor did he see potential problems inherent in the Roman political system or take into account that exceptional situations may have long-lasting consequences even after the men responsible have been removed.

The most important of his earlier fights in Cicero's view was the confrontation with the patrician L. Sergius Catilina in his consular year (63 BCE). Accordingly, he compares Antony and Catiline several times in the *Philippics*[13] and claims that he has been fighting against public enemies for 20 years (i.e. 63–43 BCE). The most prominent expression of this view is the beginning of *Philippic* 2, written in September/October 44 BCE (*Phil.* 2.1–2):

> To what destiny of mine, Members of the Senate, should I ascribe the fact that in these twenty years there was never an enemy of the Republic who did not at the same time declare war on me too? There is no need for me to mention any names. Consult your own memories. Those persons have paid me penalties greater than I should have desired. It surprises me, Antonius, that you do not dread the fate of those whose actions you imitate. In other cases I was less surprised by this

phenomenon, for none of those people became my enemy by choice; they were all challenged by me for the sake of the Republic. Whereas you, against whom I did not even say a word, have assailed me with unprovoked abuse, as though you wished to look more reckless than Catiline and madder than Clodius [i.e. another of Cicero's earlier enemies], reckoning that your alienation from me would recommend you to disloyal citizens. [2] What else am I to think? That I am held in contempt? I really fail to see anything in my life, my connections, my public record, or such modest talent as I possess, for Antonius to despise. Perhaps he thought that the senate was the place where I could most easily be disparaged? Well, this body has given many famous Romans its testimonials of good service to the Republic rendered in positions of responsibility: only to me has it given one for saving it. Can it be that he wished to meet me in an oratorical duel? That is kind of him. Could I find any richer or more rewarding theme than in defending myself and attacking Antonius? No, it must be as I said: he did not think people like himself would accept him as an enemy of his native land unless he was an enemy of mine.

Here Cicero presents himself as a victim, who has suffered on behalf of the Republic, since all these threatening characters decided to oppose him; at the same time he characterizes himself as a representative of the Republic taking all possible steps to defend and maintain it, since he interprets all these confrontations as conflicts of principle. As for Antony, Cicero highlights that, while he is a danger to the Republic and an opponent of Cicero like the others, there is less reason for him to act as he does since he has not been challenged. Cicero concludes that Antony felt that he needed to be an enemy of Cicero if he wanted to be seen as an enemy of his native land, in view of the history of Cicero's relationship with the Republic, as he is singled out as its saviour. By attributing this view to his opponent, Cicero can convey the intended image of himself more forcefully.

One key feature of the Roman Republic, which Cicero again regarded as endangered, first by Caesar (as dictator) and then by Antony, is the freedom of the citizens. Therefore Cicero ended another speech to the People on the first days of January 43 BCE with a passionate appeal to fight and die for freedom as a characteristic of the Roman People (*Phil.* 6.19):

> It is against divine law for the Roman people to be enslaved, since the immortal gods willed that they rule over all nations. The ultimate crisis is upon us; freedom is at stake. Either you must be victorious, Men of Rome, as you surely will be thanks to your patriotism and your strong united will, or – anything but slavery. Other nations can endure servitude, but the birthright of the Roman people is freedom.

Because Cicero felt determined to ensure freedom and to 'preserve' the Republic, the single individual who threatened it had to be eliminated. Since in Cicero's view this person could only be removed by military action (because of his character and the situation), he argued for immediate war even though this contradicted his earlier and well-known attitude,[14] which he felt obliged to justify,[15] and also the general assumption that peace is more agreeable than war (*Phil.* 13.1–5; 20 March 43 BCE):

> From the outset of this war, Members of the Senate, which we have undertaken against traitorous and wicked citizens, I have been afraid that a seductive proposal of peace might quell enthusiasm for the recovery of freedom. Even the name of peace is sweet; the reality beneficial, as well as agreeable. For a man who delights in strife and the slaughter of his countrymen and civil war surely holds dear neither private hearths nor public laws nor the rights of liberty. Such a man, I think, ought to be excluded from membership in the human race, banished beyond the confines of human nature. [...] [2] [...] There is no fouler thing than such a citizen, such a man, if he is to be deemed a citizen or a man, who desires a civil war. But one point has to be considered at the outset, Members of the Senate: is peace with all men possible, or is there such a thing as an inexpiable war, in which a pact of peace is a prescription for slavery? [...] But what of the present? Can there be peace with the Antonii [i.e. Mark Antony and his brothers]? [...] [5] [...] What peace can there be with him [i.e. Mark Antony]? If he were a foreign enemy,

> such a thing would scarcely be possible after such doings, but it would
> be carried off somehow or other. There would be seas, mountains, wide
> tracts of land to separate us. One would hate him without seeing him.
> But these fellows will cling to our sight and, when they get the chance,
> be at our throats.

Cicero admits that peace is generally desirable, but only if it is 'real' peace, which is not possible with all kinds of people. He argues that there can never be peace with individuals like Antony and his brothers, who have turned towards their own countrymen; they would be unbearable as citizens and cannot be trusted. In Cicero's argument this leads again to the conclusion that these enemies have to be eliminated by war,[16] but also that the war he is pursuing is essentially caused by them.

Though Cicero intended to re-establish the traditional form of the Republic he approved of, he nevertheless regarded individual initiatives and special measures (even going against Republican conventions) as justified, legitimized by his view of the clash with Antony as an exceptional temporary situation (a concept anticipated in *De re publica* 2.46). Therefore Cicero allowed men fighting on his side to be 'their own Senate', that is, to take their own decisions and not to wait for official authorization from the Senate: as long as they took what Cicero believed to be the right measures and did what was in line with his idea of the Republic, this was, according to him, appropriate in the circumstances. It is assumed that one would return to normal practice after the conflict. In this mood Cicero defended the military activities of M. Iunius Brutus and C. Cassius Longinus in 43 BCE (*Phil.* 11.26–28; second half of February 43 BCE):

> However, if Brutus finishes his business and reaches the conclusion
> that he will better serve the Republic if he pursues Dolabella [i.e. one
> of the consuls of 44 BCE, now declared a public enemy because of
> misbehaviour in a province] instead of remaining in Greece, he will
> act on his own initiative, as he has done hitherto, and not wait for
> the senate when there are so many trouble spots calling for immediate
> attention. [27] For both Brutus and Cassius [i.e. the assassins of Caesar]

have already been their own senate on a number of occasions. In such great and complete upheaval and confusion one must be guided by the circumstances, not by standard procedures. This will not be the first time for either Brutus or Cassius to regard the safety and freedom of their native land as the most sacred law and the best possible procedure. So if nothing were referred to us concerning the pursuit of Dolabella, I should still take it as the equivalent of a decree since there are eminent men, men of such valor, high standing, and nobility, whose armies in the one case are already known to us and in the other heard tell of. So did Brutus wait for our decrees when he knew our aims? For instead of going to Crete, his own province, he hastened to somebody else's, Macedonia. He considered as his everything which you would like to be yours. He raised new legions, took over old ones. He drew away Dolabella's cavalry to himself and by his personal decision judged him a public enemy, though not yet stained with so foul a murder. For were it otherwise, what right had he to draw cavalry away from a consul? [28] And did not Gaius Cassius, his equal in greatness of spirit and judgment, set out from Italy with the design of keeping Dolabella out of Syria? Under what law, by what right? By the right which Jupiter himself established, that all things beneficial to the Republic be held lawful and proper. Law is nothing but a code of right conduct derived from the will of the gods, ordaining what is good and forbidding its opposite. This law, then, Cassius obeyed when he went to Syria; another man's province, if people were following written laws, but such laws having been overthrown, his by the law of nature.

Cicero's argument makes sense in itself, but it is based on premises set by him: he allows individual decisions, unsupported by official bodies, if these are in the national interest, but he defines the actions to which this applies. A procedure such as that of Brutus, he claims, is justified on the basis of divine, natural law, which is more powerful than positive, written law. Cicero thereby touches on a fundamental philosophical problem. He may have been right that allowing some flexibility and looking to universal principles was the best way to achieve results in the circumstances, but his argument goes against the basic principles of the Republic that he aims to preserve. Besides, it provides a justification for one person making decisions, if these are to the country's benefit, with the same person determining whether this is the case. While Cicero envisaged such measures to be valid only for a limited period of time in a particular context, he thereby unwittingly provided a defence for procedures in the principate, when the Senate no longer had any real influence and the Roman emperors felt empowered to make decisions on their own. For Cicero, in addition to a philosophical or procedural grounding, this strategy of a kind of self-administered justice is supported by the expectation that individuals who have served the Republic well, including himself, should be honoured accordingly (*Phil.* 14.13–14; 21 April 43 BCE):

> For to my mind, a true, genuine triumph is only when those who have deserved well of the Republic receive the tributes of a united community. If in the shared joy of the Roman people they were congratulating one individual, that was a great mark of esteem; if they were thanking one individual, all the greater; if both, no more splendid compliment can be conceived of. Someone may say: 'Do you, then, indulge in self-applause?' It is against my will, to be sure, but a sense of injury makes me vainglorious, contrary to my habit. Is it not enough that persons ignorant of the meaning of true worth make no return of gratitude to those who deserve well? Will even those who devote all their care to the preservation of the Republic be targets for backbiting and envy? [14] You know that during the past few days there was a vast amount of talk that on Shepherds' Day, that is today, I would come down to the Forum with the fasces. I suppose that such a rumor has been concocted against a gladiator or a bandit or a Catiline, not against a man who has made sure that nothing of that kind can happen in the Republic. Was it likely that I, who hoisted, overthrew, and dashed down Catiline when he made such an attempt, should suddenly reveal myself a Catiline? With what auspices was I, an augur, to have accepted those fasces, how long was I going to keep them, to whom should I have handed them over? Could anyone have been so wicked as to invent this tale or so mad as to believe it?

Unsurprisingly, the outstanding position that Cicero appropriated for himself in the conflict with Antony led to unintended reactions among the Roman public: while he claims that he has done a service to the Republic, he is faced with feelings of ingratitude and rumours that he is striving for dictatorial power, which he rejects outright.

Cicero was, however, able to enjoy a brief spell of success of the kind he was longing for: when news of the victory over Antony in northern Italy reached Rome on 20 April 43 BCE, a great crowd escorted Cicero from his house to the Capitoline Hill and to the speaker's platform in the Forum;[17] on 26 April 43 BCE the Senate declared Mark Antony and his followers public enemies and honoured the victors.[18] Yet, soon afterwards, power relations changed, and Cicero was dead by the end of 43 BCE.

During this last year of his life, while being politically active with negotiations, Cicero found the time to continue a series of philosophical writings he had embarked upon since about 46 BCE, his 'second philosophical period'. In 44 BCE alone he finished *De natura deorum* (*On the Nature of the Gods*), *De divinatione* (*On Divination*), *Cato maior de senectute* (*Cato or On Old Age*), *De fato* (*On Fate*), *Laelius de amicitia* (*Laelius or On Friendship*), *Topica* (*Methods of Drawing Conclusions*) and *De officiis* (*On Duties*). Many of these works address topics that also appear in Cicero's letters and political speeches from the period.

Most conspicuous in the contemporary political context is the treatise *De officiis* written in the second half of 44 BCE, after Caesar's assassination. The work is addressed to Cicero's son Marcus, as a substitute for conversations father and son would have had if Cicero had been able to travel to Athens (where his son was a student) in the summer as originally planned. Unsurprisingly, the treatise is influenced by the recent experience of Caesar's dictatorship. Like the *Philippics*, it discusses issues such as the justification of war or the killing of a tyrant, though, in line with the genre, it takes a broader and more philosophical approach. General welfare is presented as a goal justifying various actions, even killing fellow human beings if they are tyrants.[19] Enemies can be warded off by military action if war is declared in advance and fought according to the code of war, after negotiations have proved unsuccessful.[20]

The position in *De officiis*, namely that war has to be a last resort after negotiations have failed, contradicts the policy adopted in the *Philippics*. But if war is the only way to achieve proper peace and maintain a constitutional government, it will be justified, and this again agrees with the reasoning in the *Philippics* (*Off.* 1.34–6):

> Something else that must very much be preserved in public affairs is the justice of warfare. There are two types of conflict: the one proceeds by debate, the other by force. Since the former is the proper concern of man, but the latter of beasts, one should only resort to the latter if one may not employ the former. [35] Wars, then, ought to be undertaken for this purpose, that we may live in peace, without injustice; and once victory has been secured, those who were not cruel or savage in warfare should be spared. [...] In my opinion, our concern should always be for a peace that will have nothing to do with treachery. If I had been followed in this we would still have some republican government (if perhaps not the very best); whereas now we have none. [...] [36] Indeed, a fair code of warfare has been drawn up, in full accordance with religious scruple, in the fetial [i.e. sacred] laws of the Roman people. From this we can grasp that no war is just unless it is waged after a formal demand for restoration, or unless it has been formally announced and declared beforehand.

Similarly, a sophisticated argument demonstrates that what is normally morally wrong may be justified under certain circumstances; as in the *Philippics*, special measures, even going against ordinary laws, are temporarily admitted if there is reason for such actions and they are in the national interest. This applies, for instance, to killing a fellow citizen when he is a tyrant, an implicit justification of Caesar's assassination (*Off.* 3.19):

> For often the occasion arises when something that is generally and customarily considered to be dishonourable is found not to be so.

> Let me suggest as an example something that can be more widely
> applied: what greater crime can there be than to kill not merely another
> man, but even a close friend? Surely then, anyone who kills a tyrant,
> although he is a close friend, has committed himself to crime? But it
> does not seem so to the Roman people, which deems that deed the
> fairest of all splendid deeds. Did the beneficial, therefore, overcome
> honourableness? No indeed; for honourableness followed upon what
> benefited.

At the end of his life, Cicero thus appears as a Roman citizen who defends, with all forces available to him, the political system in which he had gained an outstanding position and which he saw endangered. At the same time he not only aims to achieve results in the daily political struggle, but also intends to discuss fundamental political and moral questions by means of transposing Greek philosophy into Latin. His political success is gained, as he believes, by the techniques of oratory at his disposal. To make this fight, seen as paradigmatic, known beyond its actual sphere, he worked on a long-term publicity campaign, disseminating speeches to spread his views and to influence a wider audience, while he also thought about publishing a selection of his orations to create a political and oratorical legacy, thereby emulating the Greek orator Demosthenes. Amazingly, in this tense political situation he even found the time to reflect on the moral reasoning and justification behind political behaviour and to outline such ideas in philosophical treatises.

Whether Cicero intended these activities to be the crowning glory of his career is uncertain; at this stage he was able to take a leading role in all areas that he had been active in throughout his life. Unfortunately, his success was short-lived: a few months after the delivery of the last *Philippic Oration* Antony, Octavian and M. Aemilius Lepidus formed the so-called second triumvirate, officially sanctioned on 27 November 43 BCE; one of their first actions was to have Cicero proscribed and killed on 7 December 43 BCE, allegedly because Antony was irritated at the *Philippics*. This shows the impact of these speeches, albeit in a form different from what had been envisaged.

II

POLITICAL AND
LITERARY CAREER

IN THE PERIOD of the *Philippics* in 44–43 BCE (see Chapter I) Cicero
seems to have felt that he had reached the height of his career, having
at last gained another opportunity to influence Roman politics, as a
respected ex-consul and an accomplished orator. However, coming from
a non-noble background, it had taken him some effort to reach this
point, and his progress was mostly based on his intellect and rhetorical
skill (fig. 2.1).

Marcus Tullius Cicero was born in the Italian town of Arpinum (modern
Arpino) on 3 January 106 BCE. The family's so-called *cognomen* (personal
surname), by which he has become known, is derived from the Latin word
cicer, meaning 'chickpea'. Cicero's family was equestrian and owned some
land in the area of Arpinum, but none of its members had yet reached the
consulship in Rome, although they were well acquainted with senatorial
families. Cicero therefore did not have a line of famous ancestors upon
which to build his own position (and whose images could be displayed
in the entrance hall). Instead, he was what the Romans called 'a new man'
(*homo novus*), a newcomer to the scene of high-level politics.[1] Yet, as he says

2.1 Vincenzo Foppa, *The Young Cicero Reading* (fresco, 1464).

later, 'new men' can win fame and advancements on the basis of their own hard work and ambitions.[2]

Together with his brother Quintus, Cicero enjoyed a thorough and rounded education in Rome; in his youth he seems to have done more extensive rhetorical training than others and studied philosophy more seriously (fig. 2.2). In his boyhood Cicero already surpassed his peers as a speaker; he aspired to become one of the foremost men in oratory and politics,[3] and from an early age he engaged closely with politically important speeches.[4] Later he completed his studies with a journey to Greece and Asia (in 79–77 BCE). According to his own report, this was primarily undertaken to strengthen his body and to improve his speaking technique, but it was also instrumental in rounding off his overall rhetorical and philosophical training.[5] In Rome and during his travels Cicero met many leading Greek rhetors and rhetoricians, including Apollonius Molon, Menippus of Stratonicea, Dionysius of Magnesia, Aeschylus of Cnidus and Xenocles of Adramyttion; he also encountered important Greek philosophers of his day, such as Antiochus of Ascalon, the head of the philosophical school of the Academy; Philon of Larissa, another Academic; the Epicurean philosophers Phaedrus and Zeno of Sidon, and the Stoic philosophers Diodotus and Posidonius, a pupil of Panaetius.[6]

After Cicero had received the *toga virilis* ('a man's toga'), perhaps at the festival of the Liberalia on 17 March 90 BCE, and was thus accepted into the adult sphere, he started his practical education and became a fol-

lower of the augur Q. Mucius Scaevola (consul 117 BCE), by whom he was introduced to law. After the augur's death Cicero joined the *pontifex maximus* Q. Mucius Scaevola (consul 95 BCE). In the Social War Cicero did military service under Pompey (*c.*89 BCE), although even then he preferred political activity in Rome. Because of the political upheavals there were some speeches to listen to in Roman public life, but there was little opportunity for delivering one's own. Cicero devoted this period and the subsequent years to continuing his studies in rhetoric, law and philosophy. As he later explains in his rhetorical treatises, he regarded a profound, all-round education as an essential basis for success as an orator and politician. As

2.2   Cicero, portrait bust (Roman, first century CE).

a first fruit of this thorough engagement with rhetoric, he published the treatise *De inventione rhetorica* (*On Rhetorical Invention*) in the mid to late 80s BCE; as the title says, this is a study of the first task of the orator: 'to find' the material. In active life at this time Cicero was keen to win glory as an orator:[7] in Republican Rome this was achieved by appearing in the Forum as a lawyer and working as a politician.

After Sulla's victory in civil war (in 82 BCE) Cicero felt that the political situation had become quiet enough to allow him to make his first appearance in a court case.[8] In his mid twenties at the time (Gellius, *Noctes Atticae* 15.28.3), Cicero was older than other young men at this point, but he later claimed that he had intended to come forward into the Forum not as someone still learning, but as someone learned, thereby making an immediate impact.[9] Cicero's earliest appearance as an orator and lawyer of which an almost completely preserved speech remains (though Cicero alludes to his involvement in earlier cases)[10] is the defence of P. Quinctius (*Pro Quinctio*) in a private case in 81 BCE; the opponent was represented by Q. Hortensius Hortalus,[11] the most famous orator of the time,[12] and backed by other well-respected noblemen. Although this was essentially a private civil case, its history, with the involvement of several powerful men, meant that it had a political dimension. Cicero's comments are rather candid; this was apparently possible since the utterances of a fairly unknown young man were not given much weight.[13] Yet from the earliest moment that Cicero's activities as an orator can be traced (it may not be a coincidence that earlier speeches have not been preserved), he appears not as an ordinary lawyer dealing with petty cases; instead, politics and legal work are closely linked, based on philosophical reflections in accordance with his belief in connections between politics, lawsuits and oratory.[14] Thus Cicero can use appearances as a lawyer to further his political career and to comment on topical issues.

The next extant speech, the earliest one to be fully preserved, is the defence of Sex. Roscius from Ameria against patricide in 80 BCE (*Pro Sex. Roscio Amerino*), Cicero's first criminal case.[15] This was basically a straightforward issue, but the trial received additional tension since Cicero presented the real opponent as the freedman L. Cornelius Chrysogonus, a powerful crony of the dictator Sulla: Chrysogonus had acquired the estates of the defendant's deceased father as a result of the alleged charge of patricide and the Sullan proscriptions. Cicero therefore later mentions that in this speech he spoke 'in the face of the influence of Lucius Sulla, who was then despot' (*Off.* 2.51).

Because of the politically challenging circumstances, none of the established lawyers was ready to accept the defence. Cicero embraced this opportunity despite its inherent risks and managed to show that his client was not guilty, while he commented on the political circumstances; he toned down the criticism by using the ploy of distinguishing between Sulla and his men and by claiming that the dictator could not know about all details of what was going on.

In the opening of the speech Cicero explains the perhaps unexpected fact that such a young orator has taken on the defence (*Rosc. Am.* 1–4):

> I imagine you must be wondering, members of the jury, why it is that, when there are so many leading orators and men of the highest rank present here in court, I of all people should have stood up to address you: for neither in age, nor in ability, nor in authority do I bear comparison with these men who have remained seated. All those whom you see here supporting my client believe that in this case a wrong has been perpetrated, arising from an act of unprecedented criminality, and that it ought to be resisted; but to resist it themselves they have not the courage, considering the unfavourable times in which we live. The result is that they attend the trial because it is their duty to do so, but say nothing because they want to keep out of danger. [2] So am I the boldest man here? Far from it. Or am I more attentive to my obligations than everyone else? I am hardly so eager even for that distinction that I would wish others to be deprived of it. What is it, then, that has driven me more than anyone else to undertake the defence of Sextus Roscius? The reason is this. If any of these men whom you see here supporting my client – highly influential and distinguished figures that they are – were to speak for Roscius, and were to make any mention at all of politics, something which is unavoidable in this case, he would be assumed to be saying much more than he actually was saying. [3] With me, on the other hand, if I say openly everything that the case requires,

I shall certainly not find that my speech leaks out and becomes public knowledge to the same extent. A second reason is this. With the others, their rank and distinction is such that nothing they say passes unnoticed, while because of their age and experience no allowance would be given for any indiscreet remark they might make. But if I am the one that speaks too freely, what I say will either be ignored because I have not yet embarked on a political career, or else be pardoned on account of my youth – although not only the idea of pardon but even the custom of judicial enquiry has now been abolished at Rome! [4] There is also a third reason. It may be perhaps that the others were asked to speak in such a way that their decision seemed to them to be unaffected by any ties of obligation. In my case, however, I was applied to by men who by their friendship, acts of kindness, and position carried the greatest weight with me, and I considered that I could never ignore their kindness to me, nor disregard their rank, nor neglect their wishes.

The speech was a great success.[16] In Cicero's interpretation the situation is similar to the circumstances at the end of his life (in that, essentially, he sees the Republic suppressed or threatened by a dictator). This is the reason that some of the ideas governing the *Philippics* are present already: for instance, dictatorship can never be more than a temporary measure,[17] or supporters of the Republic must work to re-establish law and order.[18]

According to Cicero, the impact of *Pro Sex. Roscio Amerino* triggered intense activity for him as a lawyer.[19] This affected his health, as he later says in the treatise *Brutus* (46 BCE). He therefore went on a study tour to Greece and Asia (79–77 BCE), to improve his speaking techniques and to acquire a less exhausting way of delivery.[20] However, the Greek biographer Plutarch implies that fear of Sulla motivated Cicero to leave Rome.[21] During this period abroad Cicero spent time with a number of well-known Greek orators and philosophers, some of whom he had already encountered during earlier phases of his education.

Around the time of this journey Cicero married Terentia, his first wife; their daughter Tullia was born soon afterwards. Back in Rome, Cicero was again active in a number of court cases and was soon elected quaestor for

75 BCE,[22] entering office on 5 December 76 BCE. Cicero was one of those quaestors who assisted provincial governors and was assigned the area of Lilybaeum (the western part of the island of Sicily); one of his major tasks was to acquire grain to prevent price rises in Rome. In contrast to most other magistrates in this position, Cicero seems to have managed to accomplish these tasks while keeping everybody happy and to have diligently carried out his duties without making money for himself. As an ex-quaestor Cicero became a member of the Senate upon his return to Rome. Furthermore, he was again active as a lawyer and used this activity as a way to win voters and establish networks. As he later recalled in the speech *Pro Plancio* (64 BCE), the period in the province away from Rome made Cicero realize the importance of a visible presence at the centre of action (*Planc.* 64–6):

> I have no fear, gentlemen, of appearing to have too good a conceit of myself, if I say a word about my own quaestorship. My tenure of that office was successful enough, but I think that the achievements of my later tenure of the highest offices have led me to look for but a modest distinction from the credit I gained in the quaestorship; still, I am not afraid that anyone should venture to assert that any Sicilian quaestor has won greater renown or popularity. At that time I can say with most assured confidence that I thought that my quaestorship was the sole topic of conversation at Rome. [...]; [65] so I retired from the province filled with the notion that the Roman people would spontaneously lay all their distinctions at my feet. It happened that on my way back from the province I had arrived at Puteoli, intending to make the journey thence by land, just at the season when the place was thronged with fashionable people; and I nearly swooned, gentlemen, when someone asked me on what day I had left Rome, and whether there was any news. When I replied that I was on my way back from my province, he said, 'Why, of course, you come from Africa, do you not?' 'No,' I answered, somewhat coolly, for I was now in high dudgeon, 'from Sicily.' Hereupon another of the party interposed, with an omniscient air, 'What! don't you know that our friend has been quaestor at Syracuse?' To cut my story short, I dropped the dudgeon, and made myself just one of those

who had come for the waters. [66] This experience, gentlemen, I am inclined to think was more valuable to me than if I had been hailed with salvoes of applause; for having once realized that the ears of the Roman people were somewhat obtuse, but their eyes keen and alert, I ceased henceforth from considering what the world was likely to hear about me; from that day I took care that I should be seen personally every day. I lived in the public eye; I frequented the forum; neither my door-keeper nor sleep prevented anyone from having audience of me.

The next major milestone in Cicero's career came in 70 BCE with the trial of C. Verres. Verres had abused his magistrate's powers while provincial governor in Sicily (73–71 BCE). Because of their earlier close relationship, the Sicilian communities entreated Cicero to undertake the prosecution for extortion (*de repetundis*: about compensation for illegal acquisition of money or property by Roman officials abroad) on their behalf. Cicero had originally intended only to act as a defence lawyer in criminal cases,[23] but he could not reject the plea because of his obligations to the Sicilians. In any event this case promised to be an excellent occasion to demonstrate his talents, to improve his standing and to expose the administrative system in which Roman officials could exploit the provinces.

Since the current beneficiaries of this system feared the exposure of its worst representative, they took all possible steps to confront and hinder Cicero's aims: firstly, there was another candidate for the prosecution, Q. Caecilius Niger, so that Cicero had to defend his claim to take on the case in a kind of pre-trial, where he delivered the *Divinatio in Caecilium*. After Cicero had secured the role of prosecutor, the other party attempted to delay the trial into the following year, which would provide them with more favourable circumstances because different men, their allies, would then be holding important magistracies (owing to the Roman system of annual offices). In order to forestall these plans, Cicero collected the evidence for the prosecution in only 50 days, although he met with opposition also in Sicily. Still, the defence managed to move the start of the first hearing of the trial to 5 August: they anticipated that the first hearing would take up most of the time available for court proceedings until the end of the calendar year, and the second hearing would only be completed in the following year; for, because of various festival periods, the time for court cases towards the end of the year was limited.

Yet Cicero thwarted this plan: when proceedings opened, he gave a relatively short speech (*Verr.* 1), rather than the expected full-blown oration detailing all the charges, and proceeded almost immediately to presenting witnesses, so that there would be time for the required second hearing within the same calendar year. Cicero's tactic was overwhelming; Verres soon stayed away and then withdrew before the second hearing.[24] As a result, Cicero presumably never delivered the speeches intended for the second hearing, which outline all of Verres' misdeeds along with the evidence (*Verr.* 2.1–5). These orations isolate Verres as a disreputable person and characterize him (and his activities) as 'impudent and insane' and as 'an unprincipled rogue' in contrast to 'us honest and honourable men' (see for example *Verr.* 1.7–8; 2.3.7), a tactic to be repeated in the cases of Catiline and Mark Antony.

Cicero believed that 'the most honourable, incorruptible, and industrious men available should come forward to defend our laws and uphold our courts' and that the senatorial order must maintain its respect for truth, integrity, honesty and duty; therefore it was imperative for him to take on the prosecution in this trial.[25] Some of his arguments develop ideas that were voiced earlier[26] and reappear in the *Philippics*:[27] there he also stresses the obligation to fight against threats to the Republic. At the trial of Verres Cicero presents the problem not as an isolated instance, but as an issue fundamentally affecting the political system; accordingly he signals its importance in the opening words of the speech at the first hearing, trying to motivate the audience to feel that this question directly affects them and they are called upon to act in the interest of the greater good, a common rhetorical technique of Cicero's (*Verr.* 1.1–3):

> The very thing that was most to be desired, members of the jury, the one thing that will have most effect in reducing the hatred felt towards your order and restoring the tarnished reputation of the courts, this it is which, in the current political crisis, has been granted and presented to you; and this opportunity has come about not, it would appear,

by human planning, but virtually by the gift of the gods. For a belief, disastrous for the state and dangerous for you, has become widespread, and has been increasingly talked about not only among ourselves but among foreign peoples as well – the belief that, in these courts as they are currently constituted, it is impossible for a man with money, no matter how guilty he may be, to be convicted. [2] Now, at this moment of reckoning for your order and your courts, when people are ready to use public meetings and legislation to stoke up this hatred of the senate, a defendant has been put on trial – Gaius Verres, a man already convicted, according to universal public opinion, by his character and actions, but already acquitted, according to his own hopes and assertions, by his immense wealth. I have taken on this prosecution, gentlemen, with the complete support and confidence of the Roman people, not because I want to increase the hatred felt towards your order, but in order to mend the tarnished reputation which we both share. The man I have brought before you is a man through whom you will be able to retrieve the good reputation of the courts, restore your popularity with the Roman people, and gratify foreign nations – being as he is an embezzler of the treasury, a plunderer of Asia and Pamphylia [i.e. as legate and later *proquaestor* under Cn. Cornelius Dolabella in 80 BCE], a cheater of city jurisdiction [i.e. as city praetor in 74 BCE], and the disgrace and ruination of the province of Sicily [i.e. as provincial governor in 73–71 BCE]. [3] If you pronounce a fair and scrupulous verdict against this man, you will hold on to the influence which ought by rights to be yours. But if on the other hand his colossal wealth succeeds in destroying the scrupulousness and fairness of the courts, then I shall achieve at least one thing – a recognition that the country had the wrong jurors, and not that the jurors had the wrong defendant, or the defendant the wrong prosecutor.

While Cicero was preparing for the Verres trial, elections for the coming year took place: Cicero was elected curule aedile for 69 BCE. During his aedileship, which was sometimes seen as a stepping stone to higher magistracies, Cicero organized the festivals of the Ludi Ceriales, the Ludi Florales and the Ludi Romani, as holders of this office were required.[28] In summer 67 BCE Cicero was the first to be elected praetor.[29] As praetor in 66 BCE, Cicero was responsible for the extortion court (*de repetundis*), in which he had appeared as the prosecution during the Verres trial a few years earlier.

In 66 BCE Cicero delivered his first political speech: he spoke before the People in the popular assembly on the proposed bill of the tribune C. Manilius to give Pompey an extraordinary command in the war against Mithridates, king of Pontus (*De imperio Cn. Pompei* or *De lege Manilia*). In the opening remarks Cicero exploits the occasion to highlight his addressing the People as a step in his career, to mention his feelings of responsibility towards those who have elected him and to explain his qualification for the task and the oration's aims (*Leg. Man.* 1–3):

> Although I have always particularly enjoyed the sight of you thronging this place, and have always thought that the spot where I am now standing [i.e. the speaker's platform in the Roman Forum] is the most distinguished one in which a magistrate may transact business with you and the most honourable one in which a private citizen may address you, nevertheless, citizens, this means of becoming famous, which has always been fully available to every decent citizen, has until now been closed to me, not because of any wish of mine to avoid it, but rather because of the path I set myself when I embarked upon my career. For until now I have never dared to speak from this place of influence, and I was determined that I should never present anything here that was not the fruit of my mature powers and the product of long practice: hence I judged that I would do better to devote the whole of my time instead to defending my friends in their hour of need. [2] So, while this place has never been short of men ready to defend your interests, my exertions, which have been honestly and irreproachably devoted to defending private citizens, have now received the highest possible reward through the choice that you yourselves have made. For when, because of successive reruns of the election, I was formally declared, three times over, as the first of the candidates to be elected to a praetorship, and by the votes of all the centuries, then it was made very clear to me, citizens,

both what you had concluded about me personally and what you were recommending to others. Now, since I possess as much authority as, by electing me to this office, you have wished me to have, and since I also possess as much skill in legal advocacy as anyone who is reasonably energetic could acquire from almost daily practice in speaking in the courts, I will accordingly deploy whatever authority I have among those who have bestowed it upon me, and similarly, if I can achieve anything by my oratory, I will display it before those people particularly who in choosing me have judged that that art too is deserving of some reward. [3] And I am aware that I have especially good reason to be happy because, despite having no experience of making the type of speeches that are required from those who stand before you on this platform, the subject on which I now have the opportunity to address you is one on which no one could fail to be eloquent. This is because my subject is the outstanding and unique merit of Gnaeus Pompeius – a subject on which it is more difficult to finish speaking than to begin. In making my speech, therefore, my task will not be to strive after abundance so much as moderation.

In this speech Cicero could argue forcefully and elaborately for an obvious policy, show his reverence for the powerful Pompey and still try to ingratiate himself with both the People and some of the nobility; this strategy was successful. In the speech defending Cluentius in the same year (*Pro Cluentio*) Cicero voices a preliminary concept of what will develop into his ideal of *concordia ordinum* ('unanimity of orders'), here in the sense of a close cooperation between senators and knights (*Clu.* 152).

From the praetorship onwards Cicero aimed for the consulship more and more openly.[30] This was perhaps one of the reasons why he did not go on to become a *propraetor* in a province after his praetorship[31] and rather preferred to stay in Rome. His son Marcus was born in 65 BCE. At the beginning of 64 BCE Cicero's brother Quintus dedicated to him *A Handbook of Electioneering* (*Commentariolum petitionis*), where he showed his admiration for his brother's political successes up to this point and summarized practical political advice for the final steps of the election campaign, such as trying to be on good terms with everybody (Cicero, *Commentariolum petitionis* 2; 53), which Cicero had taken into account at all his public appearances:[32]

[2] Consider what city this is, what is it you seek, who you are. Every day or so, as you go down to the Forum, you must repeat to yourself: 'I am "new"; I seek the consulship; this is Rome.' For your status as a 'new man' you will compensate chiefly by your fame as a speaker. Great prestige has always attached to this; an advocate deemed worthy to defend ex-consuls cannot be thought unworthy of the consulship. [...]

[53] Above all, it must be shown in this canvass that high hopes and good opinions are entertained for your political future. Yet, during your canvass, you must not deal with politics either in the Senate or in political meetings of the People. Instead, you must keep in mind that the Senate should deem you, on your life's record, to be in future an upholder of its authority; the Roman Knights and men of worth and substance, from your past life, to be devoted to peace and quiet times; the masses, to be favourably inclined to their interests, since you have been 'Popular' at least in your speeches in political meetings and lawcourts.

Among the other candidates for the consulship, the disreputable C. Antonius Hybrida and the ambitious L. Sergius Catilina had the greatest chances of victory; but the questionable moral status of Cicero's rivals seems to have been in his favour.[33] The political situation forced the conservative noblemen to side with Cicero, since he appeared as the only one who might resist rebellious movements.[34] Cicero was aware of the tensions; he kept showing also that he was a politician defending the interests of the People, and he supported both factions, as he later made explicit in his inaugural speeches as consul.[35] Because of the amount of electoral bribery and other practices to canvass votes, the Senate proposed more severe penalties for *ambitus* ('bribery') shortly before the elections. A veto by a tribune of the People against this bill was answered by Cicero's speech *In senatu in toga candida contra C. Antonium et L. Catilinam competitores* (*In the Senate in a Candidate's Toga against the Other Candidates C. Antonius and L. Catilina*; surviving in fragments), which basically turned into an invective against Cicero's main competitors, especially Catiline. Cicero was elected unanimously for 63 BCE,[36] and C. Antonius was slightly ahead of Catiline.[37] Catiline was allowed to stand for the consulship again in the following year.

On reaching the consulship Cicero had gained a position he had been keenly aiming for throughout his career, as he later comments in his treatise on the state *De re publica* (*Rep.* 1.10; *c.*54–51 BCE):

> Again, when they deny that a wise man will take part in politics, who, I ask you, can be satisfied with their proviso – 'unless some period of crisis compels him'? As if anyone could face a greater crisis than I did. What could I have done at that time had I not been consul? And how could I have been consul if I had not followed from boyhood the career that would bring a man of equestrian birth like me to the highest office? So the opportunity of rescuing the country, whatever the dangers that threaten it, does not come suddenly or when you wish it, but only when you are in a position which allows you to do so.

His election to the consulship and his achievements during this period were a source of pride for Cicero for the rest of his life:[38] he was extremely proud of having been elected unanimously, since this agreed with his ideals of unity, and also of having won all his offices on account of his own worth rather than the reputation of his family, as he says, for instance, in a political attack against L. Calpurnius Piso Caesoninus in 55 BCE.[39] Correspondingly, Cicero claimed to have been acknowledged by the entire populace for his preservation of the Republic, without any military action, in the face of opposition, and to have received demonstrations of gratitude (*Pis.* 6–7):

> Quintus Catulus, leader of this order [i.e. the Senate] and a guiding voice in state policy, before a crowded meeting of the senate named me Father of my Country. The illustrious Lucius Gellius [i.e. a *homo novus*, consul in 72 BCE], who sits at your side, asserted in the hearing of my audience that a civic crown was due to me from the commonwealth. Though I wore but the gown of civil life [*togatus*] the senate threw open in my honour the temples of the immortal gods in an unprecedented

form of thanksgiving, distinguishing me not, as they distinguished so
many, for the good government of the state, but for its preservation. At
a public meeting, when upon laying down my office [i.e. as consul] I
was debarred by a tribune of the plebs from saying what I had intended,
and when I was by him permitted to do no more than take the usual
oath, I swore without flinching that this commonwealth and this city
had been saved by my sole efforts. [7] At that meeting the entire people
of Rome accorded to me, not a vote of thanks which would pass with
the day, but eternity and immortality, when, themselves upon oath,
with one voice and one heart, they acclaimed an oath so proud and
so memorable. And on that day my return home from the forum was
such that there seemed to be no one in the whole catalogue of citizens
who was not in my train.

The start of Cicero's consular year was not as smooth as he might have
hoped after the demonstrations of support at his election: as soon as the
tribunes of the People for 63 had entered office on 10 December 64 BCE,
one of them, P. Servilius Rullus, put forward a bill for an agrarian law.
According to Cicero's response, this proposed that areas of public land
and land bought from private proprietors should be settled and assigned
to individuals without property; the funds to implement this plan were to
come from selling public land in the provinces and collecting money and
war booty not yet handed over by generals; a powerful committee of ten
men, elected by a majority of 17 out of the 35 *tribus* (the tribes into which
voters in ancient Rome were organized), was to be set up to carry through
the plans within five years. While Cicero claims that he does not oppose
agrarian reform in principle,[40] having just become consul he was not in a
position to agree to such a major project with unforeseeable consequences
that might affect the entire Republic. He therefore adopted a position
effectively supporting the landowning nobility, although he did not become
tired of stating that he was a true defender of the People, fighting for the
interests of the entire populace. It was probably not difficult to convince the
audience in the Senate, but to persuade the People, at least some of whom
might have benefited from the bill, was presumably more challenging. Still,

Cicero's sophisticated speeches seem to have been successful: the bill was never turned into a law.[41]

Because of these developments Cicero's first speeches as consul, given in early January 63 BCE, are not straightforward inaugural orations, merely introducing himself to the Senate and the People, thanking the People for having elected him and outlining his programme for the year. They also confront the issue of the agrarian law, whence they are known as *Speeches on the Agrarian Law (Orationes de lege agraria)*. Cicero's 'programme', which he explains in addition, consists of 'peace', 'unity', 'liberty' and 'tranquillity' at home (*pax, concordia, libertas, tranquillitas, otium*), with various nuances according to the context.[42] Cicero's delicate situation as well as his aim to appear as everybody's champion and a man of the People become obvious in the opening of the speech to the People, the second of the *Speeches on the Agrarian Law* and his first speech as consul to the popular assembly. There he builds on his background as a 'new man' elevated to an illustrious position by the People's vote in order to describe his particular role and to create a special relationship with the men in the audience (essentially being 'one of them'). He exploits the political discussion around the meaning of the term 'supporter of the People' (*popularis*) and the role of such individuals, so as to show that, in contrast to others, he is a true defender of the People's interests, which implicitly presents the basis for Cicero's assessment of the agrarian law (*Leg. agr.* 2.1–7):

> It is a custom, O Romans, established by our ancestors, that those who by your favour have obtained the right to have images in their family [i.e. those whose ancestors held high offices] should, when delivering their first oration before the people, combine with an expression of gratitude for your favour some praise of their ancestors. And in such speeches some men are sometimes found to be worthy of the rank which their ancestors obtained, but the majority only make it seem that the debt due to their ancestors is so great that something is still left over to be paid to their posterity. As for myself, Romans, I have no opportunity of speaking of my ancestors before you; not that they were not such men as you see us [i.e. Cicero and his brother] to be, sprung from their

blood and brought up in their principles, but because they never enjoyed popular favour or were rendered illustrious by the honour you bestowed [i.e. elected to high offices]. [2] But to speak about myself before you I am afraid would show conceit, to remain silent ingratitude. For it is a very difficult matter to mention in regard to myself by what efforts I obtained this dignity, and yet I cannot possibly keep silence about the great favours you have bestowed upon me [i.e. by electing him]. For this reason I shall employ a careful reserve and moderation in my language so that, while recalling all the kindness I have received from you, when it comes to considering why I have been judged worthy of the highest honour you can bestow and such remarkable evidence of your esteem, I may myself state the reason, should it be necessary, in moderate terms, thinking that you who so judged me worthy will still hold the same opinion.

[3] I am the first 'new' man, after a very long interval, almost more remote than our times can remember, whom you have made consul; that position, which the nobility held secured by guards and fortified in every way, you have broken open, and have shown your desire that it should in future be open to merit, allowing me to take the lead. And you not only elected me consul, which in itself is a very high honour, but you did so in a way in which few nobles in this city have been made consuls, and no 'new' man before me.

For certainly, if you will be good enough to consult your memory in regard to 'new' men, you will find that those who were elected without rejection only obtained office after long labours and seizing a favourable opportunity, having become candidates many years after they had been praetors and somewhat later than their age and the laws allowed them; but that those who became candidates in their own year were not elected without rejection first; that I am the only one of all the 'new' men that we can remember who became a candidate for the consulship when the law allowed and obtained it the first time I applied, so that this honour which I have received from you, which I stood for as soon as I was allowed to do so, appears not to have been seized when opportunity offered in the person of another inferior candidate, nor to have been urgently demanded with continued importunity, but to have been obtained by merit. [4] And it is indeed an eminent distinction that I have just mentioned – that I was the first of the 'new' men upon whom after so many years you have bestowed this honour; that it was at the first time of asking, that it was in my regular year; and yet nothing can be more glorious and more illustrious than the fact that at the comitia [i.e. voting assembly] at which I was elected you did not hand in your voting-tablet, whose secrecy guarantees the freedom of your vote, but showed by universal acclamation your goodwill and attachment to me. Thus it was not the last sorting of the voting-tablets, but those first hastening to the polling-booths, not the individual voices of the criers, but the unanimous voice of the Roman people that proclaimed me consul. [5] [...]

[6] But if I alone were brought into danger, I could endure it, Romans, with greater equanimity; but there appear to me to be certain men who, if they think that I have made some slight mistake concerning any matter not only intentionally but even by accident, will be ready to reproach you all for having preferred me to my noble competitors. But it is my opinion, Romans, that to suffer anything is better than failing to carry on my consulship in such a manner that in everything I do, in everything I advise, what you have done for me and advised may obtain its meed of praise. In addition to this I have a most laborious and difficult task before me in the manner of carrying on my consulship; for I have made up my mind that I ought to follow a different system and principle from those of my predecessors, some of whom have specially avoided the approach to this place [i.e. the speaker's platform in the Roman Forum] and the sight of you, while others have not shown much enthusiasm in presenting themselves. But I intend not only to declare from this place, where it is very easy to do so, but in the senate itself, which did not seem to be the place for such language, I declared in that first speech of mine on the 1st of January [i.e. Cicero's *First Speech on the Agrarian Law*], that I would be a consul of the people. [7] Nor, since I am aware that I have been elected consul, not by the efforts of men of influence, not by the distinguished favours of a few,

but by the unanimous approval of the Roman people, in such a way that I was by a large majority preferred to men of the highest rank, how, I ask, could I help acting as the people's friend while I hold this office and throughout my life? But I have urgent need of your wisdom to help me to explain the force and interpretation of this word. For a great error is being spread abroad through the hypocritical pretences of certain individuals, who, while attacking and hindering not only the interests but even the safety of the people, are striving by their speeches to obtain the reputation of being supporters of the people.

Having dealt with the agrarian bill at the beginning of his consulship, Cicero was confronted with the so-called Catilinarian Conspiracy in the second half of his term of office. This conspiracy was another challenge to Cicero's realization of the ideals outlined in his inaugural speeches; although this 'programme' was pretty vague, like that of many politicians in similar situations, it was intended to eliminate internal strife.

When, in 63 BCE, Catiline was again preparing for the consular elections, Cicero made efforts to avoid the worst manipulation of the elections by initiating stricter laws, particularly against bribery. Nevertheless, Catiline stood as a candidate; but he was not elected. After his attempts to win power by ordinary procedural means had failed, Catiline attempted to gain an influential position by other routes and started to organize an uprising. Cicero tried to motivate the Senate against these measures, though initially without success. Only after there was clear evidence that Catiline planned murder and uproar in Rome did the Senate give the consuls greater powers by a special decree (*senatus consultum ultimum*) in the autumn; this was in effect a declaration of emergency and allowed the consuls to take steps to tackle the situation without going through the usual processes.

Still, Catiline and his co-conspirators made further plans for disruption in the city; Cicero was informed of these so that he was able to forestall them: he managed to report on the movements of armed forces outside Rome and on the planned activities in the city, including his own assassination, to the Senate on 8 November 63 BCE, delivering what is known as the *First Catilinarian Oration* (*Cat.* 1). Catiline attended this Senate meeting, presumably against Cicero's expectation, but left Rome straight afterwards. Cicero informed the popular assembly of the success of having 'sent Catiline out of Rome' (*Att.* 2.1.3) on the following day in the *Second Catilinarian Oration* (*Cat.* 2.1): 'this criminal we have expelled from Rome; or released; or followed with our farewells as he was leaving of his own accord. He has gone, departed, cleared off, escaped.' As on other occasions, Cicero uses reports to the People (and other summaries) to describe events with his own selected emphasis, thereby conveying his view of his role and the political circumstances.

At the end of November 63 BCE, while Cicero was busy with the Catilinarian Conspiracy, a charge *de ambitu* ('bribery') was brought forward against L. Licinius Murena, one of the consuls designate for the coming year. Cicero took on his defence, because, if Murena was convicted, the Republic would only have one consul at the start of the following year. Yet, since the prosecutors were among his political allies, Cicero had to be careful. However, his defence speech *Pro Murena* was successful in obtaining Murena's acquittal. Cicero also used it to discuss general political issues, such as the behaviour at elections or the appropriate duties of a consul. Thereby Cicero's speech in this individual case can be regarded as an additional attempt to influence political culture. As for his own political career, Cicero agreed to exchange proconsular provinces with his consular colleague C. Antonius, so that the latter received Macedonia and Cicero obtained Gallia citerior:[43] this exchange would provide C. Antonius, who was heavily in debt, with the necessary resources, but force him to loosen his collaboration with Catiline. Later in the year Cicero declined a proconsular province entirely, as he explained in a speech before the People.[44]

In the meantime Catiline and his followers were still planning an uprising in the city and communicating with the Allobroges, a tribe in Gaul. Cicero was able to ascertain the plans of Catiline and his men, to arrange for letters sent by the Catilinarians to their potential allies to be intercepted and to catch some participants red-handed. Despite advice to the contrary by other senior politicians, he did not open the letters before the Senate meeting he convened for 3 December 63 BCE; instead, he dramatically presented all the evidence there: letters describing the conspirators' intentions, statements of witnesses and the accused.[45] He vividly reports his own activities and the course of the Senate meeting to the popular assembly later in the day in the *Third Catilinarian Oration* (*Cat.* 3). The major issue left was the question of what to do with those conspirators who had been taken into custody (Catiline himself was still away from Rome). In the Senate meeting on 5 December 63 BCE various points of view were voiced; essentially the choice was between punishing the conspirators with the death penalty or keeping them in custody in towns in Italy forever. Cicero's speech from the debate in the Senate is the only extant oration by a consul commenting on a matter under discussion (*Cat.* 4), since presiding magistrates typically merely chaired the discussion. Eventually a speech by Cato, then only a junior magistrate, swayed the Senate, with the result that the death penalty was decreed in accordance with his motion.[46] Cicero, as the consul, had it carried out in the evening of the same day. The decision was backed by the state of emergency declared in the *senatus consultus ultimum* and the recent Senate decree; nevertheless, Roman citizens were put to death without trial, which violated Roman laws.

Cicero was proud of having averted the danger and 'saved the city' without civil war and bloodshed;[47] he therefore liked to call himself 'civilian leader and commander' (*togatus dux et imperator*; *Cat.* 2.28; 3.23) and wanted to be seen as an 'exceptionally diligent consul' (*Cat.* 2.14) or a 'watchful consul' (*Mur.* 82). Cicero denied that his success was due to chance; instead he insisted that it was based on his energetic action.[48] His speech in the following year for the defence of P. Cornelius Sulla makes this explicit (*Sull.* 33; 62 BCE):

> When an army of traitorous citizens, herded together for secret crime [i.e. mainly in Rome and Etruria], had prepared for the country a most cruel and terrible end, and when, for the overthrow and destruction of the state, Catiline had been made commander in the camp and Lentulus [i.e. P. Cornelius Lentulus Sura, one of the conspirators] commander in these very temples and dwellings, I the consul, by my precaution and my toil, at the risk of my life, without a riot, without a levy, without arms, without an army, by the arrest and confession of five men only,

freed the city from conflagration, the citizens from murder, Italy from devastation, the state from ruin. I saved the lives of all the citizens, the peace of the world, this city, the home of us all, the citadel of foreign kings and nations, the light of mankind, the home of empire, by the punishment of five mad, abandoned men.

His concern that his consulship should be remembered emerges clearly at the end of the last published *Catilinarian Oration*, based on what Cicero said on 5 December 63 BCE during the discussion in the Senate of the fate of the arrested conspirators: either Cicero sensed already at this point that his deeds might find ambiguous reception and started working to promote the 'correct' assessment, or this passage was altered later, before the surviving version of the speech was circulated (*Cat.* 4.23–4):

Since that is how the matter stands, instead of a command, instead of an army, instead of the province I have given up, instead of a triumph and the other marks of honour that I have forfeited in order to keep guard over Rome and your own safety, instead of the new friends and clients that I would have acquired in a province (although in my work at Rome I devote just as much effort to maintaining my existing connections as I do to acquiring new ones), instead of all these benefits that would otherwise come to me, and in return for the exceptional efforts I have made on your behalf, and in return also for this conscientiousness with which, as you can see, I have protected the country, I ask you for nothing whatsoever – except that you hold on to the memory of this moment and of my whole consulship. As long as that memory remains fixed in your minds, I shall feel that I am defended by the strongest of walls. But if the power of traitors deceives and triumphs over my hopes, then I commend my little son to you: he will surely receive the protection necessary to ensure not just his survival, but his standing in the state – just so long as you remember that his father was a man who saved Rome at his own unique personal cost. [24] Therefore on the survival of yourselves and the Roman people, on your wives and children, on your altars and hearths, on your shrines and temples, on the houses and homes of all of the city, on your dominion and freedom, on the safety of Italy, and on the entire state you must now make your decision carefully, as you have begun to do, and courageously. You have a consul who will not hesitate to obey whatever you decree, and who will defend your decision, and answer for it personally, for the rest of his days.

Cicero may have felt that an exaggerated extolling of his achievements as a consul was necessary, to a certain extent, so as to counterbalance the agitation against him, which started as soon as the new tribunes of the People for 62 BCE entered office in early December 63 BCE. For instance, they prevented Cicero from making the customary farewell speech on the last day in office and only granted him the usual oath declaring that the consul had observed the laws. Cicero, however, made good use of this opportunity and swore that he on his own had saved the city and the Republic. This was the main idea that he wished to convey, and he claims that the audience understood this.[49] Particularly from the end of his consulship onwards Cicero promoted his self-praise and ran a publicity campaign in a variety of forms, which started to annoy even contemporaries.[50]

At the beginning of 62 BCE Catiline died in an armed conflict, while a number of court cases directed against co-conspirators took place. In some of these trials Cicero appeared as a witness or as the defence, but he tried to limit himself to acting against well-known supporters of Catiline. Moreover, he tried to canvass Pompey's support. Also in 62 BCE Cicero defended the poet Archias in *Pro Archia*, presumably since Archias had started a poem about Cicero's consulship,[51] although apparently it was never finished.[52] Atticus wrote a Greek *hypomnema* (a kind of short description) on Cicero's consulship,[53] as did Cicero himself,[54] who also planned a Latin version.[55] In addition, Cicero wrote an epic *De consulatu suo* (*On His Consulship*) in three books[56] and thought of publishing his consular speeches.[57] Later he asked his friend, the politician and historian L. Lucceius, for a historiographical treatment (*Fam.* 5.12; 55 BCE), but this never materialized. As the brief description of his consulship in a contemporary speech demonstrates, Cicero saw his consulship as a realization of unity (*Pis.* 7; 55 BCE):

> Indeed my consulship was so conducted from its beginning to its end, that I did nothing without the advice of the senate, nothing without the approval of the Roman people; upon the rostra [i.e. the speaker's platform in the Roman Forum] I constantly defended the senate, in the senate-house the people; I welded the populace with its leaders, and the equestrian order with the senate. This is a brief description of my consulship.

The following year was marked by the so-called Bona Dea scandal: on the night of 4 December 62 BCE P. Clodius Pulcher (in female clothing) entered Caesar's house during celebrations for the Bona Dea, to which only women had access. When this was discovered, Clodius was accused of a crime against religion, but was eventually acquitted by a court of law susceptible to bribery.[58] Cicero regarded the matter as a fundamental issue for the well-being of the Republic.[59] As correspondence with Atticus during this period reveals, Cicero was more confident than others and believed that he continued his efforts to create unity among the populace, working with the noblemen, while also considering the position of the People.[60]

The political situation changed when Caesar was elected consul in summer 60 BCE and soon afterwards entered into an alliance with Pompey and M. Licinius Crassus, the so-called first triumvirate.[61] Caesar made attempts to draw Cicero over to his side, but Cicero did not wish to give up his influence and independence.[62] At the same time Cicero wrote reflections on government in the form of a long letter of advice to his brother, then provincial governor in Asia.[63]

In 59 BCE Caesar granted the adoption of the patrician P. Clodius Pulcher by a plebeian, thereby allowing him to stand for election as a tribune of the People, an office only open to plebeians. Clodius was elected, and he entered office on 10 December 59 BCE. He immediately proposed four popular bills in support of the People, and he organized a number of gangs and controlled the streets. At the end of January 58 BCE Clodius put forward a bill to the effect that anyone who killed a Roman citizen without trial should be exiled.[64] Cicero's name was not mentioned, but it was clear that the bill was aimed at the events of 5 December 63 BCE. Although Cicero had made the entire Senate responsible for this action, he felt that Clodius' attack was directed at him and behaved accordingly;[65] the situation triggered demonstrations and proclamations both for and against Cicero.[66] After some hectic negotiations, Cicero eventually left the city in self-imposed exile (*Planc.* 73; Cassius Dio 38.17.4–5; Plutarch, *Cicero* 31.5–6). On the following day Clodius' bill was approved and Cicero's house on the Palatine was plundered and set on fire (*Sest.* 53–4). Cicero withdrew to southern Italy and later to Greece while his family stayed in Rome.

Soon afterwards, Pompey and Clodius fell out, and initiatives to get Cicero recalled got under way, but suffered various setbacks, owing to the activities of opponents. At last Cicero was able to begin his return to Rome in August 57 BCE, after the popular assembly had passed a law recalling him. On his way to Rome from Brundisium in southern Italy Cicero received congratulations; he arrived in Rome on 4 September, where he was met by large numbers of people applauding him, as he had been along the way.[67] On the following day, 5 September, Cicero delivered two speeches of thanks to the Senate and to the People,[68] entitled *Post reditum in senatu* or *Oratio cum senatui gratias egit* (*After His Return in the Senate* or *Speech of Thanks to the Senate*) and *Post reditum ad populum* or *Oratio cum populo gratias egit* (*After His Return to the People* or *Speech of Thanks to the People*).

Political agitation and struggles between the two main groups or 'parties' in the Roman Republic, *optimates* (denoting 'conservative noblemen, defenders of the traditional Republic') and *populares* (denoting 'the People and supporters of their interests'), continued. In early March 56 BCE Cicero used the speech *Pro Sestio* for general statements on a political programme: as tribune in 57 BCE, P. Sestius had supported Cicero's return and therefore had clashed with Clodius' gangs, whence he was prosecuted. The oration in Sestius' defence includes a long discussion on *optimates* and *populares*, the state of the Republic and options for the future (see Chapter III). Cicero still believed that maintaining the traditional order was the best system, when citizens aimed to behave responsibly and key positions were filled with reliable individuals (*Sest.* 136–8):

But to bring my speech to a close, and to make certain that I finish speaking before you finish listening so attentively, I shall conclude my remarks on the Best Sort of men [i.e. *optimates*] and on those who lead them and defend the commonwealth, and I shall stir those of you young men who are notables to imitate your ancestors and urge those who are capable of achieving notability through your manly talent to follow the course that has brought success adorned by public office and glory to many new men. [137] Believe me, there is only one path to praise, to worthy standing, to office. It lies in being praised and esteemed by patriots who are wise and sound by nature, and in understanding that the civil community was organized in the wisest possible way by our ancestors, who – because they had not been able to endure the power of kings – created the annual magistracies with this aim in view: the magistrates would ever set the senate's policy in authority over the commonwealth, but the members of that body would be chosen from the people as a whole, with access to that highest category of the citizenry open to the manly exertions of all. They put the senate in place as the commonwealth's guardian, bulwark, and defender; they intended that the magistrates rely upon the senate's authority and be the ministers, as it were, of its most weighty wisdom; moreover, they intended that the senate itself be supported by the splendid estate of the orders next in rank at the same time that it preserved and increased the plebs' liberty and material advantages. [138] The people who do what a man can do to protect this disposition are the Best Sort [i.e. *optimates*], whatever category of the citizenry they belong to; moreover, the people who most conspicuously take onto their own backs the burden of service to the commonwealth have always been considered the leaders among the Best Sort [i.e. *optimatium principes*], the civil community's guarantors and protectors.

Afterwards, Cicero was involved in other court cases, while he fluctuated between Caesar and Pompey as regards his political position and pronounced different political views in subsequent speeches (cf. *Balb.* 61–2; 56 BCE). After indicating his support for Pompey, Cicero largely withdrew from active politics in early 55 BCE. In April he travelled to his estates and consoled himself over the unhappy situation of the Republic by reading and writing books.[69] Cicero returned to Rome in September; an open confrontation with L. Calpurnius Piso, who had challenged Cicero's portrayal of his consulship and exile, ensued: this resulted in Cicero's vehement invective *In Pisonem*, a speech of strong accusation combined with a justification of his own policy (55 BCE). Soon afterwards Cicero was reconciled with powerful men like Crassus.[70]

After having attended the inauguration ceremonies of Pompey's theatre, an enormous building and the first permanent stone theatre in Rome, in autumn 55 BCE, Cicero left the city once more amid a still uncertain political situation, avoiding Senate meetings and awkward work as a lawyer. In this period Cicero's brother Q. Cicero participated in Caesar's Gallic War as a legate (54–51 BCE). In view of the political developments Cicero also sided with Caesar, who dedicated his grammatical piece *De analogia* to him;[71] at this time Cicero apparently felt that he was Caesar's friend.[72]

In Rome Cicero again acted in a number of lawsuits, including the defence of P. Vatinius, who was charged with corruption (54 BCE). Vatinius was a supporter of the men united in the triumvirate, and Cicero had launched an invective against him just a few years earlier, but he saw this defence as a way to secure his position with Pompey and Caesar.[73] Such a significant change of alliance could seem surprising in a man like Cicero; but, according to Cicero, when such a manoeuvre is due to a sound political strategy, it is justified. At any rate, Cicero claims that wise politicians do not stick to their views, but change them according to circumstances (*Planc.* 94; 54 BCE). Still, such an explanation did not stop frequent changes of opinion becoming an issue in the invective against Cicero that was transmitted under Sallust's name.[74]

While away from Rome, Cicero started the rhetorical treatise *De oratore*,[75] finished in November 55 BCE.[76] This is ostensibly a work describing the ideal orator, but because of the qualities Cicero requires for a good orator, namely accomplishment as an orator as well as accomplishment as a philosopher and statesman, it includes a good deal of political theory. Therefore it is not surprising that this treatise was followed by a work devoted to the state and political theory, *De re publica*,[77] a piece that 'concerned the ideal constitution and the ideal citizen' (*de optimo statu civitatis et de optimo cive*), as Cicero says about an earlier version of this treatise.[78]

In 53 BCE Cicero was elected augur as the successor to P. Licinius Crassus.[79] On 18 January 52 BCE Clodius was killed in a confrontation with T. Annius Milo's guard on the Via Appia; this assassination led to unrest and political negotiations. Eventually Milo was taken to court, charged with the use of force and bribery (*de vi, de sodaliciis* and *de ambitu*). Cicero was the only defence lawyer and, allegedly intimidated by Pompey's soldiers guarding the court at the trial, he made a less than impressive appearance:[80] Milo was declared guilty and went into exile. Cicero then wrote up a brilliant speech that he might have given; this extant version of the speech won much praise, but bears little relation to the one actually delivered. Milo himself is reported to have commented that he would not be able to enjoy the fine mullets in Marseilles (his place of exile) had Cicero delivered this speech.[81]

In February 51 BCE Cicero was given the proconsulship in the province of Cilicia (in Asia Minor) for one year; he left Rome on 1 May 51 BCE. Cicero was unhappy about moving away from Rome, but he found an objective in trying to embody his ideal of a provincial governor and in distinguishing himself from his predecessor by 'justice' (*iustitia*), 'self-restraint' (*abstinentia*) and 'mercy' (*clementia*). Although he found this aim hard to realize and the administrative work tedious, he was successful in his military actions against neighbouring nations and seems to have started to enjoy his duties.[82]

When Cicero returned from the province in the autumn of 50 BCE, tensions between the former allies Caesar and Pompey had increased (especially subsequent to the death of M. Licinius Crassus, the third member of the triumvirate, after his defeat at Carrhae in 53 BCE), and both canvassed for Cicero's support. Cicero came up to Rome on 4 January 49 BCE, when there were frantic negotiations to prevent a civil war; Cicero was uncertain which side to support. On 17 January 49 BCE the news reached Rome that Caesar had crossed the river Rubicon between Gaul and Italy; Pompey ordered the evacuation of Rome. Since Cicero was unhappy with Caesar's reactions to his political proposals, he joined Pompey's camp, although he was not a convinced supporter, and moved to southern Italy and later to

Greece. Cicero returned to Italy in 48 BCE, but remained in Brundisium because of the uncertainty about the future. Cicero was reconciled with the victorious Caesar in 47 BCE and got back to Rome,[83] with his life and property saved.

In this period of enforced public inactivity, as a result of political upheaval, Cicero returned to his books, his 'old friends',[84] and started writing again, allegedly also prompted by friends.[85] He composed *Brutus*, a history of Roman oratory named after M. Iunius Brutus, in early 46 BCE; soon afterwards he completed *Paradoxa Stoicorum* (on paradoxical ethical doctrines of the Stoics), which was followed by the rhetorical treatise *Orator*, also dedicated to Brutus. After Caesar's return to Rome, Cicero attended Senate meetings, but did not contribute to discussions. However, when Caesar agreed to the Senate's entreaties in late 46 BCE to pardon M. Claudius Marcellus, an opponent of Caesar, and, in so doing, took note of the Senate after a long interval, Cicero broke his silence: he thanked Caesar profusely, while also trying to influence his policy,[86] and he praised Caesar's clemency and support of the Republic. The function given to this speech, *Pro Marcello*, is obvious from its start (*Marcell.* 1–2):

> The long silence, conscript fathers, which I had maintained for all this time – not from any fear, but out of a mixture of grief and diffidence – has today been brought to an end; and today has also brought a return to my former practice of freely expressing my wishes and opinions. For such exceptional kindness, such unprecedented and unheard of clemency, such extraordinary moderation in someone who has attained absolute power over everything, and such astonishing and, one might almost say, superhuman wisdom – these are things I cannot possibly pass over in silence. [2] Now that Marcus Marcellus, conscript fathers, has been returned to yourselves and to the state, I feel that it is not just his, but my own voice and standing that have been preserved and restored to yourselves and to the state.

Addressing himself to Caesar, Cicero also spoke for the pardoning of Q. Ligarius in *Pro Ligario*, trying to commit Caesar to a policy of clemency and justifying former supporters of Pompey, and then for Deiotarus, king in Galatia, who had originally sided with Pompey, in *Pro rege Deiotaro* (46–45 BCE). In November 46 BCE Caesar left Rome to deal with the revolt of the sons of Pompey in Spain. Cicero's son originally wanted to join his cousin in Caesar's army in Spain, but then was sent on a study trip to Athens.[87]

Also in 46 BCE Cicero's daughter Tullia was divorced from her third husband Dolabella, whom she had married in 50 BCE.[88] In the same year Cicero himself got divorced from Terentia, his first wife;[89] he then married the young girl Publilia, for whom he had been appointed as a trustee, apparently for financial reasons rather than out of love.[90] When Tullia died in February 45 BCE, he was devastated. In his grief he stopped interacting with his new wife, whom he did not see sufficiently distressed,[91] and effectively ended the relationship, which left him with the difficult task of returning the dowry.

In an effort to combat his grief, Cicero turned to literary composition: he finished a consolatory piece entitled *Consolatio* (surviving only in fragments) on 8 March.[92] Soon afterwards he moved on to the production of his next philosophical work,[93] presumably a dialogue entitled *Hortensius* after the famous orator (surviving in fragments), and then to a series of further treatises discussing the views of the major philosophical schools on important ethical and theological questions: in May he finished the first version of *Academica*; at the end of June he completed the five books of *De finibus bonorum et malorum* (*On the Chief Good and Evil*) and a new version of *Academica*;[94] *Tusculanae disputationes* (*Tusculan Disputations*) and *De natura deorum* (*On the Nature of the Gods*) followed. While Cicero initially engaged with philosophy for personal reasons, he seems to have aimed increasingly at a comprehensive treatment. After having rivalled the Greeks in the areas of rhetoric and politics, during this productive period he embarked on doing the same in the field of philosophy while continuing to provide a service to his countrymen.[95] In 44 BCE Cicero completed this series of works by the treatises *De divinatione* (*On Divination*), *Cato maior de senectute* (*Cato or On Old Age*), *De fato* (*On Fate*), *Laelius de amicitia* (*Laelius or On Friendship*), *De gloria* (*On Glory* [surviving in fragments]), *Topica* (*Methods of Drawing Conclusions*) and *De officiis* (*On*

Duties). Nevertheless, Cicero still saw this enterprise as a replacement for proper political activity, or, in other words, a job to be undertaken when one was free from political or legal duties.[96]

Following Caesar's assassination on the Ides of March (15 March) 44 BCE, the political situation suddenly changed. In the subsequent struggle for power Cicero, now a senior ex-consul, was again able to play a major role in political discussions, and he fully threw himself into this task. Albeit not holding an office at the time, he delivered a series of speeches in the Senate and before the popular assembly in 44–43 BCE (*Philippics*), arguing for a coalition with Octavian (the future emperor Augustus), whom he regarded as the lesser evil, and for war against Mark Antony, the remaining consul of 44 BCE (see Chapter I).

During the last couple of years of his life Cicero once again managed to win the support of the People and eventually to have Antony declared a public enemy by means of his rhetorical power (after Antony's defeat near Mutina in Italy in April 43 BCE). Still, Cicero did not achieve his main goal, the restoration of the traditional Republic, partly because he miscalculated the role of potential partners, as he admitted in private letters. Thus, a few months after the delivery of the last *Philippic Oration*, Antony, Octavian and M. Aemilius Lepidus formed the so-called second triumvirate, officially sanctioned on 27 November 43 BCE. One of their first actions was to have Cicero proscribed; he was killed on 7 December 43 BCE,[97] like his brother and his nephew. Cicero's tragic end demonstrates that, apart from Antony's aim for revenge, his opponents regarded his oratorical powers and his consequent potential political influence as significant.

III

POLITICIAN
AND POLITICAL
PHILOSOPHER

AS THE OVERVIEW of Cicero's biography (Chapter II) shows, his entire life is closely intertwined with political developments: his aim from the beginning was to go through the Roman career ladder (*cursus honorum*) and reach an influential position in the Republic (see Chapter VII); he worked on literature during enforced periods of quiet, and many of his writings are presented as another form of service to his countrymen and deal with political questions.

During his fight against one-man rule and for the preservation of the Republic in the last two years of his life (44–43 BCE), Cicero tried to realize political ideals and to put down thoughts on the justification for war or for killing a tyrant in a treatise on (civic) duties, *De officiis* (see Chapter I). What he voices there is clearly set down in a turbulent period and is partly triggered by those circumstances, yet is essentially the result of a lifelong involvement with politics: the ideas that inform *De officiis* and that determined Cicero's attitude to Octavian and Antony as documented in the *Philippic Orations* developed over a long time; the basic principles are already expressed in earlier treatises, where Cicero discusses both the ideal form of the state and the duties of politicians and orators.

The most important of these writings on political philosophy are the treatises *De re publica* (*On the Republic*) and *De legibus* (*On Laws*), both composed during his enforced withdrawal from politics after his return from exile in the late 50s BCE (see Chapter V); *De re publica* was the first to be started and published in 51 BCE, and *De legibus* was apparently abandoned in about 52 BCE (both works survive in incomplete form). In this period Cicero felt that Rome had 'neither commonwealth nor Senate nor courts of justice' and that acting as a lawyer and devoting himself to his studies were the only options left for him.[1] Both Ciceronian works allude to writings of the Greek philosopher Plato (428/7–348/7 BCE) in their titles (*Politeia* [*Republic*], *Nomoi* [*Laws*]) and adopt the dialogic form of the Greek pieces (the third work written in this period, the rhetorical dialogue *De oratore*, is inspired by Plato's *Phaedrus*). In contrast to Plato, however, the dialogue in Cicero is not primarily a means of testing and teaching (by the philosopher Socrates); rather, it is a way of presenting different viewpoints put forward by various interlocutors (who are historical, but have speeches put in their mouths), while the author is able to step back.

The relationship between the two Ciceronian treatises and their connection to the model, Plato, is explicitly voiced by one of the interlocutors (Cicero's friend Atticus) in the introduction to *De legibus* (*Leg.* 1.15):[2]

> *Atticus*: 'If you want to know what *I* expect, it seems logical that since you have written about the best constitution you should also write about its laws. For that, I notice, is what Plato did – your idol and favourite, whom you revere above all others.'

The treatise *De re publica* takes its starting point from a definition of 'state' that has become famous: in a play with the Latin term and its original meaning, *res publica* ('state'/'republic'; literally, 'public/common matter') is defined as *res populi* ('matter of the people'). This does not imply that a 'state' has to be a 'democracy', but rather that it should take the entire populace into account and serve everybody's interests. In the words of the interlocutor Scipio Africanus, the conqueror of Carthage, the description runs as follows (*Rep.* 1.39):

> *Scipio*: 'Well, then, a republic [*res publica*] is the property of the public [*res populi*]. But a public is not every kind of human gathering, congregating in any manner, but a numerous gathering brought together by legal consent and community of interest [*coetus multitudinis iuris consensu et utilitatis communione sociatus*]. The primary reason for its coming together is not so much weakness as a sort of innate desire on the part of human beings to form communities. [...]'

The dialogue goes on to describe the three primary forms of government (monarchy, aristocracy, democracy) as well as their opposites, the negative forms into which these can degenerate (tyranny, oligarchy, ochlocracy). This leads to the question of which of these is the best form of government. Again according to Scipio, the best form is none of those on its own, but a mixture of the three positive forms (*Rep.* 1.69–70):[3]

> *Scipio*: '[...] That is why, though monarchy is, in my view, much the most desirable of the three primary forms, monarchy is itself surpassed by an even and judicious blend of the three simple forms at their best. A state should possess an element of regal supremacy; something else should be assigned and allotted to the authority of aristocrats; and certain affairs should be reserved for the judgement and desires of the masses. Such a constitution has, in the first place, a widespread element of equality which free men cannot long do without. Secondly, it has stability; for although those three original forms easily degenerate into their corrupt versions (producing a despot instead of a king, an oligarchy instead of an aristocracy, and a disorganized rabble instead of a democracy), and although those simple forms often change into others, such things rarely happen in a political structure which represents a combination and a judicious mixture – unless, that is, the politicians are deeply corrupt. For there is no reason for change in a country where everyone is firmly

established in his own place, and which has beneath it no corresponding version into which it may suddenly sink and decline. [70] [...] I hold, maintain, and declare that no form of government is comparable in its structure, its assignment of functions, or its discipline, to the one which our fathers received from their forebears and have handed down to us. So, if you approve [...], I shall describe its nature and at the same time demonstrate its superiority. Then, after setting up our constitution as a model, I shall use it as a point of reference, as best I can, in all I have to say about the best possible state. [...]'

As Scipio is made to indicate at the end of this extract, a mixed constitution is superior to each individual form, but the particular combination realized in the traditional Roman Republic is 'much the best form', as Cicero has another speaker, Scipio's friend C. Laelius, confirm (*Rep.* 1.34):

> *Laelius*: '[...] I wanted this to happen, not just because it was right that a talk about the state should be given, preferably, by a statesman, but also because I recalled that you [i.e. Scipio] used to have frequent conversations with Panaetius in the company of Polybius (the two Greeks who were possibly most expert in political theory); you would adduce numerous arguments to prove that much the best form of government was the one we had inherited from our ancestors [*optimum longe statum civitatis esse eum, quem maiores nostri nobis reliquissent*]. Since you are more *au fait* with that debate, you would do us all a favour (if I may also speak for the others) by presenting your views about the state.'

It is typical of Cicero's treatises, in contrast to those of Greek philosophers, that, although they discuss fundamental questions, they are grounded in contemporary reality; they include references to Cicero as well as to his experiences and those of his peers or the Roman tradition. As he says about Greek philosophers in *De legibus* (3.14): 'The older Stoics supplied perceptive theoretical discussions of the state, but did not offer, as I am doing, a practical guide for communities of citizens.' Cicero's works provide examples of applied philosophy: in *De re publica* the ideal state is outlined with a view to the Roman state, even though the influence of Greek thinkers, such as the Stoic philosopher Panaetius (*c.*185–109 B C E) and the historian Polybius (before 199–*c.*120 B C E), is acknowledged.[4]

Although Cicero's *De re publica* has the form of a dialogue and Cicero does not speak himself (since he pretends merely to record the conversation), it is likely that the author Cicero broadly agrees with the views expressed by the interlocutor Scipio, who is presented as a figure of authority. That the Roman Republican constitution is seen as the best form of government explains Cicero's drive to 'preserve the Republic' as well as his pride in having done so (as he claimed with respect to the struggles against Catiline and Mark Antony). Such an attitude also means that ideally everybody should be involved in public affairs, even though the Roman Republican system was not a true 'democracy' and not everyone had the same rights and influence. This is why Cicero, as a *homo novus*, worked towards belonging to the 'leading citizens' who were respected and in a position to make decisions.

This raises the question of the character and qualities of the individuals responsible for running the state. The 'art of governing' is a science in itself and can be obtained by experience, learning or a combination of the two. What Cicero presents as an ideal is to become accomplished in this art particularly by engagement with public matters as well as by study and learning ('being a major figure in scholarly research and also in governing his country' [*Leg.* 3.14]). If only one of these options is available, in line with the practical nature of the treatise, being active as a statesman is put above leading a studious life, as explained in the introduction to one of the books (*Rep.* 3.4–6):

> So let us regard those who theorize about ethical principles as great men, which indeed they are; let us grant that they are scholars and teachers of truth and moral excellence, provided we acknowledge the fact that this other branch of study is by no means contemptible, whether it was invented by men engaged in the ever-changing world of politics or was practised by those philosophers in the course of their peaceful studies – I am speaking of the art of governing and training peoples, an art which in the case of good and able men still produces, as it has so often

in the past, an almost incredible and superhuman kind of excellence. [5] If, then, someone thinks, like the men who are taking part in the discussion recorded in these books, that he should add scholarship and a deeper understanding of the world to the mental equipment which he possesses by nature and through the institutions of the state, no one can fail to acknowledge his superiority over everybody else. For what can be more impressive than the combination of experience in the management of great affairs with the study and mastery of those other arts? Who can be regarded as more completely qualified than Publius Scipio [c.185–129; consul 147 BCE], Gaius Laelius [consul 140 BCE], and Lucius Philus [consul 136 BCE] – a trio who, to make sure of including everything that brought the highest distinction to eminent men, added this foreign learning derived from Socrates to the native traditions of their forefathers? [6] Hence my opinion that anyone who achieves both objectives, familiarizing himself with our native institutions *and* with theoretical knowledge, has acquired everything necessary for distinction. If, however, one has to choose between these paths to wisdom, then, even though some people think that a life passed quietly in the study of the highest arts is happier, there can be no doubt that the statesman's life is more admirable and more illustrious.

The last book of *De re publica*, which ends with the influential *Somnium Scipionis* ('Scipio's dream'), considers the role of the statesman and presents this as the most elevated job, for which a reward is given in the afterlife (*Rep.* 6.13):

> *Scipio (recounting his dream)*: '[...] Yet, to make you all the keener to defend the state, Africanus, I want you to know this: for everyone who has saved and served his country and helped it grow, a sure place is set aside in heaven where he may enjoy a life of eternal bliss. To that supreme god who rules the universe nothing (or at least nothing that happens on earth) is more welcome than those companies and communities of people linked together by justice that are called states. Their rulers and saviours set out from this place, and to this they return. [...]'

The description of the characteristics of the ideal statesman, who is essential for the health and stability of a nation, has been prepared in earlier books (e.g. *Rep.* 2.51):

> *Scipio*: '[...] Let us contrast with him [i.e. the tyrant] the other figure – that of the good wise man who thoroughly understands what enhances the interests and prestige of the state [*bonus et sapiens et peritus utilitatis dignitatisque civilis*], who is, as it were, a guardian and overseer of his country; for those titles are due to whoever directs and steers the community [*rector et gubernator civitatis*]. Make sure you can recognize such a man, for he is the one who, by his good sense and devoted efforts, can preserve the country. [...]'

The discussion about the best rulers continues in the companion piece to *De re publica*, *De legibus*; as the title indicates, here the focus is on the laws supporting an ideal political system as well as on the nature of law and justice more generally. 'Marcus' (i.e. Cicero's persona), who is one of the interlocutors, explains (*Leg.* 3.4–5):

> *Marcus*: '[...] However, here I am providing a body of law for free communities; so I will adjust my laws to the type of government which I think best. (In the six earlier books [i.e. *De re publica*] I presented my views about the best constitution.) [5] Magistrates, then, are a necessity. Without their good sense and close attention there can be no state. In fact the whole management of a country depends on the apportionment of their functions. Not only must their authority be clearly delimited; the same applies also to the citizens' duty to obey them. A man who exercises power effectively will at some stage have to obey others, and one who quietly executes orders shows that he deserves, eventually, to wield power himself. So it must be the case that anyone who executes orders will have hopes of holding power at some time himself while the man at present in charge will bear in mind that before long he will have to obey others. [...]'

In addition to discussing details of the legal system and the function of magistrates (with reference to the traditional Roman Republic), the dialogue aims at tackling the more fundamental question of the role of law and justice in society. 'Marcus' points this out early on (*Leg.* 1.17):

> *Marcus*: 'That's right, Pomponius [i.e. Cicero's friend Atticus, one of the interlocutors]. For in this discussion, we are not asking how to frame legally binding conditions or how to answer this and that question for our clients. Let's suppose such problems are important, as indeed they are. They have been handled by many distinguished men in the past, and are now being dealt with by a person of the greatest expertise and authority. But in our present analysis we have to encompass the entire issue of universal justice and law; what we call civil law will be confined to a small, narrow, corner of it. We must clarify the *nature* of justice, and that has to be deduced from the nature of man. Then we must consider the laws by which states ought to be governed, and finally deal with the laws and enactments which peoples have compiled and written down. There the so-called civil law of our own people too will not be overlooked.'

Later it is explained that true laws derive from what is good and just according to nature and the gods and that, consequently, man-made statutes set up for nations can only properly be called 'laws' if they agree with natural principles.[5] Some passages in the *Philippics*[6] show that in actual politics, in the fight against Mark Antony, Cicero applies this principle: he states that natural law is put above positive law, but he leaves it open who decides what is right and just according to nature (apparently anything that agrees with Cicero's view of preserving the Republic) and how this can be put into operational laws.

As becomes clear in these treatises, with their emphasis on the leading men, in Cicero's view a good form of government is not only ensured by the shape of a state's constitution and its laws, but also by the character and effort of the populace. Cicero had specific views about who was or was not a good citizen (and perhaps not even a citizen at all). This is most obvious from his speeches, because he often contrasts the party he supports (upright citizens) with the party he attacks (individuals endangering the Republic); thereby he implicitly reveals his views on the condition of the Republic and the value and roles of different groups within it (see Chapter II).

The most extended passage, in which Cicero not only uses such concepts, but also provides some explanation, occurs in the speech *Pro Sestio* (56 BCE). While it has rightly been emphasized that this exposition is part of the oration's argument, rather than a separate exercise in political philosophy, it nonetheless gives an indication of Cicero's underlying thinking. At the same time it shows how such considerations may be linked to what is essentially a political conflict in the aftermath of Cicero's exile (*Sest.* 96–8):

> No doubt this is the point of the question that you addressed to me, in particular, in your speech of prosecution, when you asked what our 'breed of The Best Sort' [*natio optimatium*] is – for that's the phrase you used. The answer to your question provides an excellent lesson for the younger generation to learn, and one that it is not difficult for me to teach: I shall say a few words on the subject, judges, and what I have to say (I believe) will not be inconsistent with our listeners' advantage, your own duty, and the case of Publius Sestius itself.
>
> In this civil community of ours there have always been two sorts of people eager to engage in the people's business and conduct themselves with more than ordinary distinction therein: one set of these have wanted to be considered, and to be, 'men of the people' [*populares*], the other 'men of the best sort' [*optimates*]. Those whose words and deeds were intended to please the many were considered 'men of the people' [*populares*], whereas those who so conducted themselves that their policies were commended by all the best sort of men were considered 'men of the best sort' [*optimates*]. [97] Who, then, are 'all the best sort of men'? If you mean how many of them there are, they are beyond counting, and indeed we could have no stability were that not the case: some take the lead in public policy, others follow, some are members of the grandest categories of the citizenry, to whom the senate chamber lies open, others are Roman citizens in the towns and

countryside, some are businessmen, and there are even freedmen who are 'men of the best sort'. The full complement of men in this category is distributed geographically and by rank, as I have said; but the category as a whole (lest there be any mistake on this point) can be pinpointed and defined briefly. All men are 'men of the best sort' who do no harm, are not wicked or rabid in their nature, and are not hobbled by embarrassments in their domestic affairs. The fact of the matter, then, is that those whom you called a 'breed' are just those who are sound and sane and have their domestic affairs in good order. The men who, in piloting the commonwealth, serve the will, the interests, and the views of the latter folk are considered defenders of the 'men of the best sort' and are themselves counted the most serious men of the best sort, the most distinguished citizens, and the foremost men of the civil community. [98] What, then, is the goal of these pilots of the commonwealth [*rei publicae gubernatores*], what ought they keep in view to guide their course? The condition that is the most excellent and most desirable in the view of all who are sane, patriotic, and flourishing: tranquillity joined with worthy standing [*cum dignitate otium*]. All who desire this condition are 'men of the best sort', those who achieve it are reckoned the men of the highest calibre, the men who preserve the civil community: for it is not fitting that people either get so carried away by the worthy standing derived from public affairs that they do not provide for their own tranquillity, or embrace any form of tranquillity that is at odds with worthy standing.

Cicero distinguishes between two groups called *optimates* and *populares*, terms also employed by his contemporaries and by modern scholars to distinguish between different political views and attitudes in the late Roman Republic. The term *optimates* is generally applied to people who tended to be respected senators and/or wealthy landowners, often with noble ancestry, who pursued what could be called, in modern terminology, a more conservative and right-wing policy, concerned with upholding the traditional system. Individuals who are described by the term *populares* are found at the other end of the political spectrum: they tended to support policies likely to help the masses of ordinary people and were often represented by the tribunes of the People. Cicero, however, employs his own definitions of those groups, starting from the literal meaning of the names, and also modifies the descriptions according to context. Eventually he counts as 'men of the best sort' virtually all citizens who are honest, responsible and supportive of the traditional political and social system, irrespective of their political role and social standing; the leaders of the state are just the best and most serious men from this group. Thus Cicero can proclaim unity, explain away potential conflicts and rifts within the Republic and single out individuals who do not agree with the ideals of the 'men of the best sort' and should therefore not be called 'citizens'. Cicero often uses the term *boni* (literally 'good/honest men') for the party that agrees with his policies and supports the Republic; the word thus develops from a social into a political term. Thereby Cicero creates a terminology with moral connotations for the two opposing forces, in calling the other side *improbi* (literally 'rascals'), although this is not a straightforward contrast (as *boni* and *mali* or *probi* and *improbi* would be). He denounces opponents because of their bad morals and character and brands them as threats to the Republic, rather than responding to their political position.[7]

The aim that the 'men of the best sort' are striving for is defined in *Pro Sestio* as 'tranquillity joined with worthy standing' (*cum dignitate otium*), the earliest occurrence of the term that has developed into a hallmark of Cicero's political ideology.[8] Further well-known phrases denoting elements of Cicero's policy are the terms 'harmony of the orders' (*concordia omnium*) and 'consensus of all honest men' (*consensio omnium bonorum*), which express the notion that all well-intentioned men (as defined by Cicero), irrespective of standing, can work together to create stable and peaceful conditions (with the exception of opponents to the state in Cicero's view). Cicero apparently sees this status as being guaranteed by the traditional structure of the Republic, which prevents the concentration of power in the hands of a single individual.

The concept of unity against disruptive individuals is evident in Cicero's *Fourth Catilinarian Oration*, whose original version was delivered in the Senate on 5 December 63 BCE, on the day on which the decision was made to condemn the captured conspirators to death (without a regular trial). Cicero wanted to create the appearance that everyone was behind this decision. Therefore, in the speech given in the discussion on the fate of the Catilinarian conspirators Cicero comments on the reactions and behaviour of different sections of the populace, stressing that everyone is of the same opinion except for those few whom he does not count as citizens (*Cat.* 4.14–16):

> Everyone has come here today, people of every order, every class, and every age. The forum is packed, the temples surrounding the forum are packed, the entrances to this temple where we are now are all packed. This is the only issue since the foundation of our city on which everyone holds exactly the same opinion – excepting only those who realize that they must die, and so prefer to die along with everyone else rather than on their own. [15] I for my part am quite happy to make an exception of such people and treat them as a special case: I would not class them as wicked fellow-citizens, but as the deadliest external enemies.
>
> But as for everyone else – immortal gods! – how numerous they are, how determined they are, and how nobly they have united in defence of our common safety and honour! Do I of all people have to remind you at this point of the Roman equestrians? While they yield to you the first place in rank and deliberation, they are your rivals in their love for their country. Now, after many years of conflict, this day and this issue unite them with you, calling them back into alliance and harmony with this order. And if we can make this national unity, forged in my consulship, permanent, then I can promise you that no internal civil disturbance will ever again affect any part of our national life. I see that the treasury tribunes have courageously come forward with no less determination to defend the country. I see also that the entire body of scribes, who happen to have come to the treasury today in considerable numbers, have turned their attention from the allotment of their posts to the national security. [16] All the free-born citizens are here, even the poorest of them, in one vast crowd. In fact, is there a single person here who does not regard these temples, the sight of our city, the possession

of freedom, and indeed this light of day and the very soil of our shared homeland as not just dear to him, but a source of joy and delight? It is worth your while, too, conscript fathers, to take note of the feelings of the freedmen. They by their own merit have obtained the rights of citizens, and sincerely consider this their home – while certain others who were born here, and born to the best of families, have thought of it not as their homeland, but as an enemy city. But why do I mention these orders and individuals when their private fortunes, their common political interest, and – what is sweetest of all – their very freedom has roused them to defend their country in its hour of danger?

Cicero reminds the senatorial audience that not only the senators, but also all other parts of society, down to the lowest ranks, have united in support of the Republic. Whether there were indeed so many people from different parts of society around or, if there were, whether they turned up because something exciting was happening are historical questions that this passage does not answer. It simply shows how Cicero uses an apparent situation to strengthen his argument and persuade the audience to agree with him.

While in those passages Cicero argues that all are 'men of the best sort', he also makes attempts to achieve unity or to ingratiate himself with ordinary people: elsewhere he claims that those who call themselves 'men of the people' use the word in the wrong sense, that one can only be a 'man of the people' by supporting policies that are in the interests of the People. This is why the term *popularis* acquires a special meaning in Cicero's writings, since it can be used in different senses: depending on the context, it may denote both 'the truly popular spirit which has the people's interest at heart' (*Cat.* 4.9: *animum vere popularem saluti populi consulentem*) and 'an unreliable politician who flatters the electorate' (*Amic.* 95: *popularem, id est assentatorem et levem civem*).

Cicero begins his political strategy as consul in his first speech before the People by stressing that he is a true 'man of the people' (also implying that, as a 'new man', he is essentially one of them; see Chapter II). He comes back to this argument at the end of his life in the *Philippics* (*Phil.* 7.4):

> And those who talk in this vein are the men who because of their fickleness used to be called 'people's men' [*populares*]. Hence we can see that all along they disliked the best condition of the community, and that they were not 'people's men' by inclination. How else does it happen that the same folk who were 'people's men' in evil causes, prefer to be criminal rather than 'popular' in the most popular cause that ever was, because it is also for the good of the Republic? As you know, I have always opposed the capriciousness of the crowd, but this splendid cause has made a 'people's man' of me.

Cicero, who is arguing for immediate conflict with Antony, confronts those who accuse him of warmongering; in Cicero's interpretation this means that these opponents do not support the interests of the Republic and of the People, as he does, as the real 'man of the people' (*popularis*). This argument only works in Cicero's understanding of the term, if 'man of the people' is used in the literal sense rather than to denote a political attitude. Cicero's strategy shows how he engages with the political rhetoric of his day and cleverly uses key terms to promote his own policies. Such reasoning, designed to provoke a specific political decision, is obviously influenced by tactical concerns, but it agrees with Cicero's overall political philosophy when he presents himself as a representative of a united People.

IV

ORATOR AND RHETORICIAN

WHEN CICERO DELIVERED the *Philippic Orations* at the end of his life (44–43 BCE; see Chapter I), he presented a range of arguments in a sophisticated manner, engaged with the audience and exploited the circumstances of their delivery. While these final speeches show the full mastery of rhetorical techniques, Cicero used such strategies throughout his oratorical career and reflected on them in treatises from the 80s BCE onwards.

The importance of eloquence ('whether it be an art, a study, a skill, or a gift of nature', as he asks in the introduction to an early treatise, *Inv. rhet.* 1.2) for Cicero as well as in Roman Republican society becomes obvious from Cicero's dialogic treatise about the qualities and tasks of an orator, *De oratore* (55 BCE), in which the conversation of the interlocutors starts with a praise of oratory as a significant cultural achievement.[1] One of the speakers, the great orator L. Licinius Crassus (140–91 BCE; consul 95 BCE), is made to comment on the impressive manipulative power of oratory (*De or.* 1.30):

'Actually,' he continued, 'I think nothing is more admirable than being able, through speech, to have a hold on human minds, to win over their inclinations, to drive them at will in one direction, and to draw them at will from another. It is this ability, more than anything else, that has ever flourished, ever reigned supreme in every free nation and especially in quiet and peaceful communities. [...]'

At the same time, another interlocutor, the famous orator Marcus Antonius (143–87 BCE; consul 99 BCE; grandfather of the Mark Antony confronted by Cicero at the end of his life), stresses later in the dialogue that oratory not only has a practical function, but is also something beautiful and delightful for those exposed to it (*De or.* 2.33):

'[...] Right now, let me advance an opinion which I firmly believe: although we may not be dealing with an art, yet there is nothing more magnificent than the perfect orator. For, to pass over the practical utility of oratory, which reigns supreme in every peaceful and free community, the faculty of speaking by itself provides such delight that there is nothing that can give a more pleasant impression either to the human ear or to the human mind. [...]'

Both these points perhaps represent views that Cicero might have shared. At any rate, throughout his active life, he used oratory as his main tool to prompt decisions by influencing audiences and to improve his standing.

Oratorical strategies similar to those employed in the *Philippics* also appear in one of Cicero's early speeches, *Pro Sex. Roscio Amerino* of 80 BCE (a defence against patricide), as shown by the ending of the speech (*peroratio*), a section that tends to be particularly rhetorically refined (*Rosc. Am.* 151–4):

Is this really the purpose for which you [i.e. the judges] have been destined, is it really for this that you have been chosen – to condemn people whom purchasers of confiscated property and cut-throats have not succeeded in murdering? [...] May the gods forbid, gentlemen, that this court, to which our ancestors gave the name 'council of state' [*consilium publicum*], should be thought a bastion for purchasers of confiscated property! [152] Do you not realize, gentlemen, that the sole aim of these proceedings is to get rid of the children of the proscribed by fair means or foul, and that the first step in this process is to be achieved through your sworn oath and this attack on Sextus Roscius? Is there any doubt about who the guilty party is, when on the one side you can see someone who, besides being the prosecutor, is a purchaser of confiscated property, a personal enemy of the accused, and a cut-throat, while on the other you see an impoverished son, highly esteemed by his relations, a man to whom not only no blame at all but not even the suspicion of it can possibly be attached? Can you see anything else at all that counts against Roscius, except for the fact that his father's property has been sold? [153] [...] This new proscription, on the other hand, is directed against the children of the proscribed and against little babies in their cradles; and unless you reject it and repudiate it by your verdict in this trial, then – by the immortal gods! – think what may happen to our country! [154] Men who are wise, and endowed with the authority and power which you possess, have a particular duty to cure those ills from which our country is particularly suffering. There is no one among you who is not conscious that the Roman people, who used to be thought merciful to their enemies abroad, are currently suffering from cruelty at home. Remove this cruelty from our nation, gentlemen. Do not allow it to continue any longer in this country of ours. It is an evil thing, not only because it has done away with so many citizens in a most dreadful manner, but because it has taken away the feeling of compassion from even the mildest of men, by accustoming them to troubles. For when we are witnessing or hearing of some dreadful event every hour, even those of us who are tender-hearted by nature find that, through constant contact with unpleasantness, we lose all sense of humanity.

The case discussed in *Pro Sex. Roscio Amerino* and the confrontation with Mark Antony, which prompted the *Philippic Orations*, are not entirely comparable, since the corpus of the *Philippics* consists of political rather than forensic speeches. Moreover, even if exaggerated by Cicero, Antony's claim to power is more obviously a question affecting the health and survival of the Republic. In both instances, however, Cicero elevates the discussion beyond the level of an individual's fate and presents it as a fundamental question of wider relevance that touches upon the state of the Republic and thus the lives of the individuals in the audience. At the same time, the orator stresses that it is in the audience's hands to take the necessary action to ensure the survival of a constitution that is morally justified and in line with Roman tradition. Thereby the personal interest and involvement of the audience are addressed, and they are motivated to a particular course of action on a psychological rather than a rational level.

Stylistically, Cicero's earlier speeches display more rhetorical flourishes than the *Philippics*: there tend to be more connectors, alliterative pairs, archaisms, colloquialisms, repetitions, correlatives and instances of anaphora, a style of speaking from which Cicero distances himself in later treatises.[2] Beyond the level of phrasing, on the other hand, rhetorical strategies in this extract from *Pro Sex. Roscio Amerino* resemble those in later speeches: these include, for instance, several direct addresses to the audience, questions and exclamations in an attempt to engage them in the argument and the thought process. Further, there are appeals to Roman tradition, which they are called upon to uphold, to their own experience and importance as well as to the resulting position of responsibility. Consequently, there is hardly any mention of the specific case in the final paragraphs (such as a summary of the facts or an appeal to do justice to the unfortunate victim). Instead, the conclusion is an emotionally charged piece, stressing the principles at issue and turning the decision the jury is about to make into a highly significant one transcending the particular case.

Overall, the oration *Pro Sex. Roscio Amerino* exemplifies two aspects that Cicero takes up in treatises in the time of the *Philippics*. Firstly, perhaps prompted by the experience of Caesar's dictatorship, Cicero writes in *De officiis* in 44 BCE that the best use of oratory is to defend someone 'overwhelmed and oppressed because of the influence of some mighty individual': he illustrates this with the example of the early speech *Pro Sex. Roscio Amerino*, given at the time of the Sullan regime (*Off.* 2.51):

There is one piece of advice concerning duty which must be punctiliously observed, that is never to threaten the civic status of an innocent man by prosecution. That could not fail to be a criminal deed. Is anything so inhuman as to take the eloquence that was given by nature for the protection and safekeeping of mankind and to turn it to the destruction or ruin of good men? [...] It is indeed defending that gives the richest yield of glory and gratitude, and the more so if it happens that the man you assist appears to be overwhelmed and oppressed because of the influence of some mighty individual. I myself have done that often; in particular I did so as a young man on behalf of Sextus Roscius of Ameria in the face of the influence of Lucius Sulla, who was then despot. That speech, as you know, is still in existence.

In fact, among Cicero's known forensic speeches there are more speeches of defence than of accusation. Accordingly, when Cicero appeared as a representative of the prosecution in the trial against Verres in 70 BCE, he felt obliged to explain this move (*Div. Caec.* 1):

It may be, gentlemen, that some of you, or some of the audience, are surprised that I have departed from the line of action which I have pursued for all these years with regard to criminal proceedings; that having defended many accused persons, and attacked nobody, I have now suddenly changed my policy, and entered the arena as a prosecutor. But anyone whom this surprises has only to understand the motives that govern my action, and he will not only recognize that I am doing right, but will certainly take the view that no one can be held better fitted than myself to conduct the case before us.

Secondly, in the mid 40s BCE, when Cicero turned out a series of rhetorical and philosophical treatises (see Chapter V), he also discussed questions of rhetorical structure. That the peroration as a special part of the speech should be amplified and emotionally charged is set out at the end of *Topica*, a rhetorical treatise of 44 BCE, which claims to be based on a work of the same title by the Greek philosopher Aristotle (384–322 BCE) as memorized by Cicero,[3] but seems to draw mainly upon other Hellenistic rhetorical treatises. Cicero says about the tropes ('Places') to be used and the emotions to be aroused (*Top.* 97–9):

> Not only complete speeches, but also parts of a speech may be supported by the same kind of Places, partly peculiar, partly general; for example, in exordia [i.e. beginnings of speeches], those who listen are to be made benevolent, docile, and attentive with the help of certain Places peculiar to exordia; the same holds for narrations, for them to work towards their goal, which is that they should be plain, short, clear, credible, of controlled pace, and dignified. Although these features are meant to be in evidence in the whole speech, they are more characteristic of narration. [98] Proof follows on narration, and because proof is primarily brought about by persuasion, it has been said in the books which deal with the whole theory of public speaking which Places have the strongest force for the purpose of persuasion. The peroration [i.e. ending of a speech] has yet again certain other Places belonging to it, and in particular amplification, whose effect in this case ought to be that hearts are either stirred up or soothed, or, if they have already been affected in this way, that the speech either heightens the audience's emotions or sedates them. [99] Precepts for this part of speech, in which compassion, anger, hatred, ill-will, and the other affections of the soul are aroused, are provided in other books which you will be able to read with me when you wish.

The combination of rhetorical rules and philosophical aspects with regard to the appropriate uses of rhetoric and the necessary accomplishments of orators have become known as characteristics of Cicero's major rhetorical works, which are well known to distinguish them from ordinary rhetorical handbooks. These features are already present in this youthful work *De inventione rhetorica*, from which he later distanced himself.[4] *De inventione* includes both the standard list of the five tasks of an orator in composing and delivering a speech (*Inv. rhet.* 1.9) and the statement that the interplay of wisdom and eloquence employed in the interest of the state is best for the country (*Inv. rhet.* 1.1):

> 1.9: Therefore the material of the art of rhetoric seems to me to be that which we said Aristotle approved. The parts of it [i.e. of the art of rhetoric], as most authorities have stated, are Invention, Arrangement, Expression, Memory, Delivery [i.e. the five tasks of an orator or parts of rhetoric: *inventio, dispositio, elocutio, memoria, pronuntiatio* (or *actio*)]. Invention is the discovery of valid or seemingly valid arguments to render one's cause plausible. Arrangement is the distribution of arguments thus discovered in the proper order. Expression is the fitting of the proper language to the invented matter. Memory is the firm mental grasp of matter and words. Delivery is the control of voice and body in a manner suitable to the dignity of the subject matter and the style.

> 1.1: For my own part, after long thought, I have been led by reason itself to hold this opinion first and foremost, that wisdom without eloquence does too little for the good of states, but that eloquence without wisdom is generally highly disadvantageous and is never helpful. Therefore if anyone neglects the study of philosophy and moral conduct, which is the highest and most honourable of pursuits, and devotes his whole energy to the practice of oratory, his civic life is nurtured into something useless to himself and harmful to his country; but the man who equips himself with the weapons of eloquence, not to be able to attack the welfare of his country but to defend it, he, I think, will be a citizen most helpful and most devoted both to his own interests and those of his community.

As Cicero stresses later in the treatise *Orator* (46 BCE), the 'perfect orator' is the person 'who is able to speak in court or in deliberative bodies so as to prove, to please and to sway or persuade' (*Orat.* 69); while he must be competent in all tasks, the use of language is most important, and this is the area in which he must excel (*Orat.* 61):

We must now turn to the task of portraying the perfect orator [*perfectus orator*] and the highest eloquence [*summa eloquentia*]. The very word 'eloquent' [*oratio*] shows that he excels because of this one quality, that is, in the use of language, and that the other qualities are overshadowed by this. For the all-inclusive word is not 'discoverer' [*inventor*], or 'arranger [*compositor*], or 'actor' [*actor*], but in Greek he is called ῥήτωρ [*rhetor*] from the word 'to speak' [*eloqui*], and in Latin he is said to be 'eloquent' [*eloquens*]. For everyone claims for himself some part of the other qualities that go to make up an orator, but the supreme power in speaking [*dicere*], that is eloquence [*eloqui*], is granted to him alone.

Such ideas are treated in detail in Cicero's main rhetorical work, *De oratore* (55 BCE). In this dialogue Cicero has the greatest orators of his youth discuss the qualities and education of 'the best orator' and his technical skills. Because it is a dialogue and the focus is on the 'ideal orator',[5] the work is a reflection on oratory rather than a reference manual.[6] In going beyond the contents of earlier rhetorical handbooks, the work frees itself from a rigid treatise structure and addresses a series of topics matched with personalities, since the 'ideal orator' is presented in relation to the actual experiences of the interlocutors. Like Cicero's other great treatises of this period (*De re publica* and *De legibus*), *De oratore* looks back to Plato (*Phaedrus*), but, because of the practical aspects of its topic, it has a more direct connection to contemporary Roman public life.

The key requirement for the 'perfect orator', repeated by the interlocutors at various points in their conversation, is knowledge of all important areas such as law, history, philosophy and psychology, supplemented by technical sophistication.[7] This is expressed early in the introduction in the writer's own voice (*De or.* 1.16–21):

The truth of the matter is, however, that this faculty is something greater, and is a combination of more arts and pursuits, than is generally supposed. [...] [17] To begin with, one must acquire knowledge of a very great number of things, for without this a ready flow of words is empty and ridiculous; the language itself has to be shaped, not only by the choice of words but by their arrangement as well; also required is a thorough acquaintance with all the emotions with which nature has endowed the human race, because in soothing or in exciting the feelings of the audience the full force of oratory and all its available means must be brought into play. In addition, it is essential to possess a certain esprit and humor, the culture that befits a gentleman, and an ability to be quick and concise in rebuttal as well as attack, combined with refinement, grace, and urbanity. [18] Moreover, one must know the whole past with its storehouse of examples and precedents, nor should one fail to master statutes and the civil law. Surely I don't need to add anything about delivery? [...] What shall I say about the universal treasure-house, the memory? It is clear that unless this faculty is applied as a guard over the ideas and words that we have devised and thought out for our speech, all the qualities of the orator, however brilliant, will go to waste.

[19] Let us stop wondering, then, why there are so few eloquent speakers, seeing that eloquence depends on the combination of all these accomplishments, any one of which alone would be a tremendous task to perfect. Let us rather encourage our children, and all others whose fame and reputation are dear to us, to appreciate fully its enormous scope. They should not rely on the precepts or the teachers or the methods of practice in general use, but be confident that they can achieve their goals by means that are of a quite different order. [20] It is at least my opinion that it will be impossible for anyone to be an orator endowed with all praiseworthy qualities, unless he has gained a knowledge of all the important subjects and arts. For it is certainly from knowledge that a speech should blossom and acquire fullness: unless the orator has firmly grasped the underlying subject matter, his speech will remain an utterly empty, yes, almost childish verbal exercise.

[21] Nevertheless, it is not my intention to lay upon orators – least of all upon ours who are so intensely occupied with life at Rome – this enormous burden of having to know everything, even though the essence of the notion 'orator,' and the very claim of being able to speak well, seem to imply the definite promise to speak distinctively and abundantly about whatever subject has been put forward.

Wide-ranging knowledge is the precondition for being a 'perfect orator', but such a person also needs to be well versed in the rules of rhetoric and the tasks of the orator, as is explained later by the speaker Crassus (*De or.* 1.64):

> '[...] Accordingly, then, if we want to capture the true meaning of the word 'orator' [*orator*] in a complete definition, it is my opinion that an orator worthy of this grand title is he who will speak on any subject that occurs and requires verbal exposition in a thoughtful, well-disposed, and distinguished manner, having accurately memorized his speech, while also displaying a certain dignity of delivery [*actio*]. [...]'

One important area is the relationship to the audience, included in the orator's final task: *actio*, 'delivery' or 'performance'. Many ancient authorities highlight its significance: Demosthenes was said to have given it first, second and third place among the most important elements of oratory, and it was felt that the same speech given by different speakers could have different effects.[8] Delivery includes not only pronouncing the words of orations (the only element of which a record may be preserved), but extends to the appearance as a whole, covering details such as clothing, gait, mimicry, gesture, references to the location and reactions of the audience. These features can sometimes be inferred from the transmitted text of speeches,[9] and there is some instruction on those in the later oratorical manual *Institutio oratoria* by the rhetorician Quintilian (*c.*95 CE).

Cicero's theoretical writings reveal that, whatever the orator is going to say, his performance should be attractive in itself. Interaction with the crowd and emotional influence upon them are key elements, as 'Cicero' (as a dialogue partner) points out in *Brutus* (46 BCE), a kind of history of Roman oratory (*Brut.* 290):

> '[...] This is what I wish for my orator: when it is reported that he is going to speak let every place on the benches be taken, the judges' tribunal full, the clerks busy and obliging in assigning or giving up places, a listening crowd thronging about, the presiding judge erect and attentive; when the speaker rises the whole throng will give a sign for

silence, then expressions of assent, frequent applause; laughter when he wills it, or if he wills, tears; so that a mere passer-by observing from a distance, though quite ignorant of the case in question, will recognize that he is succeeding and that a Roscius [i.e. a famous dramatic actor in Cicero's time] is on the stage. [...]'

Owing to passages like this, an aspect of the presentation of a speech about which some details can be inferred from preserved texts is the interaction with the audience. Political speeches could be given in the Senate or before the popular assembly, and the speakers in *De oratore* acknowledge that one needs to speak differently before each body: since in the Senate orators speak to an educated group of peers and there will be a series of speeches, they should not overdo the rhetorical display and avoid the suspicion that they are showing off. Speaking before the popular assembly, however, is like being on stage; this encourages the orator to make use of all rhetorical tropes and variations at his disposal.[10]

This description may reflect the importance of having a psychological impact on the audience, irrespective of its composition. For, as the treatise explains, people tend to arrive at decisions moved by feelings and emotions rather than by rational thought and reflection.[11] Therefore it is essential to make the audience favour individuals the orator supports by presenting their character and actions positively and to denigrate the opponents.[12] In Cicero's extant speeches there are many examples of this method: he typically extols whomever he promotes and disparages the other party in his strategy of drawing up black-and-white contrasts and of arguing with a person's life and character as a whole rather than the deeds immediately relevant.

The vilified characters in Cicero's rhetorical output include Verres, Catiline, Clodius and Mark Antony. That the principle of black-and-white contrasts is ingrained in the construction of Cicero's speeches becomes obvious in the cases of Verres and Antony when it is found in orations that were probably never delivered: the speeches against Verres for the second hearing of the trial in 70 BCE (*Verr.* 2) and the second speech against Antony in 44 BCE (*Phil.* 2) were written up as given at a particular point in time, but were almost certainly never actually spoken. Still, they include prominent elements of character invective against these two men, designed to motivate the audience to hold negative feelings against them. For instance, the fifth speech for the second hearing in the Verres trial deals with his neglect of his military responsibilities as provincial governor in Sicily: Cicero does not limit himself to describing what he regards as faults, but includes digressions on Verres' general behaviour in that role, so as to illustrate his irresponsibility (*Verr.* 2.5.28):

> While we are on this subject I think I should not pass over our glorious general's outstanding, unique diligence. For I have to tell you that, in all the towns in Sicily where governors stay and hold assizes, there is none in which a woman from a respectable family was not specially selected to satisfy his lusts. Some of these were openly brought to his table, while any who were more modest in their behaviour came later at a prearranged time, avoiding the light and the crowd of people. His dinner parties were not the quiet affairs one expects with governors and generals, nor the decorous occasions that magistrates put on, but were noisy and bad-mannered events; sometimes they even descended into hand-to-hand fighting. For this strict, diligent governor, although he never obeyed the laws of the Roman people, carefully observed all the drinking rules that are prescribed at parties. And his entertainments generally ended up with someone being carried from the feast as if from the battlefield, someone else being left for dead, and the majority sprawling, with no awareness of who or where they were – so that anyone who saw them would believe that they were looking not at a governor's official dinner, but at an outrage reminiscent of Cannae [i.e. the Roman defeat in the war against Hannibal in 216 BCE].

Equally, when Cicero spoke in support of someone, he could be full of praise. There may be a contrast to a negatively presented character, as when Octavian and Caesar's assassins are praised in the *Philippics* as opposition to Mark Antony, or a positive figure may be singled out in order to make the audience agree with what Cicero is asking for. In the speech *De lege Manilia* or *De imperio Cn. Pompei*, Cicero's first political oration when he was praetor in 66 BCE, for instance, he describes Pompey as an outstanding general to convince the audience to vote for a bill of the tribune Gaius Manilius to give Pompey the command in the war against the king of Pontus, Mithridates (*Leg. Man.* 27–9):

> It remains, I think, to speak about the choice of a commander, and his appointment to this major undertaking. I only wish, citizens, that you had so many brave men of spotless reputation at your disposal that you would find it difficult to decide which of them you would prefer to put in charge of such a major undertaking, and such a great war! But as it is, Gnaeus Pompeius, and he alone, has by his own merit surpassed in glory not only everyone who is alive today, but also all the great figures of the past. In this case, then, is there anything that could possibly make any of you hesitate?
>
> [28] To my way of thinking, there are four qualities that a great commander must possess: military knowledge, ability, authority, and luck [*scientia rei militaris, virtus, auctoritas, felicitas*]. Who, then, has there ever been who had, or potentially had, greater military knowledge than he? [...] all these demonstrate that there is no aspect of military experience which can escape the knowledge of this man.
>
> [29] As regards the ability of Gnaeus Pompeius, what speech could possibly do justice to it? What could anyone say that would not be unworthy of him, already known to you, or familiar to everyone? For the attributes of a great general do not consist only of those that are commonly thought of as such: dedication in one's duties, courage in danger, thoroughness in undertaking the task in hand, speed in accomplishing it, foresight in planning – qualities that are as evident in this single man as in all the other commanders, put together, that we have seen or heard of.

However, caution is required in drawing conclusions about an orator's personal views on the basis of his arguments in public speeches, since these are determined by what appears to be the most effective and successful rhetorical strategy. For instance, there are sometimes discrepancies in Cicero's assessment of individuals between his speeches and his letters (although the latter too might not always disclose the writer's true views, depending on the addressees). In the speech *Pro A. Cluentio Habito* (66 BCE) Cicero voices this principle explicitly (*Clu.* 139):

> But it is the greatest possible mistake to suppose that the speeches we barristers have made in court contain our considered and certified opinions; all those speeches reflect the demands of some particular case or emergency, not the individual personality of the advocate. For if a case could speak for itself no one would employ a pleader. As it is, we are employed to express, not the conclusions warranted by our own judgement, but the deductions which can be made from the facts of the case.

Since there is little first-hand evidence on orators contemporary with Cicero (only fragments and comments about them, mainly by Cicero, remain), it is difficult to be sure whether the techniques observed in Cicero's speeches and discussed in his rhetorical works were common practice in his time or a speciality of his. Since Cicero went through the traditional education of well-to-do young men in Rome, discusses such rhetorical features in his theoretical writings, regards his speeches as models for aspiring young orators[13] and had oratorical success in the society of his time, it is likely that he was not doing anything unusual. However, the fact that Cicero's writings soon became a standard item on the school syllabus and a model to follow may suggest that he used the general methods in a particularly impressive and sophisticated way. At any rate he had made an effort in his youth to study with the most famous Greek and Roman orators, philosophers and politicians of his time, and he showed himself very much aware of the development and the rules of rhetoric.

Cicero's concern that his speeches should have an impact is also reflected in the fact that some of them were written up for publication. The rhetorical treatises focus on the composition of speeches and their delivery, because in Rome speeches were not normally fully written out in advance. They could, however, be written up after delivery, with some revision in relation to the original delivery (the extent of which is debated), and then be distributed for rhetorical or political impact. This gives a literary character to what was originally a persuasion technique, and for Rome Cicero was able to trace this custom back at least to Cato.[14] Publication ensured that versions of Cicero's more important speeches survived and soon became influential models.

In the rhetorical treatise *Brutus* (46 BCE) Cicero provides a history of oratory and rhetoric at Rome from the beginnings until his own time (including information on earlier orators). This is an innovative format: there is no real precedent for a history of a particular area of expertise, characterizing both the field and its individual representatives, even though interest in aspects of the history of Rome is also noticeable in works by Cicero's friends and contemporaries. Because of the political structure of the Roman Republic, a history of rhetoric is inevitably connected with a history of politics; *Brutus* contains reminiscences, combined with admiration, of famous men in Roman public life, influential because of their oratory, and some regret that they belong to the past.

Due to its chronological structure, *Brutus* ends with the orator Hortensius and then Cicero, who appears as the climax within the historical development of rhetoric at Rome. Consequently, *Brutus* is an important document not only for Roman oratory, but also for Cicero's view of himself as an orator.[15] Cicero mentions having been praised by Caesar as an orator.[16] In addition, he does not hesitate to glorify himself, distinguishing himself from others who have not worked as hard on their education and rhetorical skills (*Brut.* 321–2):

> '[...] I, on the other hand, did not cease from efforts to increase such gifts
> as I had by every type of exercise, and particularly by writing. To pass
> over much in this period and in the years which followed my aedileship,
> I was made praetor, and because of great popular favour towards me
> I stood first among the candidates chosen. For not only my constant
> activity and industry as a pleader, but also my style of speaking, more
> thoroughly considered than the conventional manner of the forum, had
> by its novelty drawn the attention of men to me. [322] I say nothing
> of myself; I shall speak rather of others. Of them there was not one

who gave the impression of having read more deeply than the average man, and reading is the well-spring of perfect eloquence; no one whose studies had embraced philosophy, the mother of excellence in deeds and in words; no one who had mastered thoroughly the civil law, a subject absolutely essential to equip the orator with the knowledge and practical judgement requisite for the conduct of private suits; no one who knew thoroughly Roman history, from which as occasion demanded he could summon as from the dead most unimpeachable witnesses; no one who with brief and pointed jest at his opponent's expense was able to relax the attention of the court and pass for a moment from the seriousness of the business in hand to provoke a smile or open laughter; no one who understood how to amplify his case, and, from a question restricted to a particular person and time, transfer it to universals; no one who knew how to enliven it with brief digression; no one who could inspire in the judge a feeling of angry indignation, or move him to tears, or in short (and this is the one supreme characteristic of the orator) sway his feelings in whatever direction the situation demanded. [...]'

What Cicero here claims for himself implicitly recalls the portrayal of the 'perfect orator' in the earlier treatise *De oratore* (55 BCE). The 'perfect orator' must have knowledge of the techniques of rhetoric and of all the subject areas that he may have occasion to speak about or that may be of relevance for a speech (such as law, history, philosophy, literature). Consequently such a person surpasses philosophers and other learned men who are specialists in a single particular field.[17]

Cicero's rhetorical treatise *Orator* (46 BCE) discusses different types of speaking, the various duties of an orator (to teach, entertain and move audiences) as well as details of style. A large part of *Orator* is devoted to sentence structure and prose rhythm (the arrangement of sequences of short and long syllables by selection and the organization of words, especially at the end of clauses), which is the most detailed treatment of this topic in ancient literature up to this period. While this is again done on the basis of depicting the 'ideal orator', this treatise is more technical and does not avoid specific rhetorical terminology. Its more didactic approach[18] has been connected with Cicero's emerging role as a 'teacher of rhetoric' for selected students among the young men of his acquaintance.[19]

Although Cicero was regarded as a great orator, he did not win unqualified acclaim throughout his life. The last decade of his life coincided with a controversy over different styles of rhetoric, known as Atticism versus Asianism. Those who regarded themselves as 'Atticists', particularly C. Licinius Macer Calvus (c.82–50 BCE), took the classical Attic writers, mainly the Greek orator Lysias (c.450–380 BCE), as models and favoured a more restrained style. Those who did not follow these principles were considered as 'Asianists', because the style of Greek orators in Asia Minor was more abundant and ornate.

In the context of such stylistic discussions Cicero describes the development of oratory in Greece and beyond and thus of the 'Attic' and 'Asiatic' styles in the piece *Brutus* (*Brut.* 49–51):

'[...] Thus, as regards Greece, you see the birth and origins of oratory, early from the standpoint of our chronology, but from theirs quite recent. For long before Athens found pleasure in the art of speaking and in the glory of its exercise, it had accomplished many memorable things both in peace and in war. The pursuit of oratory however was not shared in by Greece as a whole, but was peculiar to Athens. [50] [...] [51] But outside of Greece proper eloquence was cultivated with great ardour, and the honours awarded to excellence in this art gave distinction to the name of orator. For when once eloquence had sailed forth from Piraeus [i.e. the port of Athens] it traversed all the islands and visited every part of Asia, but in this process it contracted some stain from foreign ways and lost that wholesomeness, and what one might call the sound health, of Attic diction; indeed it almost unlearned the art of natural speech. From this source came the Asiatic orators, not to be despised whether for their readiness or their abundance, but redundant and lacking conciseness. The school of Rhodes however retained more sanity and more similarity to the Attic source. [...]'

Cicero's own rhetorical style came under attack for its 'Asianism', since some saw it as too blown up and decadent, as too rich in words, as full of long sentences and rhetorical cadences. Thereupon, in his late rhetorical treatises, written partly in response (especially *Brutus* and *Orator*), Cicero points out that the so-called 'Atticists' have a narrow view of what is 'Attic': he indicates that Demosthenes too is an Attic orator and should be the preferred model, as he is virtually a perfect orator in his view because of his refined style adapted to the respective contexts.[20] Cicero's standpoint in the rhetorical controversy can be summarized in his own words (*Brut.* 291): 'Our conclusion then will be, not that all who speak in an Attic style speak well, but that all who speak well deserve the title of Attic.' Elsewhere Cicero characterizes the different styles in greater detail: he indicates, for instance, that there are various types of Asiatic style and these are better suited to younger orators;[21] he also points out that there are different kinds of Attic style and that the contemporary Atticists have only accepted one of them.[22]

In contrast to his friends Atticus and M. Iunius Brutus, Cicero was not a convinced 'Atticist' in the 'technical' sense. Yet during his final rhetorical period he came close to that style and at the same time kept to his own beliefs, when he attempted to maintain a passionate tone despite using a more restrained style. For Cicero did not regard the two aspects as incompatible (*Att.* 15.1a.2 [18 May 44 BCE]): 'But you have only to call to mind Demosthenes' thunderbolts to realize that a speaker can be both impeccably Attic and profoundly impressive.' Therefore Cicero would not have seen himself as belonging exclusively to either side in this quarrel. Instead, he preferred a style appropriate to the circumstances and making use of all suitable elements.

These considerations of Cicero's final years can be seen in his last speeches, the *Philippics*, which are clearly modelled on (and named after) Demosthenes: they combine passionate invective and emotional outbursts with more restrained argument.

V

PHILOSOPHICAL WRITER

DURING THE LAST YEARS of his life (44–43 BCE) Cicero was heavily involved in the political struggle with Mark Antony and composed the *Philippic Orations* (see Chapter I); at the same time he wrote numerous letters and completed a sequence of philosophical works, following upon the series of rhetorical writings of 46 BCE (see Chapter IV).

The last and most significant of these philosophical pieces within the context of its time is the treatise *De officiis* (44 BCE), an exposition of 'duties' with regard to what is 'useful' and 'honest', addressed to Cicero's son Marcus. Cicero talks about the role of these concepts in a state, and he criticizes aspirations to single rule (more or less directly), clearly in response to recent experiences with Caesar.[1] That the political circumstances in the 40s BCE have influenced further philosophical treatises has also been suggested, not only in terms of their time of composition in a period of less intensive political activity, but also with respect to the topics discussed. In the years 45 and 44 BCE alone Cicero wrote *Hortensius, Academica (Academic Books), De finibus bonorum et malorum (On the Chief Good and Evil), Timaeus, Tusculanae disputationes (Tusculan Disputations), De natura deorum* (*On the Nature of the Gods*), *De divinatione* (*On Divination*), *Cato maior de senectute* (*Cato* or *On Old Age*), *De fato* (*On Fate*), *Laelius de amicitia* (*Laelius* or *On Friendship*), *De gloria* (*On Glory*) and *De virtutibus* (*On Virtues*).

This activity in his final years is remarkable, with Cicero turning out works in all the major literary genres he had been active in throughout his life (including the rhetorical piece *Topica* in 44 BCE). Although Cicero studied philosophy from his youth onwards and allegedly engaged with it continually,[2] his theoretical writings are confined to two periods, the 'first philosophical phase' in the mid to late 50s BCE and the 'second philosophical phase' in 46–44 BCE. This chronology is no coincidence: although Cicero regarded a thorough education, including philosophy, as a precondition for an accomplished orator and senior statesman (as the treatise *De oratore* in particular shows), he considered writing philosophical works as second-best (also in the context of widespread opposition to philosophy in Rome) and as a way of doing a service to the Republic when active intervention was not possible.[3]

In Cicero's view this was the case in the mid to late 50s BCE, during the tumultuous years between his return from exile and his governorship of the province of Cilicia and the civil war, and in the mid 40s BCE, during Caesar's dictatorship, until Cicero, perhaps unexpectedly, felt called upon again to take on a politically prominent position in the struggle for power after Caesar's assassination in March 44 BCE. The 'first phase', in the 50s BCE, resulted in pieces on oratory (*De oratore*; see Chapter IV) and political philosophy (*De legibus*, *De re publica*; see Chapter III). The works dealing with other areas of philosophy date from the 'second phase' in 46–44 BCE (not all of them surviving in full), when his friends Brutus and Atticus apparently also encouraged Cicero to write.[4] While some of these pieces were only finished after Cicero had returned to politics, their genesis goes back to the quieter period of the preceding years. Overall, Cicero devotes little space to logic, physics and physiology; at the same time he covers almost all other areas of philosophy, including epistemology, ethical theory, practical morality, moral psychology, theology and metaphysics, political philosophy and legal theory.

The role of philosophical writing is indicated in the prefaces to many of Cicero's philosophical works, such as that to *Academica*, a treatise presenting the views and evolution of the philosophical school of the sceptical Academy. Cicero produced two versions of this piece in 45 BCE: in one of them he stresses that at this point in time, being relegated from public life, he has the chance to devote more time to philosophy, which he had continued to do privately, and he admits the consolation this provides;[5] in the other version Cicero stresses that he only spends time on philosophy when it does not interfere with active political life (*Acad. post.* 11; *Acad. Pr.* 6):

> *Acad. post.* 11: '[...] In my own case, Varro [i.e. a learned Roman and friend of Cicero, one of the interlocutors] – to be completely frank – while I was tied up with many duties imposed by elections, public office, legal cases, and even a degree of governance of the republic over and above my solicitude for it, I kept my philosophical interests private and renewed them through reading when I could, to stop them from getting rusty. But now that I have been wounded by a very severe blow from fortune, I am looking for a balm for my sorrow from philosophy; and now that I have been freed from administering the republic, I judge this to be the most honourable relaxation for my time of leisure. Perhaps it is particularly suited to my time of life. Perhaps it is especially consistent with any praiseworthy actions I may have performed. Perhaps it's also true that nothing else is as useful for the education of our fellow-citizens. Or perhaps, if none of these reasons work, I can't see anything else I could do. [...]'

> *Acad. Pr.* 6: Moreover, if philosophy was rightly praised in one of my books, engaging with it is obviously something highly appropriate for any important or eminent man – with the single proviso that people like myself, whom the Roman people have placed in this position, should make sure that nothing is detracted from our public work through our private interests. But I never let my work stray from the public arena while it was incumbent on me to serve – I didn't even let myself write anything unconnected with the law.

From another angle, from the point of view of oratory, Cicero regards his engagement with literature and letters as a natural extension and worthy counterpart of his political and forensic activity (*Orat.* 148):

> But even if the facts were not as I have stated them, who would be hard or unfeeling enough to refuse me the favour of devoting myself to letters, now that my forensic practice and my public career have fallen in ruins, rather than to idleness, which is impossible for me, or to grief, against which I put up a bold front? Literature was once my companion in the court and senate house; now it is my joy at home; nor am I busied merely with such matters as form the subject of this book, but with even greater and weightier themes. If these are brought to completion, I am sure my forensic efforts will find a proper counterpart even in the literary labours of my seclusion.

According to Cicero the training of an orator should include philosophy (see Chapter IV) and, as he says in his treatise *On Fate*, 'there is a great affinity between the orator and the type of philosophy which I follow.' Consequently, it will be less surprising that Cicero moves seamlessly between oratory and philosophy (making use of his rhetorical training to present philosophy attractively) and that the two main areas covered in his treatises are rhetoric and philosophy (*Fat.* 3):[6]

> When we had done this, he [i.e. the interlocutor A. Hirtius, a friend of Cicero and consul in 43 BCE] said, 'Well, since you indeed have not – I hope – abandoned rhetorical exercises, though you have certainly given philosophy priority over them, can I hear something from you?' 'You can indeed', I said, 'either listen or speak yourself. For as you rightly judge, I have not abandoned that enthusiasm for rhetoric, which I fired in you too, even though it was already blazing in you when you came to me. Nor do the things I am now dealing with diminish that faculty; rather, they increase it. For there is a great affinity between the orator and the type of philosophy which I follow; he borrows subtlety in argument from the Academy, and gives back to it in return richness

of expression and rhetorical ornament. For this reason', I said, 'since both subjects are in my possession, let it be for you to choose today which you prefer to employ.'

That active involvement in politics is closely linked with philosophical considerations on the right behaviour of a citizen and statesman in Cicero's thoughts becomes obvious from a letter to Atticus in 49 BCE: there Cicero lists a long series of questions about how to act in response to despotism and says: 'Practising myself upon these questions and setting out the arguments on either side, now in Greek now in Latin, I take my mind for a while off the troubles and at the same time ponder matters of relevance.' While he claims that he is doing this as a kind of exercise, these questions are important to him in this situation and the answers to them will determine his future actions. Therefore he is writing not about any philosophical problems considered out of scholarly curiosity, but about issues of immediate significance. That he asserts that he sets out the arguments on either side, in Greek and in Latin, shows how well trained he is in literary exercises, philosophical argument and the traditions of the philosophical school of the sceptical Academy (see below) and that he can apply these rules even in a difficult situation. Cicero writes to Atticus (*Att.* 9.4 [12 March 49 BCE]):

> Though the time I spend writing to you or reading your letters brings me my only respite, I am at a loss for matter and I am sure it is the same with you. The kind of things friends usually write to one another when their minds are easy is ruled out by the times we live in, while we have already worn threadbare the topics appropriate to *them*. However, not to surrender myself wholly to bitterness of spirit, I have chosen some themes as it were, which are both political and topical, with the object of distracting my mind from its griefs and to keep it busy on the question at issue. This sort of thing:
>
> [2] Ought a man to remain in his country under a despotism? Ought he to strive for the overthrow of a despotism by every means, even if the existence of the state is going to be endangered thereby? Ought he to beware of the overthrower lest *he* be set up as despot? Ought he

to try to help his country under a despotism by taking opportunity as it comes and by words rather than by war? Ought a statesman to live quietly in retirement while his country is under a despotism or ought he to take every risk for freedom's sake? Is it right to make war against one's land and blockade it when it is under despotic rule? Ought a man to enrol himself on the side of the best citizens even if he does not approve of overthrowing the despotism by war? Ought he in politics to join in the dangers of his friends and benefactors even though he does not approve of their actions in capital matters? Ought a man who has rendered his country great service and has on that account brought himself irreparable suffering and hostility voluntarily to incur danger on his country's behalf, or may he be allowed to begin to think of himself and his family, giving up political opposition to those in power? [section written in Greek]

[3] Practising myself upon these questions and setting out the arguments on either side, now in Greek now in Latin, I take my mind for a while off the troubles and at the same time ponder matters of relevance.

Against the background of the state of philosophy in Cicero's time and his education, it is obvious that his philosophical discussions are heavily influenced by Greek philosophy, which raises the question of the relationship between the two. Cicero once says in a letter to Atticus that his writings 'are mere transcripts, requiring less work', as he 'just contribute[s] the words' (*Att.* 12.52.3 [21 May 45 BCE]). However, this understatement seems to be due to the argument, as he intends to create a contrast with Varro's contemporary treatise *De lingua Latina* (*On the Latin Language*). Elsewhere Cicero takes pride in the fact that he does not translate word for word, but rather renders the sense, though he feels free to borrow where appropriate,[7] and he overcomes the absence of a developed philosophical language in Latin by creating the necessary technical terms that the Latin language still lacked (see Chapter VI).[8] He selects material that suits him from a variety of philosophers in eclectic fashion and thereby introduces his countrymen to philosophy.[9] There were hardly any Roman philosophers of note prior to Cicero,[10] allegedly partly owing to the lack of an appropriately developed language. In Cicero's view, this deplorable situation has to be remedied: he feels that he is the right man to do so, on account of his oratorical reputation and his experience in eloquent presentation (*Tusc.* 1.5–7):

> Philosophy has lain neglected to this day, and Latin literature has thrown no light upon it: it must be illuminated and exalted by us, so that, if in the active business of life I have been of service to my countrymen, I may also, if I can, be of service to them in my leisure. [6] And I must exert myself all the more actively because there are now, it is said, a number of books in Latin written without due care by writers who with all their merits are yet insufficiently equipped. Now it is possible for an author to hold right views and yet be unable to express them in a polished style; but to commit one's reflections to writing, without being able to arrange or express them clearly or attract the reader by some sort of charm, indicates a man who makes an unpardonable misuse of leisure and his pen. The result is that such writers read their own books themselves along with their own circle, and none of them reaches any wider public than that which wishes to have the same privilege of scribbling extended to itself. For this reason, if by my assiduity I have won for our countrymen some measure of oratorical renown, I shall with far greater enthusiasm lay bare the springs of philosophy, which were also the source from which those earlier efforts of mine took their rise.
>
> [7] But just as Aristotle, a man of supreme genius, knowledge and fertility of speech, under the stimulus of the fame of the rhetorician Isocrates, began like him to teach the young to speak and combine wisdom with eloquence, similarly it is my design not to lay aside my early devotion to the art of expression, but to employ it in this grander and more fruitful art: for it has ever been my conviction that philosophy in its finished form enjoys the power of treating the greatest problems with adequate fulness and in an attractive style.

Cicero's argument does not mean that Romans contemporary with Cicero were completely unacquainted with philosophy: Greek philosophy had been known in Rome for a long time; for instance, Romans had been exposed to different philosophical views as a result of the so-called philosophers' delegation in 155 BCE (a visit to Rome by the Academic philosopher Carneades of Cyrene, the Peripatetic philosopher Critolaus of Phaselis and the Stoic philosopher Diogenes of Babylon). There are references to philosophy in early Republican drama and satire, including, among other aspects, the presentation of two different concepts of *fortuna* (as chance or an untrustworthy goddess) in a (fragmentary) tragedy by Pacuvius from the second century BCE;[11] this passage contains the term *philosophus*, which is also attested in the works of the comic poet Terence in the 160s BCE.[12] Furthermore, in Cicero's time (possibly available by the 50s BCE) there was Lucretius' didactic poem *De rerum natura* (*On the Nature of Things*), an introduction to various aspects of the theories on physics, theology and ethics of the Greek philosopher Epicurus (342/1–271/0 BCE). Moreover, Cicero's correspondence shows that men of his social and educational background were well versed in philosophical methods and doctrines. What seemed to be lacking were a systematic exposition of the main philosophical positions and the adequate technical terminology in Latin (see Chapter VI).

In Cicero's time there were four main philosophical schools, each going back to a famous Greek philosopher: the Stoics (followers of Zeno, who taught in the Stoa in Athens), the Epicureans (followers of Epicurus), the Peripatetics (followers of Aristotle and his disciples, who established a school with a walkway called Peripatos) and the Academics (followers of Plato, whose school was located near a park named after the local hero Academus). A convenient way of displaying tenets of different philosophical schools in a literary piece is the dialogue format: representatives of each view can put forward their positions with their respective attractions and possible drawbacks side by side. This method enables the author to remain in the background rather than take sides and reveal his own beliefs explicitly, while he may engage with the views proposed in prefaces or as a partner in the dialogue. Cicero's form of the dialogue has been called 'adversarial dialogue', since he often has two or more speakers argue for and against a proposition or present contrasting philosophical perspectives on the same issue. This allows the writer to introduce a range of philosophical opinions without compromising his own stance or imposing his own authority; each side is subjected to a critical examination, and the debate is often open-ended and invites readers to make up their own minds.

This structure has been explained by Cicero's inferred sympathy with the sceptical Academics, who saw their philosophical activity as a revival of the critical investigation that Socrates is portrayed as carrying out in Plato's dialogues. Longer speeches by Cicero's interlocutors tend to be punctuated by brief discussions in which other participants comment on what they have heard or discuss the next steps. For the form of the dialogue, Cicero refers to the precedents of Plato, Aristotle and the Platonist Heraclides of Pontus (*c.*390–after 322 BCE); based on these models he employs several variations on the formal shape of a dialogue, including, for example, conversations set in the past or in the present, involving or not involving the author (as an interlocutor) or featuring speeches of different types or lengths.[13] The first philosophical work in dialogue form that Cicero embarked upon was presumably *De re publica* in the mid 50s BCE, and because the structure worked well in this instance, he may have been inspired to transfer it to other topics.

Each dialogue presenting a fictional meeting of the speakers has its own chronological and geographical setting, outlined at the start, and a carefully selected set of interlocutors, who are given personalities and are described as qualified for their tasks. Cicero apparently gave some thought to the choice of speakers, so that the positions they adopt appear plausible and in line with their known characters and their time of life. For each dialogue Cicero also explains how he allegedly came to know the recorded conversation, either by being an active or a passive participant or by receiving a report from one of the people involved. As a result of these various dialogue formats the figure of Cicero can appear as a reporter of doctrines of particular philosophical schools, as a critic pointing out the problems in any school's doctrines or as an individual indicating personal views.

This method of composition means that Cicero is not at liberty to include just any speakers in his dialogues; rather, he must consider whether they are suitable for the role and fit in with the other interlocutors. Cicero explains this issue in a letter to Atticus, with reference to Varro's appearance in the second version of *Academica* (*Att.* 13.19.3–5 [29 June 45 BCE]):[14]

In the case of Varro the consideration you mention, that I might look like a tuft-hunter, would not influence me. The fact is that I had made a resolution not to put living persons in my dialogues, but because you wrote that it was Varro's wish and that he set much store by it, I have composed this work and finished off the whole subject of Academic philosophy in four books – how well I cannot say, but as conscientiously as could possibly be. In them I have given Varro the arguments admirably assembled by Antiochus [i.e. Antiochus of Ascalon, an Academic philosopher] against the denial of certitudes. I reply to those myself. You make a third in our conversation. If I had made Cotta and Varro discuss it between them, as you suggest in your last letter, I should have been a *muta persona*. [4] This is quite agreeable if the characters belong to history. Heraclides [i.e. the Platonic philosopher] did it in many works, and I myself in my six books 'On the Republic.' And there are my three 'On the Orator,' of which I entertain a very good opinion. In these too the characters were such that I had to keep silent, the speakers being Crassus, Antonius, the elder Catulus, his brother C. Julius, Cotta, and Sulpicius. The conversation is supposed to have taken place when I was a boy, so that I could not take any part. But my recent compositions follow the Aristotelian pattern, in which the other roles in the dialogue are subordinate to the author's own. In the five books which I composed 'On the Limits' [i.e. *De finibus*] I gave the Epicurean case to L. Torquatus, the Stoic to M. Cato, and the Peripatetic to M. Piso. I thought that would excite no jealousy, since none of them was still living. [5] This treatise on the Academy I had given, as you know, to Catulus, Lucullus, and Hortensius. It must be confessed that the matter did not fit the persons, who could not be supposed ever to have dreamed of such abstrusities. So when I read your letter about Varro I seized upon it as a godsend. Nothing could have been better suited to that brand of philosophy, in which he seems to me to take particular pleasure; and his role is such that I have not succeeded in making my own case appear the stronger. For Antiochus' arguments are very persuasive and I have set them out faithfully; they have the acuteness of their originator with my elegance of style, that is

> if I can claim such a quality. But please consider yet again whether you
> think this work should be given to Varro. Certain objections occur to
> me, but we shall discuss them together.

Both the consequences of the dialogue form and the importance of the
questions chosen for discussion are alluded to, for instance, in the introduction to *De finibus bonorum et malorum* (45 BCE), a dialogue presenting the
views on the highest good according to the Epicureans, the Stoics and the
Academy under Antiochus of Ascalon (*Fin.* 1.11–12):

> On the other hand, those who would rather I wrote on a different topic
> should be equable about it, given the many topics on which I have written, more indeed than any other Roman. Perhaps I shall live to write
> still more. In any case, no one who has habitually and carefully read my
> philosophical works will judge that any is more worth reading than this
> one. For nothing in life is more worth investigating than philosophy
> in general, and the question raised in this work in particular: what is
> the end, what is the ultimate and final goal, to which all our deliberations on living well and acting rightly should be directed? What does
> nature pursue as the highest good to be sought, what does she shun
> as the greatest evil? [12] [...] For my part, I consider that this work
> gives a more or less comprehensive discussion of the question of the
> highest goods and evils [*de finibus bonorum et malorum*]. In it I have
> investigated not only the views with which I agree, but those of each
> of the philosophical schools individually.

The philosophical writings produced during the years 46 to 44 BCE can
be seen as a systematic treatment of major philosophical issues. The series
starts with *Hortensius*, a dialogue (surviving in fragments) between friends
including the title character (the famous orator), Q. Lutatius Catulus and
L. Licinius Lucullus, which attempts to turn readers to philosophy (in the
style of a *protreptikos* or 'exhortation'). In retrospect, when only a few more
works are to come (in 44 BCE), Cicero organizes his writings in a scheme
and has it appear as if such a structure were planned from the beginning:

he describes the sequence of his philosophical books, adding those on oratory and political philosophy, in the introduction to the second book of *De divinatione* (45/44 BCE), a work in which 'Marcus' (Cicero's persona) and his brother 'Quintus' each present a case against and for the idea that divination is possible. The first part of the opening explains how Cicero turned to philosophy under Caesar's dictatorship, while the second part expresses the hope that Cicero might now return to active politics (*Div.* 2.1–7):

> After serious and long continued reflection as to how I might do good to as many people as possible and thereby prevent any interruption of my service to the State, no better plan occurred to me than to conduct my fellow-citizens in the ways of the noblest learning – and this, I believe, I have already accomplished through my numerous books. For example, in my work entitled *Hortensius*, I appealed as earnestly as I could for the study of philosophy. And in my *Academics*, in four volumes, I set forth the philosophic system which I thought least arrogant, and at the same time most consistent and refined. [2] And, since the foundation of philosophy rests on the distinction between good and evil, I exhaustively treated that subject in five volumes and in such a way that the conflicting views of the different philosophers might be known [i.e. *De finibus bonorum et malorum*]. Next, and in the same number of volumes, came the *Tusculan Disputations*, which made plain the means most essential to a happy life. For the first volume treats of indifference to death, the second of enduring pain, the third of the alleviation of sorrow, the fourth of other spiritual disturbances; and the fifth embraces a topic which sheds the brightest light on the entire field of philosophy since it teaches that virtue is sufficient of itself for the attainment of happiness.
>
> [3] After publishing the works mentioned I finished three volumes *On the Nature of the Gods*, which contain a discussion of every question under that head. With a view of simplifying and extending the latter treatise I started to write the present volume *On Divination*, to which I plan to add a work on *Fate*; when that is done every phase of this particular branch of philosophy will be sufficiently discussed. To

this list of works must be added the six volumes which I wrote while holding the helm of state, entitled *On the Republic* – a weighty subject, appropriate for philosophic discussion, and one which has been most elaborately treated by Plato, Aristotle, Theophrastus, and the entire Peripatetic school. What need is there to say anything of my treatise *On Consolation* [lost]? For it is the source of very great comfort to me and will, I think, be of much help to others. I have also recently thrown in that book *On Old Age* [or *Cato*], which I sent my friend Atticus; and, since it is by philosophy that a man is made virtuous and strong, my *Cato* [i.e. the lost *Laus Catonis*, 46 BCE] is especially worthy of a place among the foregoing books. [4] Inasmuch as Aristotle and Theophrastus, too, both of whom were celebrated for their keenness of intellect and particularly for their copiousness of speech, have joined rhetoric with philosophy, it seems proper also to put my rhetorical books in the same category; hence we shall include the three volumes *On Oratory* [i.e. *De oratore*], the fourth entitled *Brutus*, and the fifth called *The Orator*.

I have named the philosophic works so far written: to the completion of the remaining books of this series I was hastening with so much ardour that if some most grievous cause had not intervened there would not now be any phase of philosophy which I had failed to elucidate and make easily accessible in the Latin tongue. For what greater or better service can I render to the commonwealth than to instruct and train the youth – especially in view of the fact that our young men have gone so far astray because of the present moral laxity that the utmost effort will be needed to hold them in check and direct them in the right way? [5] Of course, I have no assurance – it could not even be expected – that they will all turn to these studies. Would that a few may! Though few, their activity may yet have a wide influence in the state. In fact, I am receiving some reward for my labour even from men advanced in years; for they are finding comfort in my books, and by their ardour in reading are raising my eagerness for writing to a higher pitch every day. Their number, too, I learn, is far greater than I had expected. Furthermore, it would redound to the fame and glory of the Roman people to be made independent of Greek writers in the study of philosophy, [6] and this result I shall certainly bring about if my present plans are accomplished.

The cause of my becoming an expounder of philosophy sprang from the grave condition of the State during the period of the Civil War, when, being unable to protect the Republic, as had been my custom, and finding it impossible to remain inactive, I could find nothing else that I preferred to do that was worthy of me. Therefore my countrymen will pardon me – rather they will thank me – because, when the State was in the power of one man, I refused to hide myself, to quit my place, or to be cast down; I did not bear myself like one enraged at the man or at the times; and, further, I neither so fawned upon nor admired another's fortune as to repent me of my own.

For one thing in particular I had learned from Plato and from philosophy, that certain revolutions in government are to be expected; so that states are now under a monarchy, now under a democracy, and now under a tyranny [see *De re publica*]. [7] When the last-named fate had befallen my country, and I had been debarred from my former activities, I began to cultivate anew these present studies that by their means, rather than by any other, I might relieve my mind of its worries and at the same time serve my fellow-countrymen as best I could under the circumstances. Accordingly, it was in my books that I made my senatorial speeches and my forensic harangues; for I thought that I had permanently exchanged politics for philosophy. Now, however, since I have begun to be consulted again about public affairs, my time must be devoted to the State, or, rather, my undivided thought and care must be fixed upon it; and only so much time can be given to philosophy as will not be needed in the discharge of my duty to the commonwealth. But more of this at another time; now let us return to the discussion with which we started.

This long preface not only gives a summary of Cicero's philosophical works, but also states his key beliefs on the nature and effect of philosophy, together with his views on how and when to engage with philosophy and to what purpose. It becomes clear that the attitude to philosophy is somewhat ambiguous: on the one hand knowledge of philosophy is regarded as essential for an orator and statesman, and engaging with philosophy is seen as providing a refuge and consolation; Cicero kept studying philosophy throughout his life, even during busy periods. On the other hand full-time devotion to philosophy is only admitted for periods in which one cannot be of greater use to the Republic through active political intervention, since philosophical studies might detract from more important tasks. Yet if it is not possible to support the state in other ways, setting out philosophy in Latin is still a service to one's countrymen.

Some of these ideas are expressed in more emotional form in the preface to Book 5 of *Tusculan Disputations* (45 BCE), which discusses the question of whether virtue is sufficient for a happy life (*Tusc.* 5.5–6):

> But the amendment of this fault [i.e. that we prefer to condemn the course of events rather than our own mistakes], as of all our other failings and offences, must be sought for from philosophy; to whose bosom I was driven from the earliest days of manhood by my own enthusiastic choice, and in my present heavy misfortunes, tossed by the fury of the tempest, I have sought refuge in the same haven from which I had first set sail. O philosophy, thou guide of life, o thou explorer of virtue and expeller of vice! Without thee what could have become not only of me but of the life of man altogether? Thou hast given birth to cities, thou hast called scattered human beings into the bond of social life, thou hast united them first of all in joint habitations, next in wedlock, then in the ties of common literature and speech, thou hast discovered law, thou hast been the teacher of morality and order: to thee I fly for refuge, from thee I look for aid, to thee I entrust myself, as once in ample measure, so now wholly and entirely. Moreover one day well spent and in accordance with thy lessons is to be preferred to an eternity of error. Whose help then are we to use rather than thine? thou that hast freely granted us peacefulness of life and destroyed the dread of death. [6] And yet philosophy is so far from being praised in the way its service to the life of man has deserved, that most men ignore it and many even abuse it. Dare any man abuse the author of his being and

stain himself with such atrocity, and be so wickedly ungrateful as to upbraid her whom he ought to have reverenced, even if his powers had not allowed him comprehension? But, as I think, this deception and this mental darkness have overspread the souls of the uninstructed, because they cannot look back far enough into the past and do not consider that the men by whom the means of human life were first provided have been philosophers.

Beyond the issue of whether engaging with philosophy is worthwhile, Cicero's works introduce the public not only to philosophy as a subject, but also to the views of the most important schools of philosophy (Stoics, Epicureans, Peripatetics and Academics). Cicero's position is often described as eclectic, since he did not follow any of the main doctrines single-mindedly. This at any rate agrees with the description of his attitude in the introduction to one of the sections of *Tusculan Disputations* (*Tusc.* 4.7):

> But let everyone defend his views, for judgment is free: I shall cling to my rule and without being tied to the laws of any single school of thought [*unius disciplinae legibus*] which I feel bound to obey, shall always search for the most probable solution in every problem [*quid sit in quaque re maxime probabile semper requiremus*].

However, as can also be inferred from this comment, Cicero was closest to the beliefs of the sceptical Academics. Cicero first got to know their theories in Rome from Philon of Larissa, who advocated a moderate scepticism. During his study trip in 79–77 BCE Cicero witnessed the differences within the Academy in Athens, the two opposing movements embodied by Philon of Larissa and Antiochus of Ascalon, who was critical of scepticism. Towards the end of his life Cicero seems to have subscribed to a qualified scepticism, which accepts some probable opinions, and to the Academic method of arguing against any thesis and on both sides of a given issue, so as to explore all perspectives. Cicero explains his position in *Academica* and in the preface to *De natura deorum* (45 BCE), a treatise presenting the views on the nature of the gods of by Stoics, Epicureans and Academics (*Nat. D.* 1.6–12):

I see that there has been a wide and varying reaction to the several books which I have published within a short period. Some people have wondered at the reason for my sudden enthusiasm for the study of philosophy, and others have been eager to know what positive beliefs I held on each issue. I became aware, too, that many found it surprising that I approved particularly of the philosophy which in their view doused the light and plunged the issues, so to say, in darkness, and that I had unexpectedly undertaken the defence of a school of thought which men had quitted and long left behind. But my interest in philosophy is no sudden impulse, for I have devoted no little attention and enthusiasm to studying it, and I was philosophizing when I least appeared to be doing so. This is attested by my speeches, which are chock-full of philosophers' maxims, and by my intimate contact with highly educated men, for my household was regularly honoured by their presence. Then too I was educated by philosophers outstanding in their field, Diodotus and Philo, Antiochus and Posidonius [i.e. Stoic and Academic teachers of Cicero]. [7] Moreover, if the injunctions of philosophy all have a bearing on how we live, I believe that in both public and private spheres I have put into practice the precepts recommended by reason and by learning. [...]

[10] Those who seek my personal views on each issue are being unnecessarily inquisitive, for when we engage in argument we must look to the weight of reason rather than authority. Indeed, students who are keen to learn often find the authority of those who claim to be teachers to be an obstacle, for they cease to apply their own judgement and regard as definitive the solution offered by the mentor of whom they approve. [...]

[11] As for those who express surprise that I have adopted the Academic system in preference to all others, I think that the four books of my *Academica* offer them a clear enough answer. It is quite untrue that I have undertaken the defence of positions now abandoned and outmoded. Maxims of individual philosophers do not perish with them, though they perhaps suffer from the absence of the light which an expositor would cast on them. For example, the philosophical method of arguing against every statement, and of refusing to offer positive judgements

about anything (an approach inaugurated by Socrates, revived by Arcesilaus [i.e. an Academic philosopher; 316/5–241/0 BCE], and reinforced by Carneades [i.e. an Academic philosopher; c.214/3–129/8 BCE]), has flourished up to our own day, though I understand that it is now left with virtually no exponent in Greece itself. But I put this down not to any deficiency in the Academy, but to general obtuseness; for if mastery of each individual system is a daunting task, how much more difficult it is to master all of them! Yet this is what we must do if in the interests of discovering the truth we decide both to criticize and to support the view of each individual philosopher.

[12] [...] We Academics are not the type of philosophers who think that nothing is true. Our claim is that certain falsehoods impinge on all true statements, and that these bear so close a resemblance to the truth that they contain no criterion by which to judge them or to lend assent to them. The outcome of this is our view that many things are *probable*, and that though these are not demonstrably true they guide the life of the wise man, because they are so significant and clear-cut.

This approach to philosophy is for Cicero a good basis on which to survey the position of each philosophical school, particularly on aspects of ethics, metaphysics and political philosophy, and thus to provide an overview for his countrymen in the philosophical treatises of the last few years of his life. At the same time the experiences of the 50s and 40s BCE and the close engagement with Greek philosophy during this period may have changed Cicero's opinions and prompted him to adopt attitudes new to traditional Roman ideology. For instance, in *De officiis*, one of his last pieces and a non-dialogic work, the concept of liberty appears to have a moral, universalistic nature, based on the judgement of individual men, rather than being guaranteed by the mixed constitution. Just as with some arguments in the *Philippic Orations*,[15] it is with such ideas that Cicero contributed to preparing the ideological basis of the principate while he continued to defend the traditional Republican structure.

VI

LITERARY PERSONA

AFTER OVERVIEWS of Cicero's career (Chapter II) as well as of his rhetorical, political and philosophical activities (Chapters III–V) it is time to consider the ways in which he presented his ideas and arguments, that is, his literary expression, understood in a broad sense to encompass all stylized utterances. It is only because of his superb command of the language and stylistic formats that Cicero could become such an influential senator as he was at the end of his life (44–43 BCE) when he delivered the *Philippics* (see Chapter I).

As shown in Cicero's rhetorical treatises, an orator's impact on the audience is not only achieved by the ideas put forward, but also by their presentation, including the selection and arrangement of words, the correct use of language, the clarity of expression and the effective employment of stylistic figures and prose rhythm.[1] In a speech, the beginning (*exordium*) and the ending (*peroratio*) are the prime sections for winning the interest and attention of audiences and moving them emotionally; therefore these passages are typically the most carefully constructed.

Of the beginnings of Cicero's speeches, one of the most famous consists in the first few paragraphs of the *First Catilinarian Oration*, delivered in early November 63 BCE; this is the first surviving speech of those given in response to the Catilinarian Conspiracy, regarded by

Cicero as one of the key events of his consulship.[2] The speech starts as follows (*Cat.* 1.1–2):

> How far, I ask you, Catiline, do you mean to stretch our patience? [*Quo usque tandem abutere, Catilina, patientia nostra?*] How much longer will your frenzy continue to frustrate us? At what point will your unrestrained recklessness stop flaunting itself? Have the nightly guards on the Palatine [i.e. presumably guards hired by the wealthy residents of the Palatine Hill], have the patrols in the streets, have the feats of the people, have the gatherings of all loyal citizens, have these strongly defended premises in which this meeting [i.e. the meeting of the Senate in the Temple of Jupiter Stator] is being held, have the faces and expressions of the senators here had no effect on you at all? Do you not realize that your plans have been exposed? Do you not see that your conspiracy has been arrested and trapped, now that all these people know about it? Which of us do you think does not know what you were up to yesterday evening, what you were up to last night, where you were, whom you collected together, and what plan of action you decided upon? [2] What a decadent age we live in! [*O tempora, o mores!*] The senate is aware of these things, the consul sees them – yet this man remains alive! Alive, did I say? He is not just alive: he actually enters the senate, he takes part in our public deliberations, and with his eyes he notes and marks down each one of us for assassination. We meanwhile, brave men that we are, think that we have done enough for our country if we merely get out of the way of his frenzy and his weapons.

On the basis of a translation it is difficult to assess the linguistic and stylistic details. However, even without looking at the entire excerpt in Latin it is noticeable that the first paragraph is made up entirely of questions, which gives the opening a sense of urgency and restlessness. All the questions are directed at Catiline, who is addressed by name at the outset. These are rhetorical questions, since in a speech actual answers from other parties are not expected; therefore these questions have the function of emphatic statements: it is insinuated that Catiline does or should agree with these points. In reality, however, this is by no means clear; consequently, these items are not mere statements, but part of the argument intended to make Catiline acknowledge defeat in view of the overwhelming knowledge and power of all other parts of the community.

At the same time this is not a private conversation with Catiline, but a speech in the Senate: while Cicero hopes to have an effect on Catiline, he also aims to convince the senators of his point of view and his strategy. Therefore he characterizes Catiline negatively (e.g. 'unrestrained reckless-ness'), he creates a clear opposition between Catiline and everybody else (e.g. 'gatherings of all loyal citizens'), especially the community present (e.g. 'all these people', 'which of us'), and suggests that Catiline's initiatives are outrageous and nothing had been done against them. Cicero further indicates that all agitating activity has been coming from Catiline (e.g. 'your frenzy') and that the senators first looked at it good-naturedly (e.g. 'patience'), but now need to take action, especially since this is an opportune moment as they are all aware of these bad deeds. Moreover, Cicero spurs the audience to action by suggesting that they are all facing personal danger (e.g. 'marks down each one of us for assassination').

This forceful rhetoric seems to have had an effect at least on Catiline: he was so bold as to come to this Senate meeting, but left Rome afterwards. On this occasion Cicero made a particular effort because he felt that something should have been done long ago (hence the slight self-criticism that the consul did not do anything), but he apparently intended to become active only when he had enough information and was confident of support. In this speech Cicero was working on two audiences, Catiline and the other senators, at the same time and within a single argument. The techniques employed – such as making the audience feel personally affected, creating a feeling of unity among the audience, including the speaker, while singling out a few individuals, addressing members of the audience directly and stressing the need to take action – are strategies used in many Ciceronian speeches.

The ending of a speech may employ even more emotional rhetoric, since the argument has been made, and this is the point for a final appeal to the audience (consisting of judges in a trial or senators in a political discussion) to agree to proposals made. A good example is the ending of the defence speech *Pro Milone* (52 BCE). T. Annius Milo was accused of having killed P. Clodius Pulcher, an enemy of both Milo and Cicero, as he had been instrumental in causing Cicero's exile. At the actual trial Cicero did not give a particularly impressive speech, allegedly because of the disorderly and intimidating circumstances.[3] Cicero then rewrote the speech, and this is the oration that survives.[4] This version met with admiration, for instance from Quintilian and also Milo himself (see Chapter II).

To grasp the full rhetorical impact of this oration, which was written so that it could be delivered effectively, one should ideally also look at its shape in the original Latin. Therefore the text of the *peroratio* follows in English and in Latin (*Mil.* 102–5):

> How unhappy I am! What appalling luck I have had! You succeeded, Milo, in obtaining the help of these men in recalling me to my country; shall I be unsuccessful in obtaining their help to keep you in yours? What shall I say to my children, who count you as their second father? What shall I say to you, brother Quintus, who are now far away, but who shared those difficult times with me? That, in attempting to protect Milo's welfare, I was unable to obtain the help of the very men who had enabled Milo to secure my own welfare? Unable in what sort of cause? One that was approved by all the nations of the world. Unable to protect Milo's welfare from whom? From those who had felt the greatest relief at the death of Publius Clodius. And on whose advocacy? My own.
>
> [103] What terrible crime did I devise or what awful deed did I commit, gentlemen, when I tracked down, uncovered, exposed, and expunged those indications of our impending destruction? All my troubles, and those of those close to me, derive from that source. Why did you want me to return to Rome? Was it so that I could watch the expulsion of those by whom my restoration was secured? I beseech you, do not let my return be more painful to me than my departure was! For how can I consider myself restored if I am to be separated from those who were responsible for securing my restoration?
>
> How I wish that the immortal gods had arranged – forgive me, my country, for what I am about to say, since I am afraid that the words

which I am obliged to utter in Milo's defence will constitute a criminal attack on you – how I wish that Publius Clodius had not merely remained alive but had become praetor, consul, even dictator rather than that I should have to witness such a spectacle as this! [104] But Milo will have none of it – immortal gods, what a brave man, and one, gentlemen, whom you would do well to save! 'No, no,' he says, 'it is right for Clodius to have paid the penalty he deserved: I am prepared, if necessary, to pay one that I do not deserve.' Shall this man, born to serve his country, die anywhere other than in his country – unless, perhaps, for his country? Will you hold onto the memorials of his spirit, but allow no funerary monument within Italy to be set up over his body? Will any of you use his vote to expel from Rome a man whom every other city will welcome with open arms? [105] Fortunate the land that shall accept this man! Ungrateful Rome, if she shall cast him out! Unhappy Rome, if she shall lose him!

But I must stop now. I can no longer speak for tears – and my client has ordered that tears are not to be used in his defence. But I beg and implore you, gentlemen, when you cast your votes, to be bold enough to vote the way you feel. Believe me, your courage, fairness, and good faith will be strongly approved by the man who, when he picked this jury, was careful to select those who were the best, the wisest, and the most brave.

o me miserum, o me infelicem! revocare tu me in patriam, Milo, potuisti per hos, ego te in patria per eosdem retinere non potero? quid respondebo liberis meis, qui te parentem alterum putant? quid tibi, Quinte frater, qui nunc abes, consorti mecum temporum illorum? mene non potuisse Milonis salutem tueri per eosdem, per quos nostram ille servasset? at in qua causa non potuisse? quae est grata omnibus gentibus. a quibus non potuisse? ab eis, qui maxime P. Clodi morte adquierunt. quo deprecante? me.

[103] quodnam ego concepi tantum scelus aut quod in me tantum facinus admisi, iudices, cum illa indicia communis exiti indagavi, patefeci, protuli, exstinxi? omnes mihi meisque redundant ex fonte illo dolores.

quid me reducem esse voluistis? an ut inspectante me expellerentur ei, per quos essem restitutus? nolite, obsecro vos, acerbiorem mihi pati reditum esse, quam fuerit ille ipse discessus. nam qui possum putare me restitutum esse, si distrahor ab his, per quos restitutus sum?

utinam di immortales fecissent – pace tua, patria, dixerim: metuo enim ne scelerate dicam in te quod pro Milone dicam pie – utinam P. Clodius non modo viveret, sed etiam praetor, consul, dictator esset potius quam hoc spectaculum viderem! [104] o di immortales! fortem et a vobis, iudices, conservandum virum! 'minime, minime'; inquit 'immo vero poenas ille debitas luerit: nos subeamus, si ita necesse est, non debitas.' hicine vir patriae natus usquam nisi in patria morietur, aut, si forte, pro patria? huius vos animi monumenta retinebitis, corporis in Italia nullum sepulcrum esse patiemini? hunc sua quisquam sententia ex hac urbe expellet, quem omnes urbes expulsum a vobis ad se vocabunt? [105] o terram illam beatam, quae hunc virum exceperit, hanc ingratam, si eiecerit, miseram, si amiserit!

sed finis sit; neque enim prae lacrimis iam loqui possumus, et hic se lacrimis defendi vetat. vos oro obtestorque, iudices, ut in sententiis ferendis, quod sentietis, id audeatis. vestram virtutem, iustitiam, fidem, mihi credite, is maxime comprobabit, qui in iudicibus legendis optimum et sapientissimum et fortissimum quemque elegit.

Like the opening of the *First Catilinarian Oration*, this section contains numerous questions, but here there are also exclamations; the sentences are mostly short, mainly main clauses; the passage does not present a real argument, but rather invokes a series of scenarios. There are stylistic features such as anaphora (subsequent clauses or phrases starting with the same word), contrast (for instance, between 'you' and 'me' by emphasizing the respective pronouns and the use of the same verb in different forms in both parts of a sentence), addresses to the audience of judges, repetition of key words in subsequent sentences, (asyndetic) sequences or tricola (lists of three items), quotation of direct speech by someone else and an address to the personified Patria/'Country' (who appears also in the *Catilinarian Orations*). Moreover, the words in the Latin are arranged in such a way that the final sentence has a rhythmic ending in the shape of a frequent so-called *clausula* (a recognized metrical scheme).

Although this is a defence of Milo, Cicero's argument has recourse to his personal experiences: it would be ungrateful and unimaginable if he could not help Milo, who had helped him when he was in exile; this would affect also his children (for whom Milo is characterized as a 'second father') and his brother, and there would be no point in his having been brought back if he would not intervene. With a series of short questions Cicero illustrates the character of the case and the corresponding responsibilities, highlighting his own. The entire conflict between Clodius and Milo is briefly evoked, with Milo presented as the morally superior person, who is ready to accept even undeserved penalties for the sake of the country (the final element in the defence). This is meant to give rise to the question of how the judges could consider expelling such a person whom every other country would be delighted to accept. To sway the audience on a psychological level, forensic speeches could end with someone in tears or the presentation of a miserable client or his dependants. Cicero avoids such a stereotyped and conventional appeal to the emotions by saying that his client has not allowed this, and he will stop before he himself bursts into tears. Thereby he uses elements of this technique and makes an emotional appeal, but indicates the qualities of the client, who does not need to fall back on ordinary methods.

The ending feels effective since it uses all the standard techniques; yet Cicero gives them subtle twists in line with the particular situation and thus makes them more likely to capture attention: he puts himself in the position of the defendant, alludes to customary techniques, but does not use them, and presents the defendant charged with murder as the saviour of the country. As comparisons between Cicero's rhetorical treatises and his actual procedure show, from his earliest youth onwards he was familiar with the doctrines of school rhetoric and also confident enough to adapt them as required. Such techniques are likely to be employed in an extremely sophisticated fashion in an oration composed to vindicate an earlier unsuccessful appearance. If Cicero had given this speech, he might indeed have been successful in the trial!

When *Pro Milone* was written, it was clear that the speech would never be delivered; still it is shaped for the specific situation of the trial. Something similar applies to orations written up after delivery and distributed to a wider audience. While they are likely to have been polished stylistically and perhaps modified to some extent during the writing-up process, these speeches continue to evoke the circumstances of the original delivery and thereby can have an immediate effect on the reading public by document-ing events vividly. This is particularly true for collections of thematically coherent groups of speeches. In those cases, in addition to the rhetorical style, the selection and the format of distribution influence the impact of the orations. For instance, in 60 BCE, three years after his consulship, Cicero describes a project of 'consular speeches' in a letter to his friend Atticus. He envisages a group of speeches selected out of those that he has delivered during that year, which would show 'both what he did and what he said' and present him as a statesman-like orator like Demosthenes (*Att.* 2.1.3 [*c.*3 June 60 BCE]):

> I'll send my little speeches, both those you ask for and some more besides, since it appears that you too find pleasure in these performances which the enthusiasm of my young admirers prompts me to put on paper. Remembering what a brilliant show your countryman Demosthenes made in his so-called *Philippics* and how he turned away from this argumentative, forensic type of oratory to appear in the more elevated role of statesman, I thought it would be a good thing for me too to have some speeches to my name which might be called 'Consular.' They are: (1) delivered in the Senate on the Kalends of January; (2) to the Assembly, on the agrarian law; (3) on Otho; (4) in defence of Rabirius; (5) on the children of persons proscribed; (6) delivered when I publicly resigned my province; (7) when I sent Catiline out of Rome; (8) to the Assembly the day following Catiline's flight; (9) at a public meeting the day the Allobroges turned informers; (10) in the Senate on the Nones of December. There are two further short pieces, chips, one might say, from the agrarian law. I shall see that you get the whole corpus, and since you like my writings as well as my doings, the same compositions

will show you both what I did and what I said. Otherwise you shouldn't
have asked – I was not forcing myself upon you.

The selection was to include the four *Speeches on the Agrarian Law* (Cicero's
inaugural speeches as consul, of which three survive), the oration *Pro Rabirio
perduellionis reo* (a speech defending the senator Rabirius in a political trial
provoked by Caesar) and the four *Catilinarian Orations* (speeches against
Catiline by which Cicero 'saved the Republic') and a few others that have
not been fully preserved. It is not known whether the project of assembling
such a corpus was ever realized and how it may relate to possible earlier
publications of individual speeches. In any case it illustrates Cicero's view
of these orations: as a group, he saw them as illustrating his statesman-like
behaviour in critical situations.

Cicero's forensic and political speeches are one type of written works in
which his linguistic and stylistic mastery can be seen. These characteristics also come to the fore in his innovative philosophical writings. For, as
Cicero claims, previously there were no or hardly any pieces in Latin that
presented the philosophy of the Peripatetics, Academics and Stoics; reasons
may include that the material was complex or that Romans were busy with
practical matters or that it was regarded as impossible to bring philosophy
to the uninitiated. According to Cicero, so far the only noteworthy action
had been taken by a C. Amafinius and other Epicureans who had presented
the doctrines of Epicurus; they achieved a great effect, probably, as Cicero
envisages, because they were able to spread these views without any compe-
tition and a philosophy based on pleasure sounded simple and attractive.[5]
Stylistically, Cicero saw these works as lacking in art since they presented the
subject matter in ordinary language, not taking account of the conventions
of the art of oratory and the rules of philosophical discourse (*Acad. post.* 5).
    When it came to writing about Greek philosophy in Latin, Cicero found
that the Latin language lacked many of the necessary technical terms. Like
Lucretius, the contemporary Epicurean philosopher (*c.*95–55 BCE), who
famously complained about the 'poverty of the native language' (*patrii
sermonis egestas*; Lucretius 1.136–9; 1.830–3; 3.258–61) in his poem about

natural philosophy (*De rerum natura*), Cicero was confronted with a linguistic problem: he therefore felt that Romans 'have to find a new vocabulary and invent new terms to match new concepts'. In one of the prefaces to sections of his philosophical treatise *De finibus bonorum et malorum* (45 BCE) he justifies this practice (*Fin.* 3.3–5):

> The Stoics, on the other hand, as you [i.e. Brutus, the dedicatee of the treatise] well know, have a way of arguing which is not so much subtle as obscure, even for the Greek reader, and thus far more so for us Romans who have to find a new vocabulary and invent new terms to match new concepts. This need will surprise no one of even moderate learning once it is recognized that any field of knowledge whose exercise involves a degree of specialization has a large range of new terms set up to designate the subject-matter of the relevant field. [4] Thus logic and physics use terminology unknown even to the Greeks. Geometry and music, as well as grammar, have their own language. Even the art of rhetoric, despite being thoroughly public and familiar, still uses a vocabulary for the purposes of instruction which is pretty much its own.
>
> These refined and noble arts aside, not even artisans could preserve their crafts without using terminology unknown to the rest of us but familiar to them. Agriculture too, a topic which quite resists fine writing, has none the less coined new terms to delineate its themes. How much more, then, does philosophy need to do this! Philosophy is the art of life, and it cannot take ordinary language as the basis for its discussions.
>
> [5] The Stoics have been the greatest innovators of all philosophers in this regard, and Zeno their founder was more an inventor of new words than new ideas. The most learned people, working in a language which is generally considered to be richer than our own, are still allowed to use unfamiliar terms when dealing with recondite material. All the greater is the allowance that should be made for us who are so bold as to tackle these topics for the first time. We have often stated, in the face of complaints not only from Greeks but also from people who would rather be considered Greek than Roman, that our language does not come a poor second to Greek in wealth of vocabulary, and indeed is

actually superior. So we must work hard to demonstrate this truth not just in our native arts, but in those of the Greeks themselves. Now there are certain words which by venerable tradition we treat as Latin, such as 'philosophy' itself [*philosophia*], 'rhetoric' [*rhetorica*], 'dialectic' [*dialectica*], 'grammar' [*grammatica*], 'geometry' [*geometria*] and 'music' [*musica*]. One could use Latin alternatives, but these words have been adopted through long usage and we should treat them as our own.

Cicero's observation that all technical disciplines have their own jargon, by creating specific terms or using ordinary words with a particular meaning, is obviously true. It is also clear that Latin has borrowed some of these words from Greek. Cicero seems to feel that, since he is only in the process of creating a philosophical discourse in Latin, it is necessary to develop the appropriate terminology. He justifies this procedure by the precedent of Greek philosophers, and he claims that terminology taken from Greek at an earlier stage has now been naturalized in Latin. While the names for the different branches, as listed above, and some other key terms were adopted from the Greeks, other Greek terms were translated into Latin. As with translations today, the question arises which of the existing words in the target language best matches the concept expressed in the source language. For some important concepts Cicero raises the issue explicitly at various points in *De finibus* 3, where he has the interlocutor M. Porcius Cato explain Stoic doctrines (*Fin.* 3.26, 35, 39–40):

> *Cato*: '[...] [26] Let us now see how evidently the following points flow from what I have just laid down. The final aim (I think you realize it is the Greek word *telos* [τέλος] I have long been translating, sometimes as what is "final" [*extremum*], sometimes "ultimate" [*ultimum*] and sometimes "supreme" [*summum*], though one may also use "end" [*finis*] for what is final or ultimate) – the final aim [*extremum*], then, is to live consistently and harmoniously with nature [*congruenter naturae convenienterque vivere*]. This being so, all who are wise necessarily live happy, perfect and blessed lives, with no impediment or obstacle, lacking nothing. The controlling idea behind not only the philosophical

system I am discussing but our lives and destinies too is the belief that what is moral is the only good. [...]

[35] Emotional disturbances, which make the lives of the unwise a harsh misery (the Greeks call such disturbances *pathē* [πάθη], and I could have literally translated the word as "illnesses" [*morbi*], but it would not suit all cases. One does not usually call pity [*misericordia*] or indeed anger [*iracundia*] an "illness" [*morbus*], but the Stoics call each a *pathos* [πάθος]. So let our term be "disturbance" [*perturbatio*] – the very name seems indicative of vice.) – all these disturbances fall into one of four categories, each with numerous subcategories. The four are: sorrow [*aegritudo*], fear [*formido*], lust [*libido*] and what the Stoics call *hēdonē* [ἡδονή], a term applicable to body as well as mind. I prefer to speak of "elation" [*laetitia*], meaning the sensuous delight of the exultant mind. There is nothing natural about the force that arouses these disturbances [*perturbationes*]; they are all mere beliefs and frivolous judgements [*opiniones ac iudicia levitatis*]. The wise person will always be free of them. [...]

[39] [...] The results we are talking about are not bodily damage but the immoral acts which flow from the vices [*e vitiis*] (these the Greeks call *kakiai* [κακίαι]; but I prefer to call them "vices" [*vitia*] rather than "bad things" [*malitiae*]).'

[40] 'How lucidly your language conveys your exact meaning, Cato', I exclaimed. 'You seem to me to be teaching philosophy Latin and, as it were, granting her Roman citizenship. Previously she had looked like a mere visitor to Rome, unable to express herself in our idioms, particularly in the case of Stoic doctrine with its elaborate and subtle use of both ideas and terminology. [...] I am concentrating closely on what you say, and committing to memory all of the vocabulary you are using to express your themes. It may well be that I shall have to make use of it myself. In my view your choice of "vices" [*vitia*] as the contrary of "virtues" [*virtutes*] is absolutely right, and in the idiom of our language. Whatever is "vituperable" [*vituperabile*] in its own right is thereby called "vice" [*vitium*], or perhaps "to be vituperated" [*vituperari*] is derived from "vice" [*a vitio*]. If you had rendered "*kakia*" [κακία] as "badness" [*malitia*], Latin idiom would have pointed us towards one particular

vice [*unum certum vitium*]. As things are, vice [*vitium*] is the correct
contrary for virtue in general [*omnis virtus*].'

Evidently, some thought has gone into creating appropriate Latin philosophical terms: it is not always a literal translation of the Greek word that
is required since this may be inappropriate in a Latin context or trigger
unwanted associations; instead, a concept that expresses the sense may be
more suitable. That is in line with Cicero's views on 'translation' from Greek
into Latin, which he discusses elsewhere.[6] He feels entitled to borrow from
Greek philosophers where necessary, but does not intend to transpose texts
in a literal fashion (*Fin.* 1.7):

> Even if I were to translate Plato or Aristotle literally, as our poets did with
> the Greek plays, I hardly think I would deserve ill of my fellow-citizens
> for bringing those sublime geniuses to their attention. Though I have
> not thus far adopted this method, I do not consider that I am disbarred
> from doing so. If I think fit, I will translate certain passages, particularly
> from those authors I just mentioned, when it happens to be appropriate,
> as Ennius often does with Homer or Afranius with Menander.

Cicero followed such principles even in his more literal translations of
speeches by the Greek orators Aeschines and Demosthenes,[7] of which only
the introductory discussion exists (entitled *De optimo genere oratorum*). He
also translated Greek verses from epic, tragedy and philosophy quoted in
his treatises (including those by Homer, Aeschylus, Sophocles, Euripides
and Solon), where he tends to keep closer to the original.

There is no problem with this method since in Cicero's opinion the Latin
language is perfectly capable of nuanced expression, a view he defended
against others who regarded Greek as the superior language.[8] Thus Cicero
describes the capabilities of Latin (*Fin.* 1.10):

> This is certainly not the place for a lecture on the subject, but my view
> is, as I have often argued, that, far from lacking in resources, the Latin
> language is even richer than the Greek. When, after all, have we, or rather

our good orators and poets, lacked the wherewithal to create either a full or
a spare style in their work, at least since they have had models to imitate?

These considerations and their realization in the treatises, along with the
rhetorical virtuosity of the speeches, show that Cicero was very much attuned
to the possibilities of expression in the Latin language; he also felt that good
Latin versions were worth reading just as much as Greek literature.

In addition, Cicero proudly claimed that he surpassed any Greek writer
by having achieved something in the areas of both rhetoric and philosophy
(*Off.* 1.3–4):

> I strongly urge you, therefore, my dear Cicero [i.e. Cicero's son Marcus],
> assiduously to read not only my speeches, but also the philosophical
> works, which are now almost equal to them. The language is more forceful
> in the former, but the calm and restrained style of the latter ought also
> to be cultivated. Furthermore, I see that it has not happened to this day
> that the same Greek has laboured in both fields, pursuing both forensic
> oratory and also the other, quieter, sort of debating. Perhaps Demetrius
> of Phalerum [i.e. a Greek orator, politician and philosopher; *c.*360–
> 280 BCE] can be counted as doing so, a man of precise argument and an
> orator who, though not over-vigorous, spoke so pleasantly that you can
> recognise him as a pupil of Theophrastus [i.e. a Peripatetic philosopher;
> *c.*371/0–287/6 BCE]. My achievement in either field is for others to
> judge, but there is no doubt that I have pursued them both. [4] I certainly
> think that Plato, if he had wanted to try his hand at forensic oratory,
> would have been able to speak weightily and expansively. Conversely, if
> Demosthenes had held on to the things he learned from Plato, and had
> wanted to articulate them, he could have done so elegantly and with
> brilliance. I make the same judgement about Aristotle and Isocrates
> [i.e. a Greek logographer and teacher of rhetoric; 436–338 BCE]; each,
> because he so enjoyed his own pursuit, despised the other one.

Besides speeches, by which he demonstrated his political influence, and
philosophical treatises, by which he tried to introduce his fellow citizens to

Greek philosophy through works in their native language, Cicero wrote a large number of letters over many years to a wide range of addressees and on all sorts of topics, in a corresponding variety of styles. Less formal pieces may contain a number of Greek words, colloquial expressions or incomplete sentences. Extant pieces include short missives to Cicero's friend Atticus, which may be notes on trivial subjects, possibly covering a series of different points without much attempt at linking them or creating an argument;[9] carefully phrased requests, reports or congratulations to fellow magistrates or more senior politicians;[10] justifications of Cicero's political behaviour;[11] or reflections on political or literary issues almost in the form of mini-essays.[12]

An example of a more essayistic piece is a letter written to one of Cicero's friends, the politician and historian L. Lucceius, in 55 BCE (*Fam.* 5.12), in which the author tries to persuade the addressee to write a historiographical piece about his consulship. In this context Cicero considers conventions of historiography, such as writing truthfully and without ornament, and how they could be ignored in this case. He seems to have thought highly of this delicate letter, since he later recommends it to friends as 'a very pretty piece' (*Att.* 4.6.4 [*c.*19 April 55 BCE]). Cicero himself, in the end, never wrote a work of historiography, but he also discussed its nature elsewhere.[13]

What Cicero did write was poetry; the ancient biographer Plutarch even reports that 'he got the reputation of being not only the best orator but also the best poet among the Romans' (Plutarch, *Cicero* 2.4).[14] It is difficult nowadays to comment on this, since little of Cicero's poetry has survived. For someone who wanted to appear as an active statesman, even defended his philosophical writings by their usefulness for himself and for his countrymen and only devoted time to them in periods when he was free from commitments as a politician or advocate, studying or even writing poetry might seem out of character. Cicero used the speech *Pro Archia* (62 BCE) for statements on the value of poetry: however, since he defended the Greek poet Archias and argued for him to be given Roman citizenship, it is not a surprise that he pointed out the beneficial contribution that poets make when they celebrate the glory and renown of the Roman People.[15]

Cicero further argues that poetry is one branch of culture, all of which he embraces, that literary studies help him to unwind and also to improve his oratory (and thus serve a useful purpose). Consequently, engaging with poetry is not a waste of time, considering that others spend extended periods on worthless and non-intellectual recreation, particularly since his interest in literature has never prevented him from fulfilling his duties (*Arch.* 2; 12–13):

> [2] But in case anyone is surprised to hear me say this, given that my client's talents lie not in the theory and practice of oratory but in another direction, I should point out that I have never devoted myself exclusively to this one art. For all branches of culture are linked by a sort of common bond and have a certain kinship with one another. [...]
>
> [12] You will no doubt ask me, Grattius [i.e. the prosecutor], why I am so delighted with this man. The answer is that it is he who enables my mind to recover from the din of the courts and gives my tired ears a rest from the shouting and abuse. How do you imagine I could find material for my daily speeches on so many different subjects if I did not train my mind with literary study, and how could my mind cope with so much strain if I did not use such study to help it unwind? Yes, I for one am not ashamed to admit that I am devoted to the study of literature. Let others be ashamed if they have buried their heads in books and have not been able to find anything in them which could either be applied to the common good or brought out into the open and the light of day. But why should I be ashamed, gentlemen, given that in all the years I have lived my private pastimes have never distracted me, my own pleasures have never prevented me, and not even the need for sleep has ever called me away from helping anyone in his hour of danger or of need? [13] Who, then, can justly censure or reproach me if I allow myself the same amount of time for pursuing these studies as others set aside for dealing with their own personal affairs, celebrating festivals and games, indulging in other pleasures, and resting their minds and bodies, or as much as they devote to extended partying and to playing dice and ball? And I have all the more right to engage in such studies because it is from them that I am able to improve such oratorical ability as I have, an ability which has always been at the disposal of my friends when faced with prosecution. But even if my oratorical powers seem

not to amount to much, I do at least recognize the source from which
all that is highest in them has been drawn.

When Cicero describes himself as an example of someone who has benefited from poetry, this claim is intended to support his client by a positive
presentation of his occupation, but there may be some truth behind this.
Cicero presumably studied poetry from his schooling onwards. In addition to
poetic translations of Greek epic and tragedy, he produced a poetic rendering
of *Phaenomena* by the Greek Hellenistic poet Aratus (third century BCE),
a poem *Marius* on Marius (*c.*157–86 BCE; a fellow townsman and *homo
novus*, seven-time consul and opponent of Sulla) and two works (at least
planned) about his own experiences, the epics *De consulatu suo* (*c.*60 BCE;
about his consulship in 63 BCE) and *De temporibus suis* (*c.*56–54 BCE; about
his time in exile in 58–57 BCE), as part of the wider publicity campaign
after his consulship. These attempts in hexameter proved important for the
development of this metre at Rome; it then appears in sophisticated form
in Vergil's epic *Aeneid* in the Augustan period.

Of *De temporibus suis* no fragments are extant; therefore it has been
questioned whether it was ever realized. Of *De consulatu suo* there remain
a long speech by the Muse Urania, quoted by Cicero in *De divinatione*, and
several shorter fragments. The speech of the Muse Urania indicates, as does a
divine council in the same work (a traditional element in ancient epics since
Homer), that the events during Cicero's consulship were presented as prede-
termined and supported by the gods. For instance, Cicero has Urania make
a great deal of the fact, as does Cicero in his own voice in the *Catilinarian
Orations*,[16] that a long-planned statue of Jupiter was set up during Cicero's
consulship, at the very time when he successfully countered the conspiracy.
This extract from Urania's speech, translated into English prose, obviously
cannot reproduce the effects created by rhythm and the repetition of sounds,
but gives an idea of the argument (*Div.* 1.20–1):

> They [i.e. omens] all warned that a huge disaster and evil, that would
> affect the state and had begun from noble ancestry was looming, or in
> unvarying terms they announced the overthrow of the laws and ordered

us to snatch the temples of the gods and the city from the flames and to fear a terrible slaughter and massacre? These things were fixed and determined by an unyielding fate, unless a holy and well-proportioned statue of Jupiter were set up on a high column and looked to the bright east. Then the people and holy Senate would be able to discern hidden plots, once that statue, turned now to the sunrise, could see the seats of the Senators and people. [21] This statue, long delayed and after many hold-ups, was finally set up in its exalted position during your consulship and at the very moment in time that had been fixed and marked, when Jupiter made his sceptre shine on the lofty column, the destruction of our country, prepared with torch and sword, was revealed to Senators and people by the words of the Allobroges [i.e. a nation in Gaul that the conspirators tried to win as allies].

Of the shorter extracts from *De consulatu suo* the most famous ones are: 'Let arms yield to the toga, let laurels yield to praise (or: words)' (*cedant arma togae, concedat laurea laudi* or *linguae*)[17] and 'O happy Rome, born in my consulship' (*o fortunatam natam me consule Romam*).[18] These lines were frequently quoted and mocked even by contemporaries and slightly later writers for their poetic form and for their blunt self-glorification (see Chapter VIII). The verses do not refer to divine support implicitly or explicitly, but they express the notion that Cicero's consulship was a great benefit, leading to the 'rebirth' of Rome, and that he achieved great successes without military action.

Even if the self-glorification can be criticized, it is obvious that Cicero, as a poet too, was an accomplished writer, closely familiar with the relevant techniques, and was able to use them to support his argument. For instance, in the original Latin the verses just quoted are organized into two parts and there is effective distribution of sounds. However, there is far more evidence of Cicero's mastery as an orator and philosophical writer than as a poet, and it was in the disciplines of oratory and philosophy that he became a stylistic model. Via his transfer of key terminology from Greek into Latin, many of the expressions created in this context were taken over into several European languages.

VII

PERSONALITY

WHILE MODERN READERS can get a fairly good idea of Cicero's likely political and philosophical views from his public statements in the form of speeches or treatises, it is difficult to tell what Cicero's personality was like. Although Cicero is one of the individuals from the ancient world from whom a large amount of writings in different genres are extant, personal documents such as private diaries have not survived, and there are no unofficial comments from people who had close personal connections with him such as his wife or his children. Nevertheless, there is a consensus that there is abundant information about him, mainly because a large body of private correspondence (about 900 letters) is available. For in the case of other ancient writers with a considerable number of letters extant, notably Pliny the Younger (late first century CE), these were written with a view to publication from the outset and are therefore even more stylized and less personal than Cicero's. Cicero only seems to have thought of publishing a selection of letters towards the end of his life.[1] But his secretary M. Tullius Tiro kept copies of his letters, and Cicero's friend Atticus apparently collected letters sent to him. The editions of Cicero's correspondence published after his death probably derive from the material assembled by Atticus and Tiro; consequently these texts are less likely to have been shaped for publication by the author.

With the help of Cicero's letters, in connection with his other writings, it is possible to reconstruct his movements fairly closely, down to days and sometimes hours, to find out whom he knew and met and whether he was confident of the political actions he promoted in public speeches (since there are sometimes interesting differences). It is also obvious that Cicero was particularly open in letters to his friend Atticus. Nevertheless, one can never be sure whether Cicero is completely candid and honest, since, whenever he writes with a particular audience in mind (even if this is just the addressee of a personal letter), he may be adopting a pose and wish to appear in a certain light. As a result, modern readers cannot easily access Cicero's innermost thoughts. Despite this caveat, Cicero's writings, and his letters in particular, allow some conclusions about Cicero's personality to be drawn: inferences can be made when issues are mentioned frequently and/or in a particular way or when Cicero allows himself more personal remarks when addressing his family, his friend Atticus or his secretary Tiro.

An interesting example of the difference between statements in letters and those in public is Cicero's assessment of the young Octavian, since his comments in his correspondence contrast with the policy pursued in the speeches: in the period of the *Philippics* Cicero's orations are fully supportive of Octavian from the time he starts appearing in public in December 44 BCE with the aim of provoking decisive action against Antony (*Phil.* 3). However, soon after Caesar's assassination, Cicero, in letters to Atticus, is sceptical as to whether Octavian can be trusted as a citizen and will be able to achieve anything (*Att.* 14.12.2 [from Puteoli in southern Italy, 22 April 44 BCE]):

> Octavius [i.e. Octavian] is with me here – most respectful and friendly. His followers call him Caesar, but Philippus [i.e. Octavian's stepfather] does not, so neither do I. My judgement is that he cannot be a good citizen. There are too many around him. They threaten death to our friends and call the present state of things intolerable. What do you think they will say when the boy comes to Rome, where our liberators [i.e. Caesar's assassins] cannot go safe? They have won eternal glory, and happiness too in the consciousness of what they did; but for us, if

I am not mistaken, there is only humiliation ahead. So I long to be away 'Where nevermore of Pelops' line ...', as the poet says [i.e. a quotation from an unknown Latin play].

Even in November, shortly before the beginning of his campaign, Cicero, in private letters, is doubtful because of Octavian's youth and political naivety; yet he acknowledges that Octavian has won popular support (*Att.* 16.11.6 [from Puteoli in southern Italy, 5 November 44 B C E]):

> I have not buried myself down at Pompeii as I wrote that I should, partly because the weather is abominable, partly because I get letters every day from Octavian urging me to put my shoulder to the wheel, come to Capua, save the Republic a second time, and at all events return to Rome at once. 'Durst not refuse for shame, for fear accept.' [i.e. a quotation from Homer's *Iliad*]. He has certainly shown, and continues to show, plenty of energy, and he will go to Rome with a large following; but he is very much a boy. Thinks the Senate will meet at once. Who will come? And who, supposing he comes, will run up against Antony in so uncertain a situation? On the Kalends of January [i.e. 1 January] he may be some protection; or perhaps the issue will be fought out before then. The boy is remarkably popular in the towns. On his way to Samnium he passed through Cales and stayed the night at Teanum [i.e. places in southern Italy]. Amazing receptions and demonstrations of encouragement. Would you have thought it? For this reason I shall return to Rome sooner than I had intended. I shall write as soon as I decide definitely.

Such comments in letters show that 'Cicero the man' was more sceptical as regards Octavian and his desire for power than 'Cicero the politician' claimed to be, for tactical reasons. Octavian's invitation to Cicero to save the Republic a second time (if Octavian indeed phrased it like this) highlights precisely the point that would resonate with Cicero since it implied the recognition of his earlier achievements (as Cicero saw them) and the expectation that he was the only one who would be able to do this. The compliment implied in this invitation agreed with Cicero's constant aiming for an influential and respected position and the accompanying glory.

Cicero felt immensely proud whenever he had achieved something, and, correspondingly, he was offended and disappointed if others were not of the same opinion. This is why, for instance, he defends the praise of himself in the epic on his consulship (see Chapters VI, VIII), which was attacked by contemporaries (*Off.* 1.77–8):

> The best expression of all this is the verse which, I gather, is often attacked by shameless and envious men: 'Let arms yield to the toga, and laurels to laudation.' To mention no others, when I held the helm of the republic, did not arms then yield to the toga? Never was there more serious danger to the republic than then, and never was there greater quiet. Through my vigilance and my counsel the very arms swiftly slipped and fell from the hands of the most audacious citizens. Was any achievement of war ever so great? What military triumph can stand comparison? [78] I am allowed to boast to you, Marcus my son. For yours it is both to inherit my glory and to imitate my deeds. Pompey himself, indeed, whose military exploits won lavish praise, paid me the tribute of saying in the hearing of many that he would have won his third triumph in vain had my service to the republic not ensured that he had somewhere to celebrate it. Therefore the courageous deeds of civilians are not inferior to those of soldiers. Indeed the former should be given even more effort and devotion than the latter.

Cicero's self-glorification may be understood as vanity. At the same time it can be explained easily: starting from the position of a *homo novus*, he had gained a role where he could influence events in the Republic; accordingly, he was all the more disappointed when he did not meet with the expected appreciation[2] and therefore tried to force it. How much Cicero longed for recognition is clear not only from his own efforts to celebrate his consulship, but also from his attempts to enlist others to do so (see Chapter VI). In his speech in defence of the poet Archias (62 BCE) he even admitted his desire for glory openly. Obviously, in this context he set out to demonstrate the importance of poetry, but there may still be some true feelings underlying the argument (*Arch.* 28–30):

> So that you will do this all the more readily, members of the jury, I shall now reveal my feelings to you and own up to what I may call my passion for glory – a passion too intense, perhaps, but nevertheless an honourable one. The measures which I took during my consulship, with your collaboration, for the security of this city and empire, for the lives of our citizens, and for the country as a whole, these have become the subject of a poem on which Archias has now started work. When I heard what he had written I thought it was an important project and an agreeable one, and so I engaged him to complete the task. For merit looks for no reward for the toil and danger which it has to face, save only praise and glory. If you take that away, gentlemen, what incentive do we have, in life's brief and transitory career, to involve ourselves in great undertakings? [29] Certainly, if the mind had no prior conception of posterity, and if it were to confine all its thoughts within those same bounds in which the span of our life is contained, then it would not crush itself under such enormous labours, nor would it be troubled by so many sleepless responsibilities, nor have to fight so often for life itself. But as things are, there exists in every good man a kind of noble instinct which excites the mind night and day with the spur of fame and reminds it that the memory of our name must not be allowed to disappear when our life is ended, but must be made to last for ever. [30] Or are we all to appear so small-minded as to think that all our achievements will cease to exist at the same moment as we do ourselves – we who undergo toil and mortal danger in the service of the state, and who throughout our whole lives never once stop to draw breath in peace and tranquillity? Many distinguished men have been careful to leave statues and portraits behind them, likenesses not of their minds, but of their bodies: ought we not greatly to prefer to leave behind us a representation of our designs and characters, moulded and finished by artists of the highest ability? For my part, even when I was actually carrying out the actions I took, I considered that I was

spreading and disseminating a knowledge of them for the world to remember for ever. And whether I shall have no awareness, after I have died, of the world's memory of me, or whether, as the wisest men have maintained, that recollection will indeed touch some part of my being, I do at least derive pleasure at this moment from the thought and hope that my achievements will be remembered.

Considering that Cicero was striving for involvement in public life and the renown gained thereby, it may come as a surprise that in a letter of late 54 BCE he tells his friend Atticus that the dire state of the Republic does not concern him, that he instead enjoys his books and studies, as long as his private circumstances are in order (*Att.* 4.18.2 [from Rome, between 24 October and 2 November 54 BCE]):[3]

You'll wonder how I take all this. Pretty coolly, I assure you, and I plume myself highly on doing so. My dear friend, not only have we completely lost the vital essence of the free state – even its outward complexion and aspect is gone. There is no Republic any longer to give me joy and solace. Can I take that calmly? Why yes, I can. You see, I have the memory of the proud show she made for the short time that I was at the helm, and the thanks I got in return. My withers are unwrung by the spectacle of one man all-powerful, which chokes the persons who found it distasteful that *I* should have any power at all. I have many consolations. All the same, I do not move away from my position, but turn back to the life that is most congenial, to my books and studies. The labour of pleading is compensated by the pleasure that oratory gives me. My house in town and my places in the country are a source of delight. I do not remember the height from which I fell but the depth from which I have risen. If I can have my brother's company and yours, then so far as I am concerned these people can go to the devil. I can philosophize and you can listen. That place in my mental anatomy which used to contain my spleen grew a tough skin long ago. Providing only that my private and domestic circumstances give me pleasure, you will find my equanimity quite remarkable. It largely

depends, believe me, on your return. There is no one in the world with
whom I hit it off quite so happily.

In this letter it sounds as if Cicero is telling himself that he does not care
(while he does), that he is quite surprised at his own equanimity and that
he throws himself into literary studies as a replacement activity. That writing treatises is a way of doing something useful while one cannot take an
active role within the Republic transpires from the introductions to Cicero's
philosophical treatises (see Chapter V), though it may well be the case that
he also enjoyed this kind of occupation. At any rate, the exchange with
Atticus provided him with emotional support.[4] That Cicero was in need
of this again illustrates that what is visible of his activities from the outside
does not always convey a full picture of his emotions. His ability for close
friendship allows an insight into areas of his personality that is not revealed
by political alliances.

Another personal side of Cicero becomes obvious from the correspondence with his secretary Tiro, which is assembled in Book 16 of the collection
Epistulae ad familiares (*Letters to Friends*), probably arranged by Tiro. Tiro
was a slave in Cicero's household and a close confidant of Cicero and his
brother. In Cicero's service Tiro fulfilled a variety of functions: he recorded
his speeches, for which he devised a kind of shorthand (the so-called Tironian
notes); he deciphered Cicero's handwriting for scribes;[5] he was called the
'canon' of Cicero's writings,[6] and he looked after Cicero's financial affairs.[7]
The level of openness in Cicero's dealings with Tiro is remarkable, and Cicero
apparently felt supported by his assistance.[8] Tiro accompanied Cicero on
his proconsulship in the province Cilicia, but could not stay with him for
the whole time since he was frequently ill. Several times Cicero pushes Tiro
to accept money for medical treatment.[9] Concern for Tiro marks the entire
correspondence between the two men,[10] as evidenced by Cicero's letter to
Tiro from Leucas in Bithynia (*Fam.* 16.4.3–4 [7 November 50 BCE]):

Your services to me are beyond count – in my home and out of it,
in Rome and abroad, in private affairs and public, in my studies and
literary work. You will cap them all if I see you your own man again, as

I hope I shall. I think it would be very nice, if all goes well, for you to sail home with Quaestor Mescinius [i.e. L. Mescinius Rufus, Cicero's quaestor in Cilicia in 51 BCE]. He is not uncivilized, and he seemed to me to have a regard for you. But when you have given every possible attention to your health, *then* my dear Tiro, attend to sailing arrangements. I don't now want you to hurry in any way. My only concern is for you to get well.

[4] Take my word for it, dear Tiro, that nobody cares for me who does not care for you. Your recovery is most important to you and me, but many others are concerned about it. In the past you have never been able to recruit yourself properly, because you wanted to give me of your best at every turn. Now there is nothing to stand in your way. Put everything else aside, think only of your bodily well-being. I shall believe you care for me in proportion to the care you devote to your health.

On Tiro's fiftieth birthday on 28 April 53 BCE Cicero intended to set him free on his country estate. However, Tiro fell ill once again and was not able to come; therefore, Cicero travelled to Tiro, so that he could set him free on that day.[11] This episode, insignificant in relation to the political upheavals of the period, illustrates an aspect of Cicero's personality not visible otherwise.

A large number of Cicero's extant letters are connected to politics: he informs friends and acquaintances not in Rome, or in another centre of activity, of what is going on, or he asks about developments when he is away. Accordingly, he talks about the political situation in Rome and the Roman constitution more generally, provides details about individual Senate meetings, popular assemblies, court cases and speeches, and relates gossip and reports about public events such as dramatic performances. Depending on the addressee, the letters reveal his own activities and feelings, his reactions to developments, thoughts and plans as well as indications of political operations behind the scenes. Cicero seems to assume that his correspondents are equally interested in such matters, while providing his own reports allows him to present matters according to his own views and level of involvement. This focus is not a surprise considering that Cicero's entire life was inextricably linked to political circumstances. Hence what is found in the letters often includes details about historical events combined with information about Cicero's views.

For instance, Cicero tells a friend (Marcus Marius), who was not in Rome at the time, about the lavish spectacles at the opening of Pompey's theatre in 55 BCE, the first permanent stone theatre in Rome (*Fam.* 7.1.2–3 [*c.* September (?) 55 BCE]):

> To be sure, the show (if you are interested) was on the most lavish scale; but it would have been little to your taste, to judge by my own. To begin with, certain performers honoured the occasion by returning to the boards, from which I thought they had honoured their reputation by retiring. Your favourite, our friend Aesopus [i.e. a famous actor], gave a display which everyone was willing should be his finale. When he came to take an oath and got as far as 'if I knowingly swear false', he lost his voice! I need not give you further details – you know the other shows. They did not even have the sprightliness which one mostly finds in ordinary shows – one lost all sense of gaiety in watching the elaborate productions. These I don't doubt you are very well content to have missed. What pleasure is there in getting a *Clytemnestra* [i.e. a tragedy] with six hundred mules or a *Trojan Horse* [i.e. another tragedy] with three thousand mixing bowls or a variegated display of cavalry and infantry equipment in some battle or other? The public gaped at all this; it would not have amused you at all. [3] If you were listening to your man Protogenes [i.e. an attendant, reading aloud to the addressee] during those days (so long as he read you anything in the world except my speeches), you have certainly had a good deal better time of it than any of us. As for the Greek and Oscan shows, I don't imagine you were sorry to miss *them* – especially as you can see an Oscan turn on your town council, and you care so little for Greeks that you don't even take Greek Street to get to your house! Or perhaps, having scorned gladiators, you are sorry not to have seen the athletes! Pompey himself admits that they were a waste of time and midday oil! That leaves the hunts, two every day for five days, magnificent – nobody says otherwise. But what

pleasure can a cultivated man get out of seeing a weak human being torn to pieces by a powerful animal or a splendid animal transfixed by a hunting spear? Anyhow, if these sights are worth seeing, you have seen them often; and we spectators saw nothing new. The last day was for the elephants. The groundlings showed much astonishment thereat, but no enjoyment. There was even an impulse of compassion, a feeling that the monsters had something human about them.

Clearly, this is not an objective, unbiased description of the inauguration of Pompey's theatre, although a record of the main events is provided. The tone and style show Cicero's mastery of wit and sarcastic innuendo, even when writing about political processes, in cases where he could be fairly sure that the addressee shared his assessment.

Still, Cicero's letters not addressed to close friends are different from those to members of his family and to his friend Atticus, since in the latter he seems to express his feelings more explicitly. Among the surviving letters the close relationship to his family comes to the fore most strongly when Cicero writes home to Atticus and his family after he had to leave Rome to go into exile in 58–57 BCE. A letter addressed to his wife Terentia and also his daughter Tullia (affectionately called Tulliola) and his son Marcus shows how devastated he was about his fate and about leaving his family behind, causing uncertainty and grief for them (*Fam.* 14.1 [from Thessalonica, mid November, and Dyrrachium, 25 November 58 BCE]):

> From Tullius to his dear Terentia and to dear Tulliola and to dear Marcus greetings.
>
> [1] Many folk write to me and everybody talks to me about you, what amazing courage and fortitude you show, how no trials of body or spirit wear you out. Ah me, to think that my brave, loyal, true, gentle wife should have come by such misery because of me! And to think that our Tulliola should be suffering so much grief on account of her papa, who used to give her so much pleasure! As for Marcus, what can I say? Bitter sorrow and suffering has been his portion since the earliest dawn of intelligence. If I thought all this was the work of fate, as you say, I

should find it a little easier to bear. But I am to blame for everything. I thought I was loved by people who were only jealous of my success, while I refused to follow those who sought my friendship. [2] If only I had relied upon my own judgement instead of paying so much attention to the talk of friends, whether fools or knaves, how happy I might have been! As things are, since our friends tell us to hope, I shall take care not to let my health let your efforts down. I well understand the magnitude of the task, and how much easier it would have been to stay at home than it is to return. However, if we have all the Tribunes on our side, if Lentulus is as zealous as he seems, and if we also have Pompey's and Caesar's good will, we ought not to despair. [...]

[6] Take care of yourself and send me couriers, so that I know what is doing and what you and the children are doing. To be sure, I have not long to wait now. Give my love to Tulliola and Marcus. Good-bye to you all.

[7] I have come to Dyrrachium [i.e. a place on the Adriatic] because it is a Free City, and anxious to serve me, and the nearest point to Italy. But if I find there are too many people about for my liking, I shall go somewhere else and send you word.

Cicero suffered from the exile, not only because he was separated from his family, and the achievements of his consulship were called into question thereby, but also because it meant removal from home. His dislike of being away becomes clear from letters sent while he was provincial governor in Cilicia in 51–50 BCE, when he was disappointed at the distance from Rome and longed to return to the capital. This desire is shown, for instance, by a letter to the curule aedile M. Caelius Rufus, whom he advises to stay in Rome (*Fam.* 2.12.2–3 [*c.*26 June 50 BCE]):

Rome! Stick to Rome, my dear fellow, and live in the limelight! Sojourn abroad of any kind, as I have thought from my youth upwards, is squalid obscurity for those whose efforts can win lustre in the capital. I knew this well enough, and I only wish I had stayed true to my conviction. I do assure you that in my eyes all I get from the province is not worth a single stroll, a single talk with you. [3] I hope I have won some credit for integrity, but I should have gained as much of that by despising the province as I have by saving it from ruin. You suggest the hope of a Triumph. My Triumph would have been glorious enough; at any rate I should not have been so long cut off from all that is dearest to me. However, I hope to see you soon.

This emphatic embrace of life in Rome might be caused by his mood at the time, provoked by the fact that he had to fulfil his duties in Cilicia and could not travel to Rome at any time. At other times he enjoyed a stay in the countryside: there were lighter times in Cicero's life when he talked about the pleasure he gained from his villas or the consequences incurred after having had particular food at a dinner party. So he writes to M. Fabius Gallus in October 46 BCE (*Fam.* 7.26):

For ten days my stomach had been seriously out of order, but as I did not have a fever I could not convince the folk who wanted my services that I was really sick. So I took refuge here at Tusculum, after two days of strict fasting – not so much as a drop of water! Famished and exhausted, I was craving your good offices rather than expecting you to demand mine. I am terrified of all forms of illness, but especially of the one over which your master Epicurus gets a rough handling from the Stoics – for complaining of trouble with his bladder and his bowels, the latter being according to them a consequence of overeating and the former of an even more discreditable indulgence! Well, I was really afraid of dysentery. However, I think I am better for the change, or maybe the mental relaxation; or perhaps the malady is simply wearing itself into abatement.

[2] But in case you wonder how this happened or what I did to deserve it, the Sumptuary Law [i.e. a law of Caesar's, intended to curb luxury], supposed to have brought plain living, has been my downfall. Our *bons vivants*, in their efforts to bring into fashion products of the soil exempted under the statute, make the most appetizing dishes out of fungi, potherbs, and grasses of all sorts. Happening on some of these at

an augural dinner at Lentulus' house [i.e. P. Cornelius Lentulus Spinther the Younger, died 42 BCE], I was seized with a violent diarrhea, which has only today begun (I think) to check its flow. So: oysters and eels I used to resist well enough, but here I lie, caught in the toils of Mesdames Beet and Mallow! Well, I shall be more careful in future. As for you, you heard of it from Anicius [i.e. a senator] (he saw me in the qualms), and that should have been reason enough for a visit, let alone a letter.

I intend to stay here until I have convalesced, having lost strength and weight. But I expect I shall recover both easily enough, once I have thrown off the attack.

As far as one can tell on the basis of the surviving and perhaps biased evidence, Cicero was on the one hand 'an ordinary man', emotionally approachable, who could enjoy nice surroundings, cultivated dinner parties, discussions with friends, reading, writing and studying as well as domestic happiness. On the other hand, living during turbulent times and ambitiously aiming for political involvement and a respected public position, he was a versatile politician with extraordinary intellectual capacities (not only in the area of politics), yet tended to express an exaggerated opinion of himself.

VIII

LEGACY AND RECEPTION

RESPONSES TO CICERO started during his lifetime and have continued until the present day; they relate to his personality as well as his political roles and the different types of his literary output. Naturally, the immediate reaction to Cicero was closely connected with his historical personality and involvement in contemporary events, while later his intellectual legacy was valued in its own right, though an interest in Cicero as an individual remained. Because of the high number of instances of engagement with Cicero, the following survey, organized partly chronologically and partly thematically, can only sketch a broad outline and present a few telling examples.

Since Cicero was eager to disseminate his literary pieces, he sent writings to numerous acquaintances and invited feedback; he dedicated some to friends, sometimes in return for their works dedicated to him (as in Varro's case, *Att.* 13.10), and he shaped some of his treatises as dialogues in which he had friends and family members appear, creating a portrait of their interaction with him. Cicero claims that he wrote some pieces for the benefit of his countrymen and especially for aspiring orators. Above all, he was concerned about his image in history (which he tried to influence with appropriate presentations of himself): 'And what will history say of me a thousand years hence? I am far more in awe of that than of the tittle-tattle of my contemporaries.' (*Att.* 2.5.1 [April 59 BCE]).

The earliest reactions to Cicero can be found in his writings or inferred from them. Apart from details on personal relationships, these contain information on other people's opinions of Cicero's policies or literary attitudes. From his letters it appears that some of his friends did not agree with all his policies: for instance, as regards the political conflict during the last couple of years of Cicero's life, M. Iunius Brutus and Varro were more sceptical about the success of the strategy of siding with the young Octavian.[1] Some friends had different opinions on rhetorical style: Brutus, for example, favoured a more 'Attic' style than Cicero in the debate on rhetorical styles in the mid first century BCE.[2] When Cicero confronted opponents in court cases and political conflicts, their positions mainly emerge from what Cicero says about them, which is, of course, biased. Beyond the circle of Cicero's acquaintances, there was ridicule of Cicero's glorifying epics virtually from the point in time at which they became available.[3]

As soon as the second triumvirate of Octavian, Mark Antony and M. Aemilius Lepidus was formed in 43 BCE, they had Cicero proscribed and killed; his head and hands were exhibited on the speaker's platform in the Roman Forum, since these parts of Cicero's body were seen as responsible for the *Philippic Orations*, which had angered Antony and led him to seek revenge.[4] When the political situation changed and the Republic became the principate under Octavian (later Augustus), Cicero, the outspoken defender of the Republican system, was not highly regarded because of his political stance. Accordingly, Cicero is presented rather negatively in the works of Augustan historiographers, such as Livy and Asinius Pollio. At the same time, Octavian was consul in 30 BCE together with Cicero's son, an achievement that Marcus was widely perceived to owe to his father.[5] Octavian's more relaxed attitude towards Cicero and his family is also illustrated by the following anecdote: when Octavian, now emperor Augustus, came upon his grandson reading Cicero, and the boy tried to hide the book, the emperor picked it up, read a great deal of it and then said: 'An eloquent man, my boy, and a patriot' (Plutarch, *Cicero* 49.5).[6] At his death Augustus left 'an account of what he had accomplished, which he desired to have cut upon bronze tablets and set up at the entrance to the Mausoleum' (Suetonius, *Divus Augustus* 101.4),[7] a document now known as *Res gestae* (or *Monumentum Ancyranum*): Augustus' appreciation of Cicero is indicated by the fact that this record includes ideas and phrases borrowed from Cicero's *Philippics*.[8]

Cicero's struggle against Mark Antony came to be one of the most decisive elements in his life. That the *Philippics* and the fight against Antony caused Cicero's death was a widespread opinion among ancient authors.[9] Cicero's death developed into a theme for historians and rhetoricians. Propositions such as 'Cicero deliberates whether to beg Antony's pardon' and 'Antony promises to spare Cicero's life if he burns his writings: Cicero deliberates whether to do so' became topics for declamation in rhetorical schools (Seneca, *Suasoriae* 6; 7).[10] Almost all orators of whom potential speeches on these propositions have been transmitted argued that Cicero's writings were most important.

Appreciation of Cicero as a writer is also evident in the work of the early imperial historian Velleius Paterculus (20/19 BCE–after 30 CE), who feels obliged to insert an excursus on Cicero in his historical narrative, emphasizing that the assassination ordered by Mark Antony did not affect Cicero's lasting fame as an orator (Velleius Paterculus 2.66.3–5):[11]

> But you accomplished nothing, Mark Antony – for the indignation that surges in my breast compels me to exceed the bounds I have set for my narrative – you accomplished nothing, I say, by offering a reward for the sealing of those divine lips and the severing of that illustrious head, and by encompassing with a death-fee the murder of so great a consul and of the man who once had saved the state. [4] You took from Marcus Cicero a few anxious days, a few senile years, a life which would have been more wretched under your domination than was his death in your triumvirate; but you did not rob him of his fame, the glory of his deeds and words, nay you but enhanced them. [5] He lives and will continue to live in the memory of the ages, and so long as this universe shall endure – this universe which, whether created by chance, or by divine

> providence, or by whatever cause, he, almost alone of all the Romans, saw with the eye of his mind, grasped with his intellect, illumined with his eloquence – so long shall it be accompanied throughout the ages by the fame of Cicero. All posterity will admire the speeches that he wrote against you, while your deed to him will call forth their execrations, and the race of man shall sooner pass from the world than the name of Cicero be forgotten.

At this time Cicero's political beliefs were becoming less important, and he was developing into a stylistic model. In Lucan's (39–65 CE) epic on the Roman civil wars, written under emperor Nero, Cicero appears as 'the chief model of Roman eloquence, Cicero, beneath whose civilian authority fierce Catiline dreaded the axes of peace' (7.62–4).[12]

Since Cicero was the last orator of the Roman Republic and the scope of activity for orator–politicians was much reduced in the principate, there was no direct continuation of his oratory in that orators of the next generation would have immediately followed his example in public life. Cicero's impact was more noticeable in the schools of rhetoric. This is particularly obvious in the work of the rhetorician Quintilian (c.35–100 CE), Rome's first 'professor' of rhetoric, who wrote a rhetorical handbook (*Institutio oratoria*) towards the end of the first century CE: this work clearly shows the influence of Cicero's rhetorical treatises, to which Quintilian reacts, and Cicero's speeches and rhetorical works are often quoted. Although being separated in time by more than 100 years, Quintilian's discussion of delivery methods, for which otherwise little evidence remains, can shed a light on possible procedures in Cicero's time. At any rate, Quintilian's appreciation demonstrates that Cicero became a canonical author in the area of rhetoric very soon (e.g. Quintilian, *Institutio oratoria* 10.1.111–12):[13]

> And all the time these excellences, any one of which could hardly be attained by an ordinary person, however much he concentrated his effort, flow from Cicero without strain, and his oratory, than which nothing more beautiful has ever been heard, nevertheless displays all the marks of felicitous ease. [112] It was not without reason that his

contemporaries said he was 'king' of the courts, and that for posterity
Cicero has become not so much the name of a man as a synonym for
eloquence itself. Let us fix our eyes on him, let him be the model we
set before ourselves; if a student comes to love Cicero, let him assure
himself that he has made progress.

The only extant political speech from the first century C E is the *Panegyricus*
of Pliny the Younger (*c*.61/2–115 C E), a speech of thanks when Pliny was
made suffect consul (*consul suffectus*) in 100 C E under emperor Trajan; it
bears similarities in motifs to Ciceronian speeches given on similar occasions:
it includes praise of individuals to prompt them to actions favoured by the
speaker, and it promotes the idea that rulers should act for the common
welfare and subject themselves to the needs of the community and the rules
of the constitution.[14]

Pliny is well known as a writer of letters, and he sets his own letters
against the paradigm of those of Cicero,[15] which demonstrates that by this
time Cicero was regarded as a canonical letter writer. Pliny also sees Cicero
as a model and standard for oratory,[16] for the relationship to poets and
poetry[17] and for a public career.[18] Cicero as a model letter writer reappears
in the letters of M. Cornelius Fronto (*c*.90/95–167 C E), the tutor of the
future emperor Marcus Aurelius, in the second century C E.[19] Pliny's uncle,
Pliny the Elder (23/4–79 C E), had praised Cicero as a great orator and literary person who 'advanced so far the frontiers of the Roman genius' (Pliny,
Naturalis historia 7.116–17).

Cicero soon became a key author in the school syllabus (together with
Terence, Sallust and Virgil); thus he continued to be read throughout
late antiquity and into the Christian period. This lasting popularity is
one of the reasons why Cicero is among the few classical authors who
were commented upon rather early and for whom at least some of those
notes survive: there is a commentary on a selection of speeches by Q.
Asconius Pedianus (*c*.9 B C E–76 C E), a commentary on the *Somnium
Scipionis* (the final part of *De re publica*) by the Neoplatonic philosopher
and grammarian Macrobius (early fifth century C E), a commentary on
the rhetorical treatise *Topica* by the politician and philosopher Boethius

(*c.*480–524 CE) as well as various versions of Scholia (collections of notes) on some of Cicero's speeches.

As a result of this standing, Cicero's writings are assessed as examples in rhetorical works. The anonymous author of *On the Sublime*, a Greek treatise on rhetorical style, presumably dating to the first century CE, presents a comparison between Demosthenes and Cicero, the two most famous orators on the Greek and the Roman side respectively, which is likely to be one of the earliest reactions of a Greek writer to Cicero's style ([Longinus], *On the Sublime* 12.4–5):[20]

> It is in the very same respect – so I feel, my dear Terentianus, if indeed we Greeks may be allowed an opinion – that Cicero differs from Demosthenes in his grand effects. Demosthenes' strength is usually in rugged sublimity, Cicero's in diffusion. Our countryman with his violence, yes, and his speed, his force, his terrific power of rhetoric, burns, as it were, and scatters everything before him, and may therefore be compared to a flash of lightning or a thunderbolt. Cicero seems to me like a widespread conflagration, rolling along and devouring all around it: his is a strong and steady fire, its flames duly distributed, now here, now there, and fed by fresh supplies of fuel. [5] You Romans, of course, can form a better judgement on this question, but clearly the opportunity for Demosthenes' sublimity and nervous force comes in his intensity and violent emotion, and in passages where it is necessary to amaze the audience; whereas diffuseness is in place when you need to overwhelm them with a flood of rhetoric. The latter then mostly suits the treatment of a commonplace, a peroration, a digression, and all descriptive and epideictic passages, as well as historical and scientific contexts, and many other types of writing.

Cicero is often quoted and referred to by the Church Fathers and other early Christian writers. For instance, in the works of Augustine (354–430 CE) Cicero is the pagan author most often referred to, and Augustine records how reading Cicero's philosophical treatise *Hortensius* was an influential experience for him and turned him towards philosophy and the Christian God.[21]

The Christian writers Minucius Felix (first half of the third century CE) and Lactantius (*c.*300 CE) followed Cicero's writings in form and engaged with their contents. However, while Cicero continued to be the standard for Latin prose style and an important source of information on Roman Republican politics and classical philosophy, the early Christian writers were confronted with the problem of having a pagan author among their chief models. This conflict is described most memorably by Jerome/Hieronymus (345–420 CE) in one of his letters (Jerome, *Epistulae* 22.30.3–5),[22] a story that has often been retold and illustrated:

> While the old serpent was thus having sport with me, in about Mid-Lent a fever attacked my enfeebled body and spread to my very vitals, what I say is almost beyond belief, but without cessation it so wrought havoc upon my wretched limbs that my flesh could scarcely cling to my bones. [...] Suddenly I was caught up in the spirit and dragged before the tribunal of the Judge. Here there was so much light and such a glare from the brightness of those standing around that I cast myself on the ground and dared not look up. [4] Upon being asked my status, I replied that I was a Christian. And He who sat upon the judgment seat said: 'Thou liest. Thou art a Ciceronian, not a Christian. *Where thy treasure is, there is thy heart also.*' I was struck dumb on the spot. Amid the blows – for He had ordered me to be beaten – I was tormented the more by the flame of conscience. I repeated to myself the verse: *And who shall confess thee in hell?* However, I began to cry aloud and to say with lamentation: 'Have mercy on me, Lord, have mercy upon me.' The petition re-echoed amid the lashes. [5] Finally, casting themselves before the knees of Him who presided, the bystanders besought Him to have mercy on the young man, granting me opportunity to repent of my error and then to exact the penalty if I ever again read books of pagan literature. Being caught in such an extremity, I would have been willing to make even greater promises. I began to take an oath, swearing by His name, saying: 'O Lord, if ever I possess or read secular writings, I have denied thee.' After I had uttered the words of this oath, I was discharged and returned to the world above.

Despite the tension with Christian beliefs, Cicero's works continued to be read and sought after in late antiquity and beyond. Engagement with Cicero decreased in the sixth and seventh centuries CE, when, for instance, Pope Gregory the Great (540–604 CE) lamented that the charm of Cicero's style prevented young people from reading the Bible and therefore thought that the works of the pagan author should be destroyed.

Interest in Cicero increased again in the so-called Carolingian Renaissance. Early medieval scholars in this period produced collections of thematically organized excerpts from Cicero's works. Later there were attempts to combine Cicero's philosophy with Christian thinking, and his works were seen to provide guidance in questions of ethical and political philosophy. Predominantly, Cicero was regarded as a model for rhetoric, and in this more technical area there was no clash with Christian doctrines. For instance, Cicero could be an element in presentations of the seven liberal arts, combined with the relevant ancient scholars, like the figures of 'Cicero' and 'Rhetoric' on Chartres Cathedral from the mid twelfth century or in a later German manuscript, where 'Rhetoric' polishes the wood of the speech and 'Magister Tullius' provides the rules (fig. 8.1).

When Geoffrey Chaucer (c. 1343–1400), in *The Canterbury Tales*, includes an apology for simple diction in 'The Prologe of the Frankeleyns Tale', the person from whom the speaker could have learned rhetorical polish is, of course, Cicero:[23]

Thise olde gentil Britouns in hir dayes	In their own day those noble old Bretons
Of diverse aventures maden layes,	Made ballads of all kinds of happenings,
Rymeyed in hir firste Briton tonge,	Rhymed in the original Breton tongue;
Whiche layes with hir instrumentz they songe	Ballads, romances, which were either sung
Or elles redden hem for hir pleasaunce;	Accompanied by musical instruments,
And oon of hem have I in remembraunce,	Or read for pleasure. I have in remembrance
Which I shal seyn with good wyl as I kan.	One I'll be pleased to tell, as best I can.
But, sires, by cause I am a burel man,	But, gentlemen, as I'm a plain, blunt man,
At my bigynning first I yow biseche,	Before beginning I must first beseech
Have me excused of my rude speche.	That you excuse my homely style and speech.
I lerned nevere rethorik, certeyn;	I never studied rhetoric, that's certain;

Thyng that I speke, it moot be bare and pleyn.	And so the things I say are bare and plain.
I sleep nevere on the Mount of Pernaso,	I never made of Parnassus my pillow,
Ne lerned Marcus Tullius Scithero.	Or studied Marcus Tullius Cicero.
Colours ne knowe I none, withouten drede,	Colours of rhetoric – I pass them by;
But swiche colours as growen in the mede,	The colours that are used for paint and dye,
Or elles swiche as man dye or peynte.	Or grow in field, those colours I can see.
Colours of rethoryk been to me queynte;	Colours of speech are too far-fetched for me;
My spirit feeleth noght of swich mateere.	They're something I've no feeling for at all.
But if yow list, my tale shul ye heere.	But if you like, then you shall hear my tale.

From the thirteenth century Cicero had again become an important figure: for instance, the scholastic philosopher and theologian Thomas Aquinas (1225–74) refers frequently to Cicero in his major works *Summa theologica* and *Summa contra gentiles*, partly engaging with Cicero directly, partly via Augustine. The Italian poet Dante Alighieri (1265–1321) quotes from Cicero more than fifty times and develops stories and motifs from him; in Dante's *La divina Commedia* Cicero appears with other classical authors in the first circle of the unbaptized (*Inferno* 4.141).

Prior to the fifteenth century the most frequently read Ciceronian works were the rhetorical and rather technical treatises *De inventione* and the Pseudo-Ciceronian *Rhetorica ad Herennium* (then widely thought to be by Cicero). Cicero was thus seen as a guide in the area of style and structure for literary texts. The full texts of Cicero's other rhetorical writings (*De oratore*, *Brutus* and *Orator*) were only rediscovered at Lodi (Lombardy) in 1422 (copies made from this manuscript survive). Cicero's *Epistulae ad Atticum* (*Letters to Atticus*), *Epistulae ad Brutum* (*Letters to Brutus*) and *Epistulae ad Quintum fratrem* (*Letters to Brother Quintus*) were unearthed by the Italian humanist Petrarch/Francesco Petrarca (1304–74) in a library in the Italian city of Verona in 1345. This discovery dramatically changed Petrarch's view of Cicero, since he was shocked to see human faults in Cicero (*Fam.* 24.2–4), but it inspired Petrarch to publish his own collections of letters. In 1392 another Italian humanist, Coluccio Salutati (1331–1406), found Cicero's *Epistulae ad familiares* (*Letters to Friends*); he was so influenced by

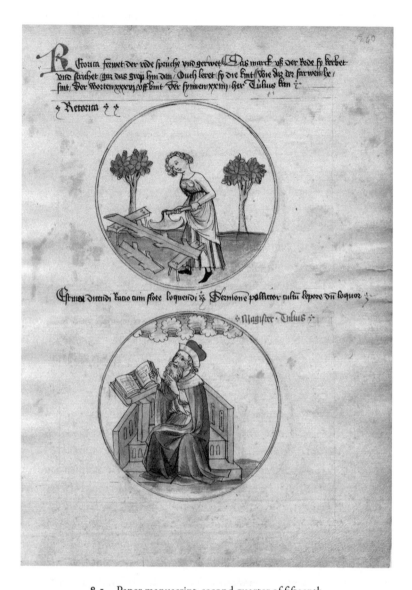

8.1 Paper manuscript, second quarter of fifteenth
century, from the area of Lake Constance.
TOP: depiction of Rhetoric ('Retorica' as one of the seven *Artes
liberales*) shaping wood (i.e. the text); German inscription (quoted
after a text by Heinrich von Mügeln, a German medieval poet) about
rhetoric, naming 'Mr Cicero' as a master ('her Túlius kan').
BOTTOM: depiction of Cicero as a scholar ('Magister Tulius'); Latin inscription
('Retorica' speaking): 'Est mea dicendi racio cum flore loquendi /
Sermone(m) polliceor cultu(m) lepore d(omi)n(a) loquor.' ('My way of speaking is to talk with
embellishment, / I promise a speech refined with charm: I talk as a mistress').

Cicero's style that he was called 'Cicero's monkey', albeit in a positive sense. The scholar and writer Gian Francesco Poggio Bracciolini (1380–1459) and others discovered the texts of speeches believed to have been lost. *De re publica* was only made accessible in the nineteenth century by Angelo Mai (1782–1854), who recovered it from a palimpsest (a reused manuscript).

The very first classical text to be printed was Cicero's *De officiis*, at Mainz (Germany) in 1465. Alexander Minutianus published a complete edition of Cicero's works in four volumes at Milan in 1498–9. The first Ciceronian work to become available in English was *De amicitia*, in a translation by John Tiptoft, Earl of Worcester (1427–70), printed by William Caxton in 1481. In the fifteenth century a single Latin edition of a Ciceronian text was produced in Britain, the first edition (*editio princeps*) of the speech *Pro Milone*, published by the German Theodoricus Rood at Oxford around 1483; this was also the first classical text to be printed in England. The first scholarly comprehensive edition was prepared by the Swiss classical scholar Johann Caspar von Orelli (1787–1849), partly in collaboration with others: this edition in seven volumes (1826–38) includes the text of all of Cicero's works, the notes of scholiasts, a biography of Cicero, a bibliography of earlier editions and several indexes. Since then Ciceronian texts have been available as objects of scholarly study.

Changes in the amount of accessible material, together with developments in attitude and intellectual outlook, meant that views of Cicero developed over time: in the early Middle Ages Cicero was predominantly seen as a personification of eloquence (with his more standard works on rhetoric used as textbooks), while further dimensions of his personality and works were acknowledged from the late Middle Ages onwards.

For the subsequent intellectual development in Europe the emergence of an educational programme of *humanitas*, derived from Cicero's writings, was significant. The starting point was Cicero's statement in *De inventione* 'that wisdom without eloquence does too little for the good of states, but that eloquence without wisdom is generally highly disadvantageous and is never helpful' (*Inv. rhet.* 1.1). This means that philosophical education must be combined with training in eloquence. The term 'humanist', which appeared in fifteenth-century Italy, was originally a description of teachers and students of classical subjects; it later became a general term for people educated in the humanities with an emphasis on classical literature and the associated worldview.

This reliance on Cicero as a thinker and a rhetorical model meant that his works played a key role in education during the Renaissance. This is illustrated by what the Swiss student Conrad ab Ulmis reports (1 March 1552) about his studies at Oxford to his patron John Wolfius:[24]

> Receive therefore a brief account of my studies. I devote the hour from six to seven in the morning to Aristotle's politics, from which I seem to derive a two-fold advantage, both a knowledge of Greek and an acquaintance with moral philosophy. The seventh hour I employ upon the first book of the Digests or Pandects of the Roman law, and the eighth in the reconsideration of this lecture. At nine I attend the lecture of that most eminent and learned divine, master doctor Peter Martyr [i.e. Peter Martyr Vermigli or Pietro Martire Vermigli, 1499–1562, an Italian theologian who converted to Protestantism and became a teacher in Oxford]. The tenth hour I devote to the rules of Dialectics of Philip Melancthon [i.e. Philipp Melanchthon, 1497–1560, a German humanist, theologian, philologist and poet] *de locis argomentorum* [i.e. Book 4 of his *Erotemata dialectices* of 1547]. Immediately after dinner I read Cicero's Offices [i.e. *De officiis*], a truly golden book, from which I derive no less than a two-fold enjoyment, both from the purity of the language and the knowledge of philosophy. From one to three I exercise my pen, chiefly in writing letters, wherein, as far as possible, I imitate Cicero, who is considered to have abundantly supplied us with all instructions relating to purity of style. At three I learn the institutes of civil law, which I so read aloud as to commit them to memory. At four are read privately, in a certain hall in which we live, the rules of law, which I hear, and learn by rote as I do the institutes. After supper the time is spent in various discourse: for either sitting in our chamber, or walking up and down some part of the college, we exercise ourselves in dialectical questions. You have now a brief account of my studies, with which I think you will be pleased.

The appreciation of Cicero as an important figure even led to the composition of further orations by 'Cicero', such as a *'Fifth Catilinarian Speech'*, and to coins being minted in the Renaissance, allegedly bearing ancient depictions of Cicero (fig. 8.2). That Cicero was regarded as a key model led to a debate called the 'Ciceronian controversy', which addressed the question of literary imitation, including the issue of whether or not Cicero should be the only model and how closely he should be followed. After the topic had been discussed by several generations of Italian humanists from about the 1480s, it was most famously presented by the Dutch humanist Desiderius Erasmus of Rotterdam (*c.* 1466–1536) in the satirical dialogue *Ciceronianus* (1528), in a discussion of the Ciceronian Nosoponus with Bulephorus and Hypologus. Towards the beginning of the dialogue Nosoponus' devotion to Cicero is presented:[25]

8.2   Imitation Roman coin with a portrait of Cicero, recorded in the inventory of Basilius Amerbach (1533–91) as 'Ciceronis nummus falsus' ('false coin of Cicero').

SIDE A: portrait of Cicero; Latin legend: M T CICERO.

SIDE B: picture of Roman goddess Minerva; Latin legend: MINERVE

NO. Now I shall reveal the mysteries to those consecrated, as it were, to the same god. For seven whole years I have touched nothing except Ciceronian books, refraining from others as religiously as the Carthusians refrain from flesh. – BU. Why so? – NO. Lest somewhere some foreign phrase should creep in and, as it were, dull the splendour of Ciceronian speech. Also I have enclosed in their cases and removed from sight all other books lest I should sin inadvertently; and hereafter there is no place in my library for any one except Cicero. – BU. How neglectful I have been! Never with such care have I cherished Cicero. – NO. Not only in the chapel and library but also in every doorway have I a picture of him beautifully painted, and I wear one engraved on a gem so that he may be in my thoughts. No other vision comes to me in sleep except that of Cicero. – BU. I do not wonder. – HYP. Among the apostles in my calendar I have given a place to Cicero. – BU. Quite right. For they used to call him the god of eloquence. – NO. I have been so diligent too in reading and rereading his writings that I have learned by heart almost all of them. – BU. What industry! – NO. Now I am girded for imitation. – BU. How much time have you allotted to this? – NO. As much as for the reading. – BU. It is too little for such an arduous task. Would that there might fall to my lot, even at the age of seventy, the glory of so illustrious a name! – NO. But hold, I am not content with this. There is not a word in all the books of that divine man which I have not set in order in an alphabetical lexicon. – BU. A huge volume it must be. – NO. Two strong carriers well saddled could scarcely carry it on their backs. – BU. Whew! I have seen them at Paris who could carry an elephant. – NO. And there is a second volume even bigger than this in which I have arranged alphabetically the phrases peculiar to Cicero. – BU. Now, at last, I am ashamed of my laziness. – NO. There is a third. – BU. Whew! A third too? – NO. It had to be. In this I have gathered all the metrical feet with which Cicero ever begins or ends his periods and their subdivisions, the rhythms which he uses in between and the cadences which he chooses for each kind of sentence, so that no little point could escape.

Such a dictionary, illustrating Cicero's use of language with examples and explanations, was provided by Mario Nizolio (1498–1576), whose work *Observationes in M.T. Ciceronem* (1535) later became popular under the title *Nizolius sive Thesaurus Ciceronianus.* The movement that only regarded Latin written in Cicero's style as 'correct' contributed significantly to Latin becoming fixed as a 'dead language'.

Cicero continued to be regarded as a stylistic model, even by people writing in other languages and on different topics. For instance, Edward

Gibbon (1737–94), the author of *The History of the Decline and Fall of the Roman Empire* (1776–89), records that he read almost all of Cicero's works and admired them:[26]

> I read, with application and pleasure, *all* the epistles, *all* the orations, and the most important treatises of rhetoric and philosophy; and as I read, I applauded the observation of Quintilian, that every student may judge of his own proficiency, by the satisfaction which he receives from the Roman orator. I tasted the beauties of language, I breathed the spirit of freedom, and I imbibed from his precepts and examples the public and private sense of a man. Cicero in Latin, and Xenophon in Greek, are indeed the two ancients whom I would first propose to a liberal scholar; not only for the merit of their style and sentiments, but for the admirable lessons, which may be applied almost to every situation of public and private life.

In the middle of the nineteenth century (14 April 1869), John Henry Newman (1801–90), later Cardinal Newman, stated:[27]

> As to patterns for imitation, the only master of style I have ever had (which is strange considering the differences of the languages) is Cicero. I think I owe a great deal to him, and as far as I know to no one else.

The attitude towards Cicero in Germany in the eighteenth and nineteenth centuries was different. The influential German ancient historian Barthold Georg Niebuhr (1776–1831) admired Cicero and called one of his children 'Marcus'. By contrast, the German classicist Theodor Mommsen (1817–1903), influenced by the historian Wilhelm Drumann (1786–1861), condemned Cicero. Theodor Mommsen published an important *History of Rome* (in three volumes: 1854, 1855 and 1856), for which he received the Nobel Prize in Literature in 1902, one of the few non-fiction works to do so and the only work by a Classicist so far. Because Theodor Mommsen did not agree with Cicero's political position, he could not see any positives in him and famously described him as follows:[28]

This was Marcus Cicero, notoriously a political trimmer, accustomed to flirt at times with the democrats, at times with Pompeius, at times from a somewhat greater distance with the aristocracy, and to lend his services as an advocate to every influential man under impeachment without distinction of person or party (he numbered even Catilina among his clients); belonging properly to no party or – which was much the same – to the party of material interests, which was dominant in the courts and was pleased with the eloquent pleader and the courtly and witty companion. [...]

Thus oratorical authorship emancipated from politics was naturalized in the Roman literary world by Cicero. We have already had occasion several times to mention this many-sided man. As a statesman without insight, idea, or purpose, he figured successively as democrat, as aristocrat, and as a tool of the monarchs, and was never more than a short-sighted egotist. Where he exhibited the semblance of action, the questions to which his action applied had, as a rule, just reached their solution; thus he came forward in the trial of Verres [i.e. in 70 BCE] against the senatorial courts when they were already set aside; thus he was silent at the discussion on the Gabinian [i.e. a law similar to the Manilian Law in 67 BCE], and acted as a champion of the Manilian, law [i.e. in the speech *De lege Manilia* or *De imperio Cn. Pompei* in 66 BCE]; thus he thundered against Catilina [i.e. in 63 BCE] when his departure was already settled, and so forth. He was valiant in opposition to sham attacks, and he knocked down many walls of pasteboard with a loud din; no serious matter was ever, either in good or evil, decided by him, and the execution of the Catilinarians in particular was far more due to his acquiescence than to his instigation. In a literary point of view we have already noticed that he was the creator of the modern Latin prose; his importance rests on his mastery of style, and it is only as a stylist that he shows confidence in himself. In the character of an author, on the other hand, he stands quite as low as in that of a statesman. He essayed the most varied tasks, sang the great deeds of Marius and his own petty achievements in endless hexameters, beat Demosthenes off the field with his speeches, and

Plato with his philosophic dialogues; and time alone was wanting for him to vanquish also Thucydides. He was in fact so thoroughly a dabbler, that it was pretty much a matter of indifference to what work he applied his hand. By nature a journalist in the worst sense of that term – abounding, as he himself says, in words, poor beyond all conception in ideas – there was no department in which he could not with the help of a few books have rapidly got up by translation or compilation a readable essay. His correspondence mirrors most faithfully his character.

Mommsen's assessment proved to be influential for a long time, both in Germany and elsewhere. In the last few decades, however, scholars have moved away from such a judgemental approach and now tend to see Cicero more objectively, making an effort to distinguish between their personal political beliefs, the assessment of Cicero's political agenda and his intellectual and organizational achievements.

Cicero has frequently been a point of reference in literature too, as the allusion to Cicero in Charles Dickens' *Dombey and Son* (see Preface) or the comment in Geoffrey Chaucer's *Canterbury Tales* (see above) demonstrate. These passing comments illustrate Cicero's status at the time of composition of these pieces. Beyond these, there are entire works dedicated to Cicero, such as a drama published anonymously in England in 1651, entitled *The Tragedy of that Famous Roman Oratour Marcus Tullius Cicero* (reissued in paperback in 2011). In eighteenth-century France Voltaire (1694–1778) wrote a drama entitled *Rome sauvée, ou Catilina* (1752), in which Cicero is the protagonist. This was a reaction to a drama *Catilina* by Prosper Jolyot de Crébillon (1674–1762), first performed in 1748. Voltaire did not think highly of this rival dramatist and royal censor, and altogether he wrote five dramas in response to themes treated by de Crébillon. In the twentieth century the American author Upton Sinclair (1878–1968), who won the Pulitzer Prize for the Novel (now renamed Fiction) for *Dragon's Teeth* in 1943, composed a play called *Cicero: A Tragedy of Ancient Rome* (1960), which, however, did not gain popularity.

Naturally, most dramatic representations of Cicero deal with a single major event in his life, particularly his confrontation of the Catilinarian conspiracy in his consular year and his fight for the Republic in the last years of his life. The most recent literary presentation of Cicero, however, aims at covering his entire life. The British novelist Robert Harris (b. 1957) has set out to narrate Cicero's life in a trilogy, of which the first two volumes have been published: *Imperium* (2006), which covers the years 79–64 BCE, and *Lustrum* (2009), which deals with the consulship in 63 BCE and the four subsequent years. As Harris says in these books, they are fiction, but he has tried to be faithful to the sources ('Author's Note'). The trilogy purports to be the story of Cicero's life as told by his private secretary M. Tullius Tiro (*c.*103–4 BCE), who is said to have written a biography of Cicero now lost.[29]

Elsewhere Cicero is acknowledged not only as a politician and orator, but also as a writer of helpful philosophical works, as an allusion to Cicero's *Consolatio*, written after the death of his daughter Tullia in 45 BCE, suggests. In the novel *Tristram Shandy* (1759–67) Laurence Sterne (1713–68) inserts the following considerations on how to cope with the loss of friends or children:[30]

> My father managed his affliction otherwise; and indeed differently from most men either ancient or modern; for he neither wept it away, as the Hebrews and the Romans – or slept it off, as the Laplanders – or hanged it, as the English, or drowned it, as the Germans, – nor did he curse it, or damn it, or excommunicate it, or rhyme it, or lillabullero it. –
>
> – He got rid of it, however.
>
> Will your worships give me leave to squeeze in a story between these two pages?
>
> When Tully [i.e. Cicero] was bereft of his dear daughter Tullia, at first he laid it to his heart, – he listened to the voice of nature, and modulated his own unto it. – O my Tullia! my daughter! my child! – still, still, still, – 'twas O my Tullia! – my Tullia! Methinks I see my Tullia, I hear my Tullia, I talk with my Tullia. – But as soon as he began to look

into the stores of philosophy, and consider how many excellent things might be said upon the occasion – no body upon earth can conceive, says the great orator, how happy, how joyful it made me.

My father was as proud of his eloquence as Marcus Tullius Cicero could be for his life, and for aught I am convinced of to the contrary at present, with as much reason: it was indeed his strength – and his weakness too. – His strength – for he was by nature eloquent; and his weakness – for he was hourly a dupe to it; and, provided an occasion in life would but permit him to shew his talents, or say either a wise thing, a witty, or a shrewd one – (bating the case of a systematic misfortune) – he had all he wanted. – A blessing which tied up my father's tongue, and a misfortune which let it loose with a good grace, were pretty equal: sometimes, indeed, the misfortune was the better of the two; for instance, where the pleasure of the harangue was as ten, and the pain of the misfortune but as five – my father gained half in half, and consequently was as well again off, as if it had never befallen him.

On a more serious note, Cicero as a transmitter of Greek philosophy exerted an impact on many early modern thinkers, including the Protestant reformer Martin Luther (1483–1546), who admired Cicero and particularly the treatise *De officiis*, the French political philosopher Montesquieu (1689–1755), the French Enlightenment writer Voltaire (1694–1778), the Scottish philosopher David Hume (1711–76) and the British liberal political philosopher John Stuart Mill (1806–73).

In 1712 the Irish rationalist philosopher and freethinker John Toland (1670–1722) published a work, *Cicero illustratus, dissertatio philologico-critica: sive Consilium de toto edendo Cicerone, alia plane methodo quam hactenus unquam factum* (*Cicero Illustrated, a Philological and Critical Interpretation: Or Considerations on Editing All of Cicero by a Method Totally Different from What Has Ever Been Done Before*), which was an advertisement and part of a campaign to raise funds for a planned edition of Cicero's complete works. In this work on Cicero Toland presents him as a key figure of the Enlightenment and discusses scholarly views on Cicero from the early

Renaissance up to his own time. Even if the envisaged edition was never realized, this treatise gives insight into the development of scholarship at the time and the exploitation of Cicero's views for contemporary philosophy.

Elsewhere Cicero had a profound influence on politicians in the period that witnessed the rise of the early-modern democratic state, for instance on speeches made in the context of the French Revolution or by the American Founding Fathers at the end of the eighteenth century. In addition to the fact that the Classics, including Cicero, were still a standard element in the education of these men, there was also felt to be a relationship between their ideals and the Roman Republic.

John Adams (1735–1826), the second president of the United States (1797–1801), is known to have studied Cicero's speeches carefully and to have admired them, as his diaries demonstrate. It can be shown that in some of his most famous orations, such as his speech in the Boston Massacre Trial (1770) and his inaugural address as president (1797), he employed a number of strategies similar to those used by Cicero. For instance, in the latter oration (delivered on 4 March 1797) Adams, like Cicero on the same occasion, mentioned that he felt honoured at his election, stressed peace and prosperity and praised his nation's political institutions:[31]

> Returning to the bosom of my country after a painful separation from it for ten years, I had the honor to be elected to a station under the new order of things, and I have repeatedly laid myself under the most serious obligations to support the Constitution. The operation of it has equaled the most sanguine expectations of its friends, and from an habitual attention to it, satisfaction in its administration, and delight in its effects upon the peace, order, prosperity, and happiness of the nation I have acquired an habitual attachment to it and veneration for it.
>
> What other form of government, indeed, can so well deserve our esteem and love?
>
> There may be little solidity in an ancient idea that congregations of men into cities and nations are the most pleasing objects in the sight of superior intelligences, but this is very certain, that to a benevolent

human mind there can be no spectacle presented by any nation more pleasing, more noble, majestic, or august, than an assembly like that which has so often been seen in this and the other Chamber of Congress, of a Government in which the Executive authority, as well as that of all the branches of the Legislature, are exercised by citizens selected at regular periods by their neighbors to make and execute laws for the general good. Can anything essential, anything more than mere ornament and decoration, be added to this by robes and diamonds? Can authority be more amiable and respectable when it descends from accidents or institutions established in remote antiquity than when it springs fresh from the hearts and judgments of an honest and enlightened people? For it is the people only that are represented. It is their power and majesty that is reflected, and only for their good, in every legitimate government, under whatever form it may appear. The existence of such a government as ours for any length of time is a full proof of a general dissemination of knowledge and virtue throughout the whole body of the people. And what object or consideration more pleasing than this can be presented to the human mind? If national pride is ever justifiable or excusable it is when it springs, not from power or riches, grandeur or glory, but from conviction of national innocence, information, and benevolence.

Even in the twentieth century politicians could be influenced by Cicero: Harry S. Truman (1884–1972), the thirty-third president of the United States (1945–53), subscribed to the Ciceronian ideal of an orator who knows about his subject and believes in what he says, and looked up to Cicero as a model, as he revealed in an interview after having left office:[32]

How would you define the effective speaker?

I would say that the effective speaker is one who accomplishes what he sets out to do. To do that, he should know more about the subject than his audience. And he *must* believe what he is saying. These, in my opinion, are the two essentials. I can't emphasize too strongly the importance of getting the true facts; a man must know what he is talking about and know it well. As for sincerity, the public is quick to detect and reject the charlatan and the demagogue. It may be deceived for a brief period, but not for long.

In my opinion, mere talent without intellectual honesty and accurate information is not enough to make a successful speaker. I've never said anything in a speech that I did not firmly believe to be right.

Would you care to mention any speaker, living or dead, as being especially worthy of emulation?

I believe an audience approves of Cicero's method, which was to state his case and then prove it. That is what I always tried to do. Charlie Ross [Charles Griffith Ross, 1885–1950; White House Press Secretary, 1945–50] and I used to translate Cicero's orations from the Latin. I guess I have read almost all of his speeches. They are models of clarity and simplicity. I wish I could do half as well.

However, it is not only politicians up to the middle of the twentieth century for whom Cicero is important. While it is not known to what extent contemporary politicians study Cicero's writings and may model their own public statements on this precedent (consciously or unconsciously), similarities between Ciceronian speeches and modern ones have been observed. After Barack Obama (b. 1961) was first elected president of the United States in November 2008, his rhetoric and appearance were often compared to Cicero in the media. An example is an article by Charlotte Higgins in the British national newspaper the *Guardian* of 26 November 2008, entitled 'The new Cicero', which includes the following comments:[33]

More than once, the adjective that has been deployed to describe Obama's oratorical skill is 'Ciceronian'. Cicero, the outstanding Roman politician of the late republic, was certainly the greatest orator of his time, and one of the greatest in history. A fierce defender of the republican constitution, his criticism of Mark Antony got him murdered in 43BC.

During the Roman republic (and in ancient Athens) politics was oratory. In Athens, questions such as whether or not to declare war on an enemy state were decided by the entire electorate (or however many bothered to turn up) in open debate. Oratory was the supreme political skill, on whose mastery power depended. Unsurprisingly, then, oratory was highly organised and rigorously analysed. The Greeks and Romans, in short, knew all the rhetorical tricks, and they put a name to most of them.

It turns out that Obama knows them, too. [...]

It is not just in the intricacies of speechifying that Obama recalls Cicero. Like Cicero, Obama is a lawyer. Like Cicero, Obama is a writer of enormous accomplishment – *Dreams From My Father*, Obama's first book, will surely enter the American literary canon. Like Cicero, Obama is a 'novus homo' – the Latin phrase means 'new man' in the sense of self-made. Like Cicero, Obama entered politics without family backing (compare Clinton) or a military record (compare John McCain). Roman tradition dictated you had both. The compensatory talent Obama shares with Cicero, says Catherine Steel, professor of classics at the University of Glasgow, is a skill at 'setting up a genealogy of forebears – not biological forebears but intellectual forebears. For Cicero it was Licinius Crassus, Scipio Aemilianus and Cato the Elder. For Obama it is Lincoln, Roosevelt and King.'

Steel also points out how Obama's oratory conforms to the tripartite ideal laid down by Aristotle, who stated that good rhetoric should consist of pathos, logos and ethos – emotion, argument and character. [...]

In English, when we use the word 'rhetoric', it is generally preceded by the word 'empty'. Rhetoric has a bad reputation. McCain warned lest an electorate be 'deceived by an eloquent but empty call for change'. Waspishly, Clinton noted, 'You campaign in poetry, you govern in prose.' The Athenians, too, knew the dangers of a populace's being swept along by a persuasive but unscrupulous demagogue (and they invented the word). And it was the Roman politician Cato – though it could have been McCain – who said 'Rem tene, verba sequentur'. If you hold on to the facts, the words will follow.

Cicero was well aware of the problem. In his book *On The Orator*, he argues that real eloquence can be acquired only if the speaker has attained the highest state of knowledge – 'otherwise what he says is just an empty and ridiculous swirl of verbiage'. The true orator is one whose practice of citizenship embodies a civic ideal – whose rhetoric, far from empty, is the deliberate, rational, careful organiser of ideas and argument that propels the state forward safely and wisely. This is clearly what Obama, too, is aiming to embody: his project is to unite rhetoric, thought and action in a new politics that eschews narrow bipartisanship.

During Obama's first term in office the interest in such comparisons subsided, but Cicero was still seen as relevant in the presidential election campaign in 2012, when Obama stood for re-election. For instance, James Carville (b. 1944), who led the successful election campaign for President Bill Clinton (b. 1946) in 1992, published an article in various versions, entitled 'Why Cicero should be every campaign strategist's mentor'. There he pointed out the striking similarities between the advice given to Cicero (when he stood for the consulship in 64 BCE) by his brother Quintus in *Commentariolum petitionis* (*Handbook of Electioneering*) and the strategies used by leaders of present-day election campaigns; he ends with the wish:[34] 'I just hope my opponent in the next campaign doesn't get a copy [i.e. of Quintus' text].'

In any event, Cicero can appear in all sorts of expected and unexpected contexts: for instance, it has been claimed that the idea of a broad liberal education goes back to Cicero. 'Cicero' is also used as an acronym, as well as the name of a magazine, language schools, restaurants, organizations and places, including a town in Onondaga County, New York, north of Syracuse, and a town in Cook County, Illinois.

CONCLUSION:
THIS IS CICERO?

HAVING LOOKED AT key aspects of Cicero's life and works (though much more detail could be added), one may want to go back to the initial question of 'Who is Cicero?' and try to provide an answer. However, it soon becomes clear that answering this question does not necessarily become easier after studying Cicero more closely: a detailed look at his career and the wide variety of his works only demonstrates that there are many sides to Cicero. Depending on which aspect is highlighted, the assessment may change, though ideally all of them would be taken into account for a comprehensive evaluation. The very fact that Cicero is a versatile and multifaceted individual means that he cannot readily be described by a single term.

In his letters Cicero appears as a caring family man, who is worried about the fate of his wife and his young son and daughter when he goes into exile and who is devastated at the death of his daughter. Yet towards the end of his life he divorced his first wife, marrying a young girl probably for financial reasons, and his reaction to the death of his daughter also conveys the impression of exaggerated and self-pitying grief. Cicero is concerned for the welfare of his secretary Tiro, who apparently had a weak constitution, and does not shy away from incurring expenses on this slave's behalf. However, this may not have been entirely disinterested care since Cicero relied on Tiro's assistance in literary and more practical matters. Cicero was loyal to his friend Atticus, though again he needed his support and advice when he was frequently uncertain about what to do. Being a *homo novus*, Cicero worked hard to advance on the career ladder and win a respected position for himself, but this also led to frequent self-glorification of his past achievements, which already met with the disapproval of contemporaries.

Unquestionably, Cicero was an illustrious personage of his time, as a politician, as a forensic and political orator and as an author of philosophical treatises. Engaged in so many fields, he soon found admirers, but he also met rejection and enmity, both during his lifetime and in later periods. This was partly because, despite his enormous achievements, his behaviour was open to criticism: he went through a series of political offices, which he conscientiously administered, and as a senator he successfully initiated a number of Senate decrees; he fought for the preservation of the traditional Republican structure. At the same time he made tactical moves arguing for policies he did not completely believe in (as evidence in letters reveals) and was perhaps over-keen to acquire a respected position. Cicero was active in the law courts, and he mostly achieved the desired outcome for his clients; but he was also keen to take on cases for political ends and for furthering his own standing. Cicero delivered numerous speeches in the Senate, before the popular assembly and at trials; those that were published are considered rhetorical masterpieces and became models for aspiring orators, even if the underlying aims and strategy may be tactical, and – among rhetoricians – the style may be debated. Cicero studied philosophy and explained the views of various Greek philosophical schools for his countrymen, which had not been done before. Thereby he managed to establish an appropriate Latin terminology for philosophy in Rome; while he may not have added a large number of novel and original ideas, he introduced Romans to Greek philosophy and provided vivid scenarios of fictional discussions in Roman Republican society, thus suggesting a tradition of philosophical interests in Roman intellectual life.

Cicero is the figure from classical antiquity with the largest number of personal letters, orations and literary publications extant. Consequently, numerous details about the conduct of his life and his personality can be reconstructed, in contrast to the lives of other ancient figures. Perhaps Cicero would not appear so multifaceted and extraordinary in some respects (both positive and negative) if there were more comparative material about his contemporaries. The detailed knowledge about Cicero influences the attitude to him and his (extant) writings, which can clearly be seen in Petrarch's disappointment after having discovered Cicero's letters.

The works produced in the last year of Cicero's life (including the *Philippics*, philosophical treatises such as *De officiis* and numerous letters) perhaps provide the fullest image of this multi-sided personality: Cicero appears as having clearly expressed views on the political situation and as fighting for what he thinks is the right course of action against opposition by means of brilliant speeches and literary writings; at the same time, deep at heart he is unsure about the possibilities of success and the consequences for himself, initially wavers and needs advice from trusted friends; he is proud of his acceptance by the People when he achieves short-term successes, but in the long term his policy fails, as he recognizes himself when the coalition with Octavian does not lead to the expected results.

In sum, Cicero emerges as a human being with outstanding abilities, especially verbal ones, but with several weak points in his character that affect his decisions. Nevertheless, he remains remarkable among figures from the ancient world because, as a representative of ancient culture, he was of particular significance for subsequent intellectual developments in Europe and beyond. His philosophical works in Latin enabled access to Greek philosophers for later generations who were not in a position to read Greek texts in the original language; the linguistic shape of his works was seen as illustrating a classic and ideal form of Latin; his rhetorical texts provided a guideline for later orators and rhetoricians.

The feeling that Cicero's works have been read uninterruptedly was already expressed almost 500 years ago. In 1568, Roger Ascham (*c.*1515–68), a graduate of St John's College, Cambridge, and tutor in Greek and Latin to Queen Elizabeth I when she was young, stated in his well-known pedagogic work *The Scholemaster*:[1]

But now, master Cicero, blessed be God and his Son Jesus Christ, whom you never knew, except it were as it pleased Him to enlighten you by some shadow, as covertly in one place ye confess, saying, *Veritatis tantum umbram consectamur*, as your master Plato did before you: blessed be God, I say, that sixteen hundred years after you were dead and gone, it may truly be said, that for silver, there is more comely plate in one city of England, than is in four of the proudest cities in all Italy, and take Rome for one of them: and for learning, beside the knowledge of all learned tongues and liberal sciences, even your own books, Cicero, be as well read, and your excellent eloquence is as well liked and loved, and as truly followed in England at this day, as it is now, or ever was since your own time, either at Arpinum, where ye were born, or else at Rome, where ye were brought up. And a little to brag with you, Cicero, where you yourself, by your leave, halted in some point of learning in your own tongue, many in England at this day go straight up, both in true skill and right doing therein.

It is unclear whether it is still true that Cicero's 'eloquence is [...] followed in England at this day' (or in other countries, for that matter), but his works continue to be read (though not necessarily in the original Latin): there are many recent paperbacks and e-books of Cicero's works and on Cicero. So, while Cicero certainly never expected that his writings would be read in such formats, advances in technology mean that his works have become even more accessible. It is now possible for all interested individuals to gain a view of Cicero directly from the sources and then, on the basis of the varied evidence, to try to answer the question 'Who is Cicero?' for themselves.

GLOSSARY

This glossary includes historical and literary figures, political terms and geographical locations relevant to this book. The brief explanations provide basic information and describe the significance of these individuals and concepts in Cicero's life.

Historical and literary individuals are listed under the best-known form and part of their names. All dates are BCE unless otherwise indicated. Biographical information has been taken from major reference works.

actio / 'delivery'	Fifth task of orator: delivery of a speech, including pronunciation, facial expression and gestures.
aedilis / 'aedile'	Roman magistrate; responsible for maintenance of public buildings and organization of public festivals (*see*: *cursus honorum*).
Aeschines	Greek orator and politician (*c.*399/89–322/15).
Aeschylus of Cnidus	Greek rhetorician (first century).
Amafinius (C. Amafinius)	Roman Epicurean philosopher (*c.* early first century).
Antiochus of Ascalon	Academic philosopher; adherent of the 'Old Academy' in contrast to Philon (*see*: Philon of Larissa), teacher of Cicero (*c.*130–68/7).

Antonius (C. Antonius Hybrida)	Consul in 63, with Cicero.
Antonius (M. Antonius)	Famous orator; grandfather of Mark Antony (143–87, consul 99).
Antony, Mark (M. Antonius)	Cicero's opponent in the *Philippics*; consul in 44; member of the 'second triumvirate' in 43 (82–30).
Apollonius Molon	Greek rhetorician; teacher of Cicero and Caesar (second/ first century).
Appian of Alexandreia	Greek historian; author of a history of Rome in Greek (*c.*90/95–160 CE).
Aratus	Greek didactic poet; author of *Phaenomena* (third century).
Arcesilaus	Academic philosopher; representative of the 'Middle Academy' (316/5–241/0).
Archias (A. Licinius Archias)	Greek poet; came to Rome in 102; defended by Cicero in 62.
Aristotle (Aristoteles)	Important Greek philosopher; founder of the school of the Peripatetics (384–322).
Arpinum	Town in Latium in central Italy, Cicero's birthplace.
Asconius (Q. Asconius Pedianus)	Commentator on Cicero's speeches (*c.*3–88 CE).
Asianism	Rhetorical style (known for flowery and bombastic language); opposite of Atticism (*see*: Atticism).
assembly	*See: contio* and *comitia*.
Atticism	Rhetorical style (known for rather plain language and reference to the classical Attic orators); opposite of Asianism (*see*: Asianism).
Atticus (T. Pomponius Atticus)	Cicero's friend; spent a large part of his life in Athens (110–32).

augur / 'augur'	One of a group of religious officials who interpreted the will of the gods by studying the flight of birds.
Augustus	*See:* Octavian.
boni / lit. 'good', 'honest men'	Supporters of the Republic in Cicero's terminology.
Brutus (**D. Iunius Brutus Albinus**)	Involved in conspiracy against Caesar; besieged in Mutina (in Italy) by Mark Antony in 43 (*c.*81–43).
Brutus (**M. Iunius Brutus**)	Supporter of the Republic; one of Caesar's assassins; dedicatee of rhetorical works by Cicero (*c.*85–42).
Caecilius (**C. Caecilius Niger**)	Quaestor of Verres in Sicily; candidate for Verres' prosecution in 70.
Caelius (**M. Caelius Rufus**)	Defended by Cicero (*c.*88–48, praetor 48).
Caesar (**C. Iulius Caesar**)	Appointed dictator for life and later assassinated; author of *commentarii* (100–44).
Calvus (**C. Licinius Macer Calvus**)	Roman poet and orator; proponent of Atticism (*see:* Atticism) in Rome (*c.*82–54).
Carneades of Cyrene	Academic sceptic; one of three philosophers visiting Rome in 155 (*c.*214/3–129/8).
Cassius (**C. Cassius Longinus**)	Involved in conspiracy against Caesar (*c.*90–42).
Cassius Dio (**Cassius Dio Cocceianus**)	Roman senator; author of a Roman history in Greek (*c.*164–235 CE).
Catiline (**L. Sergius Catilina**)	Unsuccessful candidate for consulship; launched 'conspiracy' during Cicero's consulship in 63 (*c.*108–62).

Cato the Elder **(M. Porcius Cato)**	Censor, best-known early Roman orator and author of the earliest surviving work of Latin prose, *De agricultura* (234–149).
Cato the Younger **(M. Porcius Cato Uticensis)**	Great-grandson of Cato the Elder; Stoic; opponent of Caesar in civil war (95–46).
Catullus **(C. Valerius Catullus)**	Roman Neoteric poet; author of a collection of poetry (*c.*86–56).
Catulus **(Q. Lutatius Catulus)**	Leader of the *optimates* (*see*: *optimates*) in the 70s and 60s; character in Cicero's dialogic treatises (consul 78).
censor / 'censor'	Senior Roman magistrate, responsible for census.
Chrysogonus **(L. Cornelius Chrysogonus)**	Influential freedman of Sulla; opponent in the trial of Sex. Roscius (first century).
Cicero **(M. Tullius Cicero)**	*See:* 'Key Dates' (106–43).
Cicero **(M. Tullius Cicero)**	Cicero's son (*c.*65–after 25).
Cicero **(Q. Tullius Cicero)**	Cicero's younger brother; proscribed like his brother (102[?]–43).
Cilicia	Roman province on the southern coast of Asia Minor; run by Cicero as provincial governor in 51–50.
Clodius **(P. Clodius Pulcher)**	Attended Bona Dea cult celebrations (only open to women), disguised as a woman, in 62; as *tribunus plebis* active against Cicero and prompted his exile; died in a fight between his escort and that of Milo (*c.*93–52, *tribunus plebis* 58).
Cluentius **(A. Cluentius Habitus)**	Roman knight; defended by Cicero (first half of first century).

comitia	Legislative assembly of Roman citizens for decision making.
concordia ordinum / 'unanimity of orders'	Cicero's ideal.
consul / 'consul'	Most senior Roman magistrate; two consuls elected annually (*see: cursus honorum*).
contio	Popular assembly for conveying information.
Cornelius Nepos	Roman writer of biographies and historiographical works; an acquaintance of Cicero and Atticus (*c.*100–24).
Cotta (C. Aurelius Cotta)	Interlocutor in Cicero's dialogues *De oratore* and *De natura deorum* (*c.*124–74, consul 75).
Cotta (L. Aurelius Cotta)	As praetor proposed *Lex Aurelia* for a reform of the composition of juries; in 63 requested honours for Cicero's role in fighting the Catilinarian Conspiracy; later did not recognize the legality of Cicero's exile (praetor 70).
Crassus (L. Licinius Crassus)	Famous Roman orator; interlocutor in Cicero's dialogue *De oratore* (140–91, consul 95).
Crassus (M. Licinius Crassus)	Member of the 'first triumvirate' in 60 (115–53, consul 77, 55).
Crassus (P. Licinius Crassus)	Younger son of Marcus; Cicero's predecessor as augur.
Critolaus of Phaselis	Peripatetic philosopher; one of three philosophers visiting Rome in 155 (first half of second century).
cursus honorum	Sequence of (annual and collegial) public offices: quaestor, aedile, praetor, consul.
curule magistrate	Senior magistrate, such as a consul or praetor.
Deiotarus	King in Galatia, ally of the Romans, defended by Cicero (*c.*105–40).

Demetrius of Phalerum	Greek orator, politician and philosopher (*c.*360–280).
Demosthenes	Famous Greek orator and politician, highly regarded by Cicero (384–322).
dictator / 'dictator'	Extraordinary magistrate, with exceptional yet (ordinarily) temporary power in cases of emergency.
Diodotus	Stoic philosopher; friend and teacher of Cicero; lived in Cicero's house (first century).
Diogenes of Babylon	Important Stoic philosopher; one of three philosophers visiting Rome in 155 (*c.*230–150).
Dionysius of Magnesia	Greek rhetor (second/first century).
dispositio / 'organization'	Second task of orator: arrangement of arguments in a speech.
Dolabella (P. Cornelius Dolabella)	Unsteady politician, Cicero's son-in-law (*c.*70–43, *consul suffectus* 44).
elocutio / 'expression'	Third task of orator: presentation of the material.
Epicurus	Greek philosopher; founder of the philosophical school of Epicureanism (342/1–271/0).
equites / 'knights'	Second highest social class in ancient Rome.
Fabius Gallus (M. Fabius Gallus)	Roman Epicurean and friend of Cicero.
fasces	Bundles of rods and a single-headed axe; carried by *lictores* escorting magistrates, whose status was demonstrated by the number of *lictores* (*see*: *lictores*).
Florus	Roman writer and historian; author of a brief sketch of the history of Rome based on Livy (first/second century CE).
Forum (Romanum)	Public square for political, religious, juridical and commercial activities in the centre of Rome.

Fronto **(M. Cornelius** **Fronto)**	Roman orator, rhetorician and advocate; tutor to princes; representative of archaism (*c.*90/95–167 CE).
Gellius **(L. Gellius)**	Intervened unsuccessfully against the rebellious slaves led by Spartacus in 72; later legate of Pompey; supporter of Cicero's action against the Catilinarians in 63 (consul 72).
Heraclides of **Pontus**	Platonic philosopher (*c.*390–after 322).
Hirtius **(A. Hirtius)**	Politician and historian; friend of Cicero; fought against Mark Antony in 43 (consul 43, with C. Vibius Pansa Caetronianus).
homo novus	Political 'newcomer'; a man whose ancestors did not hold high public offices and hence did not belong to the nobility.
Hortensius **(Q. Hortensius** **Hortalus)**	Famous Roman orator (favouring Asianism; *see*: Asianism); gradually pushed to second place by Cicero (114–50, consul 69).
hostis / 'public enemy', 'enemy of the state'	Used by Cicero as a label for his political enemies, especially Mark Antony.
improbi / lit. 'rascals'	Opponents of *boni* (*see*: *boni*) in Cicero's terminology.
inventio / 'finding of ideas'	First task of orator: assembling the material and developing arguments.
Isocrates	Famous Greek orator and founder of the first school of rhetoric (436–338).
Laelius **(C. Laelius)**	Politician with philosophical and literary interests; interlocutor in Cicero's dialogues; friend of Scipio Aemilianus (*c.*190–after 129; consul 140).
legatus	Ambassador of the Roman Republic appointed by the Senate or coming to Rome from other countries; general of senatorial rank in the Roman army.
Lentulus **(P. Cornelius** **Lentulus Sura)**	Roman politician; important member of Catilinarian Conspiracy; executed on 5 December 63 (consul 71).

Lepidus (M. Aemilius Lepidus)	Roman politician; follower of Caesar; member of the 'second triumvirate' in 43 (*c.*89–12).
lictores	Attendants of magistrates as an expression of magisterial authority and for protection (*see*: *fasces*).
Ligarius (Q. Ligarius)	Follower of Pompey, but pardoned by Caesar; allowed to return to Rome after Cicero's speech in 46.
Lucan (M. Annaeus Lucanus)	Roman epic poet; author of *Pharsalia*/*Bellum civile* (39–65 CE).
Lucceius (L. Lucceius)	Historian (praetor urbanus 67).
Lucretius (T. Lucretius Carus)	Roman Epicurean poet and philosopher; author of the didactic poem *De rerum natura* (*c.*96–55).
Lucullus (L. Licinius Lucullus)	Optimate politician and general; supporter of Cicero in 63; rich and later known for his extravagant lifestyle; character in Cicero's dialogic treatises (*c.*117–57/6, consul 74).
Lysias	Greek logographer (*c.*459/8 or 445–380).
magister equitum / 'master of the horse'	Roman official serving as the dictator's main lieutenant.
Marcellus (M. Claudius Marcellus)	Roman politician; opponent of Caesar; pardoned by him in 46 when Cicero delivered a speech of thanks (died 45, consul 51).
Marius (C. Marius)	A *homo novus* from Arpinum like Cicero; Roman statesman and seven-time consul; successful general; opponent of Sulla in civil war (*c.*157–86).
memoria / 'memorizing'	Fourth task of orator: the process of memorizing a speech.
Menippus of Stratonicea	Greek orator; highly regarded by Cicero (second/first century).

Milo (**T. Annius Milo**)	Supporter of Pompey; opponent of P. Clodius Pulcher, charged with his assassination; defended by Cicero without success and went into exile (died 48, *tribunus plebis* 57, praetor 55).
Murena (**L. Licinius Murena**)	Defended against the charge of obtaining office by devious means (as consul designate) by eminent orators including Cicero (consul 62).
Nicolaus of Damascus	Greek historian, biographer and philosopher; later in the service of emperor Augustus (born *c.*60).
nobiles / 'noblemen'	Highest social class at Rome; typically people whose ancestors had held high offices, especially the consulship.
Octavian (**C. Octavius / C. Iulius C. f. Caesar**)	Future emperor Augustus (63 BCE–14 CE).
optimates / 'best men'	Roman 'leadership class', 'defenders of the traditional Republic'; opposed to *populares* (*see*: *populares*).
Panaetius of Rhodes	Stoic philosopher; acquaintance of Laelius and Scipio; a source for Cicero's *De officiis* (*c.*185–110/09).
peroratio / 'conclusion'	Final part of a speech.
Phaedrus	Epicurean philosopher; acquainted with Cicero, who may have used Phaedrus' *On Gods* in *De natura deorum* (*c.*138–70).
Philippus (**L. Marcius Philippus**)	Octavian's stepfather; remained neutral in the civil war between Caesar and Pompey; later involved in the struggle between Octavian and Mark Antony (*c.*102–after 43; consul 56).
Philon of Larissa	Academic philosopher, representing the sceptical school of thought; head of the Academy from 110/9; lectured on rhetoric and philosophy in Rome (88), where Cicero was among his pupils (159/8–84/3).
Philus (**L. Furius Philus**)	Friend of P. Cornelius Scipio Aemilianus; interlocutor in Cicero's dialogue *De re publica* (consul 136).

Piso (**L. Calpurnius Piso Caesoninus**)	Caesar's father-in-law; Epicurean; politician attacked by Cicero because of his involvement in the events leading to Cicero's exile (consul 58).
Piso (**M. Pupius Piso Frugi Calpurnianus**)	Politician and orator; supporter of Clodius in 61; represents Peripatetic views in Cicero's *De finibus bonorum et malorum* (born *c.*114, consul 61).
Plato	Famous Greek philosopher; student of Socrates; writer of philosophical dialogues (e.g. *Politeia* and *Nomoi*); founder of the Academy in Athens (428/7–348/7).
Pliny the Younger (**C. Plinius Caecilius Secundus**)	Roman politician; served as an imperial magistrate under Trajan; well-known writer of letters; influenced by Cicero in oratory and epistolography (*c.*61/2–115 CE).
Plutarch	Greek writer, biographer (*Parallel Lives*), philosopher (Middle Platonist) and essayist (*c.*45–125 CE).
Polybius	Greek statesman and historian; hostage in Rome; client of the Scipios; author of a history describing Rome's rise to a 'world power' (before 199–*c.*120).
Pompey the Great (**C. Pompeius Magnus**)	Important military and political leader; originally member of the 'first triumvirate' in 60; later adversary of Caesar in civil war (106–48, consul 70, 55, 52).
pontifex maximus / 'greatest pontiff'	Leader of the most eminent college of priests in Rome.
populares	'Politicians in the late Roman Republic supporting the interests of the People'; opposed to *optimates* (*see*: *optimates*).
Posidonius	Stoic philosopher; pupil of Panaetius; teacher at Rhodes; Cicero studied with him (*c.*135–51).
praetor / 'praetor'	Roman magistrate below the consuls; assigned various duties in Rome (jurisdiction) or in provincial government (*see*: *cursus honorum*).
proscription	Public proclamation of outlawry, leading to killings and confiscation of property.

Publilia	Cicero's ward; his young second wife for a short period, married in 46.
quaestor / 'quaestor'	Most junior Roman magistrate; administrator of the state treasury and supporter of provincial governors (*see*: *cursus honorum*).
Quintilian (**M. Fabius Quintilianus**)	Teacher of oratory; first professor of rhetoric at Rome; author of rhetorical handbook *Institutio oratoria*; provides a description of oratory and rhetoric influenced by Cicero (*c.*35–100 CE).
res publica / 'Republic'	Literally 'the public thing'; Roman republic; Roman state.
Roscius (**Sex. Roscius**)	From Ameria; in 80 charged with patricide by a freedman of Sulla; defended by Cicero.
rostra	Speaker's platform in Roman Forum.
Rullus (**P. Servilius Rullus**)	As tribune proposer of an agrarian law; opposed by Cicero in four speeches at the beginning of his consulship (*tribunus plebis* 63).
Sallust (**C. Sallustius Crispus**)	Roman politician and historian; author of e.g. *De coniuratione Catilinae*, an account of the Catilinarian Conspiracy (86–34).
Scaevola (**Q. Mucius Scaevola**)	Roman politician; called 'augur' to distinguish him from his relative of the same name; considered as an outstanding lawyer; teacher of Cicero; a figure in several of Cicero's dialogues (*c.*170–87, consul 117).
Scaevola (**Q. Mucius Scaevola**)	An exemplary politician and lawyer; called *pontifex maximus* to distinguish him from his relative of the same name; teacher of Cicero (*c.*140–82, consul 95).
Scipio (**P. Cornelius Scipio Aemilianus Africanus**)	An important politician and military leader in Rome; conquered Carthage in 146; a man with cultural interests and supporter of poets; friend of Laelius; interlocutor in Cicero's dialogues *De re publica* and *Laelius de amicitia* (*c.*185–129, consul 147).

senatus / 'Senate'	Roman Senate, important governmental body in the Roman Republic, consisting of former magistrates (since Sulla); meant to advise senior magistrates, but in fact controlling key areas of politics and administration.
senatus consultum ultimum / 'ultimate decree of the Senate'	Senate's declaration of a state of emergency, which suspended civil government and gave magistrates extraordinary power.
Seneca the Elder (L. Annaeus Seneca)	Father of Stoic philosopher Seneca the Younger; Roman rhetor and historian; regarded Cicero highly (*c.*55 BCE– 39/40 CE).
Sestius (P. Sestius)	Roman politician; supported Cicero's return from exile; when charged for this reason, successfully defended by Cicero in 56 (born *c.*95, *tribunus plebis* 57, praetor *c.*55).
Sicily	Roman province; Cicero quaestor there in 75.
Sulla (L. Cornelius Sulla Felix)	Important military leader and politician; opponent of Marius in civil war; dictator in 82; initiator of a number of laws; infamous for his reign of terror (138–78, consul 88).
Sulpicius (P. Sulpicius Rufus)	Orator and politician; opponent of Sulla; killed by him; interlocutor in Cicero's dialogue *De oratore* (*c.*124/3–88, *tribunus plebis* 88).
Terentia	Cicero's first wife, from a prominent family; married in 80/77; mother of Tullia and Marcus; divorced from Cicero in 46; later married again and died at an advanced age.
Theophrastus	Greek philosopher; successor of Aristotle in the Peripatetic school (*c.*371/0–287/6).
Tiro (M. Tullius Tiro)	Slave in Cicero's family; his confidant and secretary; freed in 53; publisher of some of Cicero's works and letters; inventor of a shorthand system (*c.*103–4).
Torquatus (L. Manlius Torquatus)	Roman politician; Epicurean interlocutor in Cicero's dialogue *De finibus* (*c.*90–46, praetor *c.*49).

tribunus plebis / 'tribune of the People'	Elected plebeian official in the Roman Republic, representing the interests of the plebeians, being able to propose laws and exercising the power of intervention.
triumvirate (*triumviri*) / 'three-men board'	Originally a term for special commissions in Rome; in the late Republic denoting two three-man political alliances, the so-called 'first triumvirate' (Caesar, Pompey, Crassus), established in 60, and the 'second triumvirate' (Octavian, Mark Antony, Lepidus), established in 43.
Tullia	Cicero's daughter with his wife Terentia; married three times, eventually to Dolabella (79/76–45).
Varro (M. Terentius Varro Reatinus)	Roman polymath and prolific writer (but many of his works are lost); friend of Cicero (116–27).
Velleius Paterculus	Roman historian; author of a history of Rome including a detailed description of the time of Augustus and Tiberius (20/19 BCE–after 30 CE).
Verres (C. Verres)	73–71 propraetor in Sicily; abused his position, hence prosecuted in 70 by Cicero; thereafter living in exile until proscribed by Mark Antony (*c.*115–43).
Xenocles of Adramyttion	Greek rhetor using the Asiatic style; teacher of Cicero (second/first century).
Zeno of Citium	Stoic philosopher; founder of Stoicism (*c.*335–263).
Zeno of Sidon	Epicurean philosopher; teacher of Cicero at Athens (*c.*150–75).

Note on Sources
and Abbreviations

Throughout the volume, the discussion is supported by references to the works of Cicero or other ancient texts where relevant as well as by identifications of the sources for quotations (in brackets in the main text or in endnotes). Names of ancient authors other than Cicero and the titles of their works are generally given in full. Works by Cicero are typically mentioned by their (abbreviated) Latin titles, and the author's name is only added where it is needed for clarity. Works by Cicero have been abbreviated according to the *Oxford Classical Dictionary* (4th edn, 2012, pp. xxvii–liii); for works not included in *OCD* abbreviations of a similar style have been developed. Accordingly, the abbreviations used for the works of Cicero are as follows:

Acad. post.	*Academica posteriora / Academic Books*
Acad. Pr.	*Academica priora (Catulus and Lucullus) / Academic Books*
Ad Brut.	*Epistulae ad Brutum / Letters to Brutus*
Amic.	*Laelius de amicitia / Laelius or On Friendship*
Arch.	*Pro Archia / On Behalf of Archias*
Att.	*Epistulae ad Atticum / Letters to Atticus*
Balb.	*Pro Balbo / On Behalf of Balbus*

Brut.	*Brutus / Brutus*
Caecin.	*Pro Caecina / On Behalf of Caecina*
Cael.	*Pro Caelio / On Behalf of Caelius*
Cat.	*In Catilinam / Against Catiline, Catilinarians, Catilinarian Speeches*
Clu.	*Pro Cluentio / On Behalf of Cluentius*
Deiot.	*Pro rege Deiotaro / On Behalf of King Deiotarus*
De or.	*De oratore / On the Ideal Orator*
Div.	*De divinatione / On Divination*
Div. Caec.	*Divinatio in Caecilium / Against Caecilius*
Dom.	*De domo sua ad pontifices / On His House before the Priests*
Fam.	*Epistulae ad familiares / Letters to Friends*
Fat.	*De fato / On Fate*
Fin.	*De finibus bonorum et malorum / On the Chief Good and Evil*
Flac.	*Pro Flacco / On Behalf of Flaccus*
Font.	*Pro Fonteio / On Behalf of Fonteius*
Har. resp.	*De haruspicum responsis / On the Responses of the Haruspices*
Inv. rhet.	*De inventione rhetorica / On Rhetorical Invention*
Leg.	*De legibus / On Laws*
Leg. agr.	*De lege agraria / On the Agrarian Law*
Leg. Man.	*De lege Manilia, De imperio Cn. Pompei / On the Manilian Law, On the Command of Pompey*
Lig.	*Pro Ligario / On Behalf of Ligarius*
Marcell.	*Pro Marcello / On Behalf of Marcellus*
Mil.	*Pro Milone / On Behalf of Milo*
Mur.	*Pro Murena / On Behalf of Murena*
Nat. D.	*De natura deorum / On the Nature of the Gods*
Off.	*De officiis / On Duties*
Opt. gen.	*De optimo genere oratorum / On the Best Type of Orators*
Orat.	*Orator / The Orator*
Par.	*Paradoxa Stoicorum / Paradoxes of the Stoics*

Part. or.	*Partitiones oratoriae / The Divisions of Oratory*
Phil.	*Orationes Philippicae / Philippics, Philippic Orations*
Pis.	*In Pisonem / Against Piso*
Planc.	*Pro Plancio / On Behalf of Plancius*
Prov. cons.	*De provinciis consularibus / On the Consular Provinces*
Q Fr.	*Epistulae ad Quintum fratrem / Letters to Brother Quintus*
Q Rosc.	*Pro Q. Roscio comoedo / On Behalf of Q. Roscius, the Comic Actor*
Quinct.	*Pro Quinctio / On Behalf of Quinctius*
Rab. perd.	*Pro Rabirio perduellionis reo / On Behalf of Rabirius*
Rab. Post.	*Pro Rabirio Postumo / On Behalf of Rabirius Postumus*
Red. pop.	*Post reditum ad populum, Oratio cum populo gratias egit / After His Return to the People, Speech of Thanks to the People*
Red. sen.	*Post reditum in senatu, Oratio cum senatui gratias egit / After His Return in the Senate, Speech of Thanks to the Senate*
Rep.	*De re publica / On the Republic*
Rosc. Am.	*Pro Sex. Roscio Amerino / On Behalf of Sex. Roscius from Ameria*
Scaur.	*Pro Scauro / On Behalf of Scaurus*
Sen.	*Cato maior de senectute / Cato or On Old Age*
Sest.	*Pro Sestio / On Behalf of Sestius*
Sull.	*Pro Sulla / On Behalf of Sulla*
Tim.	*Timaeus / Timaeus*
Top.	*Topica / Methods of Drawing Conclusions*
Tull.	*Pro Tullio / On Behalf of Tullius*
Tusc.	*Tusculanae disputationes / Tusculan Disputations*
Vat.	*In Vatinium / Against P. Vatinius*
Verr.	*In Verrem / Against Verres, Verrines, Verrine Orations*

The English translations of Cicero's works have mostly been taken from the Loeb Classical Library (LCL) series (which provides the Latin text with an English translation), except for works for which more recent translations elsewhere seemed preferable. The following translations have been used:

Acad. post. / Pr.   *Academica posteriora / Academica priora*

Charles Brittain (trans.), *Cicero: On Academic Scepticism. Translated, with Introduction and Notes* (Indianapolis, IN, and Cambridge, 2006).

Arch.   *Pro Archia*

Dominic H. Berry (trans.), *Cicero: Defence Speeches. Translated with Introduction and Notes* (Oxford, 2000).

Att.   *Epistulae ad Atticum*

David R. Shackleton Bailey (ed. and trans.), *Cicero: Letters to Atticus*, 4 vols, Loeb Classical Library (Cambridge, MA, and London, 1999).

Brut.   *Brutus*

George L. Hendrickson and Harry M. Hubbell (eds and trans.), *Cicero: Brutus: With an English Translation by G.L.H.; Orator: With an English Translation by H.M.H.*, Loeb Classical Library (Cambridge, MA, and London, 1939).

Cat.   *In Catilinam*

Dominic H. Berry (trans.), *Cicero: Political Speeches. Translated with Introduction and Notes* (Oxford and New York, NY, 2006).

Clu.   *Pro Cluentio*

Humfrey G. Hodge (ed. and trans.), *Cicero: The Speeches with an English Translation: Pro lege Manilia, Pro Caecina, Pro Cluentio, Pro Rabirio perduellionis*, Loeb Classical Library (Cambridge, MA, and London, 1927).

De or.   *De oratore*

James M. May and Jakob Wisse (trans.), *Cicero: On the Ideal Orator (De oratore). Translated with Introduction, Notes, Appendixes, Glossary and Indexes* (New York, NY, and Oxford, 2001).

Div.   *De divinatione*

Book 1: David Wardle (trans.), *Cicero: On Divination: De divinatione, Book 1. Translated with Introduction and Historical Commentary*, Clarendon Ancient History Series (Oxford, 2006).

Book 2: William A. Falconer (ed. and trans.), *Cicero: De senectute, De amicitia, De divinatione*, Loeb Classical Library (Cambridge, MA, and London, 1923).

Div. Caec.   *Divinatio in Caecilium*

Leonard H.G. Greenwood (ed. and trans.), *Cicero: The Verrine Orations*, 2 vols, Loeb Classical Library (Cambridge, MA, and London, 1928/35).

Fam.   *Epistulae ad familiares*

David R. Shackleton Bailey (ed. and trans.), *Cicero: Letters to Friends*, 3 vols, Loeb Classical Library (Cambridge, MA, and London, 2001).

Fat.   *De fato*

Robert W. Sharples (ed. and trans.), *Cicero: On Fate (De fato) and Boethius: The Consolation of Philosophy (Philosophiae Consolationis) IV.5–7, V. Edited with an introduction, translations and commentaries* (Warminster, 1991).

Fin.   *De finibus*

Julia Annas (ed.) and Raphael Woolf (trans.), *Cicero: On Moral Ends*, Cambridge Texts in the History of Philosophy (Cambridge, 2001).

Inv. rhet.   *De inventione rhetorica*

Harry M. Hubbell (ed. and trans.), *Cicero: De inventione, De optimo genere oratorum, Topica*, Loeb Classical Library (Cambridge, MA, and London, 1959).

Leg.   *De legibus*

Niall Rudd (trans.) and Jonathan Powell (ed.), *Cicero: The Republic and The Laws. Translated by N.R. With an Introduction and Notes by J.P. and N.R.* (Oxford and New York, NY, 1998).

Leg. agr.   *De lege agraria*

John H. Freese (ed. and trans.), *Cicero: The Speeches with an English Translation: Pro Publio Quinctio, Pro Sexto Roscio Amerino, Pro Quinto Roscio comoedo, De lege agraria I, II, III*, Loeb Classical Library (Cambridge, MA, and London, 1930).

Leg. Man.   *De lege Manilia*

Dominic H. Berry (trans.), *Cicero: Political Speeches. Translated with Introduction and Notes* (Oxford and New York, NY, 2006).

Marcell.   *Pro Marcello*

Nevile H. Watts (trans.), *Cicero: The Speeches with an English Translation: Pro T. Annio Milone, In L. Calpurnium Pisonem, Pro*

M. Aemilio Scauro, Pro M. Fonteio, Pro C. Rabirio Postumo, Pro M. Marcello, Pro Q. Ligario, Pro Rege Deiotaro, Loeb Classical Library (Cambridge, MA, and London, 1931).

Mil.   *Pro Milone*

Dominic H. Berry (trans.), *Cicero: Defence Speeches. Translated with Introduction and Notes* (Oxford, 2000).

Nat. D.   *De natura deorum*

Peter G. Walsh (trans.), *Cicero: The Nature of Gods. Translated with Introduction and Explanatory Notes* (Oxford, 1997).

Off.   *De officiis*

Miriam T. Griffin and E.M. Atkins (trans.), *Cicero: On Duties*, Cambridge Texts in the History of Political Thought (Cambridge, 1991).

Orat.   *Orator*

George L. Hendrickson and Harry M. Hubbell (trans.), *Cicero: Brutus: With an English Translation by G.L.H.; Orator: With an English Translation by H.M.H.*, Loeb Classical Library (Cambridge, MA, and London, 1939).

Phil.   *Orationes Philippicae*

David R. Shackleton Bailey (ed. and trans.), *Cicero: Philippics. 2 vols. Edited and Translated by D.R.S.H. Revised by J.T. Ramsey and G. Manuwald*, Loeb Classical Library (Cambridge, MA, and London, 2009).

Pis.   *In Pisonem*

Nevile H. Watts (trans.), *Cicero: The Speeches with an English Translation: Pro T. Annio Milone, In L. Calpurnium Pisonem, Pro M. Aemilio Scauro, Pro M. Fonteio, Pro C. Rabirio Postumo, Pro M. Marcello, Pro Q. Ligario, Pro Rege Deiotaro*, Loeb Classical Library (Cambridge, MA, and London, 1931).

Planc.   *Pro Plancio*

Nevile H. Watts (ed. and trans.), *Cicero: The Speeches with an English Translation: Pro Archia poeta, Post reditum in senatu, Post reditum ad Quirites, De domo sua, De haruspicum responsis, Pro Plancio*, Loeb Classical Library (Cambridge, MA, and London, 1923).

Rep.	*De re publica*
	Niall Rudd (trans.) and Jonathan Powell (ed.), *Cicero: The Republic and The Laws. Translated by N.R. With an Introduction and Notes by J.P. and N.R.* (Oxford and New York, NY, 1998).
Rosc. Am.	*Pro Sex. Roscio Amerino*
	Dominic H. Berry (trans.), *Cicero: Defence Speeches. Translated with Introduction and Notes* (Oxford, 2000).
Sest.	*Pro Sestio*
	Robert A. Kaster (trans.), *Marcus Tullius Cicero: Speech on Behalf of Publius Sestius. Translated with Introduction and Commentary*, Clarendon Ancient History Series (Oxford, 2006).
Sull.	*Pro Sulla*
	Louis E. Lord (ed. and trans.), *Cicero: The Speeches with an English Translation: In Catilinam I–IV, Pro Murena, Pro Sulla, Pro Flacco*, Loeb Classical Library (Cambridge, MA, and London, 1937).
Top.	*Topica*
	Tobias Reinhardt (ed. and trans.), *Cicero: Topica. Edited with a Translation, Introduction, and Commentary*, Oxford Classical Monographs (Oxford, 2003).
Tusc.	*Tusculanae disputationes*
	John E. King (ed. and trans.), *Cicero: Tusculan Disputations*, Loeb Classical Library (Cambridge, MA, and London, 1927).
Verr. 1; 2.5	*In Verrem*
	Dominic H. Berry (trans.), *Cicero: Political Speeches. Translated with Introduction and Notes* (Oxford and New York, NY, 2006).

References for translations of the works of other ancient authors and the sources for quotations from writers after classical antiquity are given in the respective places.

The Latin texts of Cicero's works (without critical apparatus; a full critical apparatus is provided in the Oxford Classical Texts [OCT] and the Teubner series) can be found online in *The Latin Library* (http://www. thelatinlibrary.com/cic.html); electronic versions of older editions of the Latin texts and some English translations are presented in the *Perseus Greek and Roman Materials* collection (http://www.perseus.tufts.edu/hopper/

collection?collection=Perseus:collection:Greco-Roman). A range of older books, including some Loeb editions, is accessible via the digital library of the Internet Archive (http://archive.org/search.php?query=cicero). In the near future all of Cicero's works in the Loeb Classical Library (LCL) series will also be accessible electronically (http://www.hup.harvard.edu/features/loeb/digital.html).

More information on Cicero, including texts, translations, biography and bibliography, is assembled on dedicated Cicero pages: http://www.utexas.edu/depts/classics/documents/Cic.html (by A.M. Riggsby) and http://courses.missouristate.edu/josephhughes/cicero.htm (by J. Hughes).

It is not only Cicero's works that constitute a sizeable body of material, but also the number of works written on Cicero since antiquity is considerable. Naturally, this volume relies on a wide range of detailed and sophisticated contributions by other scholars, to which it is greatly indebted. However, owing to the character of this book, the chapters do not have endnotes pointing to secondary literature or providing discussions of details.

To allow readers to explore particular areas nonetheless, a select bibliography has been provided, organized thematically and including comments on individual works where necessary. From the huge bibliography on all aspects of Cicero's writings this list presents a selection of books and articles (mainly in English) that have the character of introductions or overviews or discuss a work or group of works more generally rather than studies on questions of detail, which can be found with the help of the items listed.

KEY DATES

1. CICERO: BIOGRAPHY

DATE (BCE)	LIFE	WORKS
106	birth (3 January) in Arpinum	
*c.*102	birth of brother Quintus	
90s–80s	education in Rome	
*c.*89	military service in Social War	
mid to late 80s		*De inventione rhetorica* (first rhetorical treatise)
81		*Pro Quinctio* (first surviving oration, delivered in a civil trial)
80		*Pro Sex. Roscio Amerino* (first appearance in a criminal trial)
79–77	study trip to Athens, Rhodes and Asia Minor	
80/77	marriage to Terentia	
79/76	birth of daughter Tullia	
77		*Pro Roscio comoedo*
75	quaestor in Lilybaeum (Sicily); henceforth member of the Senate	

DATE (BCE)	LIFE	WORKS
71		*Pro Tullio*
70		*Orationes Verrinae*
69	aedile	*Pro Fonteio*
		Pro Caecina
68–44		*Epistulae ad Atticum*
68	purchase of villa in Tusculum	
66	praetor	*De imperio Cn. Pompei* (= *De lege Manilia*) (first political oration)
*c.*65	birth of son Marcus	
64	candidate for consulship	*Oratio in toga candida* (in fragments)
		[Quintus Cicero's *Commentariolum petitionis*]
63	consul	*De lege agraria* I–IV
		Pro Rabirio perduellionis reo
		In Catilinam I–IV
		Pro Murena
62–43		*Epistulae ad familiares*
62		*Pro Sulla*
		Pro Archia
60		*De consulatu suo* (in fragments)
		plan of a cycle of consular speeches (*Att.* 2.1.3)
59		*Pro Flacco*
58–57	exile in Greece, on P. Clodius Pulcher's instigation	

DATE (BCE)	LIFE	WORKS
57	return to Rome (4 September)	*Post reditum in senatu*
		Post reditum ad populum
		De domo sua
56–54		*De temporibus suis* (only testimonia)
56		*Pro Sestio*
		In Vatinium
		Pro Caelio
		De haruspicum responsis
		De provinciis consularibus
		Pro Balbo
55		*In Pisonem*
55–51	first phase of rhetorical and philosophical writing	*De oratore*
		De re publica
		De legibus
54		*Pro Scauro*
		Pro Plancio
		Pro Rabirio Postumo
53	election to college of augurs	
52		*Pro Milone*
51–50	provincial governor in Cilicia	
50	marriage of daughter Tullia and P. Cornelius Dolabella	
49	on Pompey's side in civil war between Caesar and Pompey	
48	return to Italy from Pompey's camp and stay in Brundisium due to uncertainty about future	

DATE (BCE)	LIFE	WORKS
47	pardon by Caesar and return to Rome	
46–44	second phase of rhetorical and philosophical writing	
46–45		*Orationes Caesarianae*: *Pro Marcello, Pro Ligario, Pro rege Deiotaro*
46	divorce from Terentia, marriage to the young Publilia	*Partitiones oratoriae* (?)
		Brutus
	divorce of daughter Tullia and P. Cornelius Dolabella	*Paradoxa Stoicorum*
		De optimo genere oratorum
		Orator
45	death of daughter Tullia	*Consolatio* (in fragments)
	separation from Publilia	*Hortensius* (in fragments)
		Academica priora / posteriora
		De finibus bonorum et malorum
		Timaeus (in fragments)
		Tusculanae disputationes
		De natura deorum
44		*De divinatione*
		Cato maior de senectute
		De fato
		Laelius de amicitia
		Topica
		De officiis
44–43		*Orationes Philippicae*
43		*Epistulae ad M. Brutum*
	death (7 December)	

2. CICERO: WORKS

This list gives the titles of all Ciceronian works that are extant in full (or in large parts) organized by genres and then by chronology (all dates BCE). Each entry consists of the date of composition (sometimes approximate), the Latin title(s) and the standard English translation(s) of the title of the work.

(A) SPEECHES

81	*Pro Quinctio* / *On Behalf of Quinctius*
80	*Pro Sex. Roscio Amerino* / *On Behalf of Sex. Roscius from Ameria*
c.77–76	*Pro Q. Roscio comoedo* / *On Behalf of Q. Roscius, the Comic Actor*
71	*Pro Tullio* / *On Behalf of Tullius*
70	*Divinatio in Caecilium* / *Against Caecilius*
	In Verrem I, II.1–5 / *Against Verres, Verrines, Verrine Orations*
69	*Pro Fonteio* / *On Behalf of Fonteius*
69–68	*Pro Caecina* / *On Behalf of Caecina*
66	*De lege Manilia, De imperio Cn. Pompei* / *On the Manilian Law, On the Command of Pompey*
	Pro Cluentio / *On Behalf of Cluentius*
63	*De lege agraria* I–IV / *On the Agrarian Law*
	Pro Rabirio perduellionis reo / *On Behalf of Rabirius*
	Pro Murena / *On Behalf of Murena*
	In Catilinam I–IV / *Against Catiline, Catilinarians, Catilinarian Speeches*
62	*Pro Sulla* / *On Behalf of Sulla*
	Pro Archia / *On Behalf of Archias*
59	*Pro Flacco* / *On Behalf of Flaccus*

57	*Post reditum in senatu, Oratio cum senatui gratias egit* / *After His Return in the Senate, Speech of Thanks to the Senate*
	Post reditum ad populum, Oratio cum populo gratias egit / *After His Return to the People, Speech of Thanks to the People*
	De domo sua ad pontifices / *On His House before the Priests*
56	*Pro Sestio* / *On Behalf of Sestius*
	In Vatinium / *Against Vatinius*
	Pro Caelio / *On Behalf of Caelius*
	De haruspicum responsis / *On the Responses of the Haruspices*
	De provinciis consularibus / *On the Consular Provinces*
	Pro Balbo / *On Behalf of Balbus*
55	*In Pisonem* / *Against Piso*
54	*Pro Scauro* / *On Behalf of Scaurus*
	Pro Plancio / *On Behalf of Plancius*
54–53	*Pro Rabirio Postumo* / *On Behalf of Rabirius Postumus*
52	*Pro Milone* / *On Behalf of Milo*
46	*Pro Marcello* / *On Behalf of Marcellus*
	Pro Ligario / *On Behalf of Ligarius*
45	*Pro rege Deiotaro* / *On Behalf of King Deiotarus*
44–43	*Orationes Philippicae* I–XIV / *Philippics, Philippic Orations*

(B) RHETORICAL TREATISES

late to mid 80s	*De inventione rhetorica* / *On Rhetorical Invention*
55	*De oratore* / *On the Ideal Orator*
c. mid 50s or 40s	*Partitiones oratoriae* / *The Divisions of Oratory*
46	*Brutus* / *Brutus*
	Orator / *The Orator*
*c.*46	*De optimo genere oratorum* / *On the Best Type of Orators*
44	*Topica* / *Methods of Drawing Conclusions*

(C) PHILOSOPHICAL TREATISES

*c.*54–51	*De re publica* / *On the Republic* (sections lost)
*c.*52	*De legibus* / *On Laws* (surviving in parts)
46	*Paradoxa Stoicorum* / *Paradoxes of the Stoics*
46/45	*Hortensius* / *Hortensius* (surviving in a few fragments)
45	*Consolatio* / *Consolation* (surviving in a few fragments)
	Academica priora (*Catulus* and *Lucullus*) / *Academic Books* (surviving in parts)
	Academica posteriora / *Academic Books* (surviving in parts)
	De finibus bonorum et malorum / *On the Chief Good and Evil*
	Tusculanae disputationes / *Tusculan Disputations*
	De natura deorum / *On the Nature of the Gods*
*c.*45	*Timaeus* / *Timaeus* (surviving in fragments)
45/44	*De divinatione* / *On Divination*
44	*Cato maior de senectute* / *Cato or On Old Age*
	De fato / *On Fate* (surviving in parts)
	Laelius de amicitia / *Laelius or On Friendship*
	De gloria / *On Glory* (surviving in fragments)
	De officiis / *On Duties*
	De virtutibus / *On Virtues* (surviving in fragments)

(D) LETTERS

68–44	*Epistulae ad Atticum* / *Letters to Atticus*
62–43	*Epistulae ad familiares* / *Letters to Friends*
*c.*60–54	*Epistulae ad Quintum fratrem* / *Letters to Brother Quintus*
43	*Epistulae ad Brutum* / *Letters to Brutus*

(E) POETRY

	Phaenomena / *Celestial Phenomena* (translation of Aratus' work; in fragments)
60	*De consulatu suo* / *On His Consulship* (surviving in fragments)
56–54	*De temporibus suis* / *On His Times* (only testimonia)

NOTES

PREFACE

1   Charles Dickens, *Dealings with the Firm of Dombey and Son, Wholesale, Retail, and for Exportation, with Forty Illustrations by 'Phiz' and an Introduction by H.W. Garrod*, The Oxford Illustrated Dickens (Oxford, 1950; repr. 1981), ch. 11 ('Paul's introduction to a new scene'), pp. 142–3, 147.

I. CULMINATION OF A LIFE IN POLITICS AND WRITING

1   *Phil.* 1.38; 2.118–19.
2   *Phil.* 2.2; 4.15–16; 6.2.
3   *Phil.* 2.34; 2.89; 2.117–18; *Att.* 14.4.1; 14.5.2–3; 14.6; 14.9.2; 14.10.1; 14.11.1; 14.12.1; 14.14.2–5; 14.18.4; 14.21.3; 14.22.2; 15.4.2–3; 15.11.2–3; *Fam.* 10.28.1; 12.1; 12.3.1; 12.4.1; *Ad Brut.* 1.15.4; 2.5.1–2; *Off.* 1.35.
4   e.g. *Att.* 14.5.2; 14.13.4; 14.19.6; 14.22.2; 15.25.
5   e.g. *Att.* 14.10.3; 16.9; 16.15.3; *Ad Brut.* 1.4a.2–3.
6   *Att.* 16.9; *Ad Brut.* 1.15.9; 1.18.3–4.
7   *Phil.* 1.7–10; 2.76; *Att.* 14.1; 14.2; 14.3; 14.5.2; 14.9; 14.13; 14.19.6; 14.22.2; 15.5.2–3; 15.8.1; 15.25; 15.26.1; 16.7.1; *Fam.* 10.1.1; *Ad Brut.* 1.10.4; 1.15.5–6; *Off.* 3.121; Plutarch, *Cicero* 43.4; Cassius Dio 45.15.4.
8   *Ad Brut.* 2.3.4; 2.4.2.
9   e.g. *De Or.* 1.260; 3.28; 3.71.
10 *Phil.* 3.37–9.
11 *Phil.* 3.3–5 (20 December 44 BCE).
12 *Att.* 14.12.2 (22 April 44 BCE); 15.12.2 (*c.*10 June 44 BCE); 16.8 (2 or 3 November 44 BCE); 16.14.1 (*c.*12 November 44 BCE).
13 e.g. *Phil.* 2.1–2; 2.118; 4.15; 13.22.
14 Cf. also *Fam.* 5.21.2.
15 *Phil.* 7.7–9 (mid January 43 BCE).
16 *Phil.* 13.7; 13.15.
17 *Phil.* 14.12–13; 14.16; *Ad Brut.* 1.3.2.
18 *Ad Brut.* 1.3a; 1.5.1; 1.15.8–9; Velleius Paterculus 2.62.4–5; 2.64.4; Livy, *Periochae* 119; Cassius Dio 46.39.3; 46.41.5.
19 e.g. *Off.* 3.19; 3.32.
20 e.g. *Off.* 1.34–6; 1.80.

II. POLITICAL AND LITERARY CAREER

1   *Verr.* 2.5.180.
2   *Clu.* 111; *Off.* 1.116; 2.45.
3   e.g. *Q Fr.* 3.5.4; *Sull.* 11.
4   *Brut.* 122; 127; 129; 164.
5   *Brut.* 313–16.
6   *Brut.* 306; 312; 315; 316; *Nat. D.* 1.6; 1.59; *Acad. Pr.* 115; *Acad. post.* 46; *Fin.* 1.16; 5.1; *Tusc.* 2.61; *Att.* 2.20.6; *Fam.* 13.1.2; Plutarch, *Cicero* 4.1; 4.5.
7   *Brut.* 314.
8   *Brut.* 311; Plutarch, *Cicero* 3.3.
9   *Brut.* 311.
10 *Quinct.* 4.
11 *Quinct.* 1.
12 *Brut.* 317–30.
13 *Rosc. Am.* 3.
14 e.g. *Inv. rhet.* 1.1–5.
15 *Rosc. Am.* 59.
16 *Orat.* 107; *Off.* 2.51; *Brut.* 312; Plutarch, *Cicero* 3.6; Quintilian, *Institutio oratoria* 12.6.4.
17 *Rosc. Am.* 139.
18 *Rosc. Am.* 154.
19 *Brut.* 312; 314.
20 *Brut.* 313–16.
21 Plutarch, *Cicero* 3.6; 4.4.
22 *Brut.* 318.
23 *Div. Caec.* 1; 4; 70.
24 *Verr.* 2.1.20; Pseudo-Asconius, *Argumentum in Cic. Verr.* 1; on Cic. *Verr.* 1.56.
25 *Div. Caec.* 70; *Verr.* 1.36; 2.1.4; 2.5.179.
26 *Rosc. Am.* 139.
27 *Phil.* 1.38; 7.19–20.
28 *Mur.* 40; *Off.* 2.58–9; *Verr.* 2.5.36.
29 *Leg. Man.* 2; *In toga candida,* fr. 5; *Pis.* 2; *Brut.* 321; Plutarch, *Cicero* 9.1.
30 *Att.* 1.1.1–4; 1.2.2.
31 *Mur.* 42.
32 David R. Shackleton Bailey (ed. and trans.), *Cicero: Letters to Quintus and Brutus, Letter Fragments, Letter to Octavian, Invectives, Handbook of Electioneering*, Loeb Classical Library (Cambridge, MA, and London, 2002), pp. 405, 441.
33 Cicero, *Commentariolum petitionis* 7–12.
34 Sallust, *De Catilinae coniuratione* 23.5–6; Plutarch, *Cicero* 10–11.
35 *Leg. agr.* 1.23; 2.6–7; 2.9; 2.15; 2.102.
36 *Leg. agr.* 2.4; 2.7; *Pis.* 3; *Vat.* 6; *Off.* 2.59.
37 Asconius, p. 94 Clark; Sallust, *De Catilinae coniuratione* 24.1; Plutarch, *Cicero* 11.2.
38 e.g. *Off.* 1.77–8; *Phil.* 2.1–2; 2.12–13; 6.17–18; 12.21; 14.17; 14.24.
39 e.g. *Pis.* 2–3.
40 *Leg. agr.* 2.10.
41 *Rab. perd.* 32; Pliny, *Naturalis historia* 7.116–17; Plutarch, *Cicero* 12.

42   *Leg. agr.* 1.23; 2.9; 2.102.
43   Sallust, *De Catilinae coniuratione* 26.4; Plutarch, *Cicero* 12.4.
44   *Att.* 2.1.3; *Leg. agr.* 1.26; *Cat.* 4.23; *Pis.* 5; *Phil.* 11.23; *Fam.* 15.4.13.
45   *Cat.* 3.7; *Sest.* 145.
46   Sallust, *De Catilinae coniuratione* 53.1.
47   *Cat.* 3.15; 3.25; *Sull.* 33; *Off.* 1.77–8.
48   *Fam.* 5.2.8 (January 62 BCE); *Sull.* 83.
49   *Fam.* 5.2.7; *Pis.* 6–7; *Sull.* 34; *Dom.* 94; *Rep.* 1.7; *Att.* 6.1.22; Plutarch, *Cicero* 23.1–3; Cassius Dio 37.38.2.
50   [Cic.] *Ad Brut.* 1.17.1; Quintilian, *Institutio oratoria* 11.1.24; Plutarch, *Cicero* 24.1–3; Cassius Dio 38.12.7.
51   *Arch.* 28–30.
52   *Att.* 1.16.15.
53   *Att.* 2.1.1; Cornelius Nepos, *Atticus* 18.6.
54   *Att.* 1.19.10; 1.20.6; 2.1.1.
55   *Att.* 1.19.10.
56   *Att.* 1.19.10; 2.3.4.
57   *Att.* 2.1.3.
58   *Att.* 1.16.
59   *Att.* 1.18.2–3.
60   *Att.* 1.17.8–10; 1.19.3–8.
61   Suetonius, *Divus Iulius* 19.2.
62   *Pis.* 79; *Prov. cons.* 41.
63   *Q Fr.* 1.1 (60/59 BCE).
64   Velleius Paterculus 2.45.1; Cassius Dio 38.14.4.
65   *Att.* 3.8.4; 3.9.2; 3.10.2; 3.13.2; 3.14.1; 3.15.5; Cassius Dio 38.14.5–7.
66   *Sest.* 26; *Dom.* 99; *Red. pop.* 8; Plutarch, *Cicero* 30.6–7; 31.1.
67   *Att.* 4.1.5; *Dom.* 76; *Red. sen.* 38–9; *Red. pop.* 1–2; 18; *Sest.* 131; *Pis.* 51–2; Plutarch, *Cicero* 33.7–8; Livy, *Periochae* 104.
68   *Planc.* 74; *Fam.* 1.9.4; *Att.* 4.1.5.
69   e.g. *Att.* 4.10.1; *De or.* 3.13–14.
70   e.g. *Fam.* 1.9.20.
71   Suetonius, *Divus Iulius* 56.5.
72   *Att.* 4.15.10; 4.19.2; *Fam.* 11.27.2; *Q Fr.* 3.5.4.
73   *Fam.* 1.9.6–19.
74   [Sallust], *In Ciceronem* 7.
75   *Fam.* 1.9.23 (December 54 BCE).
76   *Att.* 4.13.2.
77   *Q Fr.* 2.13.1; *Att.* 4.16.2.
78   *Q Fr.* 3.5.1–2.
79   *Brut.* 1; *Phil.* 2.4; Plutarch, *Cicero* 36.1.
80   Asconius, pp. 41–2 Clark; Plutarch, *Cicero* 35; Cassius Dio 40.54.2; Scholia Bobiensia, *Argumentum.*
81   Asconius, p. 42 Clark; Cassius Dio 40.54.2–4; 46.7.3.
82   *Att.* 5.20.6.
83   *Lig.* 7; *Fam.* 4.13.2; 6.6.8.
84   *Fam.* 9.1.2.

85   *Brut.* 19–20.
86   *Fam.* 4.4.3–4.
87   *Att.* 12.7; 12.8; 12.24.1.
88   *Fam.* 6.18.5; *Phil.* 11.10.
89   Plutarch, *Cicero* 41.2.
90   Plutarch, *Cicero* 41.4–5; Cassius Dio 46.18.3; Quintilian, *Institutio oratoria* 6.3.75.
91   Plutarch, *Cicero* 41.8.
92   *Att.* 12.14.3; *Tusc.* 1.76; 1.83; 3.71; 3.76; 4.63; *Div.* 2.3; 2.22.
93   *Att.* 12.12.2; 12.23.2.
94   *Att.* 13.13.1; 13.19.3–5.
95   *Fin.* 1.10; *Tusc.* 1.1; 1.5–6; 2.5; *Acad. post.* 11; *Div.* 2.1–4.
96   *Acad. post.* 11; *Fam.* 5.15.3–4; *Tusc.* 2.1.
97   Velleius Paterculus 2.66.2–5; [Aurelius Victor], *De viris illustribus* 81.6; Livy, *Periochae* 120; Valerius Maximus 5.3.4; Seneca, *Suasoriae* 6.17; 6.20–1, *Controversiae* 7.2; Tacitus, *Dialogus* 17; Orosius 6.18.11; Plutarch, *Antonius* 19.3; 20.2–4; *Cic.* 46–9; Appian, *Bella civilia* 4.6.21; 4.19.73–20.81; Cassius Dio 47.8.3–4; 47.11.1–2.

III. POLITICIAN AND POLITICAL PHILOSOPHER

1   *Q Fr.* 3.4.1 (24 October 54 BCE); 3.5.4 (late October/early November 54 BCE); cf. also *Rep.* 5.2.
2   Cf. also 2.14; 3.1.
3   Cf. also *Rep.* 1.45; *Leg.* 3.12.
4   Cf. also *Rep.* 1.34; 2.21–2; 2.64–6.
5   e.g. *Leg.* 1.18–19; 2.11.
6   Esp. *Phil.* 11.26–8.
7   For the contrast between *boni* and *improbi* see e.g. *Leg. agr.* 2.8; *Cat.* 1.32; 4.22; *Att.* 1.13.3.
8   Cf. also *De Or.* 1.1; *Fam.* 1.9.21 (December 54 BCE).

IV. ORATOR AND RHETORICIAN

1   *De or.* 1.30–4.
2   *Orat.* 107.
3   *Top.* 1–5.
4   e.g. *De or.* 1.5.
5   Cf. also *Orat.* 7.
6   *De or.* 1.23; similarly *Orat.* 43; *Fam.* 1.9.23 (December 54 BCE).
7   e.g. *De or.* 1.48; 3.80; 3.143; also *Orat.* 14.
8   *De or.* 3.213; *Orat.* 56.
9   e.g. *Cat.* 3.20–1; *Phil.* 6.12–15.
10 *De or.* 2.333–4; 2.338.
11 *De or.* 2.178.
12 *De or.* 2.182.
13 e.g. *Att.* 2.1.3.

14 *Brut.* 61.
15 *Brut.* 307–24.
16 *Brut.* 253–5.
17 Cf. *orator perfectus* – 'perfect orator': e.g. *De or.* 1.34; 1.59; 1.71; 1.128; 2.33; 3.71; 3.80; 3.143; *oratur summus* – 'consummate orator': e.g. *De or.* 3.84; 3.85.
18 e.g. *Orat.* 140–2.
19 e.g. *Fam.* 9.18.1–2.
20 e.g. *Brut.* 35; *Orat.* 23–4; 234.
21 *Brut.* 325–6.
22 *Brut.* 289; *Orat.* 23–4; 28–9.

V. PHILOSOPHICAL WRITER

1 e.g. *Off.* 1.26; 3.36; 3.83.
2 e.g. *Nat. D.* 1.6–7.
3 e.g. *Fin.* 1.1–2; *Tusc.* 1.1; *Div.* 2.1; 2.6–7; *Nat. D.* 1.7–9; *Fam.* 9.2.5 (*c.*22 April 46 BCE).
4 *Brut.* 19–20.
5 See also *Att.* 2.16.3 (29 April or 1 May 59 BCE); 4.10.1 (22 April 55 BCE); *Fam.* 4.3.3–4 (first half of September or perhaps earlier, 46 BCE).
6 Cf. also *Tusc.* 1.7–8.
7 *Fin.* 1.6–7.
8 *Nat. D.* 1.7–8.
9 *Tusc.* 1.1; *Div.* 2.4–6; *Acad. post.* 18.
10 *Tusc.* 4.5–7.
11 Pacuvius, *Frag. Trag.* 366–75 Ribbeck²⁻³ = *Trag. inc.* 37–46 Warmington (transmitted in *Rhetorica ad Herennium* 2.36).
12 Terence, *Andria* 57.
13 e.g. *Fin.* 2.1–3; *Tusc.* 1.8.
14 Cf. also *Att.* 4.16.2 (*c.*1 July 54 BCE).
15 Esp. *Phil.* 11.26–8.

VI. LITERARY PERSONA

1 e.g. *De or.* 3.37–51; 3.103–5; *Orat.* 134–236.
2 *Att.* 2.1.3.
3 Asconius, pp. 41–2 Clark; Plutarch, *Cicero* 35.2–5; Cassius Dio 40.54.2; Scholia Bobiensia on Cic. *Mil.* (p. 112.7–10 Stangl).
4 Scholia Bobiensia on Cic. *Mil.* (p. 112.11–13 Stangl); Quintilian, *Institutio oratoria* 4.2.25; 4.3.17.
5 *Tusc.* 4.5–7.
6 *Fin.* 1.4–7; *Acad. post.* 10; *Opt. gen.* 18.
7 Cf. esp. *Opt. gen.* 13–15; 23.
8 *Fin.* 1.8–10; 3.5.
9 e.g. *Att.* 11.17; 11.19; 16.1.
10 e.g. *Fam.* 3.3; 13.4; 15.7.

11 *Fam.* 1.9 (December 54 BCE).

12 e.g. *Q Fr.* 1.1.

13 *De or.* 2.51–4; 2.62–4; *Leg.* 1.4–5.

14 Andrew W. Lintott (trans.), *Plutarch: Demosthenes and Cicero. Translated with Introduction and Commentary*, Clarendon Ancient History Series (Oxford, 2013), p. 86.

15 e.g. *Arch.* 19–22.

16 *Cat.* 3.20–1.

17 F 11 *Fragmenta Poetarum Latinorum*⁴: cf. *Pis.* 74; *Off.* 1.77; Quintilian, *Institutio oratoria* 11.1.24; [Sallust], *In Ciceronem* 6; [Cic.] *In Sallustium* 7.

18 F 12 *Fragmenta Poetarum Latinorum*⁴: cf. *Pis.* 72–5; *Phil.* 2.20; Quintilian, *Institutio oratoria* 9.4.4; 11.1.23–4; Juvenal 10.120–6; [Cic.] *In Sallustium* 7.

VII. PERSONALITY

1 *Fam.* 7.25.1 (24 August 45 BCE); *Att.* 16.5.5 (9 July 44 BCE).

2 *Brut.* 9.

3 Cf. also *Q Fr.* 3.7.2 (December 54 BCE).

4 *Att.* 8.14 (2 March 49 BCE).

5 *Fam.* 16.22.1.

6 *Fam.* 16.17.1.

7 e.g. *Fam.* 16.23.1; 16.24.1.

8 e.g. *Fam.* 16.4.3–4.

9 *Fam.* 16.4.2; 16.14.1.

10 *Fam.* 16.4; 16.9.3; 16.12.6; 16.22.1.

11 *Fam.* 16.10.1; 16.16.

VIII. LEGACY AND RECEPTION

1 e.g. *Att.* 16.9; *Ad Brut.* 1.4a.2–3.

2 *Att.* 15.1a.2

3 Especially F 11, 12 *Fragmenta Poetarum Latinorum*⁴: cf. Cic. *Off.* 1.77; Quintilian, *Institutio oratoria* 11.1.24; [Cic.] *In Sallustium* 7; [Sallust], *In Ciceronem* 3.

4 Velleius Paterculus 2.66.1–2; [Aurelius Victor], *De viris illustribus* 81.6; Livy, *Periochae* 120; Valerius Maximus 5.3.4; Seneca, *Suasoriae* 6.17; 6.20–1; *Controversiae* 7.2; Tacitus, *Dialogus* 17; Orosius 6.18.11; Plutarch, *Antonius* 19.3; 20.2–4; *Cic.* 46–9; Appian, *Bella civilia* 4.6.21; 4.19.73–20.81; Cassius Dio 47.8.3–4; 47.11.1–2.

5 Seneca, *De beneficiis* 4.30.2.

6 Andrew W. Lintott (trans.), *Plutarch: Demosthenes and Cicero. Translated with Introduction and Commentary*, Clarendon Ancient History Series (Oxford, 2013), p. 127.

7 John C. Rolfe (trans.), *Suetonius, Volume I. With an English Translation by J.C.R. Introduction by K.R. Bradley*, Loeb Classical Library (Cambridge, MA, and London; revised, with new introduction, 1998), p. 309.

8 e.g. Cic. *Phil.* 3.5 vs. Augustus, *Res gestae* 1.

9 e.g. Livy, in Seneca, *Suasoriae* 6.17; Juvenal 10.114–32; Martial 5.69; Plutarch, *Antonius* 20.3; *Cic.* 48.6; Cassius Dio 47.8.3.

10   Michael Winterbottom (trans.), *Seneca the Elder: Declamations*, vol. 2: *Controversiae, Books 7–10, Suasoriae*, Loeb Classical Library (Cambridge, MA, and London, 1974), pp. 561, 595.

11   Frederick W. Shipley (trans.), *Velleius Paterculus: Compendium of Roman History; Res gestae divi Augusti*, Loeb Classical Library (Cambridge, MA, and London, 1979), p. 193.

12   James D. Duff (trans.), *Lucan: The Civil War, Books I–X (Pharsalia)*, Loeb Classical Library (Cambridge, MA, and London, 1928), p. 373.

13   Donald A. Russell (ed. and trans.), *Quintilian: The Orator's Education. Books 9–10*, Loeb Classical Library (Cambridge, MA, and London, 2001), p. 313.

14   e.g. Pliny, *Panegyricus* 62–6; 76; 93.

15   e.g. Pliny, *Epistulae* 9.2.

16   e.g. Pliny, *Epistulae* 1.2.4; 1.5.11–13; 1.20; 9.26.8.

17   e.g. Pliny, *Epistulae* 3.15.1; 5.3.5; 7.4.3–6.

18   e.g. Pliny, *Epistulae* 4.8.4–5.

19   Fronto, *Epistulae ad Antonium imperatorem*, 3.7–8.

20   William H. Fyfe (ed. and trans.), *Longinus: On the Sublime*, in *Aristotle: Poetics. Edited and Translated by Stephen Halliwell. Longinus: On the Sublime. Edited and Translated by W.H. Fyfe, Revised by Donald Russell. Demetrius: On Style. Edited and Translated by Doreen C. Innes, Based on W. Rhys Roberts*, Loeb Classical Library (Cambridge, MA, and London, 1995), p. 209.

21   Augustine, *Confessiones* 3.4.

22   Charles C. Mierow (trans.), *The Letters of St. Jerome. Introduction and Notes by Thomas Comerford Lawler*, vol. 1: *Letters 1–22*, Ancient Christian Writers: The Works of the Fathers in Translation 33 (Westminster, MD, and London, 1963), pp. 165–6.

23   Middle English: Larry D. Benson (ed.), *The Riverside Chaucer* (Oxford, 1988), p. 178, vv. V (F) 709–28; modern English: David Wright (trans.), *Geoffrey Chaucer: The Canterbury Tales. A Verse Translation with an Introduction and Notes* (Oxford, 1986), p. 362.

24   Charles H. Williams (ed.), *English Historical Documents*, vol. 5: *1458–1558* (London, 1967), p. 1073.

25   Izora Scott (trans.), *Ciceronianus or A Dialogue on the Best Style of Speaking by Desiderius Erasmus of Rotterdam. Translated by I.S. With an Introduction by Paul Monroe* (New York, 1908), pp. 23–4.

26   Edward Gibbon, *The Miscellaneous Works of Edward Gibbon, Esq., with Memoirs of His Life and Writings, Composed by Himself: Illustrated from His Letters, with Occasional Notes and Narrative by John, Lord Sheffield* (London, 1837), p. 40.

27   John Henry Newman, *The Letters and Diaries of John Henry Newman*, vol. 24: *A Grammar of Assent, January 1868 to December 1869. Edited at the Birmingham Oratory with Notes and an Introduction by Charles Stephen Dessain and Thomas Gornall* (Oxford, 1973), p. 242.

28   William P. Dickson (trans.), *The History of Rome by Theodor Mommsen. Translated with the Sanction of the Author by W.P.D. A New Edition Revised throughout and Embodying Recent Additions*, vol. 4 (London, 1912), p. 470; vol. 5 (London, 1913), pp. 504–5.

29   Asconius on Cic. *Mil.* 38; Tacitus, *Dialogus* 17.2; Gellius, *Noctes Atticae* 4.10.6; Plutarch, *Cicero* 41.4; 49.4.

30   Laurence Sterne, *The Life and Opinions of Tristram Shandy Gentleman, with an Introduction by P. Quennell*, The Chiltern Library (London, 1948), Book V, ch. 3, pp. 277–8.

31 John Adams, 'Inaugural address', 4 March 1797. Available at http://www.presidency. ucsb.edu/ws/?pid=25802#axzz2gCLyU4wh (accessed 7 April 2014).
32 Eugene E. White and Clair R. Henderlider, 'What Harry S. Truman told us about his speaking', *Quarterly Journal of Speech* 40 (1954), pp. 37–42.
33 Charlotte Higgins, 'The new Cicero', *Guardian*, 26 November 2008. Available at http:// www.guardian.co.uk/world/2008/nov/26/barack-obama-usa1 (accessed 7 April 2014).
34 James Carville, 'Why Cicero should be every campaign strategist's mentor'. Available at http://www.guardian.co.uk/commentisfree/cifamerica/2012/may/10/why-cicero-campaign-strategists-mentor (accessed 7 April 2014).

CONCLUSION: THIS IS CICERO?

1 Roger Ascham, *The Scholemaster*, in *The Whole Works of Roger Ascham, Now First Collected and Revised, with a Life of the Author, by J.A. Giles* (London, 1864–5), vol. 3, p. 256.

SELECT BIBLIOGRAPHY

I. EDITIONS, TRANSLATIONS (BESIDES *LOEB* VOLUMES), COMMENTARIES ON CICERO'S WORKS

(A) SPEECHES

Berry, Dominic H. (trans.), *Cicero: Defence Speeches. Translated with Introduction and Notes* (Oxford, 2000) [includes *Rosc. Am.*; *Mur.*; *Arch.*; *Cael.*; *Mil.*].

——(trans.), *Cicero: Political Speeches. Translated with Introduction and Notes* (Oxford and New York, NY, 2006) [includes *Verr.* 1, 2.5; *Leg. Man.*; *Cat.* 1–4; *Marcell.*; *Phil.* 2].

Crawford, Jane W. (ed.), *M. Tullius Cicero: The Lost and Unpublished Orations*, Hypomnemata 80 (Göttingen, 1984).

——(ed.), *M. Tullius Cicero: The Fragmentary Speeches: An Edition with Commentary*, American Philological Association, American Classical Studies 37 (2nd edn, Atlanta, GA, 1994).

Dyck, Andrew R. (trans.), *Marcus Tullius Cicero: Speeches on Behalf of Marcus Fonteius and Marcus Aemilius Scaurus. Translated with Introduction and Commentary*, Clarendon Ancient History Series (Oxford, 2012).

Gotoff, Harold C., *Cicero's Elegant Style: An Analysis of the Pro Archia* (Urbana, IL, 1979) [text and commentary].

——*Cicero's Caesarian Speeches: A Stylistic Commentary* (Chapel Hill, NC, and London, 1993) [includes *Marcell.*; *Lig.*; *Deiot.*].

Grant, Michael (trans.), *Cicero, Murder Trials: In Defence of Sextus Roscius of Ameria; In Defence of Aulus Cluentius Habitus; In Defence of Gaius Rabirius; Note on the Speeches in Defence of Caelius and Milo; In Defence of King Deiotarus. Translated with an Introduction* (Harmondsworth, 1975).

——(trans.), *Cicero: On Government* (London, 1993) [includes *Verr.* 2.5; *Mur.*; *Balb.*; *Rep.* 3, 5, 6; *Brut.*; *Phil.* 4, 5, 10].

Kaster, Robert A. (trans.), *Marcus Tullius Cicero: Speech on Behalf of Publius Sestius. Translated with Introduction and Commentary*, Clarendon Ancient History Series (Oxford, 2006).

McElduff, Siobhan (trans.), *Marcus Tullius Cicero: In Defence of the Republic. Translated with an Introduction and Notes* (London, 2011) [includes *Verr.* 1; *Leg. Man.*; *Leg. agr.* 2; *Cat.* 1, 2; *Arch.*; *Dom.*; *Sest.*; *Mil.*; *Phil.* 1, 2].

Manuwald, Gesine (ed. and trans.), *Cicero: Philippics 3–9. Edited with Introduction, Translation and Commentary*, vol. 1: *Introduction, Text and Translation, References and Indexes*; vol. 2: *Commentary*, Texte und Kommentare 30 (Berlin and New York, NY, 2007).

Ramsey, John T. (ed.), *Cicero: Philippics I–II*, Cambridge Greek and Latin Classics (Cambridge, 2003).

Shackleton Bailey, David R. (trans.), *Cicero: Back from Exile: Six Speeches upon His Return. Translated with Introductions and Notes*, American Philological Association, Classical Resources Series 4 (Atlanta, GA, 1991) [includes *Red. sen.*; *Red. pop.*; *Dom.*; *Har.*; *Sest.*; *Vat.*].

Siani-Davies, Mary (trans.), *Marcus Tullius Cicero: Pro Rabirio Postumo. Translated with Introduction and Commentary*, Clarendon Ancient History Series (Oxford, 2001).

Zetzel, James E.G. (trans.), *Marcus Tullius Cicero: Ten Speeches. Translated, with Notes and Introduction* (Indianapolis, IN, 2009) [includes *Verr.* 2.4; *Leg. Man.*; *Cat.* 2; *Mur.*; *Arch.*; *Cael.*; *Pis.*; *Marcell.*; *Phil.* 4, 9].

(B) RHETORICAL TREATISES

Douglas, Alan E. (ed.), *M. Tulli Ciceronis Brutus* (Oxford, 1966) [text and commentary].

Leeman, Anton D., Harm Pinkster, Hein L.W. Nelson, Edwin Rabbie, Jakob Wisse, Michael Winterbottom and Elaine Fantham, *M. Tullius Cicero: De oratore libri III: Kommentar*, 5 vols, Wissenschaftliche Kommentare zu griechischen und lateinischen Schriftstellern (Heidelberg, 1981–2008).

May, James M., and Jakob Wisse (trans.), *Cicero: On the Ideal Orator (De oratore). Translated with Introduction, Notes, Appendices, Glossary and Indexes* (New York, NY, and Oxford, 2001).

Reinhardt, Tobias (ed. and trans.), *Cicero: Topica. Edited with a Translation, Introduction, and Commentary*, Oxford Classical Monographs (Oxford, 2003).

Williams, James D. (ed.), *An Introduction to Classical Rhetoric: Essential Readings* (Malden, MA, and Oxford, 2009) [includes extracts from *Inv. rhet.*; *De or.*; *Mil.*].

(C) PHILOSOPHICAL TREATISES

Annas, Julia (ed.), and Raphael Woolf (trans.), *Cicero: On Moral Ends*, Cambridge Texts in the History of Philosophy (Cambridge, 2001).

Brittain, Charles (ed. and trans.), *Cicero: On Academic Scepticism. Translated, with Introduction and Notes* (Indianapolis, IN, and Cambridge, 2006).

Douglas, Alan E. (ed. and trans.), *Cicero: Tusculan Disputations I* (Warminster, 1985).

——— (ed. and trans.), *Cicero: Tusculan Disputations II and IV* (Warminster, 1991).

Dyck, Andrew R., *A Commentary on Cicero, De officiis* (Ann Arbor, MI, 1996).

——— (ed.), *Cicero: De natura deorum. Liber I*, Cambridge Greek and Latin Classics (Cambridge, 2003).

———*A Commentary on Cicero, De legibus* (Ann Arbor, MI, 2004).

Grant, Michael (trans.), *Cicero: On the Good Life* (London, 1971) [includes *Tusc.* 5; *Off.* 2; *Amic.*; *De or.* 1; *Somnium Scipionis*].

Graver, Margaret R. (trans.), *Cicero on the Emotions: Tusculan Disputations 3 and 4. Translated and with Commentary* (Chicago, IL, and London, 2002).

Griffin, Miriam T., and E.M. Atkins (trans.), *Cicero: On Duties*, Cambridge Texts in the History of Political Thought (Cambridge, 1991).

Inwood, Brad, and Lloyd P. Gerson (eds and trans.), *Hellenistic Philosophy: Introductory Readings. Translated, with Introduction and Notes* (Indianapolis, IN, 1988; 2nd edn, 1997) [includes selections from *Acad.*; *Fat.*; *Fin.*; *Nat. D.*; *Tusc.*].

Lacey, Walter K., and Brian W.J.G. Wilson (eds and trans.), *Res publica: Roman Politics and Society According to Cicero* (Oxford, 1970; repr. Bristol, 1978) [selections from all genres of Cicero's works in translation with a focus on 'politics and society'].

Powell, Jonathan G.F. (ed.), *Cicero: Cato maior de senectute. Edited with Introduction and Commentary*, Cambridge Classical Texts and Commentaries 28 (Cambridge, 1988).

—— (ed. and trans.), *Cicero: Laelius, On Friendship (Laelius de Amicitia) and The Dream of Scipio (Somnium Scipionis). Edited with Introduction, Translation and Notes* (Warminster, 1990).

Rudd, Niall (trans.), and Jonathan Powell (ed.), *Cicero: The Republic and The Laws. Translated by N.R. With an Introduction and Notes by J.P. and N.R.* (Oxford and New York, NY, 1998).

Rudd, Niall, and Thomas Wiedeman (eds), *Cicero: De legibus I. Edited with Introduction and Commentary* (Bristol, 1987).

Sharples, Robert W. (ed. and trans.), *Cicero: On Fate (De fato) and Boethius: The Consolation of Philosophy (Philosophiae Consolationis) IV.5–7, V. Edited with an introduction, translations and commentaries* (Warminster, 1991).

Walsh, Peter G. (trans.), *Cicero: The Nature of Gods. Translated with Introduction and Explanatory Notes* (Oxford, 1997).

—— (trans.), *Cicero: On Obligations (De officiis). Translated with an Introduction and Explanatory Notes* (Oxford, 2000).

Wardle, David (trans.), *Cicero: On Divination: De divinatione, Book 1. Translated with Introduction and Historical Commentary*, Clarendon Ancient History Series (Oxford, 2006).

Wright, Maureen R. (ed. and trans.), *Cicero: On Stoic Good and Evil: De Finibus Bonorum et Malorum Liber III and Paradoxa Stoicorum. Edited with Introduction, Translation and Commentary* (Warminster, 1991).

Yonge, Charles D. (trans.), *Marcus Tullius Cicero: Tusculan Disputations: On the Nature of Gods and the Commonwealth. Edited with Introduction, Translation and Commentary* (New York, NY, 2005).

Zetzel, James E.G. (ed.), *Cicero: De re publica: Selections*, Cambridge Greek and Latin Classics (Cambridge, 1995).

(D) LETTERS

Shackleton Bailey, David R. (ed.), *Cicero's Letters to Atticus*, 7 vols, Cambridge Classical Texts and Commentaries 3–9 (Cambridge, 1965–70).

—— (ed.), *Cicero: Epistulae ad familiares*, 2 vols, Cambridge Classical Texts and Commentaries 16/17 (Cambridge, 1977).

—— (ed.), *Cicero: Epistulae ad Quintum fratrem et M. Brutum*, Cambridge Classical Texts and Commentaries 22 (Cambridge, 1980).

—— (ed.), *Cicero: Select Letters*, Cambridge Greek and Latin Classics (Cambridge, 1980).

—— (trans.), *Cicero: Selected Letters. Translated with an Introduction* (New York, NY, London, 1982).

Stockton, David (ed.), *Thirty-five Letters of Cicero. Selected and Edited with Introductions and Notes* (Oxford, 1969).

Walsh, Peter G. (trans.), *Cicero: Selected Letters. Translated with an Introduction and Notes* (Oxford, 2008).

Willcock, Malcolm M. (ed. and trans.), *Cicero: The Letters of January to April 43 BC. Edited with an Introduction, Translation and Commentary* (Warminster, 1995).

(E) POETRY

Ewbank, William W. (ed.), *The Poems of Cicero. Edited with Introduction and Notes* (London 1933; repr. London 1997, 2003).

Soubiran, Jean (ed. and trans.), *Cicéron: Aratea, Fragments poétiques. Texte établi et traduit* (Paris, 1972).

Traglia, Antonio (ed.), *Marco Tullio Cicerone: I frammenti poetici*, Centro di Studi Ciceroniani, Tutte le opere di Cicerone 18 (Milan, 1962; 3rd edn, 1971).

2. SECONDARY LITERATURE ON CICERO AND HIS TIMES

(A) LIFE AND TIMES (MOSTLY BIOGRAPHIES)

Blom, Henriette van der, *Cicero's Role Models: The Political Strategy of a Newcomer*, Oxford Classical Monographs (Oxford, 2010).

Dorey, Thomas A. (ed.), *Cicero* (London, 1965).

Douglas, Alan E., *Cicero*, Greece and Rome: New Surveys in the Classics 2 (Oxford, 1968).

Everitt, Anthony, *Cicero: The Life and Times of Rome's Greatest Politician* (New York, NY, 2003).

Fuhrmann, Manfred, *Cicero and the Roman Republic*, trans. W.E. Yuill (Oxford and Cambridge, MA, 1992) [translation of 1990 German edition].

Gelzer, Matthias, Wilhelm Kroll, Robert Philippson and Karl Büchner, 'Tullius (29): M. Tullius Cicero', *Realenzyklopädie* VII A 1 (1939), cols 827–1274 [in German].

Habicht, Christian, *Cicero the Politician*, Ancient Society and History (Baltimore, MD, and London, 1990).

Lacey, Walter K., *Cicero and the End of the Roman Republic* (London, 1978).

Lintott, Andrew W., *Cicero as Evidence: A Historian's Companion* (Oxford, 2008).

Marinone, Nino, *Cronologia Ciceroniana, Seconda edizione aggiornata e corretta con nuova versione interattiva in Cd Rom a cura di E. Malaspino*, Collana di studi ciceroniani 6 (Rome and Bologna, 1997) [overview of events and publications in various chronological tables].

Mitchell, Thomas N., *Cicero: The Ascending Years* (New Haven, CT, and London, 1979).

——— *Cicero: The Senior Statesman* (New Haven, CT, and London, 1991).

Murrell, John, *Cicero and the Roman Republic*, Greece and Rome: Texts and Contexts (Cambridge, 2008) [introductory work for students].

Rawson, Elizabeth, *Cicero: A Portrait* (London, 1975).

Shackleton Bailey, David R., *Cicero* (London, 1971).

Steel, Catherine, *Reading Cicero: Genre and Performance in Late Republican Rome*, Duckworth Classical Essays (London, 2005).

——— (ed.), *The Cambridge Companion to Cicero* (Cambridge, 2013) [19 articles on Cicero's life, works and reception].

Stockton, David, *Cicero: A Political Biography* (Oxford, 1971).

Tempest, Kathryn, *Cicero: Politics and Persuasion in Ancient Rome* (London, 2011).

Treggiari, Susan, *Terentia, Tullia and Publilia: The Women of Cicero's Family* (London and New York, NY, 2007).

Wiedemann, Thomas, *Cicero and the End of the Roman Republic*, Classical World (London, 1994).

(B) HISTORICAL AND POLITICAL CONTEXT

Alexander, Michael C., *Trials in the Late Roman Republic, 149 BC to 50 BC*, Phoenix Suppl. 26 (Toronto, 1990) [list of trials including those in which Cicero took part].

—— *The Case for the Prosecution in the Ciceronian Era* (Ann Arbor, MI, 2002) [analyses the role of the prosecutor; covers *Font.*; *Flac.*; *Scaur.*; *Rab. Post.*; *Mur.*; *Planc.*; *Rosc. Am.*; *Clu.*; *Sull.*; *Sest.*; *Cael.*].

Arena, Valentina, 'Invocation to liberty and invective of *dominatus* at the end of the Roman Republic', *Bulletin of the Institute of Classical Studies* 50 (2007), pp. 49–73.

Beard, Mary, and Michael Crawford, *Rome in the Late Republic: Problems and Interpretations* (London, 1985; 2nd edn, 1999).

Burckhardt, Leonhard A., 'The political elite of the Roman Republic: Comments on recent discussion of the concepts *nobilitas* and *homo novus*', *Historia* 39 (1990), pp. 77–99 [on recent discussions of the role of the nobility in the Roman Republic].

Crawford, Michael, *The Roman Republic* (London, 1978; 2nd edn, London, 1992, and Cambridge, MA, 1993).

Crook, John A., Andrew Lintott and Elizabeth Rawson (eds), *The Cambridge Ancient History*, vol. 9: *The Last Age of the Roman Republic, 146–43 BC* (2nd edn, Cambridge, 1994).

Fantham, Elaine, 'Three wise men and the end of the Roman Republic', in Francis Cairns and Elaine Fantham (eds), *Caesar against Liberty? Perspectives on His Autocracy*, Papers of the Langford Latin Seminar 11 (Cambridge, 2003), pp. 96–117 [on the role of Cicero, Cato and Varro].

Flower, Harriet I. (ed.), *The Cambridge Companion to the Roman Republic* (Cambridge, 2004).

Gruen, Erich, *The Last Generation of the Roman Republic* (Berkeley, CA, 1974).

Lintott, Andrew W., *The Constitution of the Roman Republic* (Oxford, 1999).

—— *Violence in Republican Rome* (Oxford, 1968; 2nd edn, 1999).

Mackay, Christopher S., *The Breakdown of the Roman Republic: From Oligarchy to Empire* (Cambridge, 2009) [historical account of roughly the last 100 years of the Republic].

Millar, Fergus, *The Crowd in Rome in the Late Republic*, Jerome Lectures 22 (Ann Arbor, MI, 1998).

Morstein-Marx, Robert, *Mass Oratory and Political Power in the Late Roman Republic* (Cambridge, 2004).

Mouritsen, Henrik, *Plebs and Politics in the Late Roman Republic* (Cambridge, 2001).

Paterson, Jeremy, 'Politics in the late Republic', in Timothy P. Wiseman (ed.), *Roman Political Life 90 BC–AD 69*, Exeter Studies in History 7 (Exeter, 1985), pp. 21–43 [description of political circumstances in Cicero's time].

Rawson, Elizabeth, *Intellectual Life in the Late Roman Republic* (London, 1985).

Riggsby, Andrew M., *Crime and Community in Ciceronian Rome* (Austin, TX, 1999).

Rosenstein, Nathan, and Robert Morstein-Marx (eds), *A Companion to the Roman Republic* (Malden, MA, and Oxford, 2006).

Steel, Catherine, *The End of the Roman Republic 146 to 44 BC: Conquest and Crisis*, Edinburgh History of Ancient Rome (Edinburgh, 2013).

Wirszubski, Chaim H., *Libertas as a Political Idea at Rome* (Cambridge, 1960).

Wiseman, Timothy P., *New Men in the Roman Senate 139 BC–AD 14* (Oxford, 1971).

(C) RHETORICAL BACKGROUND

Clarke, Martin L., *Rhetoric at Rome: A Historical Survey* (London, 1953); 3rd edn, rev. and with a new introduction by Dominic H. Berry (London and New York, NY, 1996).

Dominik, William J. (ed.), *Roman Eloquence: Rhetoric in Society and Literature* (London and New York, NY, 1997).

Dominik, William J., and Jon Hall (eds), *A Companion to Roman Rhetoric* (Malden, MA, and Oxford, 2007) [includes 'Cicero as rhetorician' by James M. May and 'Cicero as orator' by Christopher P. Craig].

Habinek, Thomas, *Ancient Rhetoric and Oratory*, Blackwell Introductions to the Classical World (Malden, MA, and Oxford, 2005).

Kennedy, George A., *The Art of Rhetoric in the Roman World 300 BC–AD 300* (Princeton, NJ, 1972).

——*A New History of Classical Rhetoric: An Extensive Revision and Abridgment of The Art of Persuasion in Greece, The Art of Rhetoric in the Roman World and Greek Rhetoric under Christian Emperors. With Additional Discussion of Late Latin Rhetoric* (Princeton, NJ, 1994).

Lanham, Richard A., *A Handlist of Rhetorical Terms* (2nd edn, Berkeley, CA, 1991).

Lausberg, Heinrich, *Handbook of Literary Rhetoric: A Foundation of Literary Study. Foreword by G.A. Kennedy. Translated by M.T. Bliss, A. Jansen, D.E. Orton. Edited by D.E. Orton and D. Anderson* (Leiden, 1998) [translated from original German edition, first published in 1960].

Porter, Stanley E. (ed.), *Handbook of Classical Rhetoric in the Hellenistic Period 330 BC–AD 400* (Leiden, 1997).

Sloane, Thomas O. (ed.), *Encyclopedia of Rhetoric* (Oxford and New York, NY, 2001).

Steel, Catherine, *Roman Oratory*, Greece and Rome: New Surveys in the Classics 36 (Cambridge, 2006).

(D) PHILOSOPHICAL BACKGROUND

Algra, Keimpe, Jonathan Barnes, Jaap Mansfeld and Malcolm Schofield (eds), *The Cambridge History of Hellenistic Philosophy* (Cambridge, 1999).

Long, Anthony A., *Hellenistic Philosophy: Stoics, Epicureans, Sceptics*, Classical Life and Letters (London, 1974; 2nd edn, 1986).

Long, Anthony A., and David N. Sedley (eds), *The Hellenistic Philosophers*, 2 vols (Cambridge, 1987) [anthology with commentary].

The Stanford Encyclopedia of Philosophy. Available at http://plato.stanford.edu (accessed 7 April 2014).

(E) STUDIES

(i) Speeches

Albrecht, Michael von, *Cicero's Style* (Leiden and Boston, MA, 2003).

Berry, Dominic H., and Andrew Erskine (eds), *Form and Function in Roman Oratory* (Cambridge, 2010) [includes several articles on Cicero's speeches].

Booth, Joan (ed.), *Cicero on the Attack: Invective and Subversion in the Orations and Beyond* (Swansea, 2007) [eight essays on the use of invective in Cicero's speeches].

Butler, Shane, *The Hand of Cicero* (London and New York, NY, 2002) [on the role of the written word in forensic and political struggles].

Classen, Carl J., *Recht – Rhetorik – Politik. Untersuchungen zu Ciceros rhetorischer Strategie* (Darmstadt, 1985); Italian translation: *Diritto, retorica, politica. La strategia retorica di Cicerone*, trad. di Paola Landi, ed. ital. a cura di L. Calboli Montefusco, Collezione di testi e di studi, Linguistica e critica letteraria (Bologna, 1998) [paradigmatic analyses of Cicero's rhetorical strategy].

Connolly, Joy, *The State of Speech: Rhetoric and Political Thought in Ancient Rome* (Princeton, NJ, and Oxford, 2007) [on the connections between rhetoric and political thought in Republican Rome].

Corbeill, Anthony, *Controlling Laughter: Political Humor in the Late Roman Republic* (Princeton, NJ, 1996) [on the use of humour and invective in Republican oratory, especially Cicero].

Craig, Christopher P., *Form as Argument in Cicero's Speeches: A Study of Dilemma*, American Classical Studies 31 (Atlanta, GA, 1993) [looks at 'dilemma' as a rhetorical concept in *Rosc. Am.*; *Div. Caec.*; *Q. Rosc.*; *Sull.*; *Cael.*; *Planc.*; *Phil.* 2].

—— 'A survey of selected recent work on Cicero's *Rhetorica* and speeches', in James M. May (ed.), *Brill's Companion to Cicero: Oratory and Rhetoric* (Leiden, 2002), pp. 533–99.

—— 'Bibliography', in James M. May (ed.), *Brill's Companion to Cicero: Oratory and Rhetoric* (Leiden, 2002), pp. 503–31.

—— 'Cicero as orator', in William J. Dominik and Jon Hall (eds), *A Companion to Roman Rhetoric*, Blackwell Companions to the Ancient World (Malden, MA, and Oxford, 2007), pp. 264–84 [overview of major speeches with bibliography].

Gildenhard, Ingo, *Creative Eloquence: The Construction of Reality in Cicero's Speeches* (Oxford and New York, NY), 2011.

Ludwig, Walther (ed.), *Éloquence et rhétorique chez Cicéron*, Entretiens sur l'antiquité classique 28 (Vandœuvres, Geneva, 1982) [seven essays on various aspects of Cicero's oratory and rhetoric].

MacKendrick, Paul (with the technical assistance of Emmett L. Bennett, Jr), *The Speeches of Cicero: Context, Law, Rhetoric* (London, 1995) [overview of context, structure and contents of Cicero's major speeches].

May, James M., *Trials of Character: The Eloquence of Ciceronian Ethos* (Chapel Hill, NC, and London 1988) [analysis of the use of 'character' in selected speeches].

—— 'Cicero as rhetorician', in William J. Dominik and Jon Hall (eds), *A Companion to Roman Rhetoric*, Blackwell Companions to the Ancient World (Malden, MA, and Oxford, 2007), pp. 250–63 [overview of rhetorical works with bibliography].

—— (ed.), *Brill's Companion to Cicero: Oratory and Rhetoric* (Leiden, 2002) [17 essays on Cicero's oratorical and rhetorical works, with bibliography].

Powell, Jonathan, and Jeremy Paterson (eds), *Cicero: The Advocate* (Oxford, 2004) [15 essays on various aspects of Cicero's law court speeches, an introduction to Cicero's forensic speeches and a chronological list of Cicero's known appearances as an advocate].

Prag, Jonathan R.W. (ed.), *Sicilia nutrix plebis Romanae: Rhetoric, Law, and Taxation in Cicero's Verrines*, Bulletin of the Institute of Classical Studies Suppl. 97 (London, 2007).

Steel, Catherine, *Cicero, Rhetoric and Empire* (Oxford, 2002).

Stevenson, Tom, and Marcus Wilson (eds), *Cicero's Philippics: History, Rhetoric and Ideology*, Prudentia 37/38 (2008 [2009]).

Usher, Stephen, *Cicero's Speeches: The Critic in Action* (Oxford, 2008) [on the realization of Cicero's rhetorical ideals in practice].

Vasaly, Ann, 'The masks of rhetoric: Cicero's *Pro Roscio Amerino*', *Rhetorica* 3 (1985), pp. 1–20.

—— *Representations: Images of the World in Ciceronian Oratory* (Berkeley, CA, 1993) [on the role of space in Cicero's speeches].

Weische, Alfons, *Ciceros Nachahmung der attischen Redner*, Bibliothek der klassischen Altertumswissenschaften, Neue Folge, 2. Reihe, Bd. 45 (Heidelberg, 1972) [overview of Ciceronian passages likely to be influenced by Greek orators].

Wooten, Cecil W., *Cicero's Philippics and Their Demosthenic Model: The Rhetoric of Crisis* (Chapel Hill, NC, and London, 1983).

(ii) Rhetorical treatises

Craig, Christopher P., 'A survey of selected recent work on Cicero's *Rhetorica* and speeches', in James M. May (ed.), *Brill's Companion to Cicero: Oratory and Rhetoric* (Leiden, 2002), pp. 533–99.

—— 'Bibliography', in James M. May (ed.), *Brill's Companion to Cicero: Oratory and Rhetoric* (Leiden, 2002), pp. 503–31.

Douglas, Alan E., 'The intellectual background of Cicero's *Rhetorica*: A study in method', *Aufstieg und Niedergang der römischen Welt* I.3 (1973), pp. 95–138.

Dugan, John, *Making a New Man: Ciceronian Self-fashioning in the Rhetorical Works* (Oxford, 2005) [discussion of *Arch.*; *Pis.*; *De or.*; *Brut.*; *Orat.*].

Fantham, Elaine, *The Roman World of Cicero's De oratore* (Oxford, 2004) [accessible, comprehensive discussion of the treatise].

Wisse, Jakob, *Ethos and Pathos from Aristotle to Cicero* (Amsterdam, 1989) [on *De or.* and Aristotle's *Rhetoric*].

(iii) Philosophical treatises

Arena, Valentina, '*Libertas* and *virtus* of the citizen in Cicero's *De republica*', *Scripta Classica Israelica* 26 (2007), pp. 39–66.

Asmis, Elizabeth, 'A new kind of model: Cicero's Roman constitution in *De republica*', *American Journal of Philology* 126 (2005), pp. 377–416.

Baraz, Yelena, *A Written Republic: Cicero's Philosophical Politics* (Princeton, NJ, and Oxford, 2012) [on Cicero's late philosophical works].

Clayton, Edward, 'Cicero (106–43 BCE)', *Internet Encyclopedia of Philosophy*. Available at http://www.iep.utm.edu/cicero/#SH9b (accessed 7 April 2014).

Dyck, Andrew R., 'Cicero the dramaturge: Verisimilitude and consistency of characterization in some of his dialogues', in Gareth Schmeling and Jon D. Mikalson (eds), *Qui miscuit utile dulci: Festschrift Essays for Paul Lachlan MacKendrick* (Wauconda, IL, 1998), pp. 151–64.

Ferrary, Jean-Louis, 'The statesman and the law in the political philosophy of Cicero', in André Laks and Malcolm Schofield (eds), *Justice and Generosity: Studies in Hellenistic Social and Political Philosophy. Proceedings of the Sixth Symposium Hellenisticum* (Cambridge, 1995), pp. 48–73.

Fortenbaugh, William W., and Peter Steinmetz (eds), *Cicero's Knowledge of the Peripatos*, Rutgers University Studies in Classical Humanities 4 (New Brunswick, NJ, and London, 1989).

Fox, Matthew, *Cicero's Philosophy of History* (Oxford, 2007).

Gawlick, Günther, and Woldemar Görler, 'Cicero', in Hellmut Flashar (ed.), *Die Philosophie der Antike* 4/2 (Basle 1994), pp. 991–1168 [overview of Cicero's philosophical works and views, in German].

Gildenhard, Ingo, *Paideia Romana: Cicero's Tusculan Disputations*, Cambridge Classical Journal/ Proceedings of the Cambridge Philological Society, Suppl. Vol. 30 (Cambridge, 2007).

Glucker, John, 'Cicero's philosophical affiliations', in John M. Dillon and Anthony Arthur Long (eds), *The Question of 'Eclecticism': Studies in Later Greek Philosophy*, Hellenistic Culture and Society 3 (Berkeley, CA, 1988), pp. 34–69.

Harries, Jill, *Cicero and the Jurists: From Citizens' Law to the Lawful State* (London, 2006).

Inwood, Brad, and Jaap Mansfeld (eds), *Assent and Argument: Studies in Cicero's Academic Books: Proceedings of the 7th Symposium Hellenisticum (Utrecht, August 21–25, 1995)*, Philosophia antiqua 76 (Leiden, 1997) [ten essays on various aspects of Cicero's academic books].

Krostenko, Brian A., 'Beyond (dis)belief: Rhetorical form and religious symbol in Cicero's *De divinatione*', *Transactions of the American Philological Association* 130 (2000), pp. 353–91.

Leonhardt, Jürgen, *Ciceros Kritik der Philosophenschulen*, Zetemata 103 (Munich, 1999) [on Cicero's engagement with Greek philosophical schools].

Long, Anthony A., 'Cicero's politics in *De officiis*', in André Laks and Malcolm Schofield (eds), *Justice and Generosity: Studies in Hellenistic Social and Political Philosophy: Proceedings of the Sixth Symposium Hellenisticum* (Cambridge, 1995), pp. 213–40.

MacKendrick, Paul (with the collaboration of Karen Lee Singh), *The Philosophical Books of Cicero* (London, 1989) [overviews of content and structure for all philosophical treatises].

Nicgorski, Walter (ed.), *Cicero's Practical Philosophy* (Notre Dame, IN, 2012) [ten essays on different aspects of Cicero's philosophy].

North, John A., and Jonathan G.F. Powell (eds), *Cicero's Republic*, Bulletin of the Institute of Classical Studies Suppl. 76 (London, 2001) [six essays on Cicero's *De re publica*].

Powell, Jonathan G.F., 'The *rector rei publicae* of Cicero's *De republica*', *Scripta Classica Israelica* 13 (1994), pp. 19–29.

—— (ed.), *Cicero the Philosopher: Twelve Papers* (Oxford, 1995) [includes a 'List of Cicero's Philosophical Works' and an introduction to 'Cicero's Philosophical Works and Their Background' by the editor].

—— 'Cicero', in Richard Sorabji and Robert W. Sharples (eds), *Greek and Roman Philosophy 100 BC–200 AD*, vol. 2, Bulletin of the Institute of Classical Studies Suppl. 94 (London, 2007), pp. 333–45.

Rawson, Elizabeth, 'The interpretation of Cicero's *De legibus*', *Aufstieg und Niedergang der römischen Welt* I.4 (1973), pp. 335–56 [overview and interpretation of the work].

Schmidt, Peter L., 'Cicero's place in Roman philosophy: A study of his prefaces', *Classical Journal* 74 (1979), pp. 115–27.

Schofield, Malcolm, 'Ciceronian dialogue', in Simon Goldhill (ed.), *The End of Dialogue in Antiquity* (Cambridge, 2008), pp. 63–84.

Taran, Leonardo, 'Cicero's attitude towards Stoicism and Skepticism in *De natura deorum*', in Karl-Ludwig Selig and Robert Somerville (eds), *Florilegium Columbianum: Essays in Honor of Paul Oskar Kristeller* (New York, NY, 1987), pp. 1–22.

Wood, Neal, *Cicero's Social and Political Thought* (Berkeley, CA, 1988) [analysis from the point of view of social science].

(iv) Letters

Beard, Mary, 'Ciceronian correspondence: Making a book out of letters', in Timothy P. Wiseman (ed.), *Classics in Progress: Essays on Ancient Greece and Rome* (Oxford, 2002), pp. 103–144 [on the sequence of Cicero's letters].

Carcopino, Jérôme, *Cicero: The Secrets of His Correspondence* (trans. Emily Overend Lorimer), 2 vols (London, 1951) [attempt at collating information on Cicero's character from the letters].

Hall, Jon, 'Cicero to Lucceius (*Fam.* 5.12) in its social context: *Valde bella?*', *Classical Philology* 93 (1998), pp. 308–21.

—— *Politeness and Politics in Cicero's Letters* (Oxford, 2009).

Hutchinson, Gregory O., *Cicero's Correspondence: A Literary Study* (Oxford, 1998).

Murphy, Trevor, 'Cicero's first readers: Epistolary evidence for the dissemination of his works', *Classical Quarterly* 48 (1998), pp. 492–505.

Nicholson, John, 'The delivery and confidentiality of Cicero's letters', *Classical Journal* 90 (1994), pp. 33–63.

White, Peter, *Cicero in Letters: Epistolary Relations of the Late Republic* (Oxford, 2010).

Wistrand, Magnus, *Cicero Imperator: Studies in Cicero's Correspondence 51–47 BC*, Studia Graeca et Latina Gothoburgensia 41 (Gothenburg, 1979).

(v) Poetry

Goldberg, Sander M., *Epic in Republican Rome* (New York, NY, and Oxford, 1995), pp. 135–57 [on Cicero as an epic poet].

Harrison, Stephen J., 'Cicero's "De temporibus suis": The evidence reconsidered', *Hermes* 118 (1990), pp. 455–63.

Knox, Peter E., 'Cicero as a Hellenistic poet', *Classical Quarterly* 61 (2011), pp. 192–204.

Kubiak, David P., 'The Aratean influence in the *De consulatu suo* of Cicero', *Philologus* 138 (1994), pp. 52–66.

3. RECEPTION OF CICERO AND HIS WORKS

(A) PRIMARY SOURCES

DellaNeva, JoAnn (ed.), and Brian Duvick (trans.), *Ciceronian Controversies*, The I Tatti Renaissance Library 26 (Cambridge, MA, and London, 2007) [text and translation of the exchanges between Poliziano and Cortesi, Pico and Bembo, and Cinzio and Calcagnini].

Lintott, Andrew W. (trans.), *Plutarch: Demosthenes and Cicero. Translated with Introduction and Commentary*, Clarendon Ancient History Series (Oxford, 2013).

Moles, John L. (ed. and trans.), *Plutarch, The Life of Cicero. With an Introduction, Translation and Commentary* (Warminster, 1988).

Warner, Rex, and Robin Seager (trans.), *Plutarch: The Fall of the Roman Republic. Translated with Introduction and Notes by R.W., Revised with Translations of Comparisons and a Preface by R.S. Revised and Expanded Edition* (London, 2005).

(B) SECONDARY SOURCES

Baron, Hans, 'The memory of Cicero's Roman civic spirit in the medieval centuries and in the Florentine Renaissance' (orig. 1938), in Hans Baron, *In Search of Florentine Civic Humanism: Essays on the Transition from Medieval to Modern Thought*, 2 vols (Princeton, NJ, 1988), vol. 1, pp. 94–133.

Becker, Carl, 'Cicero', in *Reallexikon für Antike und Christentum* 3 (Stuttgart, 1957), cols 86–127 [on the reception of Cicero in pagan and Christian antiquity, in German].

Clarke, Martin L., '*Non hominis nomen, sed eloquentiae*', in Thomas Alan Dorey (ed.), *Cicero* (London, 1965), pp. 81–107 [on the early reception of Cicero].

Classen, Carl J., 'Cicerostudien in der Romania im 15. und 16. Jahrhundert', in Gerhard Radke (ed.), *Cicero, ein Mensch seiner Zeit. Acht Vorträge zu einem geistesgeschichtlichen Phänomen* (Berlin, 1968), pp. 198–245; repr. in Carl J. Classen, *Antike Rhetorik im Zeitalter des Humanismus*, Beiträge zur Altertumskunde 182 (Munich and Leipzig, 2003), pp. 1–71 [on the reception of Cicero in Italy and France in the fifteenth and sixteenth centuries].

Cox, Virginia, and John O. Ward (eds), *The Rhetoric of Cicero in Its Medieval and Early Renaissance Commentary Tradition*, Brill's Companions to the Christian Tradition 2 (Leiden and Boston, MA, 2006) [on the influence of *De inventione* and *Rhetorica ad Herennium*].

Fox, Matthew, 'Cicero: Gentleman and orator: Metaphors in eighteenth-century reception', in Jan Parker and Timothy Mathews (eds), *Tradition, Translation, Trauma: The Classic and the Modern*, Classical Presences (Oxford, 2011), pp. 91–108.

Gamberale, Leopoldo (ed.), *Ciceroniana XI. Atti dell'XI Colloquium Tullianum. Cassino – Montecassino, 26–28 aprile 1999* (Rome, 2000) [eight essays on various aspects of the early reception of Cicero].

Grafton, Anthony, 'Cicero and Ciceronianism', in Anthony Grafton, Glenn W. Most and Salvatore Settis (eds), *The Classical Tradition* (Cambridge, MA, and London, 2010), pp. 194–7.

Hagendahl, Harold, *Augustine and the Latin Classics*, 2 vols, Studia Graeca et Latina Gothoburgensia 20 (Gothenburg, 1967) [pp. 35–169, 479–588 on Cicero].

Hibst, Peter, 'Vida Ciceronianus – Zur Cicero-Rezeption in Vidas Dialog *De dignitate reipublicae*', *Neulateinisches Jahrbuch* 6 (2004), pp. 69–111.

Hinds, Stephen, 'Petrarch, Cicero, Virgil: Virtual community in *Familiares* 24, 4', *Materiali e discussioni per l'analisi dei testi classici* 52 (2004), pp. 157–75.

Homeyer, Helene, 'Ciceros Tod im Urteil der Nachwelt', *Das Altertum* 17 (1971), pp. 165–74.

Jones, Howard, *Master Tully: Cicero in Tudor England*, Bibliotheca humanistica & reformatorica 58 (Nieuwkoop, 1998).

Kaster, Robert A., 'Becoming "CICERO"', in Peter Knox and Clive Foss (eds), *Style and Tradition: Studies in Honor of Wendell Clausen*, Beiträge zur Altertumskunde 92 (Stuttgart and Leipzig, 1998), pp. 248–63.

Kennedy, George A., 'Cicero's oratorical and rhetorical legacy', in James M. May (ed.), *Brill's Companion to Cicero: Oratory and Rhetoric* (Leiden, 2002), pp. 481–501.

Kesting, Peter, 'Cicero, Marcus Tullius', in *Verfasserlexikon* 1 (2nd edn, Berlin, 1978), cols 1274–82 [on the reception of Cicero in the Middle Ages, in German].

MacKendrick, Paul (with the collaboration of Karen Lee Singh), *The Philosophical Books of Cicero* (London, 1989), pp. 258–315 [on the influence of Cicero's rhetoric and philosophy].

Murphy, James J., 'Cicero's rhetoric in the Middle Ages', *Quarterly Journal of Speech* 53 (1967), pp. 334–41.

Narducci, Emanuele (ed.), *Cicerone nella tradizione europea. Dalla tarda antichità al Settecento. Atti del VI Symposianum Ciceronianum Arpinas. Arpino 6 maggio 2005* (Florence, 2006) [four essays on various aspects of the reception of Cicero].

Richter, Will, 'Das Cicerobild der römischen Kaiserzeit', in Gerhard Radke (ed.), *Cicero: Ein Mensch seiner Zeit. Acht Vorträge zu einem geistesgeschichtlichen Phänomen* (Berlin, 1968), pp. 161–97 [on the reception of Cicero in the first century CE].

Rolfe, John C., *Cicero and His Influence*, Our Debt to Greece and Rome (London, [1923]) [overview of the reception of Cicero from antiquity until the early twentieth century].

Rüegg, Walter, Dietrich Briesemeister, Peter Kesting, Hans Sauer and Peter L. Schmidt, 'Cicero in Mittelalter und Humanismus', in *Lexikon des Mittelalters* 2 (Munich, 1983), cols 2063–77 [on the reception of Cicero in the Middle Ages and in the age of humanism].

Sabbadini, Remigio, *Storia del ciceronianismo e di altre questioni letterarie nell'età della rinascenza* (Turin, 1885).

Scott, Izora, *Controversies over the Imitation of Cicero as a Model for Style and Some Phases of Their Influence on the Schools of the Renaissance*, Teachers College, Columbia University, Contributions to Education 35 (New York, NY, 1910).

Steel, Catherine (ed.), *The Cambridge Companion to Cicero* (Cambridge, 2013) [includes six essays on the reception of Cicero from antiquity until the present day].

Tateo, Francesco, Bernhard Teuber and Richard E. Schade, 'Ciceronianismus', in Gert Ueding (ed.), *Historisches Wörterbuch der Rhetorik* 2 (Tübingen, 1994), pp. 225–27 [on 'Ciceronianism' in rhetoric, in German].

Weil, Bruno, *2000 Jahre Cicero* (Zurich and Stuttgart, 1962) [survey of views on Cicero from antiquity until the 1960s].

Wolfe, Ethyle R., 'Cicero's *De oratore* and the liberal arts tradition in America', *Classical World* 88 (1995), pp. 459–71.

Zielinski, Tadeusz, *Cicero im Wandel der Jahrhunderte* (Leipzig and Berlin, 1897; 4th edn, 1929) [overview of the reception of Cicero from antiquity until *c.*1800].

INDEX

This index includes the names of ancient figures who are mentioned (even if only briefly) as playing a role in Cicero's life and works (for further details see Glossary) and of people from later periods who are referred to in the reception section. Figures from the ancient world are listed under the most common form of their name (with the Greek or Latin version added in brackets if it differs substantially and/or the full name is relevant), figures from later periods under their last name.

A separate index for Cicero follows; it lists the passages from his works quoted in translation as well as major references to particular works and aspects of his life.

INDEX ON CICERO

Copyright Acknowledgements

JACOBITISM

MURRAY G. H. PITTOCK

Professor in Literature
University of Strathclyde

First published 1998 by
MACMILLAN PRESS LTD
Houndmills, Basingstoke, Hampshire RG21 6XS
and London
Companies and representatives
throughout the world

ISBN 0–333–66797–2 hardcover
ISBN 0–333–66798–0 paperback

A catalogue record for this book is available from the British Library.

This book is printed on paper suitable for recycling and made from fully managed and sustained forest sources.

10 9 8 7 6 5 4 3 2 1
07 06 05 04 03 02 01 00 99 98

Printed in Hong Kong

Published in the United States of America 1998 by
ST. MARTIN'S PRESS, INC.,
Scholarly and Reference Division,
175 Fifth Avenue, New York, N.Y. 10010

ISBN 0–312–21306–9

To Lexie and Davina

CONTENTS

Acknowledgements

This book owes its first debt to the University of Strathclyde's generosity in granting leave for its completion, among that of other projects, in the second semester of the 1996/7 session. Its genesis is of considerably longer standing: indeed, it could not have been written, nor would I have entered upon Jacobite studies, without the dynamic environment created in eighteenth-century historiography by scholars such as Eveline Cruickshanks, Jeremy Black, Frank McLynn and Daniel Szechi, whose findings, whether one agrees or disagrees with them, have made it impossible to avoid the subject of Jacobitism in this period. I am here indebted not only to their research, but also to the many conversations I have had with them and other scholars, not least Bruce Lenman, whose assessment of Jacobitism's importance is nicely balanced with his scepticism concerning the virtues of the dynasty which gave rise to it. In addition, I have benefited (as always) considerably from many years of debate and discussion with Ross Mackenzie, Property Manager at Culloden Battlefield, and the understanding I have gained of Jacobitism's historic importance to groups in Scottish society, in part at least through his good offices. There are, of course, many other approaches to the study of eighteenth-century history, and I am fortunate to have been able to keep abreast of these both through the company of distinguished colleagues at the University of Edinburgh (particularly Harry Dickinson) and now at the Research Centre for Scottish History at Strathclyde.

Thanks are, as always, due to my wife Anne, for her readiness to discuss a subject so long inflicted on the household, and to my daughters Vinnie and Lexie, whose vision of Charles Edward Stuart has been animated by David Niven's 1948 portrayal. I trust that Jacobitism has reached a stage in its study where it will no longer fade into the mist, though any inaccuracies in bringing it here into the light of day are my own. Dates used are Old Style except where otherwise indicated.

M. G. H. P.
Bearsden

INTRODUCTION

Britain in its beginnings and in the most successful period of its development was fundamentally a state founded on foreign policy and external success. Internally, it originally lacked the integrity of identity which the main island (and even to some extent Ireland) was to possess in its heyday in the eighteenth and nineteenth centuries. The invading Angles drew back from Scotland after the Picts defeated the Northumbrians at Dunnichen Moss in 685; a century later, Offa's Dyke demarcated the border with Wales; a hundred years more, and the Scots–Irish kingdom of Dalriada established a Scottish national monarchy within a few years of the similar achievement of Egbert of Wessex in the south.

When in the twelfth century, the Plantagenet monarchs of England, supported by the Arthurian mythistory of Geoffrey of Monmouth's *Historia Regum Britanniae* (1136), laid claim to overlordship of Scotland, it was in the context of an Angevin Empire straddling the British Isles and most of France. In the centuries that followed, it was mainly to France that England looked for territory and Scotland for support: in 1513, James IV fell at Flodden in the midst of thousands in defence of French interests against those of his brother-in-law, Henry VIII; forty years later, it was French aid that saved Scotland from English arms. It was the Reformation in Scotland which opened the path to a different set of political alignments, and although a strongly Francophile interest lingered long into the eighteenth century, it was the years 1688–1707 which set the seal on realignment, with the end of the British rule of a Catholic or Catholic-leaning Scottish dynasty. Externally the Revolution of 1688, which overthrew the Stuarts and became the ideological source of the modern doctrine of Parliamentary sovereignty, opened the gates to the struggle with France for world domination and to the development of a large-scale British Empire financed by sophisticated credit arrangements sourced in an ever more dominant London; internally, the state was centralized to an unprecedented degree, both economically and politically. The Council of Wales was abolished; the

1

Irish Parliament curtailed and its abolition considered; the Scottish Estates were brought into an incorporating Union with the English Parliament, and the Scottish Privy Council dissolved; the Stannaries of
Cornwall, suspected of Jacobitism, did not meet under William III and
II (of Scotland) and George I, and thereafter dwindled into desuetude.
The Convocation of Canterbury and York, 'a major representative in-
stitution', was suppressed from 1717, as the Whig state tightened its
control on the Church of England. Every occasion of major conflict
with France from 1689 to 1801 (the year of union with Ireland) led
to ever-greater concentration of government in London. Power was
centralized, and an economic and commercial powerhouse built on the
metropolis provided the credit for the massive military spending which
secured an Empire.[1]

   This was Great Britain. By contrast, those who wished to restore the
Catholic Stuarts to the throne aimed at a diversity of ends which to a
greater or lesser extent would undermine this state. There was no question, for virtually all British Jacobites, that the Stuarts would be restored
to all their three kingdoms of England, Scotland and Ireland (though
French foreign policy on occasion leant towards a restoration in Scotland and/or Ireland alone): but the Britain of James III and VIII
would, it was generally hoped, be a very different place. Irish Jacobites
frequently desired Catholic hegemony, and the end of Saxon rule in
Ireland; Scottish Jacobites wanted to restore the Edinburgh Parliament, the Episcopal Church and the status quo ante 1688; English and
Welsh Jacobites abhorred the financial revolution, higher taxes, a pro-
Hanoverian foreign policy and the threat to the Anglican High Church
posed by the Lutheran Georges. Many Jacobites also wanted religious
toleration, and an end to the oppressive enclosures of land and emphasis on property rights under the new regime, which were widely regarded as corrupt: these and other radical measures gained at least the
intermittent support of many of the poor. Some of such aims were in
conflict, and many would no doubt not have been realized in the event
of any restoration: but people risked their lives believing them, and it is
important for the modern reader to understand that Jacobitism was
thus far more than a dynastic squabble: it was regarded by its contemporaries as a major military, political and religious threat to the existence of the state itself, not least because the rescissory legislation of a
Stuart Parliament (as in 1660) might undermine the new financial, political and religious settlement. Although Charles II had accepted some
of the changes in landownership which had occurred since 1638, and
James III and VIII was at least on occasion prepared to negotiate ac-

ceptance of the National Debt, fear of the major retrospective legislation which would almost certainly have accompanied a fresh restoration was not unjustified.[2]

In the nineteenth century, the British state reached the apogee of its imperial triumph, a triumph too easily confused with destiny through natural pride, the historic claims of Anglicanism and a Gothic particularism which emphasized that the Germanic peoples (i.e. the English and by this time Lowland Scots) were 'dedicated to the pursuit of freedom'.[3] By and large the historians of that era were no more given than most of us to deprecate the state which nourished them, a process in any case rendered yet more difficult by that state's success. So-called Whig history, the incremental history which sees the nationality of the state it describes in terms of a development towards greater and greater progress and civilization and the sloughing off of barbarity and limitations, has its native roots in medieval and early modern English claims to hegemony within the British Isles, bolstered by seventeenth-century arguments over the extent and origins of the rights of Parliament and the iconization of Magna Carta and capped by the Scottish Enlightenment's teleology of civility, which argued for the progress of society towards ever more civilized norms, using eighteenth-century Scotland as an exemplar. It was chiefly developed in the work of writers such as David Hume and Adam Ferguson (though Hume's historiography was by no means Whig in the terms then understood in England), and tended to strongly reinforce English cultural ascendancy through its identification of a gap in cultural achievement between Scotland and England which operated in the latter's favour. Though numerous qualifications can be made to this view, it is almost certainly the reason why English history and historical exemplars gained such ascendancy in Scotland in the nineteenth and twentieth centuries.

Nineteenth-century English historians were nationals of a great Power, a Power greater than it had been in the previous century, which itself was an improvement on the century before, and so on. J. A. Froude's virulent anti-Catholicism, William Stubbs's Ancient (English) Constitution, his and E. A. Freeman's 'rampant Teutonism', S. R. Gardiner's unexamined Whig precepts, even the Catholic Lord Acton's anti-Papal English particularism, were the views of historians of a great nation, searching for the roots of its greatness.[4] That greatness was safeguarded by the Revolution of 1688, which had terminated the Catholic threat, protected the Ancient Constitution and guaranteed the ascendancy of Teuton over Celt in the British Isles. It was the key event. As the Irishman Edmund Burke had argued in *Reflections on the Revolution in*

France (1790), the Revolution was a uniquely enabling development in the growth of the British state, a very English compromise with the absolute notions of revolutionary change being peddled by her hereditary enemy. For much of the eighteenth century, the Jacobites had worked to overthrow that settlement. Thus they were the enemies of Britain itself, and the inheritance of its Empire. Historian after historian ridiculed or marginalized these enemies of the state: by concentrating on the last throw of the 1745 Rising, and an accompanying picturesque (and erroneous) vision of an army of Gaelic-speaking Highlanders; by saying little of Jacobite diplomacy and policy, still less of Jacobite culture; and by ignoring the Scottish and Irish nationalist dimensions of Jacobitism. For G. M. Trevelyan, the 1745 Rising was one of 'barbarians' engaged in 'a fantasia of misrule . . . in defiance of Parliament'; in 1890 Justin McCarthy described the Jacobite army as 'as savage and as desperately courageous as Sioux or Pawnees'; in 1973, Charles Chevenix Trench could still write of 'a savage Highland horde, as alien . . . as a war party of Iroquois'. Such examples could be multiplied.[5]

These views are still with us in more moderate form: in Paul Langford's 1989 Oxford history of England in the eighteenth century, the 'Forty-five was the occasion of 'the preservation of England against a Highland rabble', while in 1996, the BBC documentary *Rebellion* showed the Jacobite forces of 1745 as an army of ragged Gaels with swords interspersed with pictures of tanks, aeroplanes, and modern British Army manouevres to symbolize the might of their adversaries. This was teleology run riot, the more so since the Rising was now being described by leading revisionist historians as 'the greatest crisis that affected the eighteenth-century British State'.[6]

A countervailing, positive view of Jacobitism had been available since the romanticization of the Stuart cause at the beginning of the nineteenth century, though its high-flown sentimentalism (moderated in general only by the useful antiquarianism of the Scottish book clubs, which printed many primary sources) did little to dissuade serious historians from their view that the subject did not deserve serious treatment. The sentimentalists endorsed the image of doomed marginality which more dismissive historians had attached to Jacobitism, using it to intensify their celebration of the heroic Celt who always fought but always fell: the 'chivalry', 'loyalty' and 'audacity' which brought, in A. D. Innes's words, 'six thousand clansmen from the Highlands of Scotland within measurable distance of winning back the British crown'.[7] At the most romantic extremes of such views, serious Jacobite sentiment claimed to linger: but the *fin-de-siècle* neo-Jacobite magazines of the nineteenth century, like *The Royalist, The Legitimist Ensign, The Fiery Cross* and even *The Jacobite,* did little to enable their predecessors to be taken more seriously than they, although it was probably no coincidence that at least some of these titles were linked to an awakening Scottish nationalism.[8] Serious work did appear on individual figures, notably Charles Edward himself (e.g. Andrew Lang's *Prince Charles Edward Stuart* (1903)), but much less so if at all on the movement as a whole, though local and tangential studies of considerable merit were produced, such as John Doran's *London in the Jacobite Times* (1877) and J. C. O'Callaghan's *The Irish Brigades in the Service of France* (1870), a book in many ways still unrivalled. The Nonjurors similarly received attention (on the whole, more than they have done since) during this period in important books, including J. H. Overton's *The Nonjurors* (1902).[9]

It is a cultural commonplace of our century to say that things were never the same after the First World War. The establishment of the Irish Free State (1922), to a much lesser extent the National Party of Scotland (1928), and the beginnings of militant Welsh nationalism in the 1930s, were rents in the fabric of Great Britain which coincided with the beginnings of decline in its international status. Historians live in history, and the commencement of instability in Great Britain's prestige coincided with a partial movement away from the tendency to use the past mainly to bolster the claims of the present, and a greater readiness to see it in its own terms: definitions adopted by Herbert Butterfield in his critique of *The Whig Interpretation of History* (1931). At this stage, serious modern Jacobite studies began to appear, at first overwhelmingly from Scottish sources in company with the major literary renaissance in that country in the 1920s and 1930s. In 1933, John Lorne Campbell's *Highland Songs of the 'Forty-Five* demonstrated the depth of pro-Stuart ideology in the Gaeltachd: arguing that the Highlanders, far from being the dupes of the Jacobites, were wittingly loyal adherents, a point made with even greater determination to the brink of partiality by Audrey Cunningham in *The Loyal Clans* (1932). Sir Bruce Seton published an important (and neglected) article on Jacobite uniform in 1928, and (with Jean Arnot) extensive work on *The Prisoners of the '45* (1928–29). By far the main Jacobite scholars of this period, though, were Alistair and Henrietta Tayler, who from primary sources quite clearly demonstrated what even many historians today seek to ignore, the importance and depth of Jacobitism among ordinary middle-class Lowland Scots. Both *Jacobites of Aberdeenshire and Banffshire in the Forty-Five* (1928) and its companion volume dealing with the 'Fifteen (1934) put this beyond serious doubt, while *1715: The Story of the Rising* (1936) emphasized the importance of Scottish Jacobitism at the time: it is still one of the most important books on its neglected subject. In a wider context, Sir Charles Petrie's *The Jacobite Movement* (1st edn 1932) provided what is arguably the first modern and sympathetic reading of international Jacobitism. Sir Charles was a Roman Catholic: his sympathetic closeness to his subject is a marked feature of his work.[10]

Interest in Jacobitism waned after 1945, though George Pratt Insh provided an extremely useful and erudite Scottish counterpart to Petrie in *The Scottish Jacobite Movement* (1952). G. H. Jones's *The Main Stream of Jacobitism* (1954) and John Owen's *The Rise of the Pelhams* (1957) both signalled Jacobitism's ultimate lack of importance at the heart of British power and policy, while the writings of Sir Lewis Namier's school de-emphasized ideology to the point where it might become hard to comprehend why anyone might risk their lives for such a thing as a dynasty, never mind the whole wishlist baggage of Jacobite activism. The minimalization of the importance of not only religious, but also secular political beliefs was a position which could not long go unchallenged, though its power surely owed something not only to the familiarity of Enlightenment thought to a modern secular age, but also the idea of a peaceful and settled 'Augustanism' in the first part of the eighteenth century, a vision of a monocultural Britain of great tenacity in North America, where Jacobite revisionism has as a consequence made little headway. A few books, such as G. W. Keeton's *Lord Chancellor Jeffreys and the Stuart Cause* (1965) hinted at counter-readings, but in general without throwing down the gauntlet to the dominant view of the period.

When the major challenge came in 1970, one of its chief features was that it came not only from the centre of the British state itself, but also from the core of a Namierite enterprise: Romney Sedgwick's volumes on *The House of Commons 1715–1754* in the *History of Parliament*. The argument put forward there by Eveline Cruickshanks was that the Tory Party survived Queen Anne's death, and was thereafter a mainly Jacobite party, 'engaged in attempts to restore the Stuarts by a rising with foreign assistance'. In *Political Untouchables: The Tories and the '45* (1979), Dr Cruickshanks expanded on this position, and in her editing of four subsequent collections has done much to extend discussion of Jacobitism in cultural and religious spheres as well as those of high politics.[11]

This view was, and to an extent still is, controversial, the more so because many political historians did not believe in the effective survival of the Tories as a coherent party in the period after 1715: those that did often placing strict limitations on its scope. But time brings in its reverses, for many nineteenth-century historians had equated Toryism and Jacobitism, and had no doubt of the survival of the former, whatever they thought of the ultimate relevance of the latter. In *In Defiance of Oligarchy* (1982), Linda Colley acknowledged the presence of a continuing Tory Party, but not its Jacobitism, while in *Jacobitism and Tory Politics 1710–14* (1984), Daniel Szechi showed the importance of Jacobitism, and the influence of Scots Jacobite MPs, in the years immediately preceding Queen Anne's death. Today, in the judgement of the present writer, the balance of opinion has shifted significantly, if not decisively, in favour of a continuing Tory Party with a noteworthy, but not necessarily dominant, Jacobite element.[12]

What the 1970 volume did do, however, was for the first time to provide the basis for a revisionist evaluation of English Jacobitism. This was of major importance, since if Jacobitism was strong in England , it became far more of a persuasive threat to the British state than if it was merely the reaction of a Celtic fringe hostile to centralism. Studies on English Jacobitism, which had long lagged behind their Scottish counterparts, now outstripped them. Since English Jacobitism could hardly claim a massive military presence in the major Jacobite risings, arguments for its importance had to be drawn from other sources. Personal records were thin on the ground, due to the care with which English Jacobites destroyed their papers, but state and diplomatic archives, particularly on the Continent, provided substantial new evidence, while the techniques of 'history from below' began to uncover a wide range of plebeian Jacobite activity. Some of the documents adduced were vulnerable to scepticism, being vitiated by the self-interested projections of conspirators and adventurers: the view that English Jacobites were both unreliable and over-optimistic was felt strongly even at the time by elements in the French administration. With regard to plebeian Jacobitism, opponents continued to suggest that aristocratic manipulation of or the use of Jacobite tokens as mere irritants by the mob explained away much 'popular' Jacobite activity, in much the same way, it must be said, as evidence of political or industrial discontent was explained away as the manipulation of left-wing agitators in the 1980s tabloid press. Historians who make such excuses confer an unlovely and implausible passivity on popular Jacobitism which one may doubt they would suffer themselves to believe in, were Thomas Paine rather than James Stuart the catalyst for the demonstrations they wish to discredit.[13]

The findings of the revisionists gained ground, at least tangentially bolstered by the reappraisal of the nature of 'British' history begun by J. G. A. Pocock in the 1970s.[14] In *France and the Jacobite Rising of 1745* (1981), Frank McLynn demonstrated the seriousness of French intentions in 1743–45, while the same author's massive archival research culminated in the definitive *Charles Edward Stuart* (1988). Jeremy Black's magisterial renewal of the claims of diplomatic history in the period in many books from *British Foreign Policy in the Age of Walpole* (1985) on, set the scene for that author's reiterated view (cf. his *Culloden and the '45* (1990)) that Jacobite activity culminated in a major military threat to the very existence of Hanoverian Britain. The need for a re-evaluation of popular (mainly English popular) Jacobitism, hinted at by E. P. Thompson in a 1974 article in the *Journal of Social History*, was carried out by Nicholas Rogers in a series of scholarly articles culminating in *Whigs and Cities* (1989), though his cautious findings were far overreached by Paul Monod's claims in *Jacobitism and the English People*, published in the same year: the definitive statement of the maximalist case for Jacobitism in English culture.[15]

The re-evaluation of Jacobitism's importance in English society naturally led to a debate over the nature of that society itself, crystallized in Jonathan Clark's *English Society 1688–1832* (1985), which argued for the continuation of an unbroken *ancien régime* temper in English politics and culture up to the age of the Reform Act. In *Revolution and Rebellion* (1986), he emphasized these claims through a massive broadside aimed at traditional English historiography. Clark's central thesis remains perhaps more controversial than that of Cruickshanks: but one achievement of his work in the 1980s was that it compelled more serious treatment of religious motivation for political and cultural action. The secularization of historiography's assessment of eighteenth-century society was one of the key means whereby controversy over 1688 was minimized: yet English religious society in the eighteenth century resembled contemporary Northern Ireland more than its modern equivalent.[16]

At the same time as Jacobitism was being rediscovered in the actions of the English gentry and the gestures of their inferiors, it was re-entering literary history through the work of Howard Erskine-Hill, notably in *The Social Milieu of Alexander Pope* (1975), *The Augustan Idea in English Literature* (1983), and a number of influential articles on Samuel Johnson and other writers. The controversy over Johnson's Jacobitism which Erskine-Hill began continues, most recently and impressively in Jonathan Clark's *Samuel Johnson* (1994). Steven Zwicker's work, beginning with *Dryden's Political Poetry: the Typology of King and Nation* (1972), has helped to set the scene for a comprehensive reassessment of the cultural and literary languages of typology in the Jacobite period, explored in the present author's *Poetry and Jacobite Politics in Eighteenth-Century Britain and Ireland* (1994). Connections between Jacobitism and the more esoteric ideas of eighteenth-century culture were located by Douglas Brooks-Davies in two idiosyncratic but extravagantly learned books, *The Mercurian Monarch* (1983) and *Pope's Dunciad and the Queen of Night* (1985). In a specifically Scottish context, William Donaldson's *The Jacobite Song: Political Myth and National Identity* (1988) set the scene for a number of further studies.[17]

Revisionist studies based on Jacobitism outside England have been much slower to develop. In Scotland, Elizabeth Carmichael's work and Bruce Lenman's *The Jacobite Risings in Britain, 1689–1746* (1980) and *The Jacobite Clans of the Great Glen* (1984) displayed a much more complex vision of Scottish society in the eighteenth century than that often found in the work of earlier historians, framed in Professor Lenman's case by the author's fine blend of perspicacity and caustic wit.[18] Paul Hopkins's book, *Glencoe and the End of the Highland War* (1986), displayed in detail for the first time how important the Scottish conflict of 1689–92 was. In *Playing the Scottish Card* (1988), John Gibson provided an up-to-date account of the attempted 1708 Rising which owes its title to a Scottish National Party campaigning slogan, and both this and Donaldson's book heralded a struggle to emplace a nationalist reading of Scottish Jacobitism, first found argued at length in F. W. Robertson's *The Scottish Way 1746–1946* (1946), and developed in the present author's *The Invention of Scotland: the Stuart Myth and the Scottish Identity 1638 to the Present* (1991) and the militarily revisionist *The Myth of the Jacobite Clans* (1995), a book which interestingly chimes with neo-Whig accounts like that provided by Stuart Reid in *1745: A Military History* (1996). The appearance of Daniel Szechi's edition of George Lockhart of Carnwath's memoirs of the Union under the title *'Scotland's Ruine'* in 1995 added a further dimension to this view, contested by scholars such as Christopher Whately, while Allan Macinnes's categorization of the aftermath of the '45 as 'genocidal intent that verged on ethnic cleansing' in Michael Lynch (ed.), *Jacobitism and the '45* (1995) has scaled yet greater heights of controversy: Macinnes's fuller treatment of these themes in *Clanship, Commerce and the House of Stuart 1603–1788* (1996) tends to reinforce the nationalist case. Irish Jacobite studies have followed a similar trend, though Breandan Ó Buachalla's encompassing study of the subject is as yet only available in Irish, while Welsh Jacobite scholarship tends to depend on a few articles by Peter Thomas and Philip Jenkins, the earliest of which appeared in 1962. In the broader spectrum of revisionist study, the idea of Jacobitism's appeal in Scotland and Ireland as primarily nationalist is found in the arguments of Jonathan Clark, Frank McLynn and Daniel Szechi, who writes thus of the traditional historiography of the Revolution of 1688: 'Of course a few Scots and Irish got hurt, which was regrettable, but England was after all the most important place in the British Isles and it got off lightly. From Edmund Burke to Margaret Thatcher the mythistory of 1688 is a seamless robe.' The omission of any mention of Ireland in publicity material for the 1988 tercentenary of the Revolution lends credence to this view.[19]

Such a wave of scholarship has not gone unchallenged, and it is perhaps no coincidence that the most recent major study in this vein, Linda Colley's *Britons* (1992), lays emphasis on the unity of Britain in the eighteenth century and the coalescing force of a common Protestantism: themes which, in more triumphalist trappings, have already a long history. Paul Langford, in *A Polite and Commercial People: England 1727–1783* (1989) and *Public Life and the Propertied Englishman* (1991) displays a detailed scholarship which manages to occlude Jacobitism virtually altogether: it appears as an invasive force *in* English life, rather than being *of* it. Both Colley and Langford are inclined to minimize divisions in British society, and tend to ignore attempts to maximize them: a similar view more subtly expressed is found in the work of John Cannon (e.g. *The Whig Ascendancy* (1981)). Economic historians, for whom the temptations of teleology remain strong, because of the paradigms of 'growth' or 'improvement' emplaced in their study, tend also still to be dismissive of Jacobitism as being recidivist: for example, R. H. Campbell in *Scotland Since 1707: the Rise of an Industrial Society* (2nd edn 1985) stresses how few of the participants in Scottish economic growth joined in the Risings, though this point is seriously open to question. Other historians, such as Bill Speck in *The Butcher* (1981), have sought at least partially to defend Cumberland and the British Army from the charges of atrocities laid against them after Culloden: a point to which I shall return in Chapter 4. In Scotland, there has been a continuation of the consensus view that Jacobitism was a localized civil conflict rather than a national and international struggle: this is the position taken by the heritage industry, and its exhibitions such as *1745: Charles Edward Stuart and the Jacobites* (Glasgow Museums, 1995), *A Nation Divided* (National Library of Scotland, 1996) and *The Swords and the Sorrows* (National Trust for Scotland, 1996) with their accompanying literature. On the whole, it appears that there is little dialogue between such representations of Scottish Jacobitism and the findings of mainly English revisionism; it can also be argued that those who seek to treat Jacobitism in the traditional manner have not sufficiently interrogated the claims of their opponents.[20]

What follows in this book is the account of a writer whose views will be plain enough, in the sense that Jacobitism will be treated as an important challenge, in national and international terms, to British state development. At the same time, a degree of reservation will be shown where it is clear that serious doubts must remain concerning the extent and validity of Jacobite claims: and such judgements will be made clear in the text. The question of bias is unavoidable; but if it were ever possible, Ranke-like, to sink into the sources noiselessly on any subject, Jacobitism is not that subject. The sources lead one to take sides; even today one's stance on religious and political issues leads to taking sides; and it is a major sign of the lasting impact and relevance of Jacobitism that it is a topic fiercely contested by partisan historiographies to this day. Nothing could more clearly demonstrate its importance than the continuing debate over whether it was important, or more effectively indicate its national qualities than the hostility towards admitting them. It is the essence of the Jacobite challenge to the Britain we inherit that the subject should still be controversial. And with that reason for writing and admission of bias, this book begins.

1

A FOREIGN KING AND A PATRIOT QUEEN

Unity or Diversity? The Multi-kingdom Stuart Polity

When James VI ascended the English throne in 1603, he brought with him a large number of his fellow-countrymen who in his own reign and that of his son succeeded (to the resentment of the natives) in engrossing a significant proportion of court offices (as high as two-fifths at one point). If the ambitions of the 'Scoto-Britanes' of the King's circle for a Scottish influence in Britain equal to England's were naturally frustrated, Scotland nonetheless held a more significant place in the concerns of James and his successors than it was to do after 1688, for even if Charles I never shared his father's passion for the idea of Britain, he was still 'too much inclined to the Scots nation'.[1] The northern kingdom retained its own parliament, and to a certain extent its own royal household: the progress of James in 1617 and the coronation of his son in 1633 were splendid affairs. It was in Scotland that Charles II sought refuge in 1650 and a coronation in 1651, and a Scots army that he led to defeat at Worcester that year; it was in Scotland that he redeveloped and extended the Palace of Holyroodhouse, in which his brother took up residence as Duke of Albany during the Exclusion Crisis, attended by many of the Scots nobility: 'I do not hear of one who stays [in London]', wrote a contemporary.[2] For the Stuarts, 'it was deliberate royal policy to keep the settlement of the three kingdoms apart from each other',[3] and the post-1660 policy of bolstering Edinburgh's status as a royal capital was no doubt intended to underline the particularity of Stuart claims to authority in their 'ancient kingdom', a favourite phrase which the dynasty continued to use through many years of exile.[4]

12

This was a major difference between the Stuart administration and that which succeeded it: the notion of a multi-kingdom monarchy, which defined a Britain potentially significantly different from that achieved by the incorporating union of 1707. As one modern historian puts it: 'the regal union began with a king-emperor. . . . It ended with a little Englander queen [Anne].'[5] Certainly the Stuart monarchs displayed more consistent concern for the localities outside London than did their successors. James I and VI had even (1607) considered setting up his seat at York, where the Council of the North met until 1641, and recommended his Welsh subjects to take their grievances to the Council of Wales and the Marches at Ludlow, where their language was spoken.[6] Between 1603 and 1688 it is arguable that the Stuarts had, on the whole, a partial, ineffective and sometimes disastrous understanding of the need to treat their three realms differently: but such an understanding they nonetheless (except perhaps in 1638) possessed: for example, when Clanranald men 'liberated the Franciscan friar, Patrick Hegarty, from the custody of John, Bishop of the Isles, during 1630', no action was taken against them, a situation which it seems hard to credit would have arisen in the case of armed action in defence of recusancy in northern England.[7] In Dublin in the 1630s, in Edinburgh at the end of the 1670s, even at Ludlow, vice-regal and royal courts flourished. James VII and II's reformation of Scottish institutions and his foundation of cultural centres such as the Advocates' Library and Royal College of Physicians, combined with the Stuart emphasis on Scotland as the 2000-year-old source of their dynasty, led to his possessing great popularity in the Edinburgh of the 1680s. At the same time, his support in 1682 for the 'Commission for Securing the Peace of the Highlands' was 'a genuine effort . . . to work co-operatively . . . with the clans in general'.[8] The commission to De Wet to paint a series of portraits of the Scottish royal line dating back to the mythological Fergus carried out at Holyrood in 1684–86 both linked the Stuarts to a native monarchy, and aligned them with heroic and patriotic predecessors such as Robert the Bruce. This was a nationalistic iconography which symbolized a 'special relationship' between Scotland and the Stuarts, one on which James and his successors drew after 1688: moreover, the Irish elements in the Scottish foundation-story meant that the Stuarts were recognized as rightful rulers in Ireland, an important qualification which they shared and share with no other British dynasty.

The Stuarts were alert to such patriotic nuances elsewhere. In the 1630s, Charles I took care to cherish the 'true affections' of the 'ancient Brittaines' of Wales, and in 1642 proposed that the Prince of Wales should hold court at Ludlow. This was in deference to the tradition of the Council of Wales, 'a remarkable experiment in regional government', founded in the 1490s, which had recently been abolished by Parliament: it was seen as a tool of royal regionalist policy.[9] James II and VII likewise made particular patriotic use of Wales, not only having many Welsh advisers, but also undertaking the only post-Reformation royal pilgrimage to a Welsh shrine in 1686, and touring the Welsh border in 1687. In the meantime the Council, like the Scottish Estates, had been restored by Charles II, only to be finally abolished by the Williamite regime at the beginning of the 1690s.[10]

In Ireland, 'the twenty-five years of Charles II's reign had been a period of peace, recovery and comparative prosperity'. The Restoration land-settlement (as pursued through the Acts of Settlement and Explanation) only returned 'about a third' of land held by Catholics before the conflict of the 1640s, but a clear recognition of the special local circumstances of Irish society was nonetheless visible under the sixteen years of Ormond's viceroyalty in particular (for example, in 1663, he blocked an attempt by the Irish Parliament to extend English anti-Catholic laws to Ireland).[11] A relatively blind eye was turned to Catholicism and the activity of its hierarchy (even by the Anglican archbishop), at least until the hysteria of the Popish Plot, which led to the execution and martyrdom of the Archbishop of Armagh in London on a charge more related to the berserk anti-Catholicism of the age than any reality. On the scaffold, St Oliver Plunket recognized the gap in understanding between the two countries when he opined that even a Protestant Irish jury would have failed to convict him. Even at the height of the Popish scare in 1681, the Archbishop of Cashel could report to Rome of the moderation of the administration in Ireland. In England (except in the north) there were few Catholics and savage anti-Catholicism. In Ireland, at least 70 per cent of the population was Catholic. Already in Charles II's reign, the shape of policy in Ireland, with a largely 'tolerant king' counterbalanced by an 'intolerant parliament', foreshadowed the gulf between the multi-kingdom polity of late Stuart Britain and the more Anglocentric regime which succeeded it. Ireland was much closer to England in terms of the size of its population than it is today: it needed careful handling, something it was not to receive after James II and VII's final defeat in 1691.[12]

The size of Ireland's population naturally accentuated its status as a Catholic bogey with many Englishmen, whose fears were intensified after James commenced a gradual Catholicizing policy in the country after 1685: one which had a particularly high profile in its army, where a majority of officers were Catholic by 1688. The song, 'Lilliburlero', allegedly written (probably in 1687) by the Earl of Wharton to Purcell's tune, was said 'to have sung James out of his three kingdoms'. Subsequently, it became the air for songs as diverse as 'The Protestant Boys' and 'Rock-a-bye Baby': variants of it still seem to play a considerable part in Ulster Unionist music. The stage Hibernian of its original set show its roots in anti-Irish paranoia on the occasion of Tyrconnell's elevation to the viceroyalty:

> Ho, brother Teig, dost hear the decree
> Dat we shall have a new debittie:
> Ho, by my soul, it is a Talbot,
> And he will cut all de English throat.[13]

The beginnings of the Revolution of 1688 did not, however, lie in Stuart policy in Scotland and Ireland so much as in the perceived threat posed by James's moves to undermine the Church of England's special status in order to accord more civil and religious rights to Dissenters and especially to Catholics. Though his policy of Toleration won him unlikely friends, notably among the Quakers (to William Penn he was 'Friend James'), the alienation of a large part of the Anglican establishment, both clerical and lay, was too heavy a burden for a regime already vulnerable to anti-Catholic paranoia to bear. The successful resistance of the Church of England to Toleration was signalled by the failure of the prosecution of the Seven Bishops in 1688, when the Church resisted demands to use its own pulpits to proclaim a toleration which undermined its position. Moreover, it was feared that there might be worse to come. The possibility that the Crown might seek to return property to the Church which had been appropriated at the Reformation had caused anxiety in the 1630s, and that had been in a merely Anglican context: James's policy was seen by some, particularly in the light of renewed French persecution of Protestants, as the beginning of something even more sinister: the restitution of Catholics to power and property, and eventually of Catholicism itself. Today, the general view is that this fear was exaggerated: but such a revision has only taken place in the context of the decline of the imperial Protestant state and Empire which rested its original claim to existence on allegations of James II's double-dealing and depravity. When Queen Mary bore a Catholic son to the ageing King on 10 June 1688, a Catholic future seemed assured, and the patience of some gave way. William of Orange, the king's nephew and son-in-law, was 'invited' into England by a small and unrepresentative group of magnates. William was in any case making preparations to invade, in order to pre-empt any alliance between Louis XIV and James in the Catholic interest. The Revolution had begun.[14]

When it was known that James's kingdoms were under threat of invasion, the Scottish Privy Council ordered two divisions of their small army to be sent south to the King's aid.[15] John Graham of Claverhouse, Viscount Dundee, who had saved William's life in battle during his time in the Dutch service, had his troops in barracks in Westminster and Tower Hamlets when the Prince of Orange landed on 5 November (a symbolically redolent day), with an exotic army 15 000 strong, including not only many Catholics, but '200 negroes wearing embroidered caps with white furs and plumes of feathers as well as 200 Finlanders in bearskin and black armour'.[16] James's nerve failed on the desertion of certain of his key English officers, notably Major-General Churchill (later the Duke of Marlborough, with a continuing taste for double-dealing under future regimes). It was notable, however, that 'most of the common soldiers remained faithful'.[17] A day after Churchill's defection, on 24 November, Prince George of Denmark, James's other son-in-law, deserted with Ormond after taking dinner with the King.[18] There was now no question of fighting in James's mind, haunted by memories of the War of the Three Kingdoms and his father's death, and he fled London, only to be captured by a party of fishermen and returned thither. Dundee advised the King, if he would not give battle, to parley with William or make his way into Scotland for support from his ancestral kingdom, but James was in the mood for giving up. Mindful of his father, and fearful for his family, he told Dundee that 'there is but a small distance between the prisons and the graves of Kings'. Some days earlier, James had given orders to disband his English army: Dundee's small force remained intact and withdrew to Watford. On 23 December, the King left for France.[19]

Civil War, Separate Societies

The constitutional crisis to which William's invasion had given rise was considerably eased by James's flight, which allowed the fiction that he had abdicated or at least left his throne vacant to salve the consciences of many among the political classes, who nonetheless debated long before offering the crown jointly to William and Mary, James's elder daughter. The Revolution Settlement was however, a partial solution on two counts: first, it did not exclude James's lawful successors from the throne, and secondly, it was driven by the needs of the English Parliament. The description of 1688 as a 'Glorious Revolution', first made by an English MP on 18 November 1689,[20] was intended as a claim that it had been bloodless. Almost bloodless for England it may have been (there was some skirmishing and other small-scale clashes), but the Revolution gave rise to major warfare elsewhere, in which upwards of 80 000 troops were involved, mainly in Ireland. Scotland was expected to fall into line with the Parliamentary settlement: whereas the Convention of Estates did in 1689, their failure to do so in the face of the English Act of Settlement of 1701 (which finally excluded Catholic heirs) led to a persistent friction only brought to an end by the Union of 1707.

In this context, Jacobitism was born. As an international movement to restore a discarded dynasty, it was unusually strong and enduring, particularly in an era where political thought was beginning to take on its modern shape. That this was the case rests on two main counts and a number of other strong supporting causes. First, the claim of the main Stuart line to the crown was unique and unchallenged, save by allegations such as that of the 'warming-pan', alleging the illegitimacy of the Prince of Wales. James II and VII was the senior heir to the Saxon royal house through Malcolm III of Scotland's marriage to Princess Margaret; he was the heir of the Plantagenets, and also of the Tudors, by James IV's marriage to Henry VII's daughter. In Scotland, he was heir to the Bruce, and in Ireland, claimed descent from ancient kings. His overthrow imperilled the hereditary principle not only in government, but in society: the idea that the Revolution had undermined traditional property and inheritance rights was widespread. Moreover the sacramental status of the Stuart monarchy and its claim to special thaumaturgical powers as expressed in the Royal Touch (for the healing of scrofula and other skin complaints), set it apart from its successors. Charles II gave the Touch to 100 000 people, often at times of political crisis, and the dynasty continued its use until the beginning of the nineteenth century.[21]

By contrast, William and the Georges abandoned the practice, which Queen Anne was the last to use. The special sacramental status of the monarchy, bolstered by its Supreme Governorship of the Church of England, and the quasi-canonical status of Charles I as the martyr-king, was largely lost after 1688, and this affected many Anglicans who had had reservations about James's policies when in power. The Anglican Church itself, after all, originally had its roots in the medieval rivalry between king and pope, in which kings had sometimes sought to appear as figures with sacramental powers. Indeed, the majority of bishops who had defied the King in 1688 became Nonjurors, a group of more than 400 Anglican clergy and a number of bishops including the Archbishop of Canterbury, who refused to take oaths to the new regime and were deprived of their livelihoods. Many of the laity followed them, including the Duke of Beaufort and six earls. Contemporaries opined that High Anglicans of this stamp (for the Nonjurors continued to have fellow-travellers within the juring Anglican Church) 'would prefer a Papist' to a Dissenter like William II and III. The Nonjuring churches (up to 600 Episcopalian clergy, the vast majority, nonjured in Scotland, and there were a few Irish Nonjurors) continued to function as a separate denomination until the nineteenth century: the last Nonjuror died in 1875. Forty years earlier, some of their ideas and theology had markedly influenced Newman and Keble, the leaders of the Tractarian movement. This was an enduring schism, which showed that there were many people of high principles who would sacrifice their own livelihoods rather than abjure their king. The Stuarts in exile continued to nominate Nonjuring bishops, taking a particular interest in that confession's affairs in Scotland.[22]

The second reason for the Jacobite movement's strength and longevity lay in the destruction of the multi-kingdom monarchy and the direction of the new regime's foreign policy towards continental war, especially towards war with France, which took up half the years between 1689 and 1714, and a good number thereafter. Such wars were highly alienating to much of Scots and Irish society, not least in the former case because of the disruption of trade thus offered to the east-coast ports, which sometimes turned as a result to smuggling and contraband. Thousands of Scots and tens of thousands of Irish went abroad, often to fight for France and the Stuarts, sometimes to traffic in goods which circumvented excise taxes, particularly brandy: smuggling was an activity with marked Jacobite links in the first half of the eighteenth century. In both Scotland and Ireland, moreover, increasing English interference in internal affairs was combined with religious oppression, directed chiefly against Catholics (though also Dissenters) in Ireland, and against the Episcopal Church in Scotland, which indeed did not fully reunite with its Anglican brethren until 1867.[23]

There were other reasons to become a Jacobite. The Lutheranism of the Georges offended many Anglicans; the poverty caused by economic change inclined some towards an alternative regime, as did the repeated imposition of new indirect taxes to meet the interest accruing from vast debts increasingly being used to fund prolonged conflicts with France or her surrogates. After 1714, the exclusion of Tories from office made a number of opportunistic Jacobites: indeed it possibly prolonged the life of English Jacobitism by many years. Some Dissenters who had supported James continued to do so; at the same time, an Anglican establishment suspicious of Dissent could, at least until 1715, harbour Stuart sympathies.[24] Catholics were *prima facie* (though not in fact ubiquitously) likely to be Jacobites; and there were always desperadoes, adventurers and the nostalgic as well as those who were opposed to the financial revolution and changing social structures. Xenophobia, first against the Dutch and then the Germans, should not be underestimated as a motive: indeed, William and the first two Georges at times only seemed to use Britain as a tool in a foreign policy based on Holland or Hanover. Discussing John Childs's standard work on *The British Army of William III, 1689–1702* (1987), Daniel Szechi notes that 'Childs leaves little room for doubt that in military terms at least, William saw in England only a milch-cow for supplying the Grand Alliance with men and money. By 1697, Britain was paying for 45% of William's polyglot army in Flanders and providing 25% of its manpower.'[25]

The literary culture of Jacobitism in England often expressed itself in terms of the English countryside depicted in idealized ruralism, a topos of pro-Stuart sentiment which itself reached back to the War of the Three Kingdoms.[26] This ruralism was often linked, sometimes idealistically, sometimes directly, to folk culture itself, a culture which Catholics and High Anglicans tended to value more than Puritans and Whigs.[27] Even such an avowed aficionado of high culture and classical typology as John Dryden, James II and VII's Poet Laureate, used popular exemplars in poems such as *The Hind and the Panther*, and adopted folk-cultural topoi in indication of his hopes for a Stuart restoration in the much-circulated Jacobite poem, 'The Lady's Song'.

Following James's last walk down the Mall with the Earl of Balcarres and Viscount Dundee on 16 December 1688, a commission was promised to the loyal Viscount as the king's Lieutenant-General and commander-in-chief of the army in Scotland (an army whose separate existence was to cease in 1689).[28] Dundee remained at Watford and then at Abingdon with his troops in a watchful standoff with the deliberations of the English Parliament until early 1689. He then returned to Scotland, King William (as he now was of England, at any rate) promising that he should be undisturbed if he lived privately. William had his own difficulties with troop mutinies and a still unsubdued Ireland to concern him: Tyrconnell, the Lord Lieutenant, was playing for time while building up his forces.[29]

The Convention of the Scottish Estates met on 14 March, with Dundee in attendance: unknown to him though not unexpected by him, two days earlier James had landed at Kinsale with a fleet of 25 French ships, flying English colours at his request, 3000–5000 men and a war chest of 400000 crowns. At first matters appeared to hang in the balance, with the proceedings being opened with a prayer for 'God to have Compassion on King *James*, and to restore him' from the Bishop of Edinburgh.[30] But following a conciliatory letter from William, a haughty and unbending one from James (or the Earl of Melfort, his Secretary of State) and rumours of the intimidating presence of the western Covenanters in the capital, the outcome was clear. Anti-Catholicism was rife, and early exponents of Union ('an unspeakable Advantage', as one termed it) were urging the Scottish Estates to recognize William.[31] On 18 March, exactly a week before they did so, Dundee left, riding out of the city after a plea to the Catholic Duke of Gordon not to yield the Castle. His intention was to summon an alternative Convention at Stirling hosted by the Earl of Mar, but the latter now saw which way the wind was blowing. Many of the Scottish nobility adopted ambiguous positions, even though they 'still saw James as the keystone in the conservative Royalist political and cultural structure'. The Jacobite bark was, for the first time among many, worse than the Jacobite bite.[32] There was probably, indeed, general shock at what was just as much of a *coup de main* as a *coup d'état*. On 11 April, William and Mary were proclaimed at Edinburgh; five days later, James's lieutenant-general raised his master's standard on the top of Dundee Law, supported by no more than 50 men, including James Philp of Almericlose, who was to immortalize the subsequent campaign in a Latin epic, the *Grameid*.[33]

In Ireland, Tyrconnell had nearly 40000 soldiers under arms.[34] The King's pro-Catholic Irish reforms had had, however, more of an effect than he had perhaps bargained for. As a result James had, from the first, 'little choice but to put himself at the head of what had become a predominantly Catholic nationalist movement'.[35] The 'Patriot Parliament' which the King summoned at Dublin on 7 May (and which four bishops of the Anglican hierarchy in the country attended) demanded 'an act declaring that the English parliament had no right to pass laws for Ireland', to which the King reluctantly agreed,[36] though the Bill on 10 May 1689 to repeal the Restoration land settlement may have served to alienate many nationally minded Protestants.[37] The strongly nationalistic flavour of this Jacobite parliament, which has attracted the attention of many Irish historians, gives a flavour of that country's chief motivation for supporting the Stuarts.

Events moved rapidly: a major international war on Scottish and Irish fronts was opening up, with English, Dutch and French troops engaged. On 29 March (though the letter was not received until June), the Earl of Melfort, James's Secretary of State for Scotland, confirmed Dundee's commission as lieutenant-general, and promised over 5000 troops.[38] Melfort also requested that the Viscount should call a Convention of Estates to declare for King James. Dundee certainly needed Irish support, for he had relatively little at home: in 1715 and 1745, by contrast, opposition to the Union swelled the Jacobite ranks many times over. By 8 May, the Jacobites had only 200 men, and Dundee could merely afford himself 70 soldiers with which to take Perth two days later. But Major-General Hugh Mackay, the Williamite commander, chased the Viscount round northern Scotland for some time with little effect, and more of the clans took heart, reinforced both by the muster at Lochaber on 18 May and by a landing of 200 Irish troops at Kintyre that month, followed by a further accession of 300 under Colonel Cannon as well as the moral support provided by the King's commission. The Jacobite victory at Bantry Bay on 1 May no doubt also played its part.[39] By the end of June, Viscount Dundee had eight battalions and two companies, virtually all Highlanders: almost thirty clans were eventually to lend his forces support, though mostly only a modest proportion of their total military strength.[40] The government price on the renegade general's head grew from 18000 merks (£1000 sterling) to 20 times that sum (compare the £100000 offered for James VIII and III in 1715 and £30000 for Charles Edward 30 years later). Despite the Duke of Gordon's surrender on 13 June, by the time Dundee's little army at last essayed a breakout into the central Lowlands in July they represented a major threat.[41]

Dundee had, however, secured little in the way of support from the Scots nobility or the Episcopal Bishops, whom he sneeringly termed 'the Kirk invisible'.[42] His attempts to cajole support in the weeks before Killiecrankie have a fantastic air about them, redolent of generations of Jacobite wish-fulfilment yet to come: 'There are 20 French frigates at Carrickfergus, and 2000 men to transport from thence; 3 saill are at Dublin, the rest comes from thence; the great fleet is at sea. I have assurance of all the north. The great army is from Dublin. I believe this week the west will see strangers.'[43] In this same letter Dundee alleges that Derry has been taken (there was in fact an offer of capitulation early in July): all Ireland but Enniskillen and that city was now in James's hands. The fall of Derry would indeed have brought Dundee reinforcements beyond the Irish battalion already sent: but it did not occur. Still short of men, Claverhouse granted a commission to Colonel Patrick Stewart of Ballachan to raise Atholl: but given the Marquess's studied ambivalence, few of the 6000 men those vast estates could provide had turned out when Dundee faced Hugh Mackay down the pass of Killiecrankie on 17 July.[44]

As a battle, Killiecrankie was not dissimilar to Culloden, except that the Jacobites won. As in 1746, so in 1689 the frontline Jacobite soldiers suffered massive casualties from heavy musket-fire as they reached the government lines: but at Killiecrankie they triumphed because of the lack of good government artillery (they did not face canister and cartridge shot at close range): their charge was better co-ordinated from rising ground because many of the government soldiers carried matchlocks rather than flintlocks, and because the plug bayonet of William's army incapacitated the user's musket.[45] As it was, the rate of casualties suffered by the Jacobites would have amply justified Pyrrhus' famous apothegm, 'another victory like that and we are done for': almost 1000 from Dundee's 2500-strong army were lost or unfit to fight, and their general was dead. Twice as many were killed in the Pass as at the Boyne the next year, though fewer than a tenth of the number of troops was involved. The campaign could only continue because, heartened by success, another army as large as the first accrued in the days after Killiecrankie. This force, now poorly commanded by Colonel Cannon, was held at bay on 21 August by a Cameronian battalion in fierce street-fighting in Dunkeld; in November, James sent the more professional Major-General Buchan across from Ireland, but his leadership made little difference, and now William was free to deploy vast bodies of troops (more than half of them foreign) in Ireland itself, where the Duke of Schomberg had landed on 13 August, just over a fortnight after the Royal Navy relieved Derry.[46] Surprised at the Haughs of Cromdale in May 1690, James's army dwindled to 800 men or so, largely reduced to carrying out hit-and-run operations. More and more of Scotland submitted to the new authorities: on 2 December 1691 James himself authorized his supporters to do so, though King William's regime nonetheless made a dreadful example of the Glencoe MacDonalds in February on the grounds that their submission had been made after the 1 January 1692 deadline.[47] In June 1694, the Bass Rock fortress capitulated, and with it the last territory loyal to the Stuarts in Scotland.[48]

In Ireland, matters were going little better. The failure to take Derry in August, combined with Dundee's death, marked the beginning of a steady deterioration in Jacobite fortunes from a point where they had controlled the whole island, barring a couple of Ulster strongholds which, as a consequence, entered Orange mythology. Lack of money led to the issue of the infamous 'Gunmoney' coinage of base metal, which so undermined the Irish currency that its repercussions continued into the next century. By contrast, William's 1690 Parliament voted him £500 000 sterling for building 27 new warships, financed by taxes on 'ale, liquors, East India goods, wrought silks, wine, vinegar and tobacco'. The massive financial resources of the English state apparatus were being brought to bear.[49] Nor were the Jacobites more successful on the field. Defeat at the Boyne on 1 July 1690 disheartened James, who left for France. The central Irish garrisons fell quickly, and Limerick would have fallen too, had not Patrick Sarsfield's night attack destroyed William's artillery train. Commanded by James's natural son, the Duke of Berwick until January, when Tyrconnell replaced him, the Jacobites held out in the south-west into 1691, only to lose disastrously at Aughrim in July. Tyrconnell died on 14 August. Shortly thereafter the Jacobite forces obtained a conditional surrender under the terms of the Treaty of Limerick, ratified in February 1692.[50] Under the terms of the Treaty to form an army in exile for James, 12 000 soldiers left for France: subsequently (1697) they were either absorbed into the French army or turned off the payroll. The surrender at Limerick also provided for Catholic rights to be maintained in Ireland, either as they were under Charles II or as consistent with the laws of the country. William even enlisted a few Irishmen, whose service he quickly dispensed with, into his forces: more characteristic was the siting of Protestant colonists, such as the Huguenot veterans of Port Arlington and Lisburn, throughout Ireland.[51] It could hardly be said that the promise of this first Article on Catholic liberties was kept: it was omitted from the business of the relevant Irish Parliament in 1697, and the Penal Laws soon radically reduced the proportion of land owned by Catholics, to two-thirds of its 1688 total by 1702, and to less than one-quarter of it by the later eighteenth century (though recent revisionism has claimed that this overstates the actual position).[52] The 1704 'popery act' severely curtailed the Catholic rights and privileges that had been enjoyed under Charles II, and another article of the Treaty was breached by the 1709 Act requiring Catholic clergy to take the Oath of Abjuration against the Stuarts, at a time when the exiled dynasty was still nominating the Catholic hierarchy in the country, a role they were to continue to play for most of the

century. 'Remember Limerick and Saxon perfidy!' became a battle-cry
of the exiled Irish soldiery on the Continent. As one of Ireland's most
distinguished recent historians notes, 'it was to be many years before
Catholics regained the status and opportunities that they had briefly
enjoyed under a Jacobite administration'.[53] The seeds of an enduring
trouble had been sown in Ireland, and although some blamed James
for his failure in the war of 1689–91, the Stuarts and their continental
allies remained the main hope of Irish Jacobitism for many years to
come.

England was not immune from early attempts to restore the Stuarts.
Almost immediately after William's successes in Ireland, his regime
had to face a French invasion fleet. Morale was low among the officer
corps, who felt they were being passed over in order to promote Dutch-
men, while some of the troops, at times less than enthusiastic in Ireland,
mutinied when told they were to serve in Flanders. Already in 1689, up
to 3000 British soldiers had deserted to the French service, and this
haemorrhage continued, albeit at a slower pace.[54] Despite complaints
from the Scots authorities, William ordered the pressing of 1000 Scots
seamen, on the pretext that 'both kingdoms' were 'equally threatened'.
This was one further step in the military integration of England and
Scotland, already under way, and underlined English expectations of
Scots acquiescence in the 1689 settlement.[55] The Scots recruitment by
no means ended the new King's troubles, however, for his most able
general, Marlborough, was in all probability once again playing both
sides:

> William III knew that certain of his senior army and naval officers were in
> correspondence with the Jacobite court. . . . The plan to attack Dunkirk in
> January 1692 was probably betrayed to the French by a British officer and the
> fact that the only surviving copy of the plans is to be found in the Blenheim
> Manuscripts may be more than simply coincidence. Marlborough was dis-
> missed from all his offices on 20/30 [old/new style] January 1692. Certainly,
> two years later, Marlborough betrayed the plans and timing of Talmark's
> Brest expedition to Saint Germain and Louis XIV.[56]

If this double-dealing was intended to lead to British defeat, it did not
produce the expected result. On 19–24 May 1692, the French fleet was
defeated at Barfleur and la Hougue, where 15 of its ships were destroyed. The plan to land a Franco-Irish army in England was over; in
England itself, the plotters in what became known as the Ailesbury Plot
were already in full flight from the well-informed authorities.[57] At la
Hougue, James, flying both the crosses of St George and St Andrew,

watched his own defeat: he apparently could not forbear applauding the efforts of the English ships.[58] The seriousness of the invasion threat in 1692 is still under dispute, but there is no doubt that it was planned to take advantage of apparently widespread discontent in England, where Jacobites claimed to have up to 14000 ready to rise in the north in eight regiments.[59] Even James's renegade daughter Anne, who had encouraged belief in the Prince of Wales's illegitimacy in 1688, had written promising her support, and it was hoped by James and Louis XIV that 'she might answer for the Church, Marlborough for the army, Russell for the fleet'.[60] In this hope triumphed over expectation to a degree unusual in political affairs not connected with the restoration of the Stuarts, whose advisers had a tendency to identify every fragment of double-dealing as a wholehearted return to proper loyalties. The birth to James of a daughter on 18 June was small consolation for yet another disappointment.

Defender of the Faith

Louis XIV gave James a pension of 600000 *livres*, and the use of the royal palace at St-Germain-en-Laye, which was to be home for the Stuart court during the next twenty-five years.[61] The smallness of the chateau meant that many among James's entourage had to find lodgings in the town, where a Jacobite expatriate community grew up which outlived the court by many years. Despite the limitations of size and wealth, court culture flourished: in particular music, where Innocenzo Fede was Master of the Music and both Sir William Waldegrave and Lord Caryll were gifted amateurs.[62] Two-thirds of Louis's money was spent on salaries for the royal household and pensions for loyal supporters, but the money could not go far in satisfying the needs of as many as 40000 exiles, three-fifths of whom were Irish, more than a third English and a small remainder Scots.[63] James could reward some with titles, but he was more cautious in giving these out than has been supposed: indeed, some were awarded merely to satisfy French court protocol, for there were more high-ranking nobility in France than in England (Scotland was closer to the Continental norm).[64]

The Jacobite court was quite a close-knit unit: there is no evidence that either William or Anne successfully introduced a spy into it, although the Jacobites were able to intrude one into the English Government (William Greg, arrested in 1707–08). Espionage, indeed, was one of the ways in which the exiles could earn themselves a precarious living,[65] and its network was recognized and promoted by the salaried officials of the court,[66] Espionage attracted and created desperate men, but so did unemployment among the many exiles for whom there was no work at all. At times, St-Germain became almost a bandit town, and even the chateau was insecure: in 1703, 'jewels to the value of £15000 . . . were taken from the apartments of Mary of Modena', while the town itself was 'a community living in an atmosphere of violence, triggered off by economic difficulties, internal rivalries and disappointed hopes'.[67] In the midst of this, of course, there were still rich men: 'Lord Middleton, said to be the wealthiest man in Saint-Germain', gave his daughter a dowry of 60000 *livres*.[68]

It was increasingly clear, particularly after the debacle of Melfort's threats to the Scottish Convention in 1689, that Stuart political policy would have to change. Two main strands were visible in Jacobite thought and activity in the 1690s as awareness of the need for change developed: the 'Compounders', led by Lord Middleton, co-Secretary of State from 1 April 1693, who favoured compromise with Anglicanism, a 'general pardon and no further measures to advance Roman Catholicism'; and the 'Non-Compounders' headed by the Earl of Melfort, who believed that the King should be restored absolutely and that those who had opposed him should be punished.[69] There was never any hope of James being restored on Melfort's blank-cheque-and-treason-trials basis, and in a manifesto of 7 April 1693 the King vowed 'upon our royal word, that we will protect and defend the Church of England, as it is now established by law. And secure to the members of it, all the churches, universities, colledges [sic] and schools, together with their immunities, rights and priviledges.'[70]

On 16 May 1694, Melfort was dismissed. There were many who now wanted to believe James. The preferment of the Dutch in England, and the country's use as a tool in William's continental ambitions, had not gone unnoticed. Princess Anne described the new King's ministers as 'insolent Dutch and sneaking, mercenary Englishmen'.[71] Xenophobia against the now entirely Dutch regime seemed to grow after the death of Mary, James's daughter and co-ruler with William, in 1694. That autumn, there were rumours of a Jacobite plot in Lancashire.[72] In the following year the Jacobite Dissenter Robert Ferguson, in his *Brief Account of Some of the Late Incroachments and Depradations of the Dutch upon the English*, accused the incomers of asset-stripping and securing preferential treatment, among other vices. In 1695–96, a further Jacobite attempt (from the new-look moderate Jacobite leadership) was entertained. Sir John Fenwick and a gang of Jacobite supporters negotiated with the

French government to secure a south-coast port where a blitzkrieg French force could land and march to London. The Fenwick Plot reached an impasse in its preparations at a point which was to become familiar in later Jacobite inactivity: the French would not commit themselves until the port was seized, and Fenwick would not seize the port until the French were committed.[73] In longer and bloodier format, this was to be the story of the invasion of England in 1745. At much the same time, Sir George Barclay arrived in England as James's lieutenant-general with a commission to 'wage war', but such grandiosity quickly subsided into the shabby Assassination Plot, an offshoot of the Fenwick one, for which 40 were recruited by George Porter, Barclay's associate. This was a large number of assassins to keep quiet and happy, and unsurprisingly one of them, Thomas Prendergast, informed. The ringleaders were executed, and an Association set up to swear William as 'rightful and lawful' King, and to abjure the Prince of Wales (the future James III and VIII). James's putative 50-battalion-strong invasion force never sailed. Though the exiled King had apparently not sanctioned the assassination attempt, it did his cause no good, and boosted sympathy for William.[74] Moreover, James spurned the new King's offer of recognition for the Prince of Wales, providing he moved to England and was brought up a Protestant.[75] In 1701–02, after James's death, Lord Belhaven likewise failed 'to persuade Mary of Modena' to have the young James III and VIII brought up as a Protestant in Scotland. Nonetheless, the accession of men like Belhaven was witness to the success that the Compounders had had in attracting Whiggish politicans disgruntled by the Revolution settlement. Such Whig Jacobites were to be an important part of future Stuart machinations in England in particular.[76]

Jacobitism needed such supporters, for it was being weakened by the gradual shift towards recognizing the Revolution's legitimacy to be found in the juring Church of England and its allies, a drift towards seeing 1688 as a special act of Providence or at the least a 'fortunate Fall' which influenced Tory and much Whig thought into the following century. The Nonjurors initially made a strong case of their own in opposition to such views: over 100 Nonjuring pamphlets appeared between 1689 and 1692, and up to a third of a million 'of the many different pamphlets discussing the allegiance controversy were circulating' in the first six years of William's reign. Nonetheless, despite such powerful levels of interest and the presence of Nonjuring fellow-travellers in the Church of England, the siren voices of compromise with the *de facto* regime were being heard by 1700.[77] In Scotland, Episcopalianism was

severely weakened by its disestablishment in 1690, after the Bishop of
Edinburgh had equivocated when asked by William for his support.
Established by law on 7 June 1690, the strength of Presbyterianism continued to grow, although many local landlords had exercised the power
to protect local Episcopal incumbents. Some of course did not survive,
such as the Revd William Dunbar of Laurencekirk, deprived in 1693
for allegedly instructing his parishioners 'publickly to swear in Church
that they should never bear armes against any of the race and name of
Stuart'.[78] Nonetheless, the Episcopalian interest remained strong: at the
time of the Union, Moray and Ross were probably more than 50 per
cent Episcopalian, Caithness, Aberdeenshire, Angus and Mearns
40–50 per cent, and Perth and Stirlingshire about 20 per cent.[79] These
figures far outweighed the number of Scottish Catholics: but the two
communities nonetheless began to share the comradeship that grows
from oppression. In the north-east of Scotland in particular, Episcopalian and Catholic interests grew closer together (despite the Pope-burn-
ing in Aberdeen in 1689):[80] indeed 'James VII . . . held such Gallican
opinions of his own powers in ecclesiastical affairs' that the difference
between the two confessions could on occasion almost be glossed over.
One at least of James's Episcopal bishops, John Gordon of Galloway,
converted to Roman Catholicism: indeed, there was 'a marked upsurge in apostasy from Protestantism' in Scotland in 1685–89, which
may have continued for some time thereafter: in 1704, the Revd James
Robertson complained to the Presbytery of Kincardine O'Neil that of
the 168 Catholics in his parish, 134 were apostate Protestants.[81] Moreover, in the face of Presbyterian triumphalism, the connection between
Episcopalianism and Jacobitism strengthened: moves towards toleration for juring Episcopal practice made in 1695 and 1712 overwhelmingly failed to woo back the Church's many priests and adherents from
their determined Stuart loyalty. Like the Catholics, and in contrast to
the established Kirk, Episcopalianism tended to make 'use of the rich
medieval, religious heritage of Gaeldom to spread its gospel message'.
Both confessions thus preserved their popularity in the Gaeltachd, and
the Episcopal, 'no less than the Catholic community, were subject to
the penal laws', though in practice greater discretion was employed in
their application.[82] It was anti-Catholicism which was headlined and
promoted by the Kirk, no doubt in part because of the embarrassment
it might expose itself to if Anglicans south of the Border questioned the
treatment of their co-religionists, as they occasionally did. In 1700, the
Scots Estates offered a reward of 500 merks (£333 6s 8d Scots, about
£27 10s sterling) 'for the detection of each priest and Jesuit', while

Queen Anne issued a royal proclamation against Popery in Scotland in 1704.[83] Such anti-Catholic penal laws were evaded in Buchan, Deeside and Strathbogie, all areas where Episcopalianism was strong, suggesting a degree of protective co-operation between the confessions, reflected also in the spread of the French Catholic Quietist teachings of Mme Bourignon, Mme Guyon and Archbishop Fénélon among the faithful of both churches. Bishop Nicolson, Scotland's first Catholic bishop since 1603, set up a retreat on the Duke of Gordon's estates, and seminaries soon followed, first at Loch Morar in 1714, then at Scalan in Glenlivet three years later.[84]

My Entirely English Heart

When James died in 1701, a spate of elegies in praise of him appeared: indeed, following a number of reported miracles on the Continent, there were even calls (though not in England!) to set in train the process of canonization. In that same year, the Act of Settlement excluded his heirs from the English throne, while on 7 March 1702, the Act of Abjuration required formal renunciation of allegiance to James III and VIII.[85] If Anne, William's successor, died without heirs, the crown would pass to the Electors of Hanover. The prospect of Lutheran Germans on the throne was not calculated to damp down xenophobia, and when William died in 1702 after his horse stumbled on a molehill (Jacobites toasted the mole as 'the little gentleman in black velvet'), Queen Anne took care to present herself in as patriotic a light as possible. Her 'entirely English heart' was a theme of her coronation speech, and she was indeed to preside over a particularly English adminstration.[86]

As a young woman at James's court in Edinburgh at the end of the 1670s, Anne had had 'one of the most profound formative experiences' of her life. She saw 'not only Scotland's immense importance to English security but also the necessity of ameliorating the religious differences between the Protestants of the two kingdoms'. From the beginning, Anne saw Scotland's consequence; but she saw it entirely in terms of England's needs. Her attitude to Ireland betrayed a similar Anglo-centrism: 'she understood they had a mind to be independent, if they could; but they should not'. It is not surprising, then, that as Queen she advanced the policy of Anglo-Scottish Union which William had called for 'in his last speech to the English Parliament'. By so doing, she gave Jacobitism a major and continuing new source of support, not something Anne had a mind to do, for recent scholarship has established that she 'was the major perpetrator, and perhaps the originator, of the calumny that her stepmother's pregnancy was false'. Far from wishing to see her half-brother restored to the throne after her death, the Queen had herself done much to delate him and destroy his claim.[87]

Although the by now tamed Irish Parliament actually lobbied for Union in 1703, the Scottish Estates displayed increasing uneasiness over both the succession and the total integration of their foreign policy into English aims. A 'taxpayers' strike' was followed by large-scale Jacobite gains in the 1703 general election: together with nationalist-minded Whigs, these 'Cavaliers' made major trouble for the Anglo-Scottish relationship in the next two years.[88] The Act Anent Peace and War of 1703 provided for Scotland after Queen Anne's death to be at war or peace separately from England, while the potentially explosive Act of Security of 1704 enabled the country to choose a king 'being always of the Royal LINE of Scotland . . . Providing always, That the same be not Successor to the Crown of England'.[89] The Act was seen as an implicit threat to restore the Stuarts (despite the necessity of the new King's being a Protestant), 'unless in this or in some subsequent Parliament such conditions of Government had been enacted as should secure from English or from foreign interest the honour and independence . . . of Scotland'. The Scottish Parliament threatened to withhold taxes and disband the army if the Act was not passed.[90] This was a direct challenge to the 1701 English Act of Settlement of the crown on Hanover, and was not to be tolerated. If the Scots felt that 'the entire episode of 1689' was 'a piece of sharp practice whereby the English secured a Scottish settlement on the cheap', it was perhaps equally surprising to some in England that the Edinburgh Estates were not falling into line as meekly as they had done then.[91] There were other problems with the Act of Security, notably the free trade clause. There was widespread resentment in Scotland at the damage the War of the Spanish Succession was doing to trade with France, and this was exacerbated by the refusal of the Royal Navy to protect Scottish merchant traffic, even though the Navy was pressing recruits in Scottish towns. Eventually such resentment boiled over in the trial and execution in Edinburgh of three English sailors, including Captain Green, master of the East India trader the *Worcester*, on the charge of 'having seized a Scots trading vessel . . . and murdered her captain'. The Edinburgh mob reacted very badly even to talk of a reprieve.[92]

The English Parliament responded to Scottish legislation with sanctions on Scotland to press her towards Union, including the Alien Act of 1705, which would have made Scots 'on a par with other foreigners with respect to trade and civil rights' if they did not make moves towards Union; the Scottish administration was also rewarded with subsidies.[93] Further pressure was put on Scottish trade; on the English side there was now an increasing desire to secure Union quickly: commissioners from both countries were carefully chosen to treat for it in 1706. The year that followed was tense: the Queen was busy bolstering her status through use of the Royal Touch,[94] and armed bands were gathering in Scotland. It was only lack of effective leadership that prevented the marshalling of an anti-Union army: as it was, the mobs were dangerous enough and the capital was 'never free from the threat of violence'. Soldiers were required in Edinburgh to combat the rioting.[95] When it became clear that an incorporating rather than a federal union was going to be proposed, the Scots Commissioners were branded as 'Unionist' traitors: ordinary Scots from burghs throughout the country joined their names to petitions against it.[96] On 20 November 1706, several thousand Cameronian Presbyterians burnt the Articles of Union at Dumfries, appealing for aid to Scots regiments in service abroad. The nationalist-minded Lord Lovat had already tried to foment a Jacobite plot in 1703; now a rising in south-western Scotland was planned, but came to nothing.[97] The Jacobites tried blocking tactics, and were among those who pushed most strongly for a federal rather than an incorporating Union: but the weak leadership of the Duke of Hamilton undermined the opposition: indeed, both the putative south-western rising and one in Atholl were defused by the Duke.[98] Hamilton was indeed suspected of desiring the crown himself: as a descendant of James II of Scotland, he was a highly eligible Protestant heir.

The Union was opposed not only by the Jacobites, but also by a number of Presbyterians who were not to be bought off by the promise of establishment for the Church of Scotland. As a result, for up to twenty years after the Union, it was possible for the Jacobites to gain support from radical Presbyterian opponents of the measure: James VIII and III even issued an address in 1718 to the Cameronians, calling on their support even though they had opposed the right to the crown of both his father and uncle. Tracts like *The Smoaking Flax Unquenchable* (1706) compared 'the lesser evil of being ruled by a Stewart king with the greater evil of being suppressed by an English-Hanoverian dynasty and parliament'.[99] On the Episcopalian side, the view that the Union was the 'beginning of all the mischief' was widespread, for 'all honours and places of Trust and consequently our government itself were at the disposal of the ministers of a nation ever intent upon our ruin and destruction'. The famines which had beset Scotland for four years at the

end of the 1690s, much weakening her economic position, were themselves seen as preludes to this new disaster: the insignia of Providence
on the folly of Union. The combination of the Union and the Hanoverian succession thus greatly increased the incidence of Jacobitism:
for it appeared 'a calamity very little short of the Union it self' to have
'upon the Throne an arbitrary German prince unacquainted with our
laws and an utter stranger to our constitution'.[100]

Contemporary estimates suggested that up to 90 per cent of Scots
opposed the Union. Within a week of its taking effect on 1 May 1707,
a memorial was prepared on behalf of some of the chief nobles of
the country calling for a restoration: signatures were given by or on behalf of the Duke of Atholl, the Marquess of Drummond, the Earls of
Nithsdale, Traquair, Galloway, Home, Strathmore, Wigton, Linlithgow, Moray, Errol, Eglinton, Caithness, Aberdeen, Buchan and the
Earl Marischal, and by Lords Kenmure, Nairne, Sinclair, Semple,
Oliphant and Kinnaird, as well as many lesser barons. Signatures were
given for the loyalty of Aberdeenshire, Angus and the Mearns. The
Union was the catalyst for the prospect of a major rising,[101] this time
with the aim of restoring James VIII to rule in Scotland alone. The main
agent in the preparation of what was to be the attempt of 1708 was Colonel Nathaniel Hooke, an Irishman who had been chaplain to the Duke
of Monmouth in the latter's rebellion of 1685, but had subsequently
converted to Catholicism. Hooke was in fact a notably successful career
Jacobite, rising to be Brigadier, Maréchal de Camp and Baron de
Hooke. Simon Fraser, Lord Lovat had suggested the Scottish project to
Hooke while in exile in France.[102] The French were themselves puzzled
by the Union: as Saint-Simon wrote: 'It passes understanding how so
proud a nation, hating the English, well-acquainted with them through
past sufferings and moreover so jealous of their freedom and independence should have submitted to bow their necks beneath such a
yoke.'[103]

Colonel Hooke had first visited Scotland in 1705 to sound out
Jacobite support. It was fairly clear that 'two-thirds of Scotland were
Stuart in sympathy', but less apparent what this would amount to in
action.[104] Hamilton's prevarication was clear, and others could not be
relied on. When Hooke returned in April 1707, however, the circumstances of Union had begun to exarcerbate disaffection: the Equivalent,
Scotland's compensation for taking on its share of the National Debt,
was, according to Robert Harley's agent Daniel Defoe, described by
the people as 'the price of their country'.[105] Seeking to capitalize on this
background, the French planned to land James in Scotland. The south-

ern side of the Forth was to be 'laid waste to deter the advance of English troops', an implementation of what Hooke claimed was the advice of Robert the Bruce,[106] while the occupation of the Tyne-Tees coalfield was a second, ambitious strand, intended to cut off London's fuel and force the government to negotiate.[107]

By March 1708, a small fleet was ready, and despite James VIII's ill health, eventually reached the Fife coast, with the aim of advancing on Stirling. On shore, a good number of Jacobites appear to have been ready. Unfortunately, the Royal Navy had so closely shadowed the French fleet that it was unable to put any troops ashore. In the circumstances, the French admiral, Count de Forbin, unwilling to take the risk of landing James alone, chose rather to return to France.[108]

The attempt of 1708 foreshadowed what was to become a repeated feature of French policy: a plan to use the Stuart cause to divide the British state into two or more of its constituent parts. That this was to remain an element in French designs bears witness not only to the strong nationalist dimension of Scots and Irish Jacobitism, but also to the perceived persistence of Scottish and Irish faultlines in the apparently unitary British state. There were no countervailing plots to divide France into her ancient provinces, no doubt because the unity of Britain was clearly seen as being of another kind: artificial and precarious. Irish and Scottish soldiers fought for France and elsewhere in Europe: the former were not trusted by Britain, the latter suffered disproportionately high casualties in the service of her armies: the tendency to view Scottish troops as disposable dates back to the War of the Spanish Succession. Elements in French policy-making may have overestimated the fissiparousness of the British state: but they did not invent it.[109]

In England it was the cry of 'The Church in Danger' which was the main engine of Jacobitism in the last years of Anne. There was much distrust of a future Lutheran king, and concern over the connections between Whigs and Nonconformists. Fearful of having established Anglican power-structures undermined in favour of privileging Dissenters or Latitudinarians, High Church divines began to drift towards Jacobitism. As Geoffrey Holmes puts it:

> One must appreciate that by 1709, the apogee of the Whigs in the reigns of William III and Anne, at least four-fifths of the parish clergy in England and Wales were convinced that the ruling party, given half a chance, would sell out the Anglican inheritance to dissenters and latitude-men, if not to the enemies of Christianity itself.[110]

The central figure and icon of this process was Dr Henry Sacheverell, whose tract *In Peril of False Brethren*, with its thinly veiled Jacobite message, may have sold up to 100 000 copies in 1709–10. Impeached before the House of Lords, Sacheverell received only 'a laughable sentence', which raised tension.[111] In September 1710, Jersey signalled its willingness to accept a Stuart restoration; in the election of that autumn, the Tories returned to power in an 'electoral landslide precipitated by [the] Sacheverell impeachment'.[112] For years Sacheverell's name became a catchphrase of street Jacobite and High Church mobs,[113] while many of the clergy supported Jacobite candidates and threw themselves into the service of pro-Stuart Toryism in both the 1710 and 1715 elections.[114] Some limited success for the High Anglicans was gained under the 1710–14 Tory administration, in the shape of the 1712 toleration of Scottish Episcopalians who would accept the ruling monarch (a development in which Jacobite Scottish MPs were notably instrumental).[115] After the disorders of 1715, George I's new administration began to close down the career opportunities of High Church clergy, a process signalled by Benjamin Hoadly's elevation to the See of Bangor in December 1715 and accelerated by the failure of the 1722 plot associated with the name of Francis Atterbury, Bishop of Rochester.[116]

The French, meanwhile, were under increasing pressure to abandon the Stuarts, as the tide of events in the War of the Spanish Succession began to run against them. Under the terms of the Treaty of Utrecht in 1713, James had to move his court from France. He moved to Bar-le-Duc in the Duchy of Lorraine; Louis meanwhile helped to arrange financial support from the King of Spain, which was offered on the conditions of the restoration of Roman Catholicism and the recognition of 'certain Spanish territorial claims in Italy'.[117]

Even while the British government was negotiating the terms of Utrecht, its leaders, Robert Harley and Henry St John (the Earl of Oxford and Viscount Bolingbroke) were in the process of hedging negotiations with the Stuarts, partly perhaps undertaken in order to secure the government's position in the Commons by appeasing Jacobite MPs. Neither of them, however, was prepared to make a decisive move on Queen Anne's death when it occurred in August 1714, perhaps because of the insistence with which James had rejected their demands that he convert to Anglicanism: though the administration's slipperiness in its promises to Jacobite MPs and its declaring of a £5000 reward for James's apprehension in Britain only weeks before Anne's death cannot inspire too much confidence in any clear reading of Oxford's or Bolingbroke's conduct in 1710–14. It was in the end an Anglican bishop who came closest to declaring for the Stuarts: Francis Atterbury, Bishop of Rochester, offered to proclaim James III, but the leading figures in government were hesitant or lukewarm. Bound by Utrecht, the French could do nothing but offer James a couple of ships and no soldiers: he, wrongfooted by the suddenness of events, came to Paris on 10 August, and was sent back to Lorraine. George I thus acceded to the throne relatively peacefully, though a wave of High Tory rioting began in October.[118]

There was already seething discontent in Scotland. Glasgow was the only short-term beneficiary of Union following the expansion in colonial trade: elsewhere, 'by 1712 it appeared that Scotland had become a victim of exploitation by English traders whose merchandise was permitted to invade the north at cheap prices to the prejudice of the Scottish market'. Episcopal toleration in that year stoked a nationalist upsurge: when it was proposed in 1713 to implement the Malt Tax in Scotland in perceived defiance of the Treaty of Union, no less a peer than Argyll, in company with the Earl of Mar, Secretary of State for Scotland, presented a petition to the Queen to dissolve it, and a motion failed in Parliament by a handful of votes. Anne's chilly response: that the Scots 'drive their resentment too far. I wish they may not repent it', was as ever of a piece with her political outlook on such matters.[119] After Anne's death, a petition was launched in Scotland in pursuit of repeal of the Union. Its rejection by George I's Whig ministry guaranteed the opposition of the now nationalist-inclined Earl of Mar and a vast army of 20000 men: the Rising of 1715, to, in King James's words, 'restore the Kingdom to its ancient free and independent state . . . a free and independent Scots Parliament'.[120]

2

MILITARY GOALS AND OTHER MEANS

Redeem the Nation and Restore the King

Queen Anne had strong sympathy with traditional Anglican culture, being the last reigning monarch to use the Royal Touch (Samuel Johnson was one of the latest beneficiaries of this sacramental ritual). As a result of these elements in her character and politics, the Queen did not especially favour the Whigs, with their traditional guilt by association with the Civil War: 'Save the Queen's White Neck' was a Tory electioneering slogan. As a consequence, the Whigs sought rather to curry favour with her successor: some even suggested the possibility of a Hanoverian invasion on one occasion.[1] Given the hostility to the Hanoverian dynasty shown by even non-Jacobite Tories, foreign policy differences, the High Church character of the party and the Jacobite equivocations of many of its supporters, it is perhaps not surprising that George I inclined on his accession towards the Whigs. The Tories, deeply suspicious of a Lutheran king's intentions towards the Church of England, fought the 1715 election on the theme of the Church in Danger, with a degree of exaggerated scaremongering that might well have appeared crypto-Jacobite. The Whigs won in seats if not in votes, and proceeded to justify the paranoia of their opponents by commencing impeachment proceedings against Robert Harley, Earl of Oxford, Viscount Bolingbroke, the Earl of Strafford and the Duke of Ormond 'for their part in the secret peace negotiations with France' in the formulation of the Peace of Utrecht.[2] In March (before in fact impeachment proceedings had begun: indeed, perhaps Marlborough's recommendation to St John to fly helped provoke them) Bolingbroke fled to France. Ormond followed in the summer, thus depriving the coming English rising of its main commander. Oxford and Strafford stood their ground: both survived impeachment, and Strafford in particular became a key player in future Jacobite plots, being elevated to a Stuart dukedom in 1722.[3]

Early signs of discontent in England focused on the West Midlands in particular, where the first Jacobite club had been established in Staffordshire in 1699.[4] Slogans such as 'Sacheverell for ever, Down with the Roundheads' were shouted at riots on 20 October, George's Coronation Day,[5] while on 1 December 1714, James was proclaimed king 'in Devonshire and elsewhere'.[6] The year which followed brought prolonged disturbances, the geographical pattern of which significantly matched that of areas which had supported King Charles in the 1640s.[7] On 28 May 1715, George's birthday, crowds gathered at the Stock Exchange (a hated example of Whig principle in action), shouting 'High Church and the Duke of Ormonde', while at Cheapside they shouted 'Down with the Rump', 'No Hanoverian, no Presbyterian Government'.[8] On 29 May, the anniversary of the Restoration, the shouts at Cheapside changed to 'A Restoration, a Stewart, High Church and Ormonde' (Ormond himself had not at this time left the country: perhaps it was unsurprising that he did so soon after demonstrations such as this).[9] The time around 10 June 1715 was the peak, with extensive rioting and 500 arrests in Shropshire, Staffordshire and Worcestershire.[10] Nonconformist chapels were a major target for the High Church mob: there were attacks on them in the counties of Shropshire, Denbighshire, Montgomeryshire, Oxfordshire, Somerset, Staffordshire, Warwickshire, Yorkshire and Lancashire.[11] At Birmingham, the Coronation Day mob shouted 'Down with the Roundheads, and the Rump, no Kingkillers, Sacheverel for ever'.[12] Most of the major towns of England and Wales saw disturbance on some level: no fewer than 57 of them witnessing Jacobite rioting in 1715–22, and every town over 10000, 'Colchester and Great Yarmouth excepted', saw public displays of aversion to the new regime'.[13] In Lancashire and the West Midlands in particular, it can be argued that Jacobite activity took on the lineaments of 'a coalition of Tory gentleman and tradesmen with skilled labourers'. Although such disturbances died down rapidly in the 1720s in most areas, these two regions proved a resilient source of discontent until much later in the century.[14]

In Scotland, the situation was somewhat different. The Union had drastically curtailed the number of parliamentary seats available, thus quite probably increasing levels of corruption in the hunt to obtain them. Powerful magnates retained control over who was elected to the remaining seats to a greater degree than in England: witness the Duke of Argyll's 'iron grip' on his home county from 1707 to 1715. At the same time, there was an Anglicizing process taking place in party politics, with a tendency for the old Jacobite Cavaliers to call themselves Tories; likewise the Episcopalians who supported them sought favour under Anne's administration by describing themselves as 'the Church of England here in Scotland'.[15] Yet these Unionist trends, whose surface quiescence no doubt deceived the British authorities more than once in the first half of the eighteenth century, concealed a more complex reality. The local magistracies and the expanding professions were alike steeped in Jacobitism (the fuss when the Faculty of Advocates accepted the gift of James VIII's portrait in 1712 was evidence of this), as were many of the magnate networks outside the far north and west. Jacobite clubs, like the Easy Club at Edinburgh, hid under their English vocabulary and nomenclature a sturdy anti-Unionist Jacobitism. Allan Ramsay, one of the Club's leading lights, became a principal agent in the defence of vernacular Scots and the patriot publishing culture of this milieu. While writing for a new British market, Ramsay also composed coded calls to Scots independence and to 'James with his Golden Reign restore'. His son, who became court painter to George III, visited the Jacobite court in Rome in 1736 and may have painted Flora Mac-Donald in the late 1740s.[16] There were many less distinguished families like them: one reason why neither in 1715 nor 1745 could the government rely on those whose *prima facie* politics should have committed them to the Hanoverian cause. For one thing, in 1715 especially, many patriotic Scots of Whiggish outlook found themselves with nowhere to go other 'than Jacobitism . . . if they wished to free Scotland from English domination'.[17] In support of this James published a declaration on 15 October 1714, in which he promised 'to relieve our Subjects of Scotland, from the hardships they groan under on account of the late unhappy Union, and to restore the Kingdom to its ancient free and independent state'.[18] Opposition to the Union was the single most important issue in Scottish domestic politics in 1715, and this opposition was strongly, if not solely Jacobite. It was widely felt that the Union had been a mistake: Scotland was as much subject to English political priorities as ever, with little say in its domestic affairs and increasingly heavily taxed, with worse to come. As *A Discourse of the Necessity and Seasonableness of an unanimous Address for Dissolving the UNION* (1715) put it: 'sure I am, the Advantage that Nation has [England], is not equally sensible to them as our loss is to us'.[19] Jacobitism was the main means of expressing that discontent. Indeed, despite political pressures, 16 of the 45 Scottish seats in the 1710 election had been taken by 'committed Jacobites', representing areas such as Fife, Perthshire, Dumfriesshire, Forfarshire, Wigton Burghs, Ross-shire, Aberdeen, Aberdeenshire, Inverness Burghs, Lanarkshire, Linlithgowshire and Linlithgow.[20] The vast majority of these areas provided a plentiful supply of troops in 1715.

Civil disturbances in Scotland in this period were less pronounced than in England, but this was simply the calm before the storm. Jacobite protest tended to come in waves in English society, its high point being in 1715; in Scotland, it was more endemic: in what was, north of Forth at least, essentially a Jacobite society, there was little need for Jacobite rioting. Nonetheless, there was some disturbance. Both in 1712 and 1713 there had been large-scale celebrations of James's birthday (10 June) in Edinburgh and Leith;[21] in 1714 there were further disturbances, and a military wapenschaw at Lochmaben in the south-west. On 21 August, the Earl of Mar, at that time still Secretary of State for Scotland, commented on the unrest in favour of 'the Pretender'.[22]

Mar was not long to call James by that name. Following the failure of Scotland's anti-Union petitioning, and his own lack of success in gaining the ear of the new government, Mar set about devoting himself to developing plans for a proposed rising, which he committed to paper on 5 July 1715, a few weeks before returning to his estates to put it into action. Under this plan, James was to land on Holy Island or the coast between Newcastle and Berwick with a French force. In a rerun of the 1708 plans, the Jacobites would seize the Newcastle coalfields. Mar's plan, which he implemented at least in part unilaterally, was not properly co-ordinated with the plans for a west of England rising fomented by Ormond and now in the hands of Lord Lansdowne.[23]

Bolingbroke, from 12 July the exiled King's Secretary of State, prioritized the descent on the south-west of England, and consulted neither potential supporters in Northumbria nor Scotland in pursuing this plan, taking it for granted that they would provide a diversionary theatre only. This breakdown in communication and rift in the focus of Jacobite activity was to cost the Rising of 1715 dear, the more so when no landing was made in the south-west, and those who gathered in support of it proved amateurish and disorganized: the muster near Bath in September 1715, for example, ' saw a good number of West Country Tory gentlemen turn up, mill about, and go home when nobody appeared to take command'.[24] By this time, an increasingly well-informed government had already acted: Lansdowne was taken, as were other conspirators including Sir William Wyndham and Lieutenant-Colonel Paul of the Foot Guards who was attempting to enlist men for James.

A proclamation of the King in Cornwall went off at half-cock and by the end of September the Rising was over in the south-west, a full month before Ormond's continental preparations were ready. Meanwhile, Mar had begun the northern Rising without James's knowledge.[25] Mar was subsequently to claim that Bolingbroke had failed to supply the Scots, an accusation which, combined with the Viscount's loose talk to his French friends, destroyed his credit with the Jacobites (Mar replaced him as Secretary of State). Ormond retained his reputation despite his flight, and the fact that his secretary, Sir John Maclean, betrayed Jacobite plans to the government: as a result of his information, most of the Tory MPs in Devon and Cornwall were arrested.[26] On the other hand, Mar himself had much to cover up, having raised the standard of the Rising at a time more to do with his personal position than coherent integration with the rest of the Jacobite plans: though it could be argued that the West Country Jacobites had fatally delayed their initiative. In any case, Mar was not the man to rescue it, though once he heard of the Earl's intentions in mid-September, James tried earnestly to persuade his half-brother, the Duke of Berwick, to be Captain-General of the Rising. Unfortunately, Berwick's acceptance of French citizenship in 1704 now compromised him, as the general officer of a power formally at peace with Britain under the terms of Utrecht. What Berwick could have done with Mar's 50 battalions is only to be guessed at, but with the suspected half-Jacobite Marlborough holding no command among the Hanoverian generals entrusted with defeating Jacobite hopes, the chances are at least fair that the Duke, as one of Europe's four leading commanders, would have triumphed.[27]

By the summer of 1715, the government was wary in Scotland as well as in England, and action was initiated against some of the main Jacobite suspects. George Lockhart of Carnwath, the prime parliamentary focus of Jacobite activity in the 1710–14 administration and later one of James's chief agents in Scotland, was arrested and taken into custody in Edinburgh Castle in August: the troop of horse that came out from Carnwath ended up being commanded by a Major Fraser.[28] On 4 August, three days after Mar returned to his estates, more solid reports started to surface of Jacobite activity; by 15 August there were signs of frequent meetings between Jacobite magnates.[29] On 8 August 1715 Sir Peter Frazer of Durris wrote in concern to the Lord Justice Clerk that 'the situation of his Majesty's [i.e. George's] friends and servants is in a very bad condition in this part of Britain .... We hear of nothing but distributing commissions, receiving of arms and Linnen cloaths making for the Regiments.'[30] On his estates, Mar was viewed as impregnable. A gathering of men was arranged under cover of a *tinchal*, or hunt, and 800 arrived. Soon many more poured in, and the standard of King James was raised at Braemar on 6 September. On it (or possibly on that raised afterwards by Viscount Kenmure in the south) was the lettering *Nemo me impune lacessit* ('Wha' daur meddle wi' me') the motto of Scotland, and beneath the words 'No union'. Two pendants bore the legends 'for our wronged king and oppressed country' and 'for ourselves and liberties'.[31] As Mar promised Spalding of Ashentullie on the offer to him of a colonel's commission, 'whether James landed or not the intention was to march south, dissolve the Union and redress the grievances of Scotland'. Whether James landed or not, nationalism was the key motivating factor in the massive military strength of the '15.[32] Argyll himself noted that north of the Forth, 'excepting our few friends in the North and those of my vassals in the West Highlands, they [the Jacobites] have a hundred to one at least in their favour'. On his own estates, half of Argyll's Campbell clansmen were 'in favour of a Scottish rising against Union'.[33] In 1745, even when Jacobite nationalism was still strong, the Stuart heir took weeks of charm and handwringing persuasion to gather a small army together; 30 years earlier, thousands flocked to the standard months before James arrived in his 'ancient kingdom'. True to the nature of his support, Mar 'sent orders to all the towns to pay the taxes and duties only on the old Scots footing'.[34]

Almost at once, two marquesses and eight earls joined Mar,[35] and lost little time in seizing control of their localities. On 13 September, Brigadier Mackintosh of Borlum proclaimed 'James the Eight' at Inverness; on the 14th, Perth fell; on 20 September, the Earl Marischal proclaimed the King at the town cross in Aberdeen; two days later, the government lost control of the city.[36] James was also proclaimed on the 20th by the Marquess of Huntly at Gordon Castle; by Lord Panmure at Brechin; by Lord Ogilvy and Viscount Dundee in Dundee; by the Earl of Southesk at Montrose and by Lord Tullibardine at Dunkeld. The Master of Sinclair proclaimed the King at St Andrews, Crail, Anstruther, Elie and throughout Fife.[37] All these counties were raised.[38] Many of the local gentry and professionals lent their support, including in Aberdeen Sir James Abercromby, former MP for Banff in the Scots Parliament, James Burnett of Monboddo, father of the distinguished Enlightenment thinker Lord Monboddo, Dr Patrick Abercromby, sometime physician to James VII and II, and author of *Martial Achievements of the Scottish Nation* and the Earl of Aboyne.[39] Dr Abercromby gave 4000 *pistoles* to the cause.[40]

Thousand upon thousand rallied to the Jacobite standard. On 16 September, a beleaguered Lord Justice Clerk complained of another rendezvous at Pinkie under the Earl of Wintoun, noting also with dismay 'the Jacobite tendencies of the gentry of Dumfries'. On 14 September, the day after Argyll had received his troops at Berwick, it was clear that there was 'nobody in arms for King George; yet throughout Scotland the Rebels were either armed or ready to rise'. Argyll informed the government that if he fought, his army would be lost, but that if he retired 'the country is lost'.[41] An address was printed at Edinburgh calling for an end to 'the late unhappy union', which had resulted in a 'packed up Assembly which calls itself a British parliament'.[42] By mid-autumn, Mar had accumulated a vast host, almost the maximum size of army which could be recruited from the nation's population: as many as one in twelve adult males joined it.[43]

Nor by any means was this merely a Highland army. One government source, estimating Mar's force at 17 700, detected only 4100 Highlanders: though this is admittedly almost certainly too few, as some 75 per cent of clan fighting strength appears to have been raised, compared with 48 per cent in 1745 and a mere 35 per cent in 1689–91.[44] Nonetheless, there were certainly comparable numbers of Lowlanders involved. As Bruce Lenman puts it:

> It must be appreciated that the towns tended to be every bit as keenly Jacobite as the landward areas. The burghs had been particularly resentful at the imposition of an English-style Customs and Excise administration after the Act of Union . . . smuggling had rapidly become a well-regarded national industry. . . . Nationalist emotions . . . could only find expression in Jacobite actions.[45]

At its peak, Mar's force (including southern and English levies) had over 50 battalions: up to 20000 men.[46] Major (later Lieutenant)-General George Hamilton served as deputy to Mar, with the Marquess of Drummond and Gordon of Auchintoul also lieutenants-general; the Earl Marischal, the Marquess of Tullibardine, Viscount Kilsyth, Viscount Kenmure and by courtesy Thomas Buchan were majors-general, while Ogilvie of Boyne, Lord Inverness, the Earls of Linlithgow and Southesk and Mackintosh of Borlum were among the brigadiers.[47] The tendency to over-officer the Jacobite army was noticeable, and remarked on by the Master of Sinclair and the Revd Robert Patten: Patten, a Nonjuring priest who preached for the Jacobite forces at Kelso, went on to turn King's Evidence against them.[48]

With the West Country front undermined by Ormond's flight, Maclean's betrayal, Bolingbroke's incompetence, Jacobite hesitancy and government decision, Louis XIV's death on 21 August and the coming to power of the notably less enthusiastic Regent Orléans created further problems for the Jacobites. In Northumbria, the English Jacobites proved to have inadequate strength and (like their southern counterparts) poor co-ordination. The authorities probably took them too seriously: but they had the Pilgrimage of Grace and the northern Rising of 1570 to remember. In particular, the government fear that the keelmen of Newcastle would go over to the Jacobites seems to have shown no political judgement beyond standard establishment terror of the mob.[49] The Stuart forces made an initial rendezvous on 6 October on what is now the A68: as with Mar, government suspicion drove them to show their hand too soon. They were so short of arms that infantry volunteers were turned away.[50] After an initial success in the capture of Holy Island on 10 October, recaptured the next day when the Jacobite commander, local MP Thomas Forster, failed to reinforce it, the small army of five troops of horse dithered.[51] James III was proclaimed at Alnwick and Morpeth, but the advance on Newcastle, which alone had much meaning in military terms, was not attempted. This was no surprise, given that Forster's force consisted of no more than 350 men with 'swords and whips', and as Newcastle was not betrayed from within, the Jacobites could do little but turn aside and proclaim their king meaninglessly at Hexham. On the day James was proclaimed in Morpeth, two French ships appeared off Holy Island: if the Jacobites could have held it for a few days more, they would have received support: indeed, 'a convergence of English, Scottish and seaborne Jacobite forces' such as this promised could have changed the direction of the war.[52]

When the British army reinforced Newcastle in the third week of October, Forster had little option but to retreat to Scotland, where he joined Kenmure and Brigadier Mackintosh at Kelso on the 22nd: shortly afterwards James was proclaimed by Kenmure and the Earl of Dunfermline and a manifesto against the Union published.[53] Mackintosh had been detached from Mar's main force early in October to strike at Edinburgh and split the Duke of Argyll's government army, a move which failed as much as anything because Mar declined to attack the weakened portion remaining at Stirling, even though he outnumbered it six to one. General Gordon was likewise despatched on a fruitless mission to Argyllshire. Mar was more interested in diluting his army's effectiveness than using it.[54] As the Duke of Argyll wrote, 'if the enemy think fit to act with vigour that men of common sense would, in their circumstances, the handful of troops now in Scotland may be beat out of the country'. Subsequently Borlum, lacking precise orders, linked up with Jacobite forces in the south-west.[55]

They were not long permitted to rally there unhindered. On 27 October, General Carpenter advanced to Wooler with about 900 men: a force the Jacobites could have smashed, but with whom they declined battle in favour of a feint towards Newcastle, followed by a retreat to Dumfries. Lord Widdrington, who was second in rank only to the Earl of Derwentwater among the English Jacobites, claimed that if they crossed over into the north-west of England that 20 000 would join them: his guess was of average Jacobite accuracy, that is to say hopeless. It also, not untypically, led to a disastrous strategic decision. Instead of fighting Carpenter, the Anglo-Scottish force now spilled over the Border in pursuit of easy recruits. Whistling in the dark, they entered Brampton on 1 November. Victory over the county militia at Penrith Fell on 3 November raised Jacobite hopes, but meant little: by Kendal on the next day only three had joined. Six enlisted at Kirkby Lonsdale on 6 November, and when Lord Widdrington appeared on the road to say that 50 had been armed at Manchester, expectations had been so far reduced as to greet this 99.75 per cent reduction in support with a cheer.[56] Matters improved, however, in Lancashire, where perhaps 500 or even 1000 joined, though 'all Papists', to the disappointment of a leadership hungry for Anglican magnate support (75 per cent of all English Jacobites who rose in 1715 were Catholics, far higher than the Scottish proportion).[57] As the Jacobites pushed farther south, Forster, incredibly, relied on the 'assurances of the Lancashire Gentlemen that no force could come near them by forty miles, but they could inform him thereof'. Partly no doubt as a result of this bizarre intelligence service, the whole army was caught at Preston by General Charles Wills (who began life as 'one of the six sons of a debt-harassed Cornish yeoman').[58] Despite a gallant defence of the approach to the town by Lieutenant-Colonel Farquharson of Invercauld at the head of his Aberdeen battalion, Preston was surrounded by Wills, now joined by the undefeated Carpenter. Discounting Scots calls for a breakout, Forster unilaterally surrendered on 14 November. The Rising in England was over.[59]

Mar himself had long since built up critical mass with an army almost as large as any that had been raised in Scotland up to that time, outnumbering effective opposition by five to one: but he delayed before attempting an advance from the Jacobite heartlands into southern Scotland. Mar waited and waited: he waited for French help, he waited for the Duke of Berwick, he waited for the King, he waited for yet more recruits to make his position impregnable. His zestful patience, the product of a political rather than a military sense of timing, was admirable; his soldiers undutifully failed to admire it, and started to drift home.[60] When at last Mar did strike, it was with little decision: and this was of a piece with his life throughout, playing both sides and seldom staking his hand at a critical juncture with any effectiveness, with the result that he died mistrusted by all. Leaving Perth garrisoned by three battalions, Mar moved south on 10 November. Argyll advanced to Dunblane, and placed part of his army on the high ground of Sheriffmuir, leaving Mar with no alternative but to give battle on ground of his enemy's choosing or risk the disintegration of his own army.[61] He faced his opponent with 20 infantry battalions and 8 cavalry squadrons: even though the Jacobites fielded less than half their maximum strength (ignoring the need for concentrated force), Argyll was outnumbered by more than two to one.[62] The Jacobite front line of ten mainly Highland battalions itself probably outweighed the total of the forces opposing it.[63] It was commanded by generals Hamilton and Gordon.[64]

In the early stages of the battle, Mar sent the Earl Marischal with a battalion and two squadrons of horse to try and move Argyll's troops out of position: they succeeded, but at the price of the disorganization of the entire Jacobite line of battle.[65] This broke up and separated the cavalry, who became largely ineffective, and the victorious right wing failed to re-engage the government forces. Mar gave them no orders. The battle ended indecisively, as Mar, consistent in his wavering to the last, omitted to launch his powerful reserves against the remnant of the government forces still on the field, which they outnumbered by four to one.[66] Government losses were at least as great as those of the Jacobites, and may have outweighed them by *three* to one, but still nothing could render Mar capable of victory.[67] A frustrated Master of Sinclair (Gordon of Glenbucket according to some accounts) cried 'O, for an hour of Dundee', amidst the tentative display of badly resourced and incompetently executed military manoeuvres which squandered themselves haphazardly amid the ranks of Argyll's tiny force. With 2000 men, Montrose had won six major victories; with ten times that number, Mar could not fashion one.[68]

Mar's already timorous momentum was stalled, and he fell back on Perth, where he proposed an Association 'never to admit of Terms till the King was restored, the Union broken and the [Episcopal] Church establisht'.[69] This already sounded defensive, and worse was to come.

With Jacobite forces in tatters everywhere but in northern Scotland (admittedly at that time with far more of the country's share of population than it now contains), James landed at Peterhead on 22 December 1715, to join the Rising Mar had begun on his behalf without his orders.[70] The King brought no French support: the Duc d' Orléans was by now proving cagey about even clandestine pro-Jacobite operations.[71] James was welcomed ecstatically by the Episcopalian clergy, the spearhead of the Jacobite intelligentsia in that part of the country, who provided him with a loyal address of welcome to his 'antient kingdom of Scotland' on 29 December. Disloyal Presbyterian ministers were imprisoned.[72] The King proceeded south, making a state entry to Dundee (where the country people strove to touch him) on 6 January and to Perth on the 9th *en route* for a planned coronation at Scone: Jacobite ladies offered their jewellery for his crown, and propaganda coronation poetry was published as part of the preparations, but there is no satisfactory evidence that even a truncated ceremony took place, though a date of 23 January is sometimes given.[73] James nonetheless held a 'spartan court' in Perth for three weeks.[74] Its glory was brief, though the undefeated Argyll's advance was slow, to the chagrin of the government.[75] Eventually on 31 January, James and Mar's dissolving army began to retreat: Mar insisted that James order the burning of Auchterarder, Crieff and Blackford among other towns, in order to stay the advance of the government forces. The King reluctantly agreed to this futile and barbarous act, but insisted on leaving his remaining campaign monies as compensation. Mar's lack of energy and decision now coupled themselves once more with his customary want of scruple, and after a last plea to Orléans, James was bundled on a ship at Montrose, leaving the remnant of his forces to *sauve qui peut* (this proved to be a relatively easy task). Before he took ship, the King wrote a letter to Argyll, which he did not send: in it, he commended Scotland to the Duke, asking him 'if not as an obedient subject, at least as a lover of your country' to care for it and disburse James's remaining monies to relieve its wants. James also asserted that 'it was with the view of delivering this my Kingdom [i.e. Scotland] from the hardships it lies under and restoring it to its former happiness and independency' that he had landed. After James left, Argyll continued to pursue the remaining Jacobite forces under Lieutenant-General Gordon in a leisurely manner: his methods won him no friends in power, and the Jacobites still hoped to win him to their cause as late as the 1740s. In this they were over-optimistic: but the Duke was, after his fashion, a lover of his country, and was reluctant to be partisan. His family was, after all, the protector of a notorious Jacobite outlaw,

Rob Roy: one reason why Rob himself failed to commit his troops to Mar's military melange at Sheriffmuir.[76]

The pursuit of Jacobite fugitives in 1715 was not nearly so marked as in 1745, for at least three reasons: the government was both less secure and had been less at risk, for the terror felt when Charles Edward was at Derby and French regiments feared daily on the south coast was absent in 1715. Second, in Scotland as in Ireland in 1691, the vast bulk of the population was Jacobite, and reprisals would only feed disaffection; third, the Duke of Argyll was a moderate figure, himself more equivocal than was customary in his family towards both the Stuart cause and the Union. In Scotland the local magistracies were saturated with Jacobite sympathisers, and Jacobites were to be found in many of the areas of local government: thus when 16 Jacobite lairds surrendered at Banff in March 1716 they were 'dealt with in a very lenient spirit' by the local JPs.[77] Bonfires on 29 May (to commemorate the 1660 Restoration) and 10 June continued in the north, and reports to the Lord Justice Clerk indicated that Jacobites could move about freely and openly in Banff and Moray.[78]

Leading nobles such as the Marquess of Huntly, who took the opportunity to submit early, were reconciled to the government and quickly released, while others such as the Earls of Nithsdale and Wintoun escaped from prison. Indeed, the number of successful escapees raises suspicions of complicity, despite the notorious lack of security in eighteenth-century prisons: not only Nithsdale and Wintoun, but General Forster and Charles Radcliffe (brother to Derwentwater) walked out of prison in London, while Brigadier Mackintosh, the doughty nationalist Robert Hepburn of Keith and thirteen others found their way out of Newgate.[79] The Edinburgh mob aided escapes from the Tolbooth and Castle in Edinburgh, though one Jacobite was killed falling down the Castle rock.[80] Although nineteen Scottish and two English peers were attainted (12 earls, 3 viscounts and 6 barons), only Derwentwater and Kenmure were executed, as the principal movers in their localities. Some twenty-eight others were hanged, drawn and quartered or shot as deserters, while several hundred were transported.[81] In several cases, the pleadings of family or friends were effective, though when George Collingwood's wife proposed to plead for him, a friend advised, 'I think you are mad when you talk of saving your husband's life. Don't you know you will have five hundred pounds p.a. jointure if he's hanged?' Despite apparently ignoring this advice, Collingwood's wife failed to prevent her husband's being hanged, drawn and quartered on 25 February 1716.[82]

The dying words of those Jacobites who did suffer were widely circulated, particularly those of John Hall JP, who claimed to be 'not a traitor but a martyr' and the Anglican priest Revd William Paul: their final statements were 'sold openly in London for many years after the '15'.[83] Derwentwater's noble end passed into folk culture and the ballad tradition; the northern lights seen at the time of his death becoming known in the north as 'Derwentwater's lights'. Images of him appeared not only in prints, but more cheaply 'on watchpapers or on textiles'.[84] The Jacobites made the most of their martyrs before the government passed its Act of Indemnity in 1717.[85]

Milder purges occurred among the Scottish professional classes, which had offered widespread support to the Jacobites in 1715. Universities, town councils, schools and the clergy, even Presbyterian clergy, had all acted as collaborators with the brief Stuart regime (in Aberdeenshire and Banffshire, a third of the 58 clergy who had come out for the Jacobites were Presbyterians).[86] Among those involved were Patrick Gray, Convener of the Trades of Aberdeen, the ministers of Rothiemay, Lumphanan, Deer, Coull and Alford, James Kid, precentor and schoolmaster of Arbroath, Professor George Liddell of Marischal College, Professor William Meston, the poet, who had been a Jacobite governor; the Principal of King's College, University of Aberdeen, many councillors and deacons of trades in Perth, the father of the Governor of Pennsylvania and a collection of other academics, schoolmasters, solicitors and doctors, not to mention Robert Burns's grandfather.[87] The two universities of Aberdeen in particular were hotbeds of Jacobite sympathies and Jacobite connections (for example, Rob Roy's cousin, James Gregory, was professor of medicine at King's).[88] They were thoroughly purged by the authorities, as were the major schools. More Episcopalian clergy were dislodged (36 in Aberdeen alone, while dragoons were used against congregations in Banffshire and Aberdeenshire), and replaced in some areas by conforming Anglicans who owed their obedience to English or Irish bishops: this procedure was intensified after 1745.[89] Local magistracies likewise were to be rid of their disaffected incumbents: but this attempt proved only partially successful. Even though 261 JPs had been dismissed in August and September 1715, after the Rising had ended the majority of those remaining in the shires of Kincardine, Forfar and possibly Inverness, and 'three in ten of those in Aberdeenshire' still required to be purged.[90] The effect of these changes was to plant government sympathizers more firmly at every level of the cultural leadership of Scottish society in the Lowland counties. In England, where disaffection had been, if riotous, evanescent, isolated prosecutions and a watchful eye served the authorities just as well, except with regard to the Catholic gentry. In their case, two Acts made provision for 'estates given to super-stitious uses' to 'be forfeited' and for 'all Catholic landowners to register their real estates, and all income arising out of landed property', the same to be assessed for Jacobite war reparations. Although by 1721 there were over 1700 'appeals and claims on estates belonging to the Jacobite prisoners', many Catholics evaded the full force of this legis-lation: putting property in trust with Anglicans was one of the means whereby they did so in north-east England, which says more for gentry solidarity than sectarianism. Attempts to negotiate to take the oaths foundered, however, on government unwillingness to abrogate the least tittle of the Penal Laws.[91]

The Rising of 1715 was the reverse of that of 1745, being well manned and badly led, rather than well led and badly manned. Its results em-phasized to Scottish Jacobites what their English and Irish colleagues already knew: that a successful rising was unlikely without committed aid from a foreign power. Its conduct demonstrated the grave difficul-ties faced by the Jacobites in communication and co-ordination, both within the British Isles and across the Channel. As in 1745, a poor do-mestic intelligence service was a major factor in the Jacobite defeat, while events at Preston showed the potential for disagreement between English and Scottish Jacobites. Faced in Britain with a financially power-ful state with major seapower, the Jacobites needed speed to throttle the financial system either through control of commodities (the Newcastle coalfield) or markets (London), while ideally keeping the Navy busy with an invasion force. In 1715, they lost out through the sheer ponder-ousness and indecision of the Rising, features unique to the year when they possessed their strongest army in the field.

Plans, Agents and Ciphers

In the long term, prospects of Jacobite success depended on the con-junction of three things: a foreign alliance, an internal rising on the margins of the United Kingdom and a fifth column at its core. Due to Britain's major Continental engagements, the Jacobites often had the first; they sometimes had the second; but it was the third on which they depended and which, except in Ireland and Scotland north of the Forth, they never reliably possessed. In 1718, the Earl of Stair, 'British Ambassador to Paris, reported . . . that the Jacobites were "much better disposed to drink the Pretender's health than to fight with him"'. This was a judgement which the agents of Jacobite activity seemed incapable of reaching. Employed to find and foment the fifth column, their status depended only too often on the magnificence of their lies. For those who listened to them, Jacobitism was truly the triumph of hope over experience. From the archives a most glorious picture of Jacobite support can be conceived: one of the major comforts of communication within the outlawed movement must have been the warm glow of hyperbole. The only real hope of a fifth column emerging among the many who almost undoubtedly supported the Stuarts in England was through a French landing or a Scottish victory on English soil. Neither ever occurred.[92]

Jacobite dealings with Spain dated back to 1715, when Louis XIV had attempted to circumvent the Treaty of Utrecht by initiating links between his grandson Philip V and the Stuarts with the aim of setting up a Spanish subvention to Jacobite activity. An alliance between the Stuarts and Spain resulted, where James recognized Spanish continental ambitions and the aim of re-Catholicizing the British Isles in return for the promise of £100000, £36000 of which had been handed over by the end of 1715. The Catholicizing clause was unrealistic and unenforceable: it was also humiliating for James and a potentially major embarrassment. Almost the only face-saving aspect of the agreement was that the Spaniards did not insist on the return of Gibraltar or Minorca in the event of a restoration.[93]

After the failure of the '15, Spain (which had paid over the bulk of its subvention, though £15000 had been lost off St Andrews in January 1716) began to lose interest in the Jacobites: but Philip V granted James a secret pension as an insurance policy.[94] A commercial treaty with the Hanoverian government had been negotiated as early as December 1715, and the hope of improving relations led to Spanish attempts to recover territory lost in southern Italy, counting on British indifference. Unfortunately for Philip V and Cardinal Alberoni his chief minister, Austria resented the affront to its own position in Italy, and Austria was 'perhaps Britain's single most important European ally'.[95] Alberoni began to turn back to the Jacobites, whose hopes had in the meantime become entwined with those of Charles XII of Sweden, who was being both provoked by the Royal Navy and irritated by Hanover's attempts on former Swedish territory in Bremen and Verden. The Swedes were to agree to provide a Protestant army (a huge bonus, this) in return for money. As with Frederick the Great's Prussia later in the century, negotiations dragged, and fizzled out with the death of Charles XII in 1718.[96] Following the destruction of the main Spanish fleet by Admiral Byng in August 1718, Alberoni moved once more to give direct Spanish support to the Jacobite cause. The Duke of Ormond arrived in Madrid in December, and promoted the idea of a diversionary Scottish bridgehead as well as a landing of Spanish troops in southwestern England: he suggested the Earl Marischal as its leader. In February 1719 Marischal was promised only two ships, 2000 stand of arms (rifle, bayonet, sword), and 'a very small body of Spanish regulars' in contrast to the 5000 men and 30 000 stand promised to the main expedition.[97]

The French government, with whom Spain was at odds following a plot against the Regent Orléans, gave such information as it had to London. Major-General the Earl Marischal sailed at the end of February, arriving safely in the Outer Hebrides : the Spanish force with him was indeed a token one, being a solitary battalion's worth of 327 men in six picquets (just under 50 men plus officers, hand-picked from their parent units).[98] The Marquess of Tullibardine (Jacobite Duke of Atholl) attempted to trump Marischal's commission with his own, and there was some dissension among the leadership as a result. On Marischal's advice, the Jacobite force advanced towards Inverness without having any confirmation of Ormond's landing in the south (as a matter of fact, his fleet had been ruined in a storm).[99] Their store of *matériel* was the main strength they brought to the theatre of war in Scotland, and this was stored in an exposed position in Eilean Donan castle, and destroyed by Royal Navy bombardment on 10 May. The government acted quickly and decisively by both land and sea, Major-General Wightman advancing with 1100 men to meet the Jacobites as they moved through the West Highlands. The small armies met in Glenshiel on 10 June. Wightman's well-emplaced artillery kept the Spaniards pinned down, while the Scots Jacobites, with three or four small battalions and a couple of freestanding companies (including one led by Rob Roy) lacked the critical mass to break the British position: in any case, they were spread over too wide a front. The battle, which was mostly a firefight, ended when the Spaniards tried to escape over the pass behind them and some of the Scots levies took to their heels. Wightman took 274 Spanish prisoners, and the disastrous venture of the '19 was over.[100] It was more than a token defeat in a number of ways, for it showed Hanoverian ability to overcome the Jacobites in their heartland; moreover, although relatively few rank-and-file Jacobites had been raised to fight, quite a number of senior figures had shown their hand, among them the Marquess of Seaforth, Scotland's third most

powerful magnate in military terms (after Atholl and Argyll), and Lord
George Murray, who had some sort of conversion experience while on
the run after the battle. Cardinal Alberoni lost his office following
Spain's ill-judged support for this enterprise.[101]

James's peripatetic Court moved from Avignon to Urbino to Rome
by 1719. If this was unsettling and appeared to render him even more
marginal, his marriage to the Polish princess Clementina Sobieska in
August 1719 boosted Jacobite hopes, which were further raised by the
birth of a son, Charles Edward, on 20 December 1720. Meanwhile, the
South Sea Bubble crisis of that year renewed openings for Jacobite disaffection in England. The Bubble, England's first major stock-market
crash, was not only an economic setback for the speculating classes:
because of the South Sea Company's association with the government
through its undertaking to repay the National Debt, the administration
itself was implicated in the company's collapse, both corporately and
through the many individuals who had made money from the stock.
The Duchess of Kendal, George I's mistress, was one of two senior
noblewomen who had 'received £36000 in unpaid-for South Sea
stock'. It is even possible that King George himself was 'privy to the
frauds' which presaged the company's collapse. Indeed, Roger Knight,
'chief cashier to the South Sea Company', revealed the accounts to
King James 'as evidence . . . against George I and his German favour-
ites'. The odour of corruption was strong, and the time appeared right
for a Jacobite attempt against a discredited regime.[102]

Five peers, lords Orrery, North, Grey, Strafford and Arran were involved, besides Atterbury, the Bishop of Rochester, who was effectively 'head of James's affairs in England'.[103] The plan was to resuscitate
the Spanish connection, using foreign arms to foment a domestic rising
supported by a landing of Irish regiments, to which the French Government would 'turn a blind eye'.[104] General Dillon, the prospective commander of the invasion force, was King James's agent in Paris, while the
Scots MP Alexander Urquhart (probably a double agent) was used as
a go-between by the Jacobites in contact with the government in the
person of the Earl of Sunderland; Argyll also entered discussions with
James's supporters.[105] In April 1722, Alderman John Barber, subsequently Lord Mayor of London, 'left for Rome with £50000 in bills of
exchange': the same amount again was sent to France and Spain, from
which latter up to 12000 arms were expected. The hope was that disaffected non-commissioned officers (more senior ranks had been largely
purged at the time of the '15) could be stirred to spearhead a revolt in
which London would be raised along with much of the south of the

country. It seems in retrospect a futile hope, though large numbers of weapons were found both at Bristol and Reading and in the capital after the plot had failed to mature.[106] The Duc d'Orléans's Regency in the person of Cardinal Dubois felt obliged (as in 1719) to inform the British government of the plot once it became too visible for France to ignore, and a number of critical arrests were made, including that of Christopher Layer, the front man and a member of the Nonjuring tradition which was still very strong in his native Norfolk.[107] Layer was hanged, drawn and quartered; Atterbury was exiled for ten years along with Lords Grey and North (who later became lieutenant-general in the Spanish service), and the plot collapsed.[108] By virtue of its secret nature, however, much still remains to be discovered concerning it: one of the more intriguing features undoubtedly being the close proximity to the plot of the household and occasionally persons of some great Whig magnates, including the Earl of Burlington. The possibility certainly exists that the Atterbury Plot had quite widespread support among the disaffected in the English Establishment: whether it could have raised a popular revolt is quite another matter.[109] Nonetheless, scaremongering in connection with the Plot proved effective, especially when linked to the agricultural disturbances being promoted in the south of England by the likes of the Windsor Blacks, and severe new laws for the protection of property and an extension to the number of capital offences were the result. What E. P. Thompson called the 'complicity between the ascendancy of the Hanoverian Whigs and the ascendancy of the gallows' was the result of the persistent challenge to property rights made possible by a regime which had subverted the property rights of the Stuart monarchy, the Nonjurors, the Catholics and all who actively promoted their cause.[110]

Jacobite diplomatic successes were nearly always dependent on factors beyond the control of the Stuarts because of the inherently limited influence of an exiled and homeless dynasty, however courteously treated. Nor were they the only dynasty in this position.[111] Favoured for many years by English belligerence towards France, the Treaty of Utrecht undermined Jacobite hopes, dislodged James's court, and made the financing and equipping of the movement largely dependent on hole-in-corner relationships which could cost dearly in credibility, like that with Spain in 1715. There were persisting hopes of action from Sweden or Russia: but neither had the lasting strategic interest in the British Isles necessary to plan a serious invasion, nor the ability to deliver one if planned. The idea of Peter the Great outmanoeuvring the Royal Navy he was so keen to imitate and learn from was always an unlikely one. France and to a lesser extent Spain were the key states for Jacobite hopes: but support from both was easily undercut by conciliatory or threatening moves in British foreign policy. Sir Robert Walpole's peace policy in the 1720s and 1730s was thus deeply disabling for the Jacobites, whose opportunities, like those arising through Lord Cornbury's plot of 1733–35, were weak, feeble and transitory ones. Cornbury's designs to secure a French landing and internal rising, based on discontent with Walpole's Excise policy and French irritation with Britain's Austrian diplomacy, failed to receive official backing from Louis XV's administration and faded quietly away.[112] Like Harley before him, however, Walpole was not above staying in touch with the Jacobite bogeyman whom he so frequently invoked: for example he wrote 'a pretended offer of service' to James in 1739.[113]

Mar in exile became a double agent in an attempt to rehabilitate himself with the British government, from whom he accepted a pension of £2000 a year in 1721.[114] At the same time, he was still in James's confidence and suggesting various schemes to the King. Despite his own role in bringing the Union about, there was definitely a nationalist tinge to Mar's thought: for example, one of his plans included provision for an independent Scotland and Ireland garrisoned by French troops, though it has been suggested that this was mooted as a bait to discredit James.[115] Nonetheless, it was a theme which Mar (now a Jacobite duke) returned to more than once in his slippery career: for example, in a letter to the Cameronians of 31 October 1718, in which James through Mar promises the 'unhappy union . . . null and void from the beginning'.[116] Despite the remarkable coincidence of the usefulness of his correspondence in providing the British government with incriminating evidence in the Atterbury Plot, it was not until 1725 that Mar's double-dealing was finally brought home to James.[117]

British espionage was on the whole pretty effective, not least in times of military crisis such as the '45. Once the Jacobite court was established in Rome, a sophisticated network of informers was developed, which seems to have allowed the Government greater knowledge of Jacobite affairs than they had possessed in the days of St-Germain. This could of course cause problems: British travellers 'were from time to time embarrassed by the attempts of the Jacobite Court to help them diplomatically' by the securing of passports and so on in an area so well policed by their own government's spies. 'Minor spies' who 'would report on the day-to-day activities of the Jacobites and pry into their mail' were dealt with by the British Consul at Leghorn; 'higher officials . . . tried to fathom the political motives behind such details'.[118]

British secret agency was not without its problems, however. Not only was there defection to the other side (as with the case of Thomas Chamberlayne, British Consul at Messina, who joined the Jacobites in 1731 and was subsequently used in an assassination attempt against a British spy in Florence); there was also the vulnerability of the British civil service to downright lies. Since money was paid for information on the Jacobites, a great deal of factitious material was peddled for reward, and a stream of informers making up stories for money was a continuing difficulty for the authorities.[119] Nonetheless, they had the upper hand, for unfortunately, like most anti-establishment groups, the Jacobite intelligence service was riven by distrust of its own fifth column, a fear exacerbated by religious and national differences. This was particularly marked in disagreements between the Scots and English: 'the Scotch & English has always been like Doggs & Catts; & now worse than Ever', as the government agent John Semple put it in 1725.[120]

Letter-writing was a risky business for obvious reasons, and much Jacobite conspiracy took place *sub rosa*, in unattributable discussions 'under the rose' (both the white rose and the central rose of ceilings in the period).[121] When Jacobite correspondence was entered into, it was usually in code, some of which merely involved the substitution of one name by another, or even by a dash after an initial letter: it was as a result virtually transparent as to subject, even if individuals could not always be identified. For example, the use of 'Corsica' as a code for 'Britain' and the 'Master' for King James hardly required great resources to understand, while the Jacobite tendency to describe one of their own number as 'honest' was only one of a series of political *double-entendres* which were comprehended by and formed part of the humour of eighteenth-century society. Interest in Jacobite 'codes, cryptograms, symbols' reached its height in the aftermath of the Atterbury Plot, causing 'great public interest in the hidden significance of an apparently innocuous vocabulary'. Jonathan Swift explored and mocked the whole process in his treatment of Lagado in *Gulliver's Travels* (1726): 'A sieve signified a court lady, a lame dog an invader (an obvious reference to the evidence given in the Atterbury Plot), a chamber-pot a committee of grandees. No parody of Swift's could have exceeded the absurdities of reality.'[122]

Jacobitism could not participate fully in the controversialism of the popular press in England because of its position before the law. Nonetheless, quasi-Jacobite journals such as *Mist's* developed a considerable popularity, delivering sales of up to 10 000 copies with its coded commentary on affairs of the day: indeed, the total readership of Jacobite journals has been estimated at 200 000, of the same order as the government press.[123] Among the themes explored was the new attitude to property rights caused by the deposition of the monarch, with its undertones of challenge to primogeniture and patriarchy itself. One letter in *Mist's*, for example, suggests that the amount of money possessed by successful Whigs is less important to a marriageable woman than the corruption of the social order which they represent: 'Gold will not reconcile her to a King-killer . . . she'll never yield to be one Flesh, in Subjection to a Wretch that does not think it his Duty to be obedient to his Sovereign.' The patriarchal rights of Whig husbands are abrogated by their politics, despite the fact that they wish to be 'always absolute . . . they'll not allow the Father of the People [i.e. James]'. *Mist's* also provided coded allusions on a range of levels to the Jacobite cause and its leader.[124] James was even portrayed as a flaming sun-god, following the Augustus of Horace's Ode of renewal (*Odes* IV:5) ('Bring back the light, good leader, to the land'),[125] and the double link of the Stuart claimant to Christian symbolism (he was, like Charles I, a suffering servant) and the Aeneas of Vergil's epic lay at the core of much early eighteenth-century Jacobite high culture: the sly political symbolism of John Dryden's translation of the *Aeneid* (itself a pro-Stuart text as far back as the Interregnum) being a case in point. The double nature and dynastic ambivalence of 'Augustanism' in the early to mid-eighteenth century is as yet imperfectly realized.[126]

If Nathaniel Mist himself was not infrequently in trouble with the law, there were others yet further out on the Jacobite fringes, such as Francis Clifton, who distributed 'lost lover' ballads throughout the London area via itinerant singing men: James was the absent lover, whose return would revitalize the land (love-songs current at the time which mention 'James', 'Jamie' or 'Jemmy' are frequently linked to this amorous Jacobitism of loss). He was also a native king, the king of the oak tree and of the English countryside, which had been used as far back as the Civil War period to symbolize Stuart order.[127] Popular rural Jacobitism shared the same emphases, revolving as it did round the springtime Stuart festivals of 29 May and 10 June (rue and thyme were worn in mourning on 28 May, George I's birthday, the day before the return of the 'Garland King' in 1660).[128] One Clifton woodcut of 1720 showed

> a lady and a gentleman [James and Clementina Sobieski], roses [Stuart emblem, possibly first used in the 1340s], flaming hearts [suffering loyalty], a ship on the water [invasion], an empty throne [Hanoverian flight and Stuart restoration], a crowned king hiding in an oak tree [Charles II, renewal, fertil-

ity and patriotism] and a butler [the Duke of Ormond, whose family name was Butler].[129]

The native, patriot quality of English Jacobite propaganda was not seriously challenged until the development of the Patriot Whig opposition to Robert Walpole in the 1730s.[130] Indeed, the Patriot Whigs themselves may have drawn on the presence of a Whiggish element in Jacobite thinking, which stressed the arbitrary high-handedness of Parliament over the succession and emphasized that William's and George's primary concerns were with continental politics and priorities designed to defend the interests of Holland and Hanover.[131] There was a lot of truth in this claim, which moreover found a ready echo in the xenophobia of more traditional Jacobitism:

> O Scotland, thou'rt o'er cauld a hole
> For nursing siccan vermin;
> But the very dogs o England's court,
> They bark and howl in German.[132]

In Scotland, Jacobite propaganda unsurprisingly centred on the Union: George Lockhart of Carnwath, James's most active agent, 'was emphatic that repeal of the Act of Union had to be the main plank in the Jacobite platform', both in the 1719 Rising and subsequently.[133] This was a profitable approach because the British government insisted on making small breaches in the Union: for example the Malt Tax, which was perceived as a differential tax in England's favour. Troops were needed to quell anti-malt tax riots in Glasgow in 1725.[134] Certainly Jacobitism had a broader and more enduring base in Scotland: one can get a sense of its institutional breadth and strength from Lockhart's own correspondence, concerned as it is with the administration of Church and nation rather than the minutiae of feverish conspiracies.[135] As Bruce Lenman confirms, 'north of the Forth the great majority of the nobility and gentry retained strong Episcopalian sympathies, and the Episcopalian clergy who ministered to these sympathies themselves tended increasingly to Jacobite views of a very violent kind'.[136]

The growth of Anglican landownership in Ireland and the consolidation of a Church of Ireland ascendancy meant that 'the Catholic Irish had nowhere else to go' but Jacobitism for almost all the eighteenth century, certainly at a popular level, although the Stuart-appointed hierarchy was more equivocal: clergy nonetheless were involved in recruitment for the Irish Brigades.[137] Jacobite propaganda tended primarily to be distributed in two forms: songs and poetry prophesying the return of the Stuart king (usually with foreign aid) as Ireland's saviour from the Saxon oppressor and recruiting matter for the Irish Brigades. These troops in the French service recruited in their home country continuously during this period, despite the death penalty which they often risked. Recruitment material for the Brigades suggested that they were to be part of an invasion force to restore both the Stuarts and Ireland to their proper place. This mixture of dynastic and national patriotism was visible in Brigade culture on the Continent: for example, James Cantillon, captain of the grenadier company in Dorrington's Regiment, advanced at the head of his men at Malplaquet in 1709 (where James III and VIII himself fought as a brigadier in the Maison du Roi), shouting '*Forward, brave Irishmen ! Long live King James III, and the King of France*'.[138] Sometimes such patriotic motifs were used, as in Jonathan Swift's *A Modest Proposal* (1729), as a symbolic if oblique threat to the British government if it should fail to improve its treatment of Ireland. Swift himself, despite his Anglican office, very likely had links with the 'hidden Ireland' of the Gaelic Catholic poets, a group almost universally Jacobite.[139] Swift's own position on Jacobitism appears to have been equivocal, and still intrigues scholars:[140] but in Ireland one thing was clear, and that was that the Stuart cause's subservience to nationalism was more decisively marked even than was the case in Scotland: the transference of Jacobite messianic sentiments to Daniel O'Connell, himself the nephew of a general in the Irish Brigades, is instructive in this regard. For O'Connell himself, Jacobitism was virtually synonymous with the struggle for the restoration of Ireland's rights.[141]

The Jacobite Community

On the Continent, the Jacobite community began to fragment into a diaspora following the departure of the Court from St-Germain in 1713. The flight of a further tranche of Jacobite exiles both to Europe and North America intensified a process which was increasingly scattering James's adherents abroad. Many of those who arrived were, like their predecessors, poor and in need of financial support, which could not realistically come from the Court itself, and they were often helped by individual benefactions from within the Jacobite network, as when 'the Marquise de Mézières, formerly Eleanor Oglethorpe, established ... a refuge for recusant women who had been forced to flee England' in

1752.[142] The Scots, who had had a long tradition of helping each other abroad in foreign military service stretching back 200 years, adapted more readily than many to the need to gain their own living.

A goodly proportion of the country gentlemen in England remained attached to Jacobitism in at least a passive sense, and their reward was a tradition of caricature as bumpkins and ignoramuses generated by their Whig opponents from the 1690s through Fielding's Squire Western to Macaulay's *History*. It has been estimated that some 25 per cent of the country gentry were of Jacobite inclinations during the reigns of the first two Georges, ranging from hardly more than one in ten in Sussex to 40 per cent in Lancashire.[143] In such an environment as prevailed in the north-west and other Catholic hot spots in England, it was relatively easy for Jacobitism to develop a sophisticated system of cross-class communication and observance. In north-eastern England, long-standing Catholic gentry families made good use of their seventeenth-century experience in cautious and largely successful planning to retain both their estates and their principles, while their environment could safeguard them from prosecution: for example 100 Jacobites supported the escaped prisoner Dr Edward Charlton in an affray at Hexham in September 1718, making it effectively impossible to re-arrest him.[144] The Government spy William Cotesworth continued to report the presence of armed and mounted bands of Jacobites in the area for several years after the '15.[145]

Jacobite high culture made good use of political symbolism. White roses were an early example, and persisted after the failure of the '15, being still worn in Norwich in September the following year. Iconography was also important. Sir Watkin Williams Wynn was 'reported to have "audaciously burnt the King's picture" during election campaigns in North Wales' in 1722, while witty Oxford Fellows such as William Adams of Christ Church had 'a Room in his Lodgings . . . wch he used to call Hell, it being dark & in it were contained the Pictures of the late Prince of Orange'. After the Atterbury Plot's failure, prints of the Bishop were published showing him holding a picture of Archbishop Laud, on which was stated Laud's 'Martyrdom': the implicit connection between Charles I and James III and VIII was clear, as was the case with the Oxford antiquary Thomas Hearne's picture of James as 'EIKON BASILIKON', the martyred Charles I. Alderman John Barber, Lord Mayor of London in 1733, 'displayed pictures of the two Stuart princes at his home', while as late as 1754, a broadsheet alleged that James's or Charles's portraits 'may be seen . . . at the House of every TRUE BLUE either in Town or Country'.[146]

Irritating as this was to the authorities, prosecution sometimes resulted in juries who were unwilling to convict: this seems to have been
the case in 1723, when Robert Cotton refused to deny a charge of displaying Clementina's portrait and calling her 'the Queen of England,
King James's Queen' to visitors. Despite this, the jury returned a Not
Guilty verdict. Even where the jury convicted, there could be out-
breaks of popular support for the unfortunate Jacobite:' in 1718
... widespread sympathy was attracted by the case of James Shep-
heard, a young apprentice executed for allegedly conspiring against
the life of George I, and several prints were published, in defiance of the
authorities'. Perhaps as a result of this rather uncertain public mood,
print-sellers often got off quite lightly.[147]

Jacobite high cultural networks could be used not only to protect but
also to honour friends of the cause. When Chevalier Ramsay, formerly
tutor to Prince Charles Edward, visited England in 1729, he was elected
in rapid succession to the Fellowship of the Royal Society and to that of
the Spalding Club in Lincolnshire, in correspondence with the Society
of Antiquaries. In April 1730, Oxford University awarded him the
DCL. Such honours were no doubt due to his abilities, but perhaps
they were also a coded sign of sympathy.[148] Connections across Jacobite
society were far more complex than is usually understood.

Jacobite clubs were important locations of Jacobite contact, as were
coffee houses (particularly in Paris, where 'the English Coffee House was
"the general meeting place for those of the three nations [England, Scotland, Ireland]" ') and alehouses.[149] Some 140 clubs have been identified,
over 90 per cent of them outside Scotland, where open Jacobitism was
easier: as late as 1787, Robert Burns was the guest of the Steuart Club in
Edinburgh, and addressed it in a Jacobite spirit.[150]

As suggested in the discussion of the 1715 Rising earlier in this chapter,
Scotland north of the Forth remained a special case in mainland Britain
due to the sheer depth of militant Jacobitism there (which is not to say that
Jacobitism was not also strong in some of the southern areas of the country). Between Perth and Loch Lomond, 28 of the 35 lairds were believed
to be Jacobite, while in the cities, middle-class activites like publishing and
gentry-dominated institutions like the Royal Company of Archers were
alike heavily infiltrated by Jacobitism.[151] The east-coast ports, towns like
Arbroath, Montrose, Stonehaven, Inverbervie and Johnshaven, not to
mention Aberdeen and Leith, were ripe for disaffection as they were not
only Episcopalian strongholds, but were also suffering economically
through the long-term trend initiated by the Union which moved
Scotland's economic axis to the west and imperial trade away from the

traditional European links of the major ports on the east coast. In the Jacobite period those links remained in the shape of an extensive illegitimate smuggling trade, which was also frequently the cloak for introducing Jacobite spies and Irish Brigade recruiting officers. Montrose was one of the key ports in this regard, 'a fine loyal [i.e. Jacobite] seaport town'; its smuggling ring only started to disintegrate after the '45 when increasing pressure was put on locals to inform.[152]

The continuing strength of heritable jurisdictions in the Highlands served to consolidate Jacobitism among many of the clans there. Such jurisdictions consolidated powers of 'estate management' and 'the power to punish thieves and murderers caught red- handed' under the authority of rights of barony. An 'ethos of protection within the localities' consolidated feudal elements in Scottish society and maintained a higher degree of military capacity through the authority of the clan chief and the heads of septs (usually colonels and captains respectively in the event of a rising). At the same time, the traditional leadership of such groups was also participating in improvement and the economic transformation of their estates, even before the disastrous aftermath of the '45 Rising. Episcopalianism was here as elsewhere the motor for 'confessional nationalism': of the 50 principal clans, 18 were predominantly and another 18 significantly Episcopalian.[153]

The culture of the Church was therefore important. Because the Episcopal and other Nonjuring churches provided both the bulk of the Jacobite intelligentsia and the main conduit through which its propaganda flowed, their unity and good organization were central concerns of the Jacobite high command. At the same time, like all sects, they had a tendency to disunity which was the very flower of the unwavering adherence to principle which was its root. Occasionally, such disunity threatened major disturbance to Jacobite efforts. One of the chief of these occasions was the 'Usages' controversy of the 1720s, where the reintroduction of Catholicizing practices into the Nonjuring Church divided congregations, particularly in Scotland. In 1727, Lockhart of Carnwath 'intervened in James's name' in support of good order against the Usagers: they retaliated by publicly denouncing him.[154] The absent King took an anxious interest: he was himself responsible for nominating both Catholic and Nonjuring bishops, and indeed on occasion took advice across the religious divide: for example, Francis Atterbury was involved in recommending nominations for Catholic bishoprics.[155]

There seems to have been indeed a shadowy interconnection with Catholicism which laid the Nonjurors under some suspicion. When, in

1693, James II and VII had assured them that they were 'the true Church of England . . . that part of the clergy and people, which adhered to her doctrines and suffered for them', 'the Pope and two bishops in the Roman obedience' appear to have been consulted in connection with the continuing consecration of the Nonjuring line. The Nonjuring bishops were prone to describe themselves as 'Catholic Bishops of the English [or Scottish] Church', as for example at the consecration of the Nonjuring apologist Jeremy Collier on Ascension Day 1713 (Collier became Primus, first bishop in a Church without archbishops, in 1716: the Scottish Episcopal Church still retains this title as a relic from its Nonjuring days). Nor was such title to Catholicity mere usurpation of Roman terminology, as could be found within mainstream Anglicanism. Prominent priests such as the Revd Deacon anticipated John Henry Newman's spiritual anxieties of the 1830s: in 1721, Deacon wrote that 'when I came to consult history, the less defensible I found the Church of England'. Conversations concerning possible union with the Orthodox Church in 1717–21 underlined the intensely High Anglican characteristics of many among the Nonjurors (they continued to believe, for example, in the sacramental power of the Royal Touch), while in the 1745 Rising in particular they were suspected of working hand-in-glove with disaffected Catholics. By the 1770s, English Nonjuring was almost extinct (though its adherents lingered on in a shadowy existence for another century), and its Scottish sibling had largely followed within another fifteen years. Nonetheless, for a good part of the eighteenth century the political culture of the Nonjurors and their theological writings had made a considerable impact, not least through William Law's *Serious Call to a Devout and Holy Life* (1728), which was to be highly influential on those, like the Wesleys and Newman, who were sceptical of the Latitudinarianism of the mainstream Church of England. In secular literature, the serious moral approach of figures in or linked to the Nonjuring tradition such as Jeremy Collier, Samuel Johnson and Thomas Bowdler has had an influence on the teaching of literature and literary criticism into our own century: as Paul Monod remarks, 'the bowdlerization of Shakespeare was the outcome of a century of strict Jacobite piety'. In the Church of England itself, the Tractarians inherited the Anglo-Catholic ecclesiology of their Nonjurant predecessors, while 'the historical record of discrimination endured by the Episcopal Church . . . captured the Tractarian imagination'.[156]

Antiquarianism was strongly associated with Jacobitism throughout the eighteenth century. As Horace Walpole put it to Richard Bentley in 1753, 'my love of abbeys will not make me hate the Reformation till that makes me grow a Jacobite, like the rest of my antiquarian predeces-

sors'.[157] Among these were Richard Rawlinson, well known as 'a collect-
or of curiosities and manuscripts', from 1728 a Nonjuring bishop and
Thomas Hearne.[158] Hanoverianism was not however without its supporters among antiquaries: 'Philip von Stosch, a famous antiquarian
collector' was for 35 years a spy 'on the doings of the Stuart court'.[159] As
Jacobitism subsided as a realistic political option, antiquarianism's mu-
tation into Primitivism served to preserve a nostalgic appreciation of
the simple societies of the Celtic and English fringe and their culture
and traditions, much as earlier Stuart propaganda had emphasized folk
ways and the countryside.

Criminality, Property and Government

For some Jacobites, the absent monarch was a messianic deliverer, the
restorer of the Church, the nation's and not least their own fortunes; for
others, he was the symbol of Scottish or Irish nationality and independence. He was also the key oppositional point of focus, a figure who
could be aligned with a culture of protest based not only on nationalism
and 'country' values, but also with more broadly radical issues of resistance. Jacobitism was certainly invoked in connection with protests
against enclosure and other working-class grievances: indeed, as has
been pointed out by scholars such as Paul Monod and Philip Jenkins,
many of the towns in England and Wales which witnessed Jacobite disturbances were also radical hotbeds after the French Revolution. In
Scotland, Jacobite songs such as 'The Sow's Tail to Geordie' were
adopted by the Jacobins of the 1790s, and some of Burns's radical
poetry, such as 'Scots Wha Hae', seeks to fuse Jacobin and Jacobite
ideology.[160]

In the Jacobite period itself, the exiled monarch was presented as a
social bandit, a criminal hero and a lord of misrule who would reverse
the cultural categories of the Whig state in a restoration of customary
rights. The image of the King as fellow-rebel in the struggle to restore
true rights was reflected in Jacobite criminal subculture, chief among
whom were the smugglers and the highwaymen, some of whom, like
Tim Buckley, robbed 'pawnbrokers and stockjobbers', rather in the
fashion of those members of the Windsor Blacks who compared themselves to Robin Hood. The enlisting of men for their gang was, like the
legend of Robin Hood itself, believed by the authorities to be a cover
for Jacobite recruitment.[161] If their oft-suspected but never convin-
cingly proved links to the Atterbury Plot are ever fully uncovered, the

Blacks would be the nearest thing to the elusive Jacobite fifth column that the eighteenth century produced in England.[162]

The general run of highwaymen were often well educated: Captain Macheath (a name suggestive of Scottish and renegade officer Jacobitism) rightly says in John Gay's *Beggar's Opera* that 'Gentlemen of the road may be fine gentlemen.' As Frank McLynn has argued, the illegitimacy of the 1688 regime was seen as promoting bogus property relations, which it was the patriotic highwayman's duty to amend. A number of those caught and convicted made pro-Jacobite speeches from the scaffold: one at least, Thomas Butler, had been a Jacobite spy.[163] In Ireland, the highwaymen could even be gentry who had 'turned Tory' (become bandits). Their use of alehouses as safe points of rendezvous helped to submerge them in one of the chief locales of interchange for popular culture, itself not infrequently Jacobite in this period:

> Everywhere there were substantial numbers of Jacobites there were bound to be Jacobite alehouses, inns and taverns. Whether they were run by sympathetic landlords, or simply businessmen with an eye to the main chance, most plebeian Jacobites as a result had a 'social space' that was peculiarly their own . . . The government certainly believed these places to be nests of sedition, [and] surreptitiously organized Whig 'Mughouse' gangs to attack well-known Jacobite haunts and occasionally closed down the more notorious of them, but to no avail: the customers would simply appropriate another venue and carry on as before.[164]

Such locales were regarded as a threat partly *because* they provided points of interchange between popular Jacobitism and its high cultural ideologues. The means whereby Jacobite sympathizers kept open the historic connections between high cultural patronage and folk cultural practice sustained the network of Jacobitism as a whole: not only did criminals such as smugglers distribute high cultural propaganda such as medals, prints and portraits; they also had an 'entree to the merchant community of the French Atlantic seaboard' through their Jacobite links. Coastal ports were, as British espionage well knew, a prime locale for Jacobite spies.[165] Smugglers therefore would have made good Jacobite messengers, and there was often a welcome for them on the other side of the water: 'In England and Scotland sympathetic landowners aided and abetted smugglers for both political and economic reasons, thereby promoting some of the most difficult public-order problems British governments have ever had to deal with.'[166]

It was little wonder in the circumstances that those concerned with the administration of Hanoverian justice should, like Henry Fielding, oppose themselves to folk ways, associated as they were with such political and criminal baggage. In *An Enquiry into the causes of the Late Increase in Robbers* and *A proposal for Making an Effectual Provision for the Poor*, Fielding sought 'to demonstrate that there is abundant justification for controlling the activities of the poor', including their 'too frequent diversions'.[167] Smuggling in particular was a highly politicized crime: each of the four 'Smuggling Acts of 1698, 1717, 1721, and 1745 were passed amid great anxiety over Jacobite activity in England',[168] which had some basis in that smugglers clearly retained high cultural links (possibly, for example, among the Jacobite-inclined Independent Electors of Westminster).[169] Since a Stuart restoration would limit the National Debt if not actually cancelling it, thus lowering the indirect taxes which were raised to pay its stockholders, there were, as Frank McLynn remarks, 'good objective grounds' for smugglers to support the Stuarts, since a restoration would liberate their business.[170] Smuggling, like other Jacobite criminal activity, was often big business: its politicized nature as a crime and its degree of acceptance within the community surely played a large, if submerged, part in the fury of the Porteous Riots in Edinburgh in 1736. The town mob had tried to free a smuggler on the gallows and had been fired on by Captain Porteous's orders. Porteous had been sentenced to hang, but was reprieved: as a result, the mob lynched him and freed the prisoners in the Tolbooth in a widespread but well-organized period of rioting which alarmed the London authorities, who clearly understood its Jacobite and nationalist undertones (those active in the Porteous Riots were still excepted from pardon after 1745).[171] In Scotland the community outside the south-west was tolerant of disaffection, and in England the number of 'seditious words' prosecutions may have been fairly low, but the degree of unease reflected by the authorities was high (not least in the rapid expansion of the number of capital crimes). One folk song which may reflect popular resentment of this in some form is 'The Robber':

> I went to London one fine day
> With my sweet love to see the play,
> Where Fielding's gang did me pursue
> And I was taken
> And I was taken by the cursed crew.

The highwayman of this song, who 'Never robbed any poor man yet/ Nor was I ever in a tradesman's debt', but instead 'robbed the lords and the ladies gay' fits precisely the tradition of the Jacobite social bandit, an image reinforced in the last stanza, where he sings 'Let none but brave rogues follow me,/Give them good broadswords,/Give them good broadswords and liberty.' The broadsword, a weapon of limited use to a highwayman, was the archetypal Jacobite weapon. In addition, the highwayman of the song calls upon the 'six pretty maidens' who bear his 'pall' to 'wear white ribbons all': white was the colour of the Stuarts (as well as the Bourbons, hence its popularity in the Irish Brigades), and a ribbon set in a cockade was the badge of loyalty. 'True Blue' was also a Jacobite colour: hence Horace Walpole's phrase, 'be-James'd with true-blue ribbands'. It is interesting also to note that 'The Robber' shares a structural similarity with the Jacobite song 'Derwentwater's Farewell', where the Earl calls on 'six maids of fair Tynedale' to 'Scatter my grave with flowers'.[172]

The 'pretty maiden' theme itself had an important role to play in Jacobite activity, for not only were women widely suspected of being vulnerable to Jacobitism: the movement itself was also characterized as libidinous and predatory. Both prostitutes and gipsies were associated with Jacobite sentiments,[173] while the Highlander was routinely depicted not only as a cannibal, but as a sexually predatory and voracious male. As in the case of the growing urban working class, Jacobitism was projected by groups in power desirous of maintaining their property on to unknown, poor and numerous kinds of 'others' (including, of course, foreigners and Catholics) who were alienized as carrying a threat not only to the Hanoverian dynasty, but to civilization itself. There was plenty of genuine Jacobite criminality of course, but the equation criminal = Jacobite was one which was a short step from the belief that Jacobite = criminal, and it was frequently resorted to. The comparison of Jonathan Wild, the notorious thief-taker general, with Walpole was one all the more pertinent because of this equation: one encouraged paranoia about thieves, but secretly nourished them, and the enemies of the other suspected him of the same process with regard to Jacobites. Jacobite activity, real or suspected, was a threat revealed not only in the actions of the authorities but also in the discourse of the period: the repeated fear of disorder, of the mob and the enemy within owe a great deal to the Jacobite threat, and much of the great literature of the period, such as Alexander Pope's *The Dunciad* (1727/43), Henry Fielding's *Tom Jones* (1749) and Jonathan Swift's *Gulliver's Travels, Drapier's Letters* and *A Modest Proposal* (1723–29) reflects the nature of these concerns, as well as revealing the richness of Jacobite code and culture.

3

JACOBITE CULTURE

Literature, Artefacts and Symbolism

One of the recent gains of Jacobite scholarship has been the realization that a merely teleological account of success or failure is insufficient to explain the importance of dynastic, political, national or religious loyalty to the Stuarts in the eighteenth century, still less to account for the phenomenon of popular or plebeian Jacobitism. Within the groups who held such beliefs, rioting and enlistment in Jacobite armies was, as is surely always the case in politics, the role of a minority of activists amid a mass of sympathizers: the tip of an iceberg. It is the detail, beliefs and iconography of these sympathizers which provided the warp and woof of networking and communication for those who stood in danger of the gallows, should they be explicit. Just as the scale of non-Russian nationalism in the USSR prior to 1989 could be seriously underestimated in the West due to the lack of opportunity for its public expression, so Jacobitism can appear, as it still does to an historian so distinguished as John Cannon, to be the dog that did not bark, and hence, by implication, the dog that hardly existed. The understanding of Jacobite culture has a major role to play in qualifying this traditional cynicism, because it begins at a lower (and hence more realistic) common denominator of commitment than does a study essentially bent on identifying those ready to take up arms. The prevalence of Jacobite culture illuminates the extent of Jacobite support, even where such support was limited in times of crisis from moral principle, personal cowardice, or the sheer impossibility of organizing effectively. The term 'sentimental Jacobite' is sometimes applied to the people in such groups: this is a term which, since it seeks to reduce all essential commitment (as opposed to nostalgia) to the status of violence, should be resisted. It is insulting to term an Irish Republican opposed to the

IRA a 'sentimental nationalist': had the secret ballot been open to Jacobites, it has been the opinion of scholars as politically opposed as Samuel Johnson in the eighteenth century and Christopher Hill in the twentieth that the Stuarts would have regained their three kingdoms.[1]

Jacobite literature shared major themes in common throughout the British Isles. First, there was the portrayal of the absent monarch as a messianic deliverer whose return would awaken the land to newness of life: such a vision can be found from Scottish popular and folk song through Munster *aislings* to high cultural writing such as Alexander Pope's 'Messiah: an Eclogue'. Second, the absent monarch could be presented as a social bandit, a criminal hero, a lord of misrule who would reverse the cultural categories of the Whig state and restore customary rights: deliverance and renewal were the common themes, but the manner of their achievement crossed every register in the heroic, from the heavenly to the criminal. This pattern in itself was both cause and consequence of the cross-class traffic in Jacobite writing, born out of the criminalization of the disaffected of whatever background. Such traffic was manifested in various ways. First, there was an attempt to maintain ancient bardic traditions which themselves were increasingly interactive with folk culture due to the breakdown in the bardic schools and in networks of patronage: such was the case with the Jacobite bards patronized by Catholic gentry in 'hidden Ireland', or the support offered to the harper John Parry in Wales by Sir Watkin Williams Wynn. Second, there was the phenomenon noted by the Scottish patriot Fletcher of Saltoun, who observed that the support of a country's songs was better than that of its laws, a view still arguably true in the eighteenth century, and reflected in the distribution of Jacobite songs in Scotland and Ireland. Thirdly, the 'epidemic of Jacobite ballad-hawking ... apparently popular among artisans and labourers' was fed in a more contrived way by middle-class print controversialists such as Nathaniel Mist and Francis Clifton, who provided 'mediated texts': mass-produced Jacobite literature which made use of folk-cultural elements. Pedlars and beggars distributed such products, while Mist, 'in trouble with the law no fewer than 14 times', was himself driven by the criminalization of Jacobitism closer to the status of the many print workers and hawkers he employed who were also prosecuted. Given that in 1689–94 alone, there were perhaps a third of a million 'pamphlets discussing the allegiance controversy' alone in circulation, there was clearly a mass market to be fed by these middle-class middlemen. Evidence of ballad distribution can be found not only in London, but also in Birmingham, Northumberland and on the east coast of Scotland. In Ireland, from the 1680s on, it gave rise for the first time to a '*nationally* Gaelic ideology'.[2]

In Scotland the 'improvised oral communication' of folk culture interacted with the printed ballad, and well-known folk songs and motifs were adapted for Jacobite use: their airs could, when played without the set, reveal Jacobite sympathy publicly while rendering prosecution virtually impossible. Such a situation is evidenced in the famous song 'The Piper o' Dundee', the hero of which was reputed to be the Earl of Southesk: the song celebrates the mustering of Jacobite forces through the 'innocent' playing of Jacobite airs.[3] In the 1760s, the Irish Whiteboys were to use Jacobite airs in a similarly provoking manner.[4] The 'Bonnie Highland Laddie' song-cycle, which seems to have first appeared in the 1720s and 1730s, altered the traditional folk type of the Highlander/gipsy stealing away a respectable woman into a vision of a feminized Scotland, well dressed in English bribes, being liberated from the clothing of the 'English fop' to start a new life of sexual fulfilment, stripped by a phallically armed Highlander, symbolic of Charles Edward Stuart in later versions of the song. The pursuit of patriotic honesty is seen as leading to a renewing fertility which frees the beloved woman/nation (an equation in Irish poetry also) from the slavery of Hanoverian Union into a realm of liberated glee. Jacobite Gaelic poetry also had a vision of the heroic Highlander as metonym for the nation, being on occasion 'quite explicitly Scottish, not merely Gaelic'. The symbol of the patriot Highlander found in such literature was no doubt recognized in Charles Edward's own decision to march in the van of his troops in Highland dress. Cumberland understood the connection: he requested a version of 'Highland Laddie' for a theme song as he set out in pursuit of Charles, and Hanoverian propagandists in general accepted the image while altering its terms to those of predatory appetites and ungoverned sexuality.[5]

In Ireland, avoidance of prosecution was often guaranteed, not by the use of non-specific airs, but by virtue of the fact that the singing was in Gaelic (the same was true in the Scottish Gaeltachd, but there were hardly any authorities there with the inclination or ability to prosecute until towards the end of the Jacobite period). Mixed English and Gaelic songs helped to titillate their target audience by teasing mistranslation, as in this example from Donnacha Rua MacConmara (the true translation of the Irish alternate lines is in italics):

Come, drink a health, boys, to Royal George, our chief commander –
not appointed by Christ; and let us beseech Mother Mary to scuttle
                    himself and all his guards.
We'll fear no cannon nor loud alarms while noble George shall be our
                                                            guide –
and Christ that I may see him kicked aside by him who left us on his
                    exile to France![6]

Sets such as this indicate the politicization implicit in linguistic, as well
as religious, issues in Ireland. In addition, a whole raft of code-names
were used to apply to the messianic Stuart deliverer: he was the 'rising
falcon', 'an bricleir' (the bricklayer), 'an buachaill ban' (the fair lad),
'Spanish Cormac', 'The Blackbird', 'Mac an Cheannai' (the Redeem-
er's/Merchant's son). Sometimes the two Gaelic words for 'six' and
'mouse' were used together to indicate 'Seamus' (= James). In keeping
with the idea of the King as absent lover (an ancient one in Hiberno-
Scottish culture), the suppressed name of the hero harked back to the
traditions of *amour courtois.*[7] In the *aisling* tradition, where the poet
encounters a vision of a bereft maiden who represents the nation
mourning her absent lover, Jacobite and more ancient Irish national
symbolism conjoined. In the 1760s, a similar conjunction can be seen
betwen the *aisling* and the mystic leader of the Whiteboys, Queen Sive
Oultagh.[8]

The intimacy of referral to James and his son Charles by pet names
(e.g. 'Jemmy, lovely Jemmy') was apparently common throughout the
British Isles. The king was an absent lover, made equal to his subjects
by common misfortune (there was also a tradition of the Stuarts mixing
among their subjects on an equal footing, one which stretched back at
least to James V's supposed antics in beggar's disguise). Balladeers, as
in earlier periods of constitutional crisis, usually adopted an oppositional stance: several in fact marched with Jacobite armies: indeed one
of the most famous Jacobite songs, 'The Chevalier's Muster Roll', was
apparently specially composed for the Jacobite army on the march into
England in 1715. In Ireland, the visionary *aisling* was popular enough to
create 'a mass national public' in Leinster and Munster in support of
Daniel O'Connell two generations later, while as late as 1915 Jacobite-
derived material was being sung in Kerry. Overt Jacobite imagery in
Irish nationalist poetry continued to a very late date: Maire Bhui Ni
Laoghaire's *aisling* from the end of the eighteenth century continues
to appeal for help to Spain, even though Republican France is now
Ireland's only hope. The 'timelessness of poetry and prophecy' implicit

in the defeated narratives of typological history surely lies behind 'the tenacity of poetical Jacobitism' in Ireland. [9]

Jacobite high culture possessed its own realm, as well as the discourses it shared with more popular literature of protest, in its firm defence of the traditional symbols of nationhood and kingship which had been seriously damaged in 1688. What Paul Korshin calls 'the tumid enthusiasm of the seventeenth-century paean' entered a long diminuendo with the removal of the central legitimate line, to be extensively replaced by images of a 'King, Divine by Law and Sense', one as often as not divorced from the supernaturalism of a 'Goblin-Witchcraft, Priestcraft-Prince' of the old sacred monarchy as brought into disrepute by James II and VII. Although the imagery and ideology of the Patriot Whigs in the 1730s did much to reclaim this iconography for the Hanoverians, the damage done in 1688 had lasting effects. Augustan ambivalence and the notion of dynastic uncertainty hang heavily over the art and music of the period, even in the surprising case of Handel, as Ruth Smith has pointed out. [10]

Chief among the monarchical images of Jacobite high culture was Astraea, the embodiment of justice, whose symbolism had links to both the caesaropapist ideology of Anglicanism (the monarch as church leader was himself a type of eternal justice) and the image of the king as an agent of fertility: Astraea was *virgo spicifera*. As an icon of a renewing and ascendant monarchy, she was derived from the symbol of the virgin Astraea in Virgil's Fourth Eclogue, who heralds the arrival of Augustus (or, as some were to think, Christ) and his justice to the troubled (Roman) world. In the aftermath of the Reformation, the imagery of Astraea had been associated with Queen Elizabeth, particularly after the defeat of the Armada. The redefinition of the English monarch's role as head (later Supreme Governor) of the Church of England undertaken by Cranmer and others required a realignment of his or her position towards that of Davidic King or Christian Roman emperor, and away from the Papacy: hence the term 'caesaropapist' and the strengthening of a new iconography with ideological implications. [11]

Under James I and VI, Astraean imagery receded, but the seventeenth century saw some of her iconic force made manifest in Britannia. Like the Blessed Virgin, Britannia was portrayed as the mother of the Church: for example, a 1682 print which represents the Church of England as under attack from both Jesuit and Puritan portrays 'Britannia as Mary Dolorosa'. After 1688, unlike Astraea, Britannia appears to have been gradually emptied of supernatural symbolism: by the time of

James Thomson's famous 'Rule Britannia' of 1740, she had been more or less appropriated as a Hanoverian icon. At the same time, 'Astraea nostra' (Charles Edward) remained at the heart of Jacobite symbolism, and was so strongly associated with Jacobitism and the sacramental claims of the Stuart monarchy that she seems seldom to have been used in British royal imagery afterwards.[12]

If Astraea and Britannia represented one aspect of the struggle over British monarchical ideology, another is borne witness to by Aeneas, the founder (according to *English* foundation-myth) of the British race, and also of Rome. From Brut his grandson, all legitimate British monarchy was on this view derived, and as rightful rulers the Stuarts were likened to him. In the Interregnum, John Ogilby (whose plates Dryden used in his own Jacobitical 1697 translation of the *Aeneid*) had presented Virgil's epic in a Royalist light, as did Dryden after 1660, in *The Hind and the Panther* in particular.[13] In the aftermath of the Revolution, men such as James Philp of Almericlose and Richard Maitland, fourth Earl of Lauderdale (whose translation Dryden had read in manuscript) began to exploit the powerful symbolic impetus given to the identification of the Stuarts with Aeneas by the exile of James from his Trojan/ British kingdom in 1688: the English self-identification with Troy itself derived from the foundation-myth. Aeneas and the *Aeneid* continued as a central topos of high cultural Stuart code well into the eighteenth century, when 'AEneas & his two Sons' was a common term for James, Charles and Henry, Duke of York (as, for example, in the Gask correspondence). Charles Edward was described as a 'Trojan hero', Jacobites were 'old Trojans', and '*Fuimus Troes*' was the repeated mantra of Jacobite disappointment. Charles was Astraea, whose return was called for in Virgilian phrase by the Oxford Jacobite Dr William King, Principal of St Mary Hall, in his famous '*Redeat*' speech of the late 1740s. *Ascanius or the Young Adventurer* was a popular tract on Charles Edward couched in what must have been a highly recognizable code, which also of course subsumed the ambivalent image of Augustus, that type of Aeneas (and, like the caesaropapist monarchy, Pontifex Maximus) for whom Virgil had written.[14]

The oak tree, originally the clan badge of the Stuarts, and attached to them providentially following Charles II's miraculous escape from capture in the Boscobel oak in 1651, was eventually integrated into the general patriotic imagery of England/Britain. In the aftermath of 1688, however, it remained explicitly Jacobite: Williamite medallic iconography makes great play of images of smashed and broken oak trees over which fresh orange trees blossom, and the oak continued in use as a Jacobite symbol until the 1750s and 1760s. Oak was also associated with the ancient Britons through its role in Druid religion (this probably helped it to enter Patriot Whig discourse in the 1730s) and also with Aeneas: it was by a magical oaken bough that the Trojan hero entered the underworld in Book VI of the *Aeneid*. Oak Apple Day, the popular festival in celebration of Charles II's restoration which still endures in the once-Royalist West Midlands, did not appear to take off as a day of celebration until around 1715: it may have provided a symbolic cloak for support for more recent Stuarts.[15]

High and folk culture cross over in the case of oak symbolism, as they also do in the case of that most famous Jacobite image, the White Rose, which may have been a badge of the Scottish royal house as far back as the time of David II in the 1340s. In the seventeenth century, Charles I had been repeatedly identified in his coronation service, his masques and his martyrdom as 'The White King', and white for the Rose of York would also have been the natural badge of the Duke's men during the Exclusion Crisis, though I know of no evidence that it was worn by them then. However, shortly after 1700, white roses appear to signify Jacobite sympathies (although as Claire Lamont has pointed out, it is uncertain which rose, the full or the semi-plena, is *the* Jacobite rose: it may indeed be both, the full normally occurring in Jacobite painting and the semi-plena on glass). As with oak symbolism, the white rose and associated white cockade are genuine examples of cross-class Jacobite display: worn for example by the gentry in Bath in the 1740s, they are also found in the first half of the eighteenth century in popular protest from Dublin to Shrewsbury. In 1716, the price of white roses soared in London to feed the appetite of popular display.[16]

If oak leaves and white roses lent themselves equally to high cultural iconography and popular celebration, the ruralist theme in Jacobitism was closely associated with a dispossessed gentry and their allies. Stuart ruralism may have dated back as far as the 1620s: it was associated with the subgenre of the topographical poem, the first example of which, Sir John Denham's *Cooper's Hill*, uses an allegorical image of the deer hunt found in later Jacobite discourse. Indeed, the association of the Windsor Blacks with deer (particularly their 'activities . . . in the royal forests') could be seen as a sign of their Jacobite links, especially in the light of broadsheets such as 'The Hunting of the Newfound *Dear* with its Last Legacy', with its theme of George I as a slaughtered deer, to be divided up among his subjects as a prelude to James's restoration:

> And to some honest Tory,
> His horns I'll give away,
> To blow the tidings to the Man,
> That's o're the Raging Sea.[17]

Ruralism and retreat were later used as themes by writers such as Alexander Pope, the Countess of Winchilsea and Alexander Robertson of Struan, major-general in the 1745 Rising. Pope's hero of rural society and its folkways, John Kyrle, the Man of Ross, is depicted for example in the *Epistle to Bathurst* as helping those groups who would have been the victims of enclosure at the expense of the rising middle class. This idealized ruralism later made its way into a more general imagery of beneficient Tory landlordism and English authenticity: this is its role, for example, in the writing of Jane Austen.

The most obvious Jacobite artefact was tartan. Today, cultural pundits frequently suggest that the use of tartan as synecdochal for Scotland is a caricature of the early nineteenth century, or even (as Lord Dacre has argued) an invention. In fact, a cult of tartan can be traced back to James's court at Holyroodhouse in Edinburgh during the Exclusion Crisis, and even further, to James VI's marriage to Anne of Denmark in 1596. After 1707, the icon of the Highlander as patriot became a means of expressing dislike for the Union and associating it with a Lowland betrayal of Scotland for money and position, whereas the poor Highland gentleman despised such trappings, instead showing nobility in his pursuit of honesty, which linked both his military prowess and sexual frankness as a renewer of the now politically barren Scotland. In 1715 and more decidedly in 1745, tartan was used as a uniform for the Jacobite army, irrespective of origin. By the 1740s, English Jacobites had also taken up the tartan as a symbol of their own patriotism, Sir John Hynde Cotton having a complete bespoke set made for him in Edinburgh just before the '45. After the defeat of the rising, the ideological status of tartan was recognized in the 1747 Act, which effectively banned it in public everywhere but in the British army: but it continued to be worn as a sign of defiance both in Scotland and by English Tory squires. Eventually it was transmuted into a badge of romantic (though with hindsight, misplaced) Jacobite loyalty on the one hand, and the new and true loyalism of Scotland to the British Crown and Empire on the other. As a controlled and nostalgic means of expressing Scottish difference, tartan ended its Jacobite career in the social ritual of clan gatherings, the interior decor of Balmoral and the retail trade of Edinburgh's Royal Mile.[18]

Jacobite embroidery and plasterwork may have had some of its symbolic origins in the symbolic stumpwork of the Stuart period, just as Jacobite jewellery no doubt derived at least in part from mementoes of the martyred Charles I. Some of the most distinguished Jacobite plasterwork is found in the House of Dun, overlooking Montrose Basin, where around 1740 Joseph Enzer created for Lord Dun an allegorical Jacobite narrative of exile and restoration in a house itself designed by the Earl of Mar. Beginning in the saloon, the allegory depicts the Auld Alliance of Scotland and France, the return of the exile from overseas, hounds bringing a stag to bay (cf. *Cooper's Hill*) and an enslaved Scot with an English musket pointing at his heart. In the adjoining dining-room, oak leaves, white roses and the effulgent renovation of flowers and fertility suggest the positive outcome of the saloon's vision of the fate of Scotland and the Stuarts and the struggle to restore them, and this theme is continued elsewhere. In 1745, John Erskine, Lord Dun's brother, commanded a company in the 2nd battalion of the Forfarshire Regiment, and was one of the most efficient recruiters to the Prince's army on the east coast.[19]

Articles of clothing or personal possessions were also found decorated with Jacobite motifs: garters, for example, might bear the legend 'When this you se Remember me' (i.e. James III and VIII), while snuffboxes were made with a picture of Charles II in an oak tree on the lid and one of James inside, or with concealed portraits of Charles Edward. Beppy Byrom, the daughter of the Manchester Jacobite John Byrom, 'bought a blue and white dress to celebrate the victory at Prestonpans . . . and tradition says that she wore plaid garters'. Whigs described such women as '*Lancashire Witches*', with their 'Plaid Breast-knots, Ribbonds, and Garters . . . that above a Ladys Knee is of so attracting a Quality, that it's . . . in Danger of drawing . . . Military Gentlemen off their Duty'.[20]

The Byrom collection of Jacobite artefacts contains a saltglaze teapot in blue enamel, overpainted with the white rose, oak leaves and the monogram 'C.R.III'. Roses and oak leaves also appear on Jacobite decanters, and memorial plaques were made with the names of Jacobite martyrs in circles. The National Museum of Scotland has an example of an embroidered wall-hanging with 'a sunflower [symbol of loyalty] with the initials "JR/CR" and the date 1719 in its centre', clearly alluding to James's marriage to Clementina Sobieska. Such dates could also serve to reinforce a narrative of continuing (not merely previous) loyalty, thus encoded for those who knew where to look for it. More than 7000 Jacobite medals were issued during the 1690s alone, while Robert Strange's copper plates for Stuart banknotes were avidly collected by sympathizers after Culloden. Among other compact displays, complex Jacobite narratives of a messianic kind are found on pro-Stuart fans, no doubt a means for the many Jacobite ladies of the time to express their sympathies.[21]

Jacobite glasses from family collections are also rich in the key symbolism known to contemporaries, though undoubtedly fakes exist. Besides the rose and oak leaf, the grub and butterfly are also found. The grub may indicate the belief, referred to in the song 'By Yon Bonnie Banks', where the speaker travels 'the low road' of death, that 'the soul of a dead exiled Scot returns to his native land by an underground route':

> O ye'll tak' the high road, and I'll tak' the low road,
> And I'll be in Scotland afore ye,
> But me and my true love will never meet again
> On the bonnie bonnie banks o' Loch Lomond.

Flower symbolism is prevalent. Daffodils appear on Jacobite glass, 'as indicative of hope, honeysuckle indicating fidelity, Lily of the Valley (return to happiness), Sunflower (unswerving loyalty), Forget-me-nots and Carnation (coronation) . . . such flowered glasses appear to have been produced in sets where the initial letter of the plants can be arranged in an appropriate acrostic'. Inscriptions on the glasses frequently come from the *Aeneid*, pointing up contemporary literary interpretations of the Jacobite king as Aeneas, and on occasion identifying Cumberland with Turnus.[22]

Glass artefacts also took advantage in their inscriptions and symbolism of the altering perspective provided by moving liquid. Anamorphic portraits of Charles Edward come into view on moving the vessel, while on some glasses the crown descends on the Prince's head as they are tilted towards the mouth (a convenient symbol for passive Jacobites, since it hints that drinking the King's health will be enough to restore him). In other glasses, the Garter appears on 'the wrong breast' when the glass is held 'with the portrait away from the drinker thus reversing the figure'.[23]

Jacobite prints were also important in the communication of pro-Stuart sympathies. In *The Agreable Contrast*, for example, Charles Edward stands behind a tree fuller in blossom than does Cumberland in his butcher's apron. Flora MacDonald stands beside the Prince, and she remarks approvingly on the 'Long tail' of the suggestively phallic greyhound that accompanies him. By contrast, Cumberland is accompanied by an elephant with 'a pitteful tail', and both Flora's full basket and her name help to reinforce the symbolism of the fecund Charles and his sterile opponent, as Paul Monod points out (this kind of bawdy badinage about the opposition is found both in Jacobite and Hanoverian prints, though anti-Jacobite propaganda tries to undermine fertility claims by over-emphasizing them through depicting the 'fertile' Highlander as wanton, lascivious, libidinous and monstrous). Other prints, such as *The Highlander's Riddle*, mix images and letters in an amusing cipher.[24]

Of course, though much in the way of Jacobite artefact and display is unmistakably so, there was a large middle ground of symbols (such as the Royal Oak) which could be used openly because of their ambivalence, but by that very token were not necessarily indicative of Jacobitism. In assessing Jacobite symbolism, it is important to proceed carefully. Dr William King, the sometime leader of the Jacobite party at Oxford who subsequently became disenchanted with Charles Edward, ironized the significance of 'Jacobite' symbols as effectively as any modern historian, sceptical of revisionist claims:

How disaffected a place is *Oxford*! The *Vice-Chancellor* is a Jacobite. Why? because he reprimanded our College. In the dutiful expressions of his attachment to the King and Royal Family he certainly meant the Pretender; at least *we represented his words so to ourselves in English.* Every minute circumstance in this place is an evidence of Jacobitism. The picture-shops are stuck full of prints of Mr. *Rowney*, with a *Latin* motto under this, *Pro Patria*; which means the Pretender. One of the principal coffee-houses in the *Highstreet* is called *James's* coffee-house. Can anything be more flagrantly jacobitical? There is also an inn in the *Highstreet* called *The King's Head*; and whose Head is it? Not King GEORGE's, no, King CHARLES's. Besides all this, one of the Chief *Old Interest* inns is the *Flower de Luce*, which, by a very slight knowledge of *Inuendo*, may denote the connexions and attachment of that party.

It is noteworthy in the light of King's (himself no mean practitioner of classical Jacobite code) gentle irony of 1754 that the eighteenth century was as familiar with the concept of coded Jacobite display as are our modern scholars.[25]

Warrior Women

Just as Jacobitism's 'outsider' status tended to draw together (if only temporarily) disaffected groups, and to criminalize those ideologically opposed to the Hanoverian regime, thus driving them into cross-class alliance with criminals who themselves became politicized as a result of the connection, so there was a gendered element to Jacobite support based on the movement's association with the outsider. Not only was there a romantic appeal to Jacobite outlawry; it also offered the opportunity for action in a wider public sphere, from the running and defence of estates which might be forfeit (the Countess of Panmure went through heroic legal negotiations to secure her family's) to the recruitment and even the leadership of troops, if not actual fighting itself. Moreover, current research on the important role women have played in the Irish and Scottish national movements gives rise to another possibility: that the nationalist element in Jacobitism in these countries and the different role of women within their societies may have had an impact on the extent of female Jacobite activity. For these reasons at least, Jacobitism, as a 'subversive movement' which 'would accept all volunteers, regardless of sex', has a major role to play in the history of women in the eighteenth century. For women who wished 'to exert influence',

> there was an intense appeal in Jacobitism . . . In work for the Pretender, ladies could correspond personally with their 'King over the water', giving him encouragement and advice; they could smuggle messages back and forth across the Channel; they could use their charms to help corrupt important politicians into supporters of 'King James III'. Often they organized secret meetings in which they took leading roles and helped plan the great 'risings' for overthrowing the government and establishing their monarch's reign.

Alexander Pope's friend Mrs Charles Caesar, the Duchess of Buckingham and the Oglethorpe sisters were only a few of the women who belonged to this group: Valerie Rumbold implies that Pope's exclusion by virtue of his religion from society and its offices may have helped his participation in a network of such women as Mrs Caesar, with 'her cult of royalist virtue'.[26]

It is certainly the case that early feminists and quasi-feminists such as the Countess of Winchilsea and Mary Astell (whose patron was the Nonjuring Archbishop of Canterbury, William Sancroft) either skirted Jacobitism or were Jacobites. Winchilsea, who was a prominent figure in the Nonjuring community and its debates (for example, on the

Usages controversy with Bishop Brett (Primus in England from 1726)), associated the status of women as outsiders with the more generalized marginality of Stuart sympathizers at large ('Alas! a woman that attempts the pen/Such an intruder on the rights of men'). The woman who finds herself constrained 'by mistaken rules' is aligned with those excluded by the 'mistaken rules' of the new post-1688 regime. Both Winchilsea and her husband were forcibly secluded from the public life that they had enjoyed before James's fall (Winchilsea had been 'maid of honour to Mary of Modena', 'the sovereign mistress of my vanquished mind'): this was particularly the case after her husband's arrest for Jacobitism on 29 April 1690.[27] In true ruralist mode, Winchilsea developed a celebratory vein in her writing in praise of retreat, in particular 'The Petition for an Absolute Retreat', which contains many images suggestive both of the displaced Jacobite and displaced female poet, the fall which threatens retreat being linked both to that of the Stuart regime and also to 'Ardelia' herself ('So the sad Ardelia lay/Blasted by a storm of fate/Felt through all the British state'). Winchilsea networked with other Jacobite-leaning feminists, such as Delariviere Manley, some of her poetry being printed in Manley's *The New Atlantis*. Manley, in her turn, was close to the Jacobite Alderman John Barber, who himself was a friend of Swift, who in his turn encouraged Winchilsea to publish, Manley herself assisting Swift in some of his Tory pamphleteering.[28] In other poems, Winchilsea suggests that the materialism of stockjobbers has destroyed the honesty and openness of love, and implies an analogy between hidden Jacobite beliefs and the inability of women to express their views and feelings directly. She even put her own feminist slant on Jacobite Augustanism in her observation that 'Livia so influenced Augustus that his accomplishments in world dominion were brought about only "thro' a woman's wit"'.[29]

If Winchilsea was forced to find something to celebrate in both her and her husband's joint exile from public life, Mary Astell represented a much more decidedly women-only position: indeed, her belief that women could only be effectively educated and reach their full development in an environment separate from men might to some seem all too redolent of the Jacobite and Catholic association with nunneries: all-female communities had a history of being bleakly represented in Protestant propaganda. Jacobite women were in fact to be associated with a spectrum of all-female provision: one of the Oglethorpe family specifically founding a retreat for exiled recusant women in France in 1752.[30] Astell's own name was more closely associated with the development of charity schools, themselves feared by the government to be nurseries of Jacobitism. Although not unsympathetic at the time to the Revolution, Astell, whose maternal grandfather had been a Royalist hero, herself 'idealized Charles I as a religious and political martyr' and moved in quasi-Jacobite circles, both Atterbury and the Duchess of Ormond being among her friends.[31] Another contemporary feminist, Elizabeth Powell, founded *The Orphan Reviv'd or Powell's Weekly Journal* in 1718 as a 'High Church and Jacobite newspaper', while yet another woman writer, Lady Mary Wortley Montagu, was sister-in-law to the Earl of Mar (and thus incidentally, cousin by marriage to the Jacobite philosopher Lord Forbes of Pitsligo). As Mary Mahl and Helene Keon argue, 'writing and publishing were symptoms of unrest' among women, and it is therefore not surprising that Jacobite women were frequently writers, or even, as in the case of Mrs Ruddiman, publishers.[32]

Thrust out as it was from public action, Jacobitism was strong in the private sphere: passed on through marriage alliances and families, and by determined women who had to take responsibility for running property their menfolk had left to fight. More remarkable than this, perhaps, is the evidence for the direct involvement of women in the campaigns, and not always as camp-followers either. The most famous example is that of Colonel Anne Mackintosh (daughter of the Farquharson of Invercauld who had fought at Preston in 1715), who led out a regiment of Mackintoshes while her husband captained one of the Independent Companies on the Hanoverian side. He was subsequently captured and humorously granted by Charles Edward (with whom Hanoverian propaganda wrongly insinuated she was having an affair) to be her prisoner. The unnaturalness and threat of Jacobite women is recognized in Hanoverian depiction (most centrally perhaps in *The Female Rebels* tract of 1747): one print even goes so far as to show such women being attacked by British army soldiers with drawn swords at Culloden, apparently in a spirit of self-congratulation. A number of women were in prison in connection with the '45 in both England and Scotland (up to 2000 may have crossed the border with Charles Edward), and there are repeated references in contemporary reports to Jacobite 'Amazons': one garbled French account apparently (wrongly) suggesting that a whole regiment entirely consisting of women had been raised. 'Miss Jenny Cameron', whose image was often reproduced in prints, became the archetypal Jacobite woman soldier: depicted fully armed, 'the bold Amazon of the North' signified the sexual vigour, alien threat and role-altering qualities of an all too contemporary revolutionary movement: 'While antient Poets treat of Amazons/Our Moderns outvie them in Camerons'. Miss Cameron

was reputed to have led 200 into battle at each of the three major encounters of the '45. In allusion to *The Beggar's Opera*, the Prince was depicted between Flora MacDonald and Jenny Cameron, musing 'How
happy could I be with either/ Were t'other dear charmer away'.[33]

Although sometimes undeniably regarded as a nuisance (for example, an order went out to the 1st battalion of the Forfarshires at
Macclesfield on 22 November 1745 'against all women, but soldiers
wives'[34]), women nonetheless made important contributions to Jacobite
recruitment. For example, Lady Ogilvie assisted her husband throughout the campaign, and 'witnesses declared they saw her standing upon
the Cross of Cupar in Angus with a drawn sword in her hand, while the
Pretender was proclaimed by Lord Ogilvie's orders'. Both she and
Jean, the dowager Duchess of Perth, who died in 1773 'aged nearly
ninety', were held prisoners after the failing of the Rising, along with
others such as Lady Strathallan, who often drank 'the Pretender's
health and success to his arms in Britain'. The Countess of Errol was
also prominent in recruiting men to the cause. As *The Female Rebels* put
it: 'Delicacy of sentiment, mercy, tenderness, and compassion, the peculiar ornaments of the fair sex, were by them [Duchess of Perth and
Lady Ogilvie] exchanged for wild transports of lawless ambition, the
lust of power, cruelty, revenge, and all the wild horrors of destructive
war.' The language is clear: 'wild transports', 'lawless', 'lust' all indicate
that Jacobite disorder can be equated with immoral wantonness.[35]

There were also women active on the other side: for example, Peg
Woffington, who wrote 'The Female Volunteer, or, an attempt to make
our men Stand' in response to the Hanoverian defeat at Falkirk: in
doing so, she was writing in a subgenre familiar to both Jacobite and
Hanoverian women, the female warrior ballad, publication of which
had taken off after the Restoration 'and the loosening of restrictions on
ballad publishing'. In Scotland, however, the evidence points to such
figures being in the main Jacobite: there were women carriers who
warned lurking Jacobites of Hanoverian patrols, to say nothing of untrustworthy public servants, such as Barbara Strachan, 'the Jackobite,
postmistress off Buchan'.[36]

Charles Edward's own depiction as a woman in Hanoverian propaganda was made possible by the Betty Burke episode in 1746, when he
cross-dressed in order to conceal himself as Flora MacDonald's Irish
maid. Alongside the image of the rapacious masculinized Highlander,
another process of cultural iconization was beginning to develop: that
of the supine and feminized Celt, a characterization which was to prosper in the nineteenth century. In the Jacobite period itself, the attraction

felt by women for the Jacobite cause was known and remarked on: it
was an implicit reproach to their susceptibility. So widespread was the
view that women would tend to be Jacobites that one Edinburgh Whig
produced a detailed memorandum in 1745 in which he purported to
show that 'only' 40 per cent of ladies in the Edinburgh area were in fact
Jacobites, citing in his support a list of 328 names, with evidence for the
political affections of each.[37] Such a list might have caused inconve-
nience and indeed danger were it of men, but although female Jacobites
might be detained, incarcerated or threatened in the heat of the moment, they were immune from the most severe penalties to which the
state resorted: so they were very useful to the Jacobite movement, for
they risked less by their activities than did male Jacobites. Thus women
participated in propaganda, Nonjuring activism, publishing, espionage and military recruitment: the whole gamut of Jacobite activity.
They were, not only for the above reasons, but also because of their role
in cementing families and continuing their Jacobite traditions, important in the pursuit of the one project which made all the others possible:
that of fund-raising.

Finding the Money

All the key questions concerning the nature of Jacobitism as an international movement depended on its finances: the exiled dynasty's ability
to maintain a court, a secretariat, an espionage system, to supply and
mount risings, to produce medals and other artefacts of propaganda,
and above all to subsidize a host of penniless exiles with the wherewithal to survive for which they were always clamouring, meant that
money had continuously to be found. Yet although many studies
of Jacobitism mention sums of money in passing, virtually none deal
with the financing of the movement in its own right in the way in which
even minor campaigns and conspiracies are considered in isolated
detail. Finance, was, however, a continuous problem: part of the evidence we have for the strength of at least a passive Jacobitism in England is that bankrolling on the scale required by the Jacobite
leadership was to some extent dependent on the donations of wealthy
English Jacobites.

Immediately after 1689, Louis XIV's provision of a pension of
600 000 *livres* (around £50 000 per annum in sterling terms, £6 million
in current money) and the use of the palace at St-Germain proved sufficient to supply the needs of a modest royal household (including the

salaried officials who supported the espionage network), though not an expatriate community, who seem to have had in many instances to resort to banditry, 'a community living in an atmosphere of violence, triggered off by economic difficulties, internal rivalries and disappointed hopes'. There were, however, individual wealthy Jacobites at the court, such as Lord Middleton, who was even in a position to give his daughter a dowry of 60 000 *livres*.[38] Until 1697 (when those which France could afford were absorbed, together with Lord Mountcashel's Brigade, into the French forces), Louis also paid James's army of Wild Geese, which consisted of 15 battalions of infantry, two regiments of dismounted dragoons, two regiments of horse and two companies of Lifeguards.[39] The absorption of James's army into the French service effectively rendered the King and his successors not the pensioners only, but also the servants of French foreign policy, a situation which proved embarrassing in the extreme after the Treaty of Utrecht removed both French residence and official subsidy: the latter could only be regained through the politically damaging agreement with Spain negotiated in 1715, itself of prime importance to the funding of the Rising in that year. At this stage, Ormond's request for £100 000, troops and arms could only be met by Spain: the furthest France was prepared to go was to supply arms in secret. In response to its religious and political conditions, Spain handed over £36 000 by the end of 1715; a further £15 000 in bullion being lost off St Andrews in January 1716. At the same time, James was receiving subventions of £26 000 from Clement XI and £25 700 from the Duke of Lorraine: thus the continental backing received by the Jacobite high command during the period of the '15 totalled £100 000 (about £12 million at today's prices).[40] At the same time, significant sums were being raised in the British Isles. The Duke of Marlborough remitted £2000 to the Jacobite cause in April 1715 and a further £2000 in August, by way of an insurance premium rather than in expiation for his conduct in 1688,[41] while the English Jacobite community as a whole contributed £40 000 to the costs of the Rising: given that this was at least £25 per man raised in England, and that such volunteers generally provided their own arms and were in the field for only two months, the '15 clearly appears far closer to being a self-financing rising than was Charles Edward's attempt of thirty years later.[42] The fact that the Lancashire gentry were as much as 40 per cent Jacobite may have gone some way to providing the critical mass necessary to generate such a level of funding.[43] In addition, Derwentwater at least was fabulously wealthy, with estates valued at £200 000.[44]

One of the chief difficulties for Jacobite finance lay in the aftermath of any rising, when the clamour for relief from a flood of exiles who had risked lives and lands to no avail would be but ill stemmed by the declining contributions of Jacobitism's now disappointed European backers. Thus in 1716, Spain, which had already signed a commercial treaty with George I at the end of the preceding year, was in no hurry to pay the tens of thousands it still owed to the Jacobites. In January 1716, a paltry £2750 was proffered; in April £2200 and in October £3100.[45] In response to diminishing funds, and in pursuit of further subventions to aid the prospective Swedish invasion, the spy Captain (later Colonel) Lancelot Ord, a veteran of the '15 posing as 'Mr Downes', arrived in London in October 1716 with a request for £50000 from the English Jacobites. Although Captain Ord failed to raise anything like this amount, he received substantial pledges, such as the £20000 apparently promised by John Crowley should the King make another attempt in England. In 1717, Francis Francia, another Jacobite agent, claimed to have raised £60000, but there appears to have been little truth in this. Circumstances were, however, shortly to demonstrate that the willingness of English sympathizers to give substantial amounts of money to the cause was by no means exhausted.[46] Such support was crucial, for Scottish Jacobites were on the whole not nearly so well off as their English counterparts: only 8 out of 38 listed forfeited estates in 1716/17 produced over £1000 per annum. Magnates such as Viscount Kilsyth (£864 per annum), Lord Nairne (£740), the Earl of Nithsdale (£809) and Viscount Kenmure (£608) were only on a par with middling English squires, senior army officers and London clergy: Sacheverell had £700 per annum from his living at St Andrew's, Holborn. Senior Jacobites such as Colonel John Balfour of Fairney had only just over £150 a year, about the same as the Headmaster of Shrewsbury School and less than half the stipend of a Canon of Christ Church, Oxford.[47]

At the time of the Atterbury Plot, the English elite were, as I suggested in Chapter 2, still prepared to finance Jacobitism heavily, although the extent of the popular support they could have drawn on had the Plot come to fruition is less clear. Yet if recruitment was uncertain, finance was strong, no less than £100000 being remitted from England through intermediaries in order to secure the purchase of arms.[48] Questions have arisen as to where finance on the scale still being provided from English contributions in the 1720s could have come from (benefit concerts appear to have been one means whereby money was raised), and this has led to the identification of on the surface unlikely figures such as the Earl of Burlington as a source for Jacobite funds, a case which, if interesting, is still not proven.[49] Burlington's debts were certainly of legendary proportions: in 1717 (when Atterbury was remitting money to the Stuarts, as his archdeacon at Rochester, the Duke of Chandos's brother, had done in 1715), they were over £23000, reaching £169000 in 1738.[50] Burlington also borrowed £22000 from Hoare's bank in January 1722, at the time when money was being raised for the Atterbury Plot, while in 1725 he lent money to the Jacobitical Duke of Beaufort, who is known to have visited James III and VIII in that year. The connection of Burlington's own chaplain and the closeness of the Earl himself to some of the Plot's goings-on are among a variety of circumstances which lend credence to suspicion that Burlington may have played a part in the complex web of Jacobite funding. The exiled court certainly promised good interest: in 1731, Lord Cornbury remarked that James would give interest at 5 per cent ('payable at his Restoration') and 7–8 per cent on larger sums.[51] Though generous in an era of virtually stable prices, this was indeed no more than one of the most colossal examples of 'the cheque's in the post' in history, and was the cause of bad feeling from those who misunderstood its terms, as perhaps Lord Elcho did after 1745, when he resented Charles Edward's treating of his campaign loan as a gift, though in the circumstances it could be considered little else.[52]

In 1743–44, Lord Barrymore offered £12000 to defray the cost of a rising to be held in the expectation of a French invasion: the French force was to land at Maldon in Essex. In May 1744, France granted a pension of £1800 per annum to Charles Edward, thus making him effectively independent of his father, and this was later raised to £3000, despite the failure of the 1744 plan, which Sir Watkin Williams Wynn tried to persuade Louis XV to remount in October: in support of this, Lord Traquair was to travel to England to raise funds. In France, the Marquis d'Argenson liquidated the Prince's debts, which eventually amounted to 30000 *livres*; the whole aborted attempt of 1744 cost France 900000 *livres*, but in the next year even more was to be spent.[53]

I shall be discussing the Rising of 1745 in detail in the next chapter, but the rickety state of its finances gives a good initial indication of the enormous gamble it represented, and also emphasizes how its gamblers threw in a stronger hand at Derby in December than that they had first ventured at Glenfinnan in August. Charles's effort was privately financed and unofficially launched. Scots Jacobites estimated that for Charles to stand any prospect of success via a descent on Scotland, he required 6000 troops and the money to pay them. Unable to secure this or any other commitment from the French court, Charles borrowed money from Waters, the Paris banker, to hire ships, arms and men from Irish shipowners to whom he was introduced by Lord Clare. His initial loan of 40000 *livres* was extended to 120000 when James covered the first part of the debt. In the end, Charles scraped together enough for two ships, 3500 stand of arms, 2400 broadswords, 100 or more men and 4000 *louis d'or* to pay them and his future recruits: he lost most of these already inadequate resources *en route* to Scotland, and as a result of this and poor fund-raising in the British Isles, the '45 was hamstrung from the beginning due to lack of money.[54]

In contrast to the situation promised only a year earlier, the Rising found the English and Welsh supporters of the Stuarts very short of money, whether by accident or design (although it was subsequently claimed by Sir John Douglas that Alderman Heathcote had raised £10000 in London for Charles – for when he should reach the capital, of course).[55] Sir Watkin Williams Wynn had 'only £200 in ready money' when the Prince landed, which unfortunate circumstance (despite his having spent £120000 on two previous general elections) rendered it impossible for him either to supply a major subvention or to pay his own troops. Luckily, Sir Watkin's circumstances had recovered sufficiently to enable him to expend another £4000 on election expenses shortly afterwards.[56]

In Scotland, Charles's officials, acting as agents of a provisional government, proved more effective at raising cess monies than Mar's staff had in 1715, and significant sums were uplifted to cover the running costs of the army in this way. Although the initial war chest had run out by Perth, and Charles required Elcho's loan to keep going, matters subsequently improved. Initially, however, there was the hurdle of the banking system to overcome. As the Jacobite forces reached Edinburgh, both the Royal Bank and the Bank of Scotland (despite its reputed Jacobite connections) closed their doors. This created a problem in that some of the cess payment received by the Jacobites was in promissory notes from these banks. A fear arose that the Prince's supporters would print their own notes, thus repeating the Gunmoney debacle in Ireland in 1689–90, when silver denominations were minted in base metal to provide funds, their value collapsing after James's defeat. John Campbell of the Royal Bank of Scotland, possibly acting under the influence of his kinsman, the aged Jacobite Earl of Breadalbane, was prominent in providing a solution. After John Hay of Restalrig, the Prince's Secretary of State, brought in £5500 (of the £15000 which had been demanded) from Glasgow on 29 September, some in Royal Bank notes, a process began whereby significant sums in gold were paid over by the directors of the Bank. Despite the severe disapproval of the Lord Justice Clerk, over £15000 was provided, obtained in many cases by gaining entry to the Hanoverian-held castle, and withdrawing the gold from its vaults. Small wonder that Duncan Ban MacIntyre (a poet of Jacobite sympathies for all that he fought on the side of the government at Falkirk) later wrote a praise-poem to Campbell:

> Glad tidings to cheer me would be
> If I were to see thee tomorrow
> Invested with the Crown,
> Amid rejoicing and pomp,
> Instead of King George.[57]

Charles obtained £3000 from Cope's war chest after Prestonpans, but money still remained tight. Fencible recruits were being raised for the army at the rate of one man in lieu of £5 sterling rental, but these re-cruits had to be paid, and the rent foregone for them could not be used to pay them.[58] Jacobite captains had 2s 6d a day, 1st Lieutenants 2s, jun-ior lieutenants and ensigns 1s 2d to 1s 8d, sergeants and pipers 9d and infantry 6d (cavalry sergeants had 1s 6d and cavalry volunteers 1s). At these rates, it would have cost the Jacobite army between £175 to £200 a day in wages alone to mount the march into England. Moreover, in their absence, taxes were not effectively raised for them in Scotland.[59] By comparison, the wealth and power of Britain was immeasurable: £1 300000 was voted for the services in November 1745, and £100000 was found to pay the 6000 Hessians who arrived to help Cumberland in early 1746; in Yorkshire alone, £26000 had been raised 'by the first week of April' through loyal subscription. The disparity in resour-ces alone clearly indicates why a rapid strike at London represented Charles's best hope.[60]

France eventually provided the major funding for the 1745 Rising, as it had not in 1715: it was estimated that the hire of ships alone for the French invasion fleet cost 1 000000 *livres*, while the rescue operation cost 1 250000. Some of this might more profitably have been spent in Scotland from January 1746, when Charles Edward's shortage of funds was critical: in this context the loss of the 252000 *livres* carried by *Le Prince Charles* (the former Royal Navy *Hazard*, captured by Jacobite forces at Montrose) when it ran aground at Kyle of Tongue was of cru-cial importance. Culloden was fought because Charles was out of money, having received less than £4000 since the Battle of Falkirk on 18 January 1746. Indeed, 'most' of the subvention paid to the Jacobite army in Scotland 'was lost or captured', only £15000 reaching the Prince, a tiny sum when he had had himself to raise a loan in order to mount the Rising at all.[61] As so often in Jacobite affairs, French generosity can be read in two ways. Sir James Steuart, the Jacobite economist, estimated that France had expended £213000 on the Stuart cause in 1745–46, considerably more than the total subsidy from Continental powers in 1715. On the other hand, the recall of English and Hessian troops from Flanders 'enabled Saxe to take Brussels', which yielded booty worth £1000000; similarly, the Royal Navy's involvement in containing the Rising enabled French privateers to seize £700000-worth of British shipping. In other words, French profits from Jacobite activity exceeded their expenditure on it by a ratio of eight to one. In time of war, even major Jacobite ventures could yield stunning financial gain to the state that sponsored them. Had the French spent more of course, their profits might have been greater: as Lord George Murray put it in 1755: 'Had the Ministers of the Court of Versailles, ten years ago, been persuaded to support his Royal Highness the Prince at the beginning of his attempt, in a proper manner, I think I do not say too much if I affirm that his Royal Highness could not have failed of success.' Given the credence that even those sceptical of Jacobite hopes pay to Lord George's judgement, this is a statement worth paying attention to.[62]

France was not the only financial backer of the '45, for as the Prince's cause advanced the French court set about encouraging its political allies to contribute: the Earl Marischal, for example, securing over 41000 *livres* from the Spanish Ambassador in Paris in autumn 1745 as a down payment on a subsidy to pay the monthly wages of 2000 troops and supply 1000 arms and 10000 Spanish dollars as a cash equivalent. The Papacy had, with misgivings, helped as in 1715. James had secured a £25000 loan and Benedict XIV sent Prince Henry in Paris a significant sum after hearing of the victory at Prestonpans, but the eventual level of support was the customary 'too little, too late' that the Jacobites had come to expect from their continental allies. On his return to France, Charles (with Henry) was initially allowed 144000 *livres* a year, but this wealth (which even so, he overspent) was short-lived, given his expulsion following the Treaty of Aix-la-Chapelle in 1748.[63]

By the 1750s, Charles Edward's reputation for alcoholic excesses had done much to dry up English funds in particular (though money continued to be raised in Ireland), as had his determination never again to be used as an adjunct to French ambition, or to accept the offer of cheap diversionary forces. Since France or Spain had alone ever looked likely candidates for putting the Stuarts back on their thrones, and given that such funds as remained to be donated in the British Isles were largely predicated on a foreign-backed rising, Jacobitism was rendered bereft both of funds and the means to raise them, and was condemned to increasing political and military paralysis culminating in irrelevancy. This process was undoubtedly hastened by Charles Edward's personal behaviour, Henry's elevation to the cardinalate (the British govern- ment had tried to bribe the Pope with £150000 to make Henry a Cardinal 'even before James approached him on the subject') and not least the fresh wave of exiles seeking pensions and support after 1746. Living increasingly on capital and loans, bolstered by intermittent pensions from the French government and the papacy with which to finance its diminishing network and sporadic propaganda exercises, the Jacobite cause in the person of Charles Edward was running out of money (Henry, with 600000 *livres* a year from his benefices, was in another case altogether). By the time financial improvement came in 1766, when Charles inherited his father's money, it was too late for it to be used for the cause, except in so far as it defrayed the ex- pectations of the legions of indigent Jacobite exiles who clamoured for it.[64]

Philosophy, Theology and the Stuarts

The intellectual milieu of Jacobitism reached far beyond its political manifestations, both at high and more popular levels. Not only were certain kinds of cultural and theological discourse marginalized, not to say endangered, by developments after 1688; Stuart apologists were also seeking out new ways to express the beliefs and affections which they saw discarded around them. The result was a number of sophist- icated and often influential contributions to the philosophy, theology and imaginative literature of the long eighteenth century. The last- named I dealt with at some length in *Poetry and Jacobite Politics in Eigh- teenth-Century Britain and Ireland* (1994): in this context, one of Jacobite culture's major achievements was its role in the vernacular revival and defensive adoption of folk literature and its values, which led to the preservation and development of a distinctive Scottish literary tradi- tion in the work of Robert Fergusson, Robert Burns, James Hogg, Sir Walter Scott and others.

The Jacobite tradition also produced a number of important theologians and religious writers (William Law being among the most significant, with his powerful subsequent influence on both Methodism and Tractarianism), as well as in Sir James Steuart (author of *An Inquiry into the Principles of Political Oeconomy*, 1766), the second economist of the century and (if he be counted) in John Law, one of its premier financiers: Law, '*écossais et grand jacobite*', was responsible for 'the prototype of the Bank of France', although his project collapsed due to bad tactics and the economic immaturity of French society.[65] In philosophical and cultural speculation, Jacobite culture's often ambivalent position between secular and sacred versions of Enlightenment (notable, for example, in the strong Masonic involvement of many Jacobites), gave rise to the distinctive work of writers such as Alexander, 4th Lord Forbes of Pitsligo (1678–1762) and Chevalier Andrew Michael Ramsay (1686–1743).

Lord Forbes was the inheritor of the strongly distinctive cultural life of what has rightly been called the 'conservative north' of Scotland, whose traditionalist Scoto-Roman culture remained attached both to the Latin and the Scots language until well into the eighteenth century, a process which Jonathan Clark has recently argued can be paralleled south of the Border.[66] Figures such as Dr Arthur Johnston, who dedicated his version of the Psalms to Archbishop Laud, or Professor John Forbes of Corse with his *Spiritual Exercises* (1624–47) were a world away from the Covenanting central belt of Scotland.[67] In 1638, Aberdeen had refused the National Covenant, and during the wars which followed, troops raised in the north often melted away in desertions rather than fight King Charles.[68] When Episcopalianism was restored in 1662, of the 271 deprived ministers, only 24 were from north of the Tay; in 1690, when it was again abolished, only 4 of 200 clergy in the counties of Aberdeen, Banff, Moray, Ross and Caithness 'conformed to presbyterianism'.[69] In this situation, it was no surprise both to find extensive conversion to Catholicism in the rural areas and the growth of the French Catholic mysticism associated with the names of Mme Bourignon, Mme Guyon and Archbishop Fénélon (Lord Forbes's friend) among both Catholic and Episcopalian communities.[70] After the like-minded Dr George Garden (who emphasized the 'catholicity of the Sacraments and Creeds') was deposed from his living in 1701,[71] Pitsligo gave him 'a house at Rosehearty within a few minutes' walk of his castle, close to the Moray Firth'. Here an ecumenical religious community was set up, 'where persons of different religious persuasions lived together in the love of God and the practice of self-abnegation'.

This followed the views of Bourignon and Guyon, who 'always dis-suaded their Protestant followers from changing their church connec-tion' (though as an Archbishop, Fénélon was understandably of another opinion).[72] Lord Forbes's sympathy with such Quietist ideas can be traced in his unpublished writings on government: but his openness towards emerging secular ideas is also borne witness to in his fore-shadowing of Hutchesonian utilitarianism in his views on power and its legitimacy. It is not in fact clear that Pitsligo could reconcile these two elements in his thought, as his apologia for joining the Rising of 1745 makes clear: one's impression reading this is that the pull of the sacred Prince outweighed other considerations and that Lord Forbes's utilitar-ian justifications are retrospectives. His recorded comments may bear this out: although Pitsligo claimed he 'weighed and weighed again' his decision to rise, and that any enthusiasm was of the 'coldest kind', he is also remembered as saying 'have you ever known me be absent at the second day of a wedding?' (the first bridal of Scotland and her absent Stuart lover having been in 1715). Lord Forbes's heroic and legendary practice of his ideals in the aftermath of Culloden lends a long-recog-nized extra dimension to his two main published works, *Essays Moral and Philosophical* (1732) and *Thoughts Concerning Man's Duty in this Life and His Hopes in the World to Come.*[73]

As a young man, Andrew Ramsay had sought to join the Rosehearty community before going off to be tutor to the Earl of Wemyss. Sub-sequently, he became Fénélon's (and Mme Guyon's) secretary and wrote the *Vie de Fénélon* (1723). As a boy, he 'used to go and pray in the dark in a ruined pre-Reformation church', and so it was little surprise when he converted to Catholicism, nonetheless remaining a most ecumenical Christian. Ramsay was philosopher, theologian and political theorist rolled into one. After the publication of his *Essai philosophique sur le gouvernment civil* (1721) he was called to serve for a brief period as Charles Edward's tutor, before court intrigues and Ramsay's uncon-ventional behaviour put paid to the appointment. Shortly afterwards, he had a major success with *Les voyages de Cyrus* (*Travels of Cyrus*) (1727), which was translated into English, German, Italian, Spanish and Greek and went through 30 editions. The book's purpose was 'to outline the training of the perfect ruler', and in doing so it drew on a rich cocktail of orientalism, travel and political literature. Following an unsuccessful attempt to gain election to the Académie Française, Ramsay published *A Plan of Education for a Young Prince* (1732) and the successful *History of Turenne*, besides becoming involved in Freemasonry, the early stages of which would have suited his Christian universalism. In 1735, James created Ramsay baronet of Scotland, one of only 34 UK baronetcies granted by the Stuarts in exile. Sir Andrew's last (and posthumous) work, *Philosophical Principles of Natural and Revealed Religion*, sought to defend Christianity 'against Materialism, Deism and Socinianism'. In this it was traditionalist, but in other ways its grand analogy between different world religions placed it 'in line with the most progressive thought of his [Ramsay's] own time'. David Hume discussed its remarkable ideas of 'the pre-existence of souls and the universal salvation of men, beasts and devils', which themselves were, if most unsafe theologically for a Catholic, a tribute to the breadth of Ramsay's sympathies.[74]

The Episcopal Church's sacred mystical tradition was just as strong, as was borne witness to in Professor Henry Scougall (a friend of Ramsay's) classic, *The Life of God in the Soul of Man* (1677) or in Professor James Garden's *Comparative Theology* (1699).[75] The 1717–21 negotiations between the Nonjurors and the Orthodox still form one of the key documents in Orthodox ecclesiology, being cited even in popular works on the subject, while the 1764 eucharistic liturgy of the Episcopal Church could be seen as providing a bridge between the Nonjurors and the Tractarians.[76] The stress laid by certain among the Nonjurors on Catholicity was perhaps also reflected in works such as Robert Nelson's *Companion for the Festivals and Fasts in the Church of England* (1704), which reached its thirty-sixth edition by 1826. The (after 1689) gradually forgotten doctrines of 'Passive Obedience and . . . Non-Resistance' were kept alive by works like Revd John Kettlewell's *The Measures of Christian Obedience*, which, originally appearing in 1681, was still in print by 1714.[77] More extraordinary in its supernaturalism was the Revd Robert Kirk's *The Secret Commonwealth of the Elves and Fairies*, which allegedly led to its author's abduction by the Little People for revealing their secrets.[78]

The curious juxtaposition of 'advanced' cosmopolitan thought and sympathy for locality, tradition and longstanding practice is one of the most appealing in Jacobite writing and practice: it is yet one more dimension of the cross-class melding of interests among Jacobites which has been one of the central themes of this chapter. Before being dislocated permanently, these links were drawn on one last time, as Charles Edward launched the Rising of 1745.

4

Bonnie Prince Charlie

Welcome to the British Shore?

The Malt Tax riots in Glasgow in 1725 were caused by legislation seen as being in breach of the 1707 Treaty of Union: they were crushed by General Wade, himself at the beginning of a 16-year mission to improve roads and communications in the Highlands, to redevelop Independent Companies of Highlanders to police the area and to emplace an upgraded cadre of local law officers. In 1745, Wade's achievement was to be highly beneficial to Charles Edward's army, whose lightning pace of advance owed much to the Hanoverian general's roads.[1]

Whatever its effects in the short term, such a lengthy exercise in military administration in Scotland was a result of continuing fears about the potential for Jacobite disaffection there. Wade, who had originally been sent in response to Lord Lovat's self-serving 1724 Memoir on the State of the Highlands (though recent research suggests that fear of Malt Tax disaffection may have played a more significant part in the decision to send Wade than has been hitherto suspected), estimated (in all probability, overestimated) Jacobite military strength in the Highlands at 14000.[2] Since this was nearly a quarter of the average size of the total English and Irish military establishments in the War of the Austrian Succession, such numbers posed a clear threat. Moreover, although Wade dealt relatively comfortably with the Glasgow riots, Lowland Scotland in general was rife with disaffection, not least on the east coast, which was in economic decline as the focus of post-1707 Scotland switched from Continent to Empire. An increase in smuggling was the east-coast response to shrinking markets and discriminatory taxation, and smuggling's status as a quasi-Jacobite political offence was consequent on this.[3]

In 1739, the independent companies in the Highlands were increased in number from six to ten, and formed into a regiment, the
43rd, always known as the Black Watch. Originally intended to serve in
Scotland, they were 'decoyed . . . south to London', secretly intended
for Flanders. The resulting mutiny was put down with savagery, but the
result was that when the Rising of 1745 broke out, government lines of
defence in Scotland were thin, and the Black Watch itself was kept in the
south of England due to fears for the reliability of its soldiers.[4]

Scotland was thus as much of a military problem as it was a partner in
Union. The extension of taxation, particularly the Excise and the Malt
Tax, to the country was perceived as discriminatory and unfair: the
Jacobite leadership took great care to emphasize their commitment to
return to the lighter taxation Scotland had enjoyed prior to 1707. Widespread uneasiness and resentment at these taxes contributed to an
effective military occupation by British troops; in this context the development of the Independent Highland Companies was akin to the
use of native forces in British India, and the treatment of the Black
Watch in the early 1740s an act of incorporating colonialism. Economic
change, brought about at least in part by a realignment towards imperial markets, was contributing to demographic stagnation in east-coast
Scotland, an area whose strong Episcopalian contingent was in any
case sympathetic to Jacobitism. Walpolean patronage hardly had an
impact in Scotland beyond the benefits conferred on a small inner
circle.[5] The purges carried out against largely Episcopalian professionals in the north-east after 1715 had moreover created an 'embittered'
cadre of dispossessed intelligentsia, some of whom emigrated; those
who remained could expect to find their fellow-Jacobites embedded
in the gentry of Aberdeenshire, Banffshire, Kincardineshire, Angus,
Perthshire and Fife.[6] On the other hand, the pro-Hanoverianism of the
Presbyterians and those with a prospect, however distant, of recognition from the settled order, was increasing. Scottish society, language,
literature and culture were beginning to change in response to 40 years
of Union, though at nothing like the pace that would succeed after
Culloden. In response to these factors, Charles Edward's pragmatism
and the republican patriot iconography his propaganda was emphasizing by the 1740s portrayed a more flexible figure than that of his father.
In answer to the ambivalent rhetoric of the Patriots in the 1730s,
Charles was shown as the image of incorruptible native youth: an alternative far more attractive as a Patriot King than Frederick, Prince of
Wales. In Scotland, his messianic qualities were stressed, along with his
status as a fertility king and renewer of a barren nation. In response,

Whig propaganda was to identify him as the 'Italian Bravo' or a French dupe surrounded by bubbles, each containing a dream of an invasion which would never take place ('to bubble' meant 'to dupe with false prospects' in the language of the time).[7] Charles was shown as often as possible in conjunction with the Pope and other anti-Catholic representations: his quality as an alien, a foreigner from the land of popery and poisoning (Italy), was emphasized more heavily than had ever been the case with his father. The anti-Catholicism of the '45, so much more emphatic than that of the '15, was plausible not only because of the diminishing role of High Anglicanism in Jacobite affairs, but also on account of a determination to alienize a claimant whose youth and attractiveness were only heightened by his representation as a native prince, the 'Great Genius of Britain', in Dr William King's phrase.[8] Nationality was a key issue: the allegation that the Hanoverians put the welfare of their German electorate before that of their British kingdoms was a persisting one: for this reason alone, it was crucial that Whig propagandists destroyed Charles's claim to be a native prince. In this context, the developing imperialist identity of England may have had as its corollary a rising xenophobia conjoined with an anti-Catholicism all too conveniently applicable to the one man who threatened to overset the British state.

The leadership of Jacobitism in English society had been gradually bought off or undermined. Following the Atterbury Plot, the trend towards flooding the Anglican hierarchy with Whigs, which had begun with the elevation of Benjamin Hoadley to Bangor, intensified: by 1725 there were no virtually no Tory bishops left, and Jacobite clerical leadership in the juring Church was at an end. Similarly, although English gentlemen continued to subscribe to James's cause, that cause itself increasingly lacked direction after the death of Lord Orrery in 1731. In addition, Walpole's peace policy undermined the prospects of a fresh rising, for it was almost impossible to launch a Jacobite military venture in England without the presence of French or Irish troops (Walpole himself was keenly aware of the vulnerability of the British mainland to invasion). On the Continent, the collapse of James's marriage to Clementina Sobieska after 1726 was a propaganda disaster, and totally undermined Jacobite attempts 'to build up an anti-Hanoverian alliance of Spain, Austria and Russia'. Despite a brief flicker of opportunity on the collapse of the British–French alliance in 1731, and the outbreak of the War of the Polish Succession in 1733, James was left without any support to fight for his thrones while Europe was riven by other dynastic battles.[9]

This position, which obtained throughout most of the 1730s, altered when Walpole was 'reluctantly hounded into declaring war on the Bourbon monarchy of Spain in 1739, over the old issue of British access to areas of Spanish ascendancy in the Americas'.[10] French uneasiness over this was brought to a head when France decided to attack Britain's Austrian ally, in order to take advantage of the apparent vulnerability of Maria Theresa, who had succeeded to the throne in 1740. By 1744, two years after Walpole's fall, France and Britain were in the throes of another major war which was ravaging both sides, neither of which could claim victory nor admit defeat. Clearly, the Stuarts once again provided France with the possibility of a trump card: the more so since Cardinal Fleury, who had maintained an anti-Jacobite policy since 1726, died in the January of that year, aged 90.[11] John Murray of Broughton, Lord Barrymore and Sir Watkin Williams Wynn (along with Sir John Hynde Cotton, the main leader of the Jacobite Tories in Parliament) visited Paris.[12] Sir Watkin's own disaffection was clearly mounting: on 10 December 1742 he had declared in Parliament 'that England was made a mere province of Hanover'.[13] In response to their own perception of this opportunity, and to the pressure of Jacobite agitation, France began to prepare to invade England at the end of 1743: at the same time, increasing consideration began to be given to the possibility of pursuing an independent Scotland.[14] The aim was to land at Maldon, striking immediately thereafter at London,[15] and 15 000 silver medals were struck in support of the attempt. Tellingly, these carried the portrait of Charles Edward rather than James, for the English and Welsh Tories were increasingly of the opinion (first voiced in the 1730s) that the Prince as Regent offered a much more fresh and attractive prospect than his ageing and disappointed father.[16] On 23 December, James issued a Declaration which formally appointed his son Prince Regent and among other matters stressed the importance of Scotland's status in any Stuart restoration: 'We see a Nation always famous for valour, and highly esteemed . . . reduced to the Condition of a Province, under the specious Pretence of an Union with a more powerful Neighbour'.[17] Outwith Scotland (and possibly Ireland), there were signs that the Jacobites were out of touch. The Duke of Ormond's own manifesto emphasized 200 years of friendship between England and France prior to 1688: eirenic as it may have been, it hardly answered to the circumstances of the mortal struggle for world empire in which the two superpowers were now engaged.[18]

Charles Edward left Rome on 30 December 1743 and arrived in Paris almost a month later. Admiral de Roquefeuil set out shortly thereafter with some 22 ships to engage the British fleet and prevent them from intercepting the invasion force. However, the slowness of the preparation and the all-too-public movements of Charles Edward meant that Norris, the Royal Navy commander, was already in position to stop the French transport fleet. De Roquefeuil drove him off, but storms prevented a decisive engagement, and also damaged the waiting transports. By the end of February, further bad weather had undermined the seaworthiness of the French forces: the British government had already started making arrests at home. Indecisiveness turned to withdrawal, and the invasion was cancelled. The pension Charles Edward received from France was no compensation;[19] nor did Sir Watkin's further attempt in October to persuade Louis XV to renew invasion plans meet with success.[20] Charles himself was an embarrassment to France, who wished to downplay his importance to some of its allies, particularly Prussia.[21] Fearful of peace, for which negotiations were already under way, the Prince was determined to continue to cause trouble, a talent he long retained.[22]

The Road to Defeat

Embittered by the failure to get the 1744 invasion under way, Charles Edward decided to force France's hand in his support by mounting his own expedition to Scotland. The contacts he had developed there in connection with the 1744 attempt proved invaluable at this juncture: Murray of Broughton, the representative of the Jacobites in Scotland since 1740, met Charles in August, but made it clear that he could not expect a major Rising if he landed without French support.[23] Charles set off with only two ships, the *Du Teillay* and *Elisabeth*, 3500 guns, 2400 broadswords, 20 artillery pieces, 4000 *louis d'or* and somewhat over 100 marines raised by Lord Clare.[24] Such an expedition could be passed off as Franco-Irish privateering, and was taken little notice of: few could have thought the invasion of a country a practical proposition on such resources.[25]

On 9 July 1745, four days after setting sail for Scotland, the *Elisabeth* was badly damaged by HMS *Lyon*, a British man o'war. With 300 casualties and severe structural problems, the French ship returned to Brest, her condition too risky even to consider coming alongside *Du Teillay* to transfer *matériel*.[26] This attack, which virtually destroyed Charles's already pitiful resources, was to prove a metaphor for the whole campaign, where the Royal Navy was successful in largely cutting off supplies of both men and money. Charles's main chance lay in a dynamic thrust towards London, backed by French men and money and finally a landing on the south coast. So much was realized by his supporters on the Continent: within weeks of his landing, the Earl Marischal was demanding 10 000 infantry and arms for 30 000 from France.[27] Too few of his Scottish commanders realized this degree of urgency, or understood the extent of British naval power. The 'fortress Scotland' policy favoured by strategically inept Jacobites like Cameron of Lochiel and a source of sentimental nostalgia for succeeding generations of Jacobitically inclined Scottish nationalists, stood not a chance of success. The lesson taught to Charles I in 1642–43 and James II and VII in 1689–91 was still the same: attack London quickly or lose.[28]

Charles made landfall at Eriskay on 23 July, together with a handful of companions: the 'Seven Men of Moidart'. Despite Macleod of Macleod and Sir Alexander MacDonald of Sleat's refusal to join (they were being blackmailed by the authorities, who knew of their practice of 'kidnapping surplus tenants for sale as bond servants (virtual slaves) in America',[29] and widespread reluctance to 'come out' without French support, the Rising nonetheless began unexpectedly well for the Jacobites, even before 1300 men rallied to the standard at Glenfinnan on 19 August, amid cries of 'King James the Eight . . . prosperity to Scotland and no Union'.[30] Such stand of arms as the *Du Teillay* had brought were distributed.[31] On 14 August, Keppoch's men overcame Colonel Swithenham and his company 12 miles from Fort William; two days later, MacDonald of Tiendrish and some Glengarry men defeated two companies of the Hanoverian Royal Scots. Five days after Glenfinnan, 800 more came into the Jacobite army at Fort Augustus, and in the next week the Prince was joined by Robertson of Struan, John Roy Stewart, Lord Nairne and Mercer of Aldie; the MacGregors meanwhile surprising two companies of British troops at Inversnaid. Macpherson of Cluny, who as an Independent Company captain had been active in controlling cattle-raiding and other breaches of law in the Highland counties, joined after having been captured on 28 August. On 3 September, thanks to Wade's roads, the Jacobites reached Dunkeld, and the next day the army entered Perth, where Lord Ogilvy, Viscount Strathallan, Oliphant of Gask, the Duke of Perth and Lord George Murray joined the Prince's forces.[32]

On 25 September, Aberdeen was taken by the Jacobites, who encountered considerable popular enthusiasm, but a lack of the support among the gentry and the better sort which they had known in 1715.[33] The town authorities had been at first indifferent to James Moir, the 4th laird of Stoneywood, who began recruiting in the streets of the town: but by and by he had gathered a battalion of 300 men.[34] The hinterland of the north-east was as fruitful for Jacobite recruiting as ever, with Jacobites clustered heavily in towns such as Achmedden, Pitsligo, Fraserburgh, Inverugie and Fyvie.[35] As a hostile contemporary witness remarked of the north-east, in its early days 'the Rebellion was favoured by almost all the common people. The promise of freeing them from the Malt Tax had a surprising influence upon them . . . The Rebels . . . were looked on as the deliverers of their country.'[36] This verdict is borne out by contemporary Jacobite sources: 'We hear for certain from the North that there are whole Parishes that there are not a man left but three of four that are able to bear arms, so that if this Heroic Spirit continueth among us, you are like to have all Scotland in one side of the Forth.'[37] On 24 September, Lord George Murray requested the Jacobite Duke of Atholl (William Murray, Marquess of Tullibardine) to raise three battalions to gather the cess in Perthshire, Angus and Fife.[38]

The Jacobite army seized Edinburgh in near-farcical circumstances, and a suspicion of collusion always attended the then Lord Provost and Lord Lieutenant, Archibald Stewart, despite his being acquitted on 31 October 1747: an 'insolent' verdict according to the Lord Justice Clerk.[39] The Lord Provost was apparently allocated a place on the Jacobite Privy Council.[40] Certainly, the town fell with little trouble, and its militia were not called on to demonstrate their ineffectiveness. A deputation was sent out by the Council on 16 September and again in the early morning of the 17th to negotiate with the Jacobites, and as it returned into the city, Lochiel's Camerons rushed through the open gate behind it, 'the guard immediately dispersing'. Outside the Castle, there was little further resistance, and whatever the Lord Provost's own role, there can be little doubt that a Jacobite fifth column was present in the city, a suspicion borne out by the fact that there was recorded Jacobite unrest in the Town Guard long after Charles's army left Edinburgh. A crowd of up to 20000 greeted his entry to the capital, which was accompanied by strongly nationalist symbolism.[41] Heavily Episcopalian Leith and the Lothian hinterland were both largely Jacobite, and Charles may have raised several hundred troops there, as well as obtaining more than 1000 stand of arms for their use.[42]

Meanwhile, towards the end of August, British forces under General Cope had marched north to oppose the Jacobites at the Pass of Corrieyairack: the so-called 'well-affected Highlanders' they were to meet on the way failed to materialize, and on hearing (inaccurately) that the Jacobites had reached the Pass before them, Cope decided to make for Inverness and thence to Aberdeen (where he removed the town's cannon and small arms for safe keeping and his own use) in order to take ship for Edinburgh. He sailed on 15 September, and disembarked at Dunbar hours before the Jacobites took the capital. Cope adopted a careful position north of Tranent, covered by sea, marshland and the wall of Preston House, home to Colonel Gardiner, one of his senior officers. The Jacobite army, guided through the marsh by a sympathizer, Robert Anderson of Whitburgh, attacked at dawn on 21 September, their gunfire driving off the dragoons while wedge-shaped columns from their front line plunged through the government army like battering rams in a hail of shot and steel. Cope's artillery was not well positioned, and the speed of the attack further limited its effectiveness. As his army fled, the enclosed nature of his position became a death trap, and the Jacobite forces killed many as they attempted to fly; they also took 1500 prisoners, of whom a good number joined the Prince. The British authorities took serious alarm, being increasingly concerned at the prospect of a French or Spanish invasion. The War of the Austrian Succession was absorbing most of the country's troops, despite which the French were following up victory at Fontenoy with a string of further successes. The situation was so parlous that 6000 Dutch soldiers had been called in August, but diplomatic wrangles between France and the Netherlands prevented their use. In September, 10 battalions under Sir John Ligonier had been recalled, and after Prestonpans Cumberland was called back with a further eight battalions and nine squadrons of cavalry.[43] On 30 October, General Wade reached Newcastle, and the coalfield was safe.[44] In the Highlands, the Hanoverian laird Duncan Forbes of Culloden eventually raised 18 companies, command of this force (which was, however, not fully recruited until February) was given to the Earl of Loudon when he returned to Inverness on 11 October with those of his men who had survived Prestonpans; four days later, an unsuccessful attempt was made by Lord Lovat to capture Forbes: a crucial moment in the Rising's progress in northern Scotland.[45]

In Edinburgh, following the victory at Prestonpans, Charles attempted to consolidate the patriotic element in his support in two declarations of 9 and 10 October. The first stated that 'the pretended Union of the Kingdoms' (England and Scotland) was at an end, describing the British Parliament as an 'unlawful assembly'; the second displayed the close link in Jacobite thinking between the Union and the hateful Act of Settlement which it had imposed in Scotland in defiance of the legislation of the Scottish Parliament:

> With respect to the pretended Union of the two Nations, the king cannot possibly ratify it, since he has had repeated Remonstrances against it from each Kingdom; and since it is incontestable, that the principal Point then in View was the Exclusion of the Royal Family from their undoubted Right to the Crown, for which Purpose the Grossest Corruptions were openly used to bring it about.

Although on occasion hedged with a degree of ambivalence, such outright opposition to the Union was a strategic necessity for the Stuarts. In other clauses, Charles hedged his bets on the future status of the National Debt and the confirmation of established Churches.[46]

The distribution of Jacobite propaganda was important, and the Prince's staff were 'adept' in its arts.[47] Thomas Ruddiman the younger was 'editor and part owner and printer of the *Caledonian Mercury*', a paper which gave an essentially Jacobite gloss to the proceedings of the campaign.[48] The tartan uniform of the army and the white cockades of Jacobite sympathizers were important in profiling the presence of Stuart soldiery, as were the legendary swordblades inscribed 'Prosperity to Scotland and no Union': indeed, it was 'the principal aim of Charles's propaganda to equate Scottish nationalism with Jacobitism'.[49] Robert Strange's banknote plates (by the late 1740s much sought after by Jacobite collectors) and fans added a strong financial and domestic visual perspective.[50] The traditional cultural repertoire of singers and fiddlers was also important for distributing the message throughout the countryside: the balladeer 'Mussel-Mou'd Charlie', who was to be the last survivor of the '15 (d. 1782), celebrated the Jacobite victory at Inverurie on 23 December in verse, and fiddlers such as John Sinclair of Banff were instrumental in carrying Jacobite airs abroad.[51] Among Jacobite musicians of distinction, the young Neil Gow played in front of Charles Edward at his court in Holyroodhouse. Jacobite songs had carried their message of Charles Edward's youth and symbolic role as a fertility king far beyond Scotland's borders: in pro-Jacobite Oldham, Joshua Winterbotham sang 'My Bonny Highland Laddie' on the army's march south.[52]

It was decided to invade England by only one vote:[53] over-optimism concerning the possibility of a 'fortress Scotland' (which might be defended until French help arrived to protect it) was one factor in this; another was distrust of the English Jacobites, whom it was felt by some (though by no means all) were more given to ' "Womanish Railing, vain Boasting, and noisy Gasconades"' than to the significant support of an armed rising.[54] A decision was made to take the western route, thus avoiding Wade's army at Newcastle. As was the case with the resolution to evade rather than fight Carpenter 30 years earlier, this may well have been the wrong strategy to adopt: an outflanking manouevre, like those of 1651 and 1715, which lacked credibility because of the weakness implicit in its avoidance of confrontation. On the march south, the Earl of Nithsdale and Viscount Kenmure joined the Rising, but left it almost immediately on ascertaining that the army was only 5000 strong (with perhaps another 2000 camp-followers).[55] The fall of Carlisle on 14/15 November came as an unwelcome shock to the government, and Charles's army moved steadily south, encountering little opposition. On 23 November, Lord Derby gave up the defence of Manchester for lost; three days later at Preston, there was 'the loudest acclamation of the people you can imagine' for the Jacobites. At least two companies of men were raised in Lancashire, and a whole battalion (the Manchester Regiment) in Manchester, which the Jacobites entered on 29 November: but although the road between Preston and Wigan (the Jacobite Lord Barrymore's heartland) was lined with well-wishers, they 'declined to fight when offered arms, on the grounds of lack of training' (this suggests that it was not altogether lack of arms which held back English recruiting, as some even at the time opined).[56] A feint towards Wales by Lord George Murray drew Cumberland out of position, giving the Jacobites the advantage in any dash to London.[57] On 3 December, the Duke of Devonshire, Lord Lieutenant of Derbyshire, withdrew his forces as the Jacobites entered Ashbourne. A day later, they were at Derby.[58]

The Council of War at Derby was the critical juncture of the Rising. To those who regard the '45 as being a major threat to the British state, the decision made there to retreat was both momentous and mistaken. It had been coming, however, for some time. Lord George Murray's expectations of support in Lancashire had been, as was the case with Lord Widdrington in 1715, largely disappointed.[59] At the Council at Preston on 27 November, Charles had claimed that Sir Watkin would meet the army with 300 horse between Macclesfield and Derby, and that the Duke of Beaufort 'would meanwhile raise South Wales and seize Bristol'. This was one optimistic asseveration too many for officers who had been hearing promises of French and English help almost since the Prince had landed.[60] On the Council, only Colonel O'Sullivan and Lieutenant-General the Duke of Perth supported the Prince, many of whose natural backers were not on the Council of War. The Captain of Clanranald and Lieutenant-General the Duke of Atholl (Marquess of Tullibardine) initially supported the Prince also: Frank McLynn has argued that it was the appearance of the double agent Dudley Bradstreet, with his tale of an army between the Jacobites and London, which finally swayed the Council, as Bradstreet himself gloatingly and no doubt exaggeratedly recalled in his *Life and Uncommon Adventures* (1755).[61]

Bradstreet, an Irishman, claimed that he had persuaded the Jacobites that Cumberland would cut off their retreat, while the Duke of Richmond attacked their west flank with his cavalry and a third army barred their way to London. This was all false, a lie which, as Bradstreet boasted, was 'the only Reason and Motive for that fortunate and dreaded Army . . . to retreat, from which Period date their inevitable Ruin'. Whatever credence is given to Bradstreet's own coxcomb claims (and many historians discount them altogether), the fact was that Finchley Common, the rallying point for the troops guarding London, was poorly defended. On 3 December, orders had been given to lead out the artillery train from Woolwich; on the same day, seven companies of the Black Watch (that mistrusted regiment) moved to Enfield, together with three other companies. On the 4th and 5th, five companies of foot and a squadron of dragoons moved into position. On the 6th, directions were given to the Lord Mayor 'for the security of the city'. Alarms and signs were put in place, the trained bands were on alert and 30 field pieces had been 'mounted on Carriages at the Tower'. There were still more than 18 companies to come up, Sinclair's Royals and the 39th Foot. But that was all: four battalions' worth of regulars and the trained bands against 17 Jacobite battalions, two regiments of horse and an artillery train. Victory was surely theirs for the asking.[62]

Doubt was, however, only too readily sown in the minds of a Jacobite leadership which (unlike its opponents, who had been officially opening correspondence since 4 October) had a poor intelligence system and had been repeatedly disappointed by the Prince Regent's overoptimistic assessment of the situation.[63] The Prince, who argued that the could reach London, paralyse the government and win over the mob, was no longer believed.

Who was right ? Lord George Murray, who was among the foremost proponents of retreat, had been half a defeatist from the beginning; the clan leaders almost certainly overestimated their safety from reprisal should they return to Scotland (and although in a majority neither in the army nor the Privy Council, chiefs dominated the Council of War). Colonel O'Sullivan's reputation has long been the victim of the personality clashes between Scots and Irish in the army, the anti-Irishness of many of the Scottish Jacobite memoirs we inherit, and the over-general acceptance of Lord George's total military ascendancy, tactical and strategic: a perhaps overdue revisionist case for O'Sullivan's military abilities has recently been put forward.[64] The argument was made that the army could have been harried by snipers and militiamen on the approach to London, but that had not been its fate to date: its opponents had rather melted away. Had Charles advanced, his army would almost certainly have swept aside the force at Finchley, and entered London.[65]

Everything then depended on five variables: (i) the reaction of the London populace, especially the mob and the governing elite; (ii) the embarkation of French forces; (iii) the landfall of same; (iv) the morale of the British field army, particularly in a situation where their lines of supply and pay had been cut off; (v) a general rising in England. Not all of these complement each other: a French invasion would diminish the chances of a popular Restoration, though perhaps not by as much as is sometimes supposed; on the other hand, without it, the odds on a successful dash on London by a determined Cumberland were probably better than those on a general rising. In 1485, 1553, 1651, 1660 and 1688 there had been little popular armed involvement in England in either support or opposition to factional battles or *coups d'état*: the prognostications for a mass English rising in favour of the Stuarts were not encouraging. Charles could have been like Northumberland in 1553, who despite government backing and his seizure of the Tower and other key points, was unable to hold London against Mary's forces for more than a fortnight.[66] A successful French invasion would have brought total victory – but at what cost to long-term stability ? Given that Charles would have gained victory at Finchley and reached London, the choice comes down to either a successful French landing, which would have had a certainty of delivering short-term victory, or a victory in the field by Jacobite forces already in control of the national finances, which might have been the precursor of a long-term restoration.

What would a Stuart victory have changed ? The optimistic case, put forward (in extreme form) by Sir Compton Mackenzie, among others, is that the face of history would have been radically altered. The race with France for top-nation status would have become an amicable *rapprochement*; the American colonies, rendered free to rebel by the removal of the French threat from Canada in the Seven Years' War, would have stayed British in the absence of that war. Britain itself would have reverted to the late Stuart model of a looser monarchy of three distinct kingdoms, with diverse administrations in Edinburgh and Dublin.

Anglicanism–Episcopalianism would have been the established Church in all these kingdoms, with Toleration and early emancipation for Catholics and an early end to discrimination against Dissenters. The Irish problem would not have existed, certainly not in its post-1782 form; but the United Kingdom would have itself been a more middle-of-the-road European imperial power rather than an icon of Protestant ascendancy and Empire.[67]

On the other hand, the possibility certainly exists that things would not have changed much. James or Charles would have been absorbed into a political system now more powerful than they, and would have continued as France's rivals (as some in France feared: hence the desire to restore the Stuarts to Scotland and/or Ireland rather than all three kingdoms). The Union with Scotland might have been ended or radically altered, and the position of Catholics in Ireland improved, but Presbyterianism would have had to remain established north of the Border and disappointed Episcopalians would have had to settle for merely being allowed to exist. A third alternative, the negative view, is that a Catholic monarch would have simply proved too unstable in the eighteenth-century Anglican/Presbyterian polity, and that his tinkering or fear of his tinkering with the religious settlement would once again have led to the Stuarts being expelled. All these views have something to commend them: the first is Panglossian, and barely differs from the rosiest expectations of some contemporary Jacobites; the third takes too little account of the declining anti-Catholicism of the elite (who, after all, were responsible for the Revolution of 1688, which was no popular rebellion) and the very different personalities possessed by James or Charles in particular, as compared to that of James II and VII. It might be one answer to say that only by adopting the second approach could the Stuarts have avoided the renewed calamity of the third: but the reader will make up their own mind as to the version of this fantasy, pleasing or otherwise, which is preferred.

The retreat, when it came, was well controlled, and evaded Cumberland's forces (to evade Wade's was little enough challenge, for the septuagenarian general proved incompetent in moving his troops), but the hostility of the localities increased. Anti-Jacobite rioting at Manchester on 9 December led to a fine of £2500 being levied on the city;[68] meanwhile Cumberland was encouraging the country people to kill stray Jacobite troops, wanting no blood on his own hands lest Hanoverian prisoners were mistreated.[69] Although artillery was abandoned, in some ways (number of horses for example) the Jacobite army retreated better equipped than it had been on the march south.[70] A skirmish at

Clifton staved off the Hanoverian van, while Major-General Oglethorpe, a Hanoverian commander from a Jacobite family, showed such
unusual incompetence in failing to engage the retreating army that he
was court-martialled: although acquitted, he went on to show his true
inclinations by backing the Jacobite paper the *True Briton*.[71] On 20
December, the army re-entered Scotland, having ill-advisedly left a
force behind to defend Carlisle: such hapless tokenism crumbled rapidly before Cumberland's guns, and the defenders suffered even
harsher penalties than those to which most captured Jacobites were
subjected.[72]

During the absence of the Prince's army in England, a second and
substantial force was raised in Scotland, initially under the command of
Viscount Strathallan as major-general, who ceded to Lieutenant-General Lord John Drummond after the latter landed with his Royal Scots
at Montrose on 22 November, a day after the British capture of a second French convoy aboard the *Soleil*, which included the Earl of Derwentwater.[73] (Recruitment in Scotland for the Royal Scots had taken
place over a number of years prior to the Rising, despite the vigilance
of the authorities.[74]) Lord John did not advance into England, as
Charles wished, but continued to raise men in Scotland.[75] The strongly
Episcopalian Lowlands north of the Tay were responding readily to the
call, with few complaining of being forced: indeed, 2000 had already
come out by the time Lord John landed.[76] The Earl of Cromartie (a
noted agricultural improver) supervised recruitment and the collection
of cess in Fife;[77] Lord Lewis Gordon acted as Lord Lieutenant of
Aberdeenshire and Banffshire; Colonel Sir Alexander Bannerman
governed the Mearns in the same capacity, while Lieutenant-Colonel
James Moir raised and commanded the Aberdeen battalion and Lieutenant-Colonel Sir James Kinloch occupied Angus with the 2nd battalion of the Forfarshire Regiment, supervising the landing of troops and
equipment from France, now engaged in providing significant support:
250 carts were landed at Stonehaven in mid-October.[78] Angus was particularly fertile territory for the Jacobites: Captain Patrick Wallace,
Provost and Governor of Arbroath, raised two companies for the
Forfarshire Regiment, while Robert Wedderburn of Pearsie, the Sher-
iff Clerk for the county, raised a third and Captain James Erskine,
younger brother to Lord Dun, two more. Sir John Douglas, the MP for
Dumfries, raised money from English Jacobite sources.[79] By contrast,
the Hanoverian authorities in Scotland raised only around 1000 men in
the western and central Lowlands in addition to Loudon's 2000-strong
Highland militia, which provoked the northern army's only major

engagement at Inverurie, where in December seven companies of Loudon's were met and defeated by a larger Jacobite force, in which the two companies of Royal Scots did most of the fighting.[80]

On one level, Charles's plans had succeeded. The launch of the Rising, victory at Prestonpans and agitation by his allies in France all persuaded the French government to launch an invasion, the seriousness of which was fully revealed in Frank McLynn's masterly study, *France and the Jacobite Rising of 1745* (1981). A force consisting of 17 battalions, six of them Irish and three Scots, was assembled, and had the Prince marched on from Derby this would very likely have sailed, although France's own envoy, the Marquis d'Eguilles, who had landed in Scotland on 14 October, may not have helped his own cause by exaggerating Jacobite numbers and thus inducing French complacency about the likelihood of Charles Edward succeeding without their help.[81] Throughout December, knowledge of the impending threat spread panic in England, even with the Jacobites in retreat (for example, London underwent a further panic after 9 December, and Ligonier was ordered there to defend it): not until late in January was it finally clear that there had been no collusion between Charles Edward's movements and those of the French. Cumberland returned south to meet the French threat, leaving General Hawley in command in Scotland:[82] the period between the Jacobite victory at Falkirk over Hawley on 17 January and the Jacobite retreat to the Highlands on 1 February is the second turning-point of the campaign, and the first occasion on which it became clear that the Jacobites must lose.[83] In fact, France had already changed its mind. The doubt that supervened on news of the retreat was such that 'by 2 January [1746] not even a direct order from Louis XV to invade immediately' could succeed. By 1 February, the invasion was officially abandoned in favour of drip-feeding supplies of men, money and *matériel* into Scotland,[84] four picquets being landed at Aberdeen and Peterhead shortly afterwards.[85] This strategy was on one level clearly diversionary; on another, it may have been part of a muddled switch in policy priorities towards Scottish autonomy. Charles Edward's verdict on such moves thereafter was a constant one: '*tout ou rien*'.

In all, the Jacobites raised between 11 000 and 14 000 men, probably only about three-fifths of the number who had come out under Mar (or even fewer, given the impact of French reinforcements which Mar had not possessed), but still an impressive figure for a dynasty off the throne for almost sixty years, and in its own right a credible mass fighting force. There were, according to Stuart Reid's helpful formulation, four main categories of recruit: those who were pressed (mostly Highlanders), fencibles raised by landowners in lieu of rent, those hired out by the county (a significant proportion in sympathetic areas: one-third of the Banffshire contingent) and volunteers, mainly found among 'officers, the cavalry, and many of . . . the lowland units'.[86] In many areas recruitment was harder work than in 1715, and if it was conducted more efficiently, accession to the ranks was at a slower pace, itself vitiated by occasional lack of arms, as when Lochiel sent some Camerons home from Edinburgh for want of guns and swords.[87]

The Atholl Correspondence bears impressive witness to the fact that the Jacobite army which was waiting at Edinburgh in October 1745 took an agonizingly long time even to surpass 5000 men, the number with which it set off in November. Such loss of time and men told against the vital principle of concentration of force. Yet while it was away, another 5000 were raised, as is reflected in the 10 200 available for the battle of Falkirk and the siege of Stirling in January, a rare concentration not achieved again: the ill-advised retreat from the central Lowlands north at the beginning of February no doubt precipitated the desertion it was intended to stem. Indeed, some recruits dispersed on hearing the news.[88] Stemming from this, the ultimate failure of the northern army even in its own localities was its inability to 'hold the Angus or Aberdeenshire ports long enough to enable the big reinforcement from Dunkirk in February to get through'.[89] Had the Jacobites hung on a day or two longer, 650 troops would have landed at Aberdeen: as a result of their failure to make landfall, the regiment following them did not sail.[90]

Cumberland's bloodthirstiness bought the Jacobites some time in early 1746, for the Duke's refusal to negotiate a cartel for prisoners led to his loss of the services of the Prince of Hesse, whose 6000 troops could have decided the issue much earlier (Lord George Murray indeed made some tentative advances to Hesse in the search for a negotiated settlement).[91] Despite the transient military successes made possible by Cumberland's own difficulties, time and, more importantly, money were running out for the Jacobites.[92] Although the decision to fight on a lumpy, waterlogged moor on 16 April was a foolish one, the battle of Culloden itself could not have been avoided: there were signs in early April of the increasing desperation of the underfed and underpaid army, now trapped behind the Spey, since Charles could not afford the resources to advance on Cumberland at Aberdeen. At this stage the French informed the Prince that 'all plans for a major expedition to Scotland had been laid aside'.[93] Those who suggest that a prolonged guerrilla campaign could have been conducted use both the vocabulary and the strategy of the twentieth century in an unhelpful hindsight. Lord George Murray was not Michael Collins, nor could the Jacobite army seamlessly blend back into daily life like the latter's shadowy brigades of volunteers. A society was, in large part, 'out': its state was public, its money was low, it had nowhere to go. In this sense, *sauve qui peut* was the only decision which could be made when the relics of the army assembled at Ruthven after the battle. Although Lochiel held out for some weeks, and isolated bands continued in arms until the 1750s, the maintenance of a force of thousands was impossible.[94]

Culloden itself was principally an artillery battle, in which Cumberland's guns held sway over a clear field and level ground: moreover, their variety of shot enabled them to be effective both at close and long range. Cumberland's force of 9000, about a quarter of them Scots (principally Campbells and Munros) faced around 6000 Jacobites, perhaps 1500 of whom slept through the battle:[95] this was largely a result of the disastrous attempt at an attack on Cumberland's camp during the preceding night, which had exhausted the men. Both the Earl of Cromartie and Cluny Macpherson were absent, the former on a mission to recover the French gold wrecked on the Kyle of Reay, had forced the Jacobites to give battle,[96] and to collect monies raised for the Prince in Orkney.[97]

In the early exchange of cannonades, the government gunners had the best of it. Although many shots went over the heads of the Prince's army, morale was dented as the attack was delayed (the couriers kept getting killed).[98] Government troops were meanwhile carrying out a flanking attack. After 10 minutes, the front line eventually charged (though in a disorganized fashion, and without effective volley firing from their steel wedges) and the Hanoverian gunners changed to canister shot, causing 200 Jacobite casualties a minute, though the infantry had time for only one volley before the Scots were upon them.[99] One wing of the government line gave way, but without the collapse of the whole front rank as at Killiecrankie and Prestonpans the Jacobites could not sustain this rate of attrition, which increased when the flanking fire of muskets at close quarters was brought into play, and the Highland, Aberdeenshire and Perthshire troops found themselves depleted, with no time to reload, and facing the ferocious wall of fire characteristic of the necessarily massed force of muskets individually inaccurate, but at fifty yards collectively deadly. Meanwhile a flanking movement of the Argyll militia attacked and disorganized the remaining lines of the Jacobite army. As the Prince's attack spent its force, the

government troops closed and moved forward. Keppoch fell to their
fire at the head of his men, and Viscount Strathallan died leading the
Perthshire Horse in a heroic but vain counter-attack. The Royal Scots
and the Irish stood firm, the latter round a small knoll on the battlefield's edge, their repeated volleys of musketfire sufficient to halt
the galloping dragoons from pursuit of the fugitives for some crucial
moments before they were forced to surrender, their commanding officer mortally wounded and scores of their men casualties.[100] The sole
Jacobite successes may have come from hand-to-hand fighting. Colonel MacGillivray killed several of his opponents, while the Quaker
Jonathan Forbes subsequently remarked that he 'let daylicht into three
of the English deevils' and Sergeant-Major Grant (the last survivor of
the battle, who died in 1824) remarked to his officer, 'Oh, let's throw
awa' thae fushionless things o' guns, and we can get down upo' the
smatchets wi' oor swords.'[101] In this context, Cumberland's much-
cited reformation of bayonet use, intended to enable Jacobite soldiers
in the front line to be bayoneted under their raised sword arm by the
man diagonally opposite them, may have been less effective than is
sometimes advertised, although the heroicization of the sword common in Gaelic poetry and the unlikely high casualty figures attributed
to some of the Jacobites who used it may give pause for doubt. In an
early elegy on the battle, the fiddler William Farquharson, who arrived
late on the field, 'broke his violin over his knees and never played
again': a powerful folk-motif found (for example) in the accounts of the
deaths of the social bandit James Macpherson at Banff in 1700 and of
the hero of the Irish patriot song 'The Minstrel Boy'.[102] By evening, 'the
road to Inverness was strewn with corpses', onlookers and passers-by
as well as Jacobite soldiers. The relatively intact units who marched
south fared best: to the west there was no safety: more were killed after
the battle ended than during it.[103]

Despite the magnitude of its defeat, the Jacobite army was not the
rag-tag and bobtail it has often been taken for. There seems to have
been less trouble in securing modern equipment for much of the army
than has been sometimes supposed. Far from being a banditti armed
with pitchforks and ammunition which did not match their guns, the
Jacobite army was a conventionally regimented contemporary force,
Lochiel's and the Forfarshire and Glengarry Regiments even having
grenadier companies. There is no sign that the up to 160 Hanoverian
soldiers who joined after Prestonpans felt out of place in a regiment
commanded by a Highlander (though admittedly many deserted),
while no fewer than 98 deserters from Guise's 6th Foot were in turn

retaken by the British Army at Culloden.[104] Highlanders were apparently quite prepared to be picqueted for work with other units, as can be seen in both Captain MacLean's recently published diary and in the joint defence of Newhaven on 28–29 October 1745, carried out by a mixed force of Clanranalds and the 1st battalion, the Forfarshire Regiment. There were also Lowland officers serving in Highland units, such as Lieutenant Henry Clark of the Canongate in Lady Mackintosh's, though this practice was rare. Lord George Murray designed a 'a simple method of drill which could be easily taught and understood' by the soldiers under his command;[105] in the north-east, officers of the Irish picquets were largely responsible for drill, Major Nicholas Glascoe, for example, being military instructor to the 2nd battalion, the Forfarshire Regiment.[106]

Only the gentlemen in the front ranks of the regiments appear to have been armed with the swords which are too often held to typify the Jacobite manner of fighting: on the field of Culloden, government troops recovered 2320 Jacobite muskets, but only 190 broadswords, and in subsequent surrenders the number of guns yielded up was four times the number of swords. This was true of even classically 'Highland' units, such as Glengarry's and Keppoch's. Not only was the battle of Falkirk principally won by musketry, but Jacobite artillery action was not as lame as some have supposed: the bombardment of Fort William alone utilizing 14 artillery pieces and hundreds of shells, while Cumberland's men recovered no fewer than 30 Jacobite guns after Culloden.[107] 'Extemporised arm' as the Jacobite artillery undoubtedly was, in Sir Bruce Seton's opinion, 'the English army itself was not much better supplied'.[108] As early as October 1745, a government spy attributed the victory of the Prince's troops at Prestonpans to the fact that the Jacobites had two or more firearms each: by contrast, the 'Regular foot' are characterized as 'having nothing but the Gun and Bayonet to trust to'; a similar report from Lancaster on 24 November says that 'the Highlanders have 2 pistols on each side of their Breast & a Musket slung over their Shoulders & a Broad Sword'.[109] In October, 1500–1600 stand of arms were unloaded at Montrose for Jacobite use;[110] at Stonehaven, six Swedish cannon which were reputed to fire nine rounds a minute, and 1800 ball were landed, the fishing fleet guiding them in safe past a man o' war; on the other hand, despite these influxes, some groups of troops were short of arms.[111] On the march south, troops were issued with 'twelve shot' each:[112] 50000 bullets were ordered at Manchester.[113]

Once again, it was the Union and antipathy to it which lay at the core of Jacobite support in Scotland, whether expressed directly or through the medium of Episcopalian difference (though there were only 130 Episcopal priests by 1746 compared to over 600 in 1689). In both the north-east and the west Highlands Episcopalianism was 'closely mingled' with a strengthening Roman Catholicism, which may have increased its adherents in the Highlands by up to 80 per cent between 1709 and 1745, although Episcopalians were significantly more likely to take up arms for the Prince than Catholics.[114] The Piskies were in fact very rigid Jacobites, and in the north-east at least would not give communion to those who had heard King George prayed for in the Church of Scotland or England until they repented.[115] Both Catholics and Episcopalians remained closely linked to the prospect of a Jacobite restoration, although support from the emplaced professionals of Scotland's independent banking, legal and educational services had diminished as a result of government action after the '15: on the other hand, a nationalist revival had to some extent been ensured by government repression following the Porteous riots and many of the '15's displaced professionals had continued resentful Jacobites.[116] There was still some official involvement with the Rising in Scottish society: as in 1715, local authorities were held to be guilty of complicity with the Rising by government agents.[117] Anti-Catholicism was also stronger, ironically so in view of Charles's ecumenical and latitudinarian tendencies: there was much less chance of a Presbyterian minister lending his support to Jacobitism in 1745 than in 1715. Yet despite uneven recruitment in the localities, there was a national quality to the Rising, reflected among other ways in the strength of the misguided 'fortress Scotland' policy of such patriots as Lochiel, or in the Chevalier Johnstone's view that the Prince should have raised a 'national war' between England and Scotland. Johnstone was Lord George Murray's ADC, and it is interesting to speculate whether the implicit lack of confidence in English Jacobitism displayed by such comments affected the conduct of the campaign.[118] The use of tartan as a standard uniform for the army was, as in 1715, intended to promote ideas of an ancestral and authentic Scottish nationality held in common by Lowland and Highland alike: 'loyalty to their King, and a desire to re-establish Scotland's independence . . . had brought them to the field'.[119] This was recognized by their enemies: the Earl of Chesterfield's March 1746 letter to the Duke of Newcastle, with its assertion that 'if Scotland be not an enemy country, I don't know what country can ever be called one' being only among the more extreme of contemporary identifications of Jacobitism's national quality.[120] In the latter stages of the Rising, French plans showed signs of tending towards a separatist solution, and this was reinforced by a February memorandum from the Jacobite leadership appealing for a French landing with significant arms in return for repudiation of the Union. In Frank McLynn's words, 'there was both a moral obligation and a political expedient for France to secure Scotland for Charles Edward, to break up the United Kingdom and to provide a bulwark for George II'.[121] After Culloden, Simon Fraser, Lord Lovat advised Charles to fight on like Bruce, in order to 'win Scotland': as Bruce Lenman rightly says, 'Scottish nationalism was perhaps Simon's strongest emotion next to megalomania.'[122] Interestingly, Lovat had been among the earliest to doubt the potential of English Jacobitism, taking a Scottish perspective as early as 1705.

In early 1746, Patrick Wade crossed over to Ireland as an emissary of Charles Edward, with a message of support for the Catholic community, but they were incapable of action due to the absence of the Irish Brigades and a heavy presence of British troops. The Earl of Chesterfield, Lord Lieutenant in Ireland, had (following the retreat from Derby!) acted with energy and decision: a reward of £50 000 (£20 000 more than the mainland figure) was put on Charles Edward, with additional bounties of £1000 for individual Jacobite commanders, and Chesterfield armed four regiments of Ulster Protestant volunteers without waiting for government authorization.[123] Any disaffection in the ranks was dealt with ruthlessly: 300 strokes of the cat o' nine tails were inflicted on one dragoon sergeant simply 'for uttering disrespectful words about George II'. Such prompt action, combined with the quietism of a Catholic leadership deprived of their natural military leaders and eager not to risk their slowly improving position under the status quo, and some effective anti-Jacobite propaganda, including that of the philosopher Bishop Berkeley, quieted the country, though there were invasion scares: on 27 October 1745, 15 000 Irish militia were ordered to County Down to await a rumoured Highland attack.[124]

In the aftermath, Charles Edward had difficulty believing in the extent of Cumberland's atrocities (General Hawley alone burnt 7000 cottages, while the heaping-up of wounded Jacobites and firing cannon into them for sport was only one of the more immediate means of despatch utilized by the Duke's forces), and a number of accounts attest to the Prince's lifelong feelings of uneasiness and even guilt for the fate (discussed further in Chapter 5) the failure of the Rising had brought on Scotland.[125] Meanwhile, Louis XV was 'stung by the accusation that he had left the Stuart prince to his fate' and ordered a large-scale rescue operation, which was eventually successful.[126] The British authorities, who had an embarrassment of prisoners, selected a proportion for exemplary treatment, a tactic they were to employ again in Ireland after the Easter 1916 Rising: 270 individuals were dispatched to Carlisle (the Privy Council had decided on 15 May to risk no Scottish trials) in August 1746;[127] some 120 were subsequently executed; over forty chiefs, gentry and noblemen were attainted.[128] On 12 August 1746, a fresh Disarming Act was passed, which banned both weapons and the wearing of Highland dress 'outwith the king's service'.[129] Episcopal clergy were treated more harshly than Roman Catholics, and the meeting-houses in which they worshipped were destroyed throughout their north-eastern strongholds, while legislation was passed which effectively outlawed their holy orders; meanwhile, the power of the landlords who had once protected them was severely curtailed by the abolition of heritable jurisdictions, among other measures.[130] However, despite the fact that significant armed groups of Jacobites were still at large in the Lowlands, by and large the government forces were more lenient there than north of the Highland Line. Indeed, there seems to have been at an early stage an implicit intention to ethnicize the '45 as a Gaelic rising, and to take the harshest measures against Gaelic society. The idea that the Rising was overwhelmingly Highland is one found in both hostile and romanticized accounts: at the time, it provided an excuse for alienizing part of Scotland as unredeemably barbarous (much the same language and images were used of the Catholic Irish in the nineteenth century); later it fed a romantic image of a glamorous and remote 'other', safely removed from any relevance to either eighteenth-century international politics or Scottish nationalism. That was not the view of the government in the 1750s: both the construction of the military white elephant Fort George, arguably the largest fort in the world, and the fact that Scotland was effectively under army occupation for a decade after the Rising testify to this.[131]

The English Jacobites

Jeremy Black has tellingly compared the situation in England in 1745 to that of the Bosworth campaign 260 years earlier, 'with most of the political nation inactive'.[132] Since the result in 1745 maintained, rather than destroyed the status quo, this inaction has frequently been conflated with opposition to the Jacobites: if no change occurs, those who do not overtly align themselves with its failed forces are held to have been against it; on the contrary, in cases where attempts at change are successful (e.g. 1688), the equal inactivity of the majority is held to show their consent to the change. This is the 'heads-I-win, tails-you-lose' version of history, which continues to have some very eminent practitioners. Such details as can be ascertained from England and Wales in 1745–46 do not altogether bear it out, nor is it easy now to appreciate the degree of genuine panic felt by many as the Jacobite army moved closer to its goal. As early as 28 September, only a week after Prestonpans, and with the Prince's forces still firmly north of the Border, many in England had stopped paying the land tax, and collateral from an association of London merchants was required to save the Bank of England's ability to pay out specie.[133] Bank of England stock fell by 10 per cent in two months,[134] and as early as 11 October, Lord George Murray presciently if perhaps exaggeratedly remarked that 'credite [sic] is at a stand; the greatest Banquiers have stopt payment; all would go to our wish if we could but march immediately'.[135] There was talk of a possible *coup d'état* precipitated by 'National Debt fund-holders',[136] and the Bank of England protected its stock by paying out to its agents in sixpences, which it then recycled to continue the process. On the other hand, some who were confident, like General Sir John Ligonier, saw market falls as a buying opportunity.[137]

There was certainly a degree of popular Jacobite display. Charles 'was greeted like a hero in Stockport', and the same was true at Preston;[138] at Ormskirk, 'two hundred Jacobite sympathizers assembled in the night . . . plying for volunteers at drumbeat and proclaiming King James'.[139] But private good wishes and rumours of a French landing seem to have been more typical responses, in a discourse already geared more to passive expectation than active preparation.[140] Whereas there were Jacobite riots and demonstrations aplenty after 1746, at Lichfield, Walsall and Exeter to name but three,[141] in the Year of the Prince itself the carnival spirit of English Jacobitism failed to develop its displays into decisions as the prospect of real change and the threat of the ultimate penalty from a frightened government both drew closer. Indeed, even in strongholds such as Manchester, there was significant anti-Jacobite feeling, while London saw pro-Hanoverian demonstrations on 30 October (George II's birthday) and 5 and 12 November.[142]

Recruitment remained weak, although it was claimed by some that there were 1500 English recruits with the Jacobites at Derby who melted away on the retreat, and by Lochiel that had arms been available, many more would have joined. Many who have studied the period find their stock of credulity too low to accept these claims, and note the convenient arrival of Sir Watkin and Lord Barrymore's messenger at Derby two safe days after the Jacobite retreat began. On the other hand, it could be argued that sending the messenger was in itself highly risky; yet the sceptic could answer that the message itself, that 'they would join in the capital or each in their own counties', was vague to the detriment of real commitment.[143] In 1732, Sir Watkin had raised 800–900 men to attack Chester's Whigs, but now nothing; even though Charles's 'now is the time or never' letter of 11 November failed to reach Lord Barrymore, it is hard to imagine the septuagenarian Earl doing much about it: though had 10 000 Irish or French regulars been with the Prince, it might have been otherwise.[144] Certainly there were sceptics in both the naval and war ministries in France, and John Hynde Cotton's acceptance of a place in the 'Broad Bottom' administration was viewed in some circles there as yet further evidence of the transient and unstable qualities of English Jacobite support: indeed, decreasing belief in the reality of English Jacobitism may have been instrumental in the increasing attention French policy began to pay to Scottish and/or Irish separatist solutions.[145] Although Barrymore, Cotton and Wynn 'had committed themselves to bring their levies to support Saxe's French invaders' in 1744, had the French landed (a real possibility) in December 1745, it is hard to believe that they would have been able to do very much at all, despite the fact that they had already demanded help from Versailles.[146] At least six other leading Tories had had some cognizance of the 1744 invasion plan, but they were of no effect.[147] Indeed, although Charles's Proclamation at Edinburgh on 9 October clearly stated that all who attended Parliament 'would be deemed guilty of "an overt Act of Treason and Rebellion"', Tory MPs practically tripped over one another to get to Westminster' eight days later. They would have been liable to arrest had they not gone: but they certainly took George's threats more seriously than Charles's.[148] Lord Clare was suspicious of Sir Watkin's lack of preparation, and in the end frankly told Maurepas that 'it was useless to expect anything of a party of which not a single member rose when the Stuart prince crossed half England and was so near London'.[149]

Doubt has been expressed concerning the uneven and unpredictable sentiments of the urban mob, especially in the capital. Uncertainty over the trustworthiness of the London poor is borne witness to in a number of sources, most strikingly by Hogarth's painting *The March to Finchley*, which depicts the preparations for the defence of London had Charles marched on from Derby: the townscape through which the soldiers uncertainly and apprehensively pass is littered with subversive iconography, suggestive of fears of mob recidivism. Jeremy Bentham later commented that 'multitudes of the citizens of London were friendly to the Stuarts . . . even in the corporation there were aldermen waiting to bring about the restoration of the exiled family', and this suggestion is echoed elsewhere: we know that there were serious Jacobite sympathizers in the London administration, as evidenced by the Independent Electors of Westminster. Moreover, a significant body of MPs at least, and possibly the majority of Tories, were opportunistically or otherwise well disposed to the Stuarts.[150] The good intentions towards the Jacobite cause visible in the continuing subventions made to the Stuarts by the Tory elite are certainly striking enough to suggest the sincerity of their Jacobitism on one level at least. Yet they could not be turned from subscribers into organizers, while the nature of the doubtful temper of the London mob is considerably more questionable: the evidence of the Gordon Riots and the depth of populist anti-Catholicism displayed on other occasions is hardly suggestive of a hotbed of Jacobitism, and Nicholas Rogers concludes that in London in 1745 (as opposed to 1715), Jacobitism 'had assumed a marginal, ethno-religious character. It was to be found among Catholics, principally the London Irish, but had lost ground among the wider community'. Anti-Popery propaganda may have had its effect: by 1745, 'anti-Catholicism struck . . . a responsive chord' as 'it did not in 1715'.[151] Henry Fielding's *True Patriot* (though it later moderated its tone) was not untypical: the 19 November issue castigated the advancing Jacobites as having 'the bloody hearts of Popish priestly bigots and barbarians', a fine example of alliteration, if not much else.[152] As had been the case in 1722, members of the elite sympathetic to the Jacobites may have overestimated popular support, and the fears of anti-Jacobites as to the sentiments of the mob may have simply been the terror of the Other manifest in alarm concerning a Jacobite fifth column in the dockyards, a largely unjustified anxiety over a group of key workers reminiscent of concerns over the loyalty of the Newcastle keelmen thirty years before.[153]

The London and provincial press adopted a determinedly pro-Hanoverian tone, though occasionally with reluctance, as in the case of the *Norwich Gazette* (Norwich, like the east coast ports in Scotland which lent so much support to the Jacobites, was in economic decline). There was even talk of an uprising there, and 'a number of leading Tories refused to join the local subscription'. On the other hand, there was a pro-Hanoverian demonstration in Bristol on 5 November,[154] and similar activity in Oxfordshire later in the month (though the north of the county was pro-Jacobite), but the government had less confidence in Chester's loyalty (in 1747, Cheshire was still 'officially denounced as a

"Jacobite and Popish county"').[155] Two years before, 'a faint attempt
had been made by the more adventurous Tory squires . . . to raise the
Stuart standard'. Warrington was also strong in its support, and
Cumberland's troops experienced at first hand the traditional West
Midlands Jacobitism of Staffordshire, one of his men remarking that
'the people here [Stafford] make no bones of telling us they would
rather see the Highlanders among them than the King's troops'.[156]

English Jacobitism was, by 1745, clearer on its problems than their
solutions. Neither in England nor Wales was there a national question,
potently combined with religious division and repression, to the extent
that obtained in Scotland or Ireland. Resentment at Hanoverian high-
handedness and presumptions of their bias towards the Electorate
in foreign policy were hardly grounds for revolution; the exclusion
of the Tories from office might make them prone to dabble in Jacobitism, but equally reluctant to form its vanguard; and the excision of
the juring High Church from the Anglican polity left only Nonjuring
ideologues and those with deep economic grievances as the core of a
Jacobite fifth column and fighting force. Whereas many might welcome the return of the Stuarts (and this is not to be lost sight of), in few
areas of England was there the critical pressure to spark an armed rising: the West Country might be one, Lancashire and Cheshire another;
but neither of these would move to any significant degree without
French help or a Jacobite victory on English soil, and preferably one
close to London.

Remember Limerick and Saxon Perfidy

Jacobitism and affection for the Stuarts were deeply woven into Irish
society throughout the eighteenth century: indeed 'until . . . 1766, all
but a handful of bishops appointed to vacant Irish sees were chosen on
the nomination of the Stuarts'. In 1756, 'Archbishop Michael O'Reilly
was arrested on a charge of aiding the Pretender', though it appears suspicion was in this case groundless.[157] Such levels of fear on the one side
and sympathy, hope and support on the other were sustained by the
increasing gravity and oppressiveness, at least in theory, of the Penal
Laws against Catholics. As late as 1758, 'the chief baron of the Irish ex-
chequer . . . declared that Irish law did not presume a Catholic to exist,
except for the purpose of punishment'.[158] It was small wonder that,
for Ireland's Catholics, 'a "restoration of the Stuarts" was, for a long
period, the only occurrence to which the oppressed majority of the Irish

nation could look for a permanent deliverance from the penal *regime* of the Revolution'.[159] In Irish (and usually in French) eyes the main vehicle of that restoration was to be the Irish Brigades in the service of France.

After the removal of 12 000 Irish soldiers to France following the surrender of Limerick, recruitment into the Brigades proceeded fairly steadily, combined with associated ventures such as the extensive use of Irish merchants and Irish-captained and crewed privateers. An Irish regiment had been raised for the French service in 1671,[160] so there was already a tradition upon which to build. The military Irish community abroad became known as the 'Wild Geese' from at least the early eighteenth century. It was romanticized by those who stayed in Ireland, from whom it recruited heavily: perhaps a total of 450 000 joined the Brigades during their existence. There were also major desertions from the British army: 1000 leaving Marlborough in the War of the Spanish Succession, for example.[161] In periods of peak recruitment such as 1711–14, at least 10 000, and possibly double this number of men joined the Brigade, while in the 1720s and 1730s up to 1000 a year entered their ranks. In 1714, 'men enlisted in Dublin were told "that they should immediately march to Lorraine and see the young king"', while those signing up in County Wexford 'were assured that "they were to serve King James the Third and that they should not fight a battle till they landed in England or Ireland"'. Rising concern led to a 1723 bill 'making it a felony to enlist in, or recruit for, any foreign service without licence'. As a result of this legislation, hundreds may have been hanged. As the Duke of Newcastle was informed by Archbishop Boulter, the Church of Ireland Primate, in 1730, 'all recruits raised here for France or Spain . . . are generally considered as persons that may some time or other pay a visit to this country as enemies. That all who are listed here in those services hope and wish to do so there is no doubt'.[162] Further legislation followed after the '45.[163] However, despite this fear and draconian use of the 1723 law, the possibility remains that 'the English might secretly have been glad of the [Irish] Brigade, as its net effect was to lessen the impact of Jacobitism in Ireland'.[164] By this reasoning, the messianic longing for the Brigade's return in triumph was a disabling one, which effectively rendered Irish Jacobitism in Ireland a passive phenomenon, expecting great things from abroad and thus unable to do anything at home.

Almost from its formation, the Irish Brigade had a reputation for ferocity: its soldiers were 'chosen in 1694 as the troops most suitable for employment in the suppression of the Camisards'.[165] In 1697, the

scaling-down of the French military establishment led to the full incor-
poration of some of the Brigade soldiers in the French army, and the
disbanding of other units, diminishing the total number in the French
service from 15 000 to 6000 (Brigade strength only fell slightly thereafter). As a result, an exodus began which scattered Irish soldiers and officers among the major powers of Europe, as well as leaving many
'homeless wanderers throughout France'. Many went to Spain, where
Ormond commanded them as Captain-General from 1718 to 1732:
both there and in France, officers and men continued to take a double
oath to James as well as to the monarch of their adoptive country.[166]
Recruits to other nations found a ready (and sometimes a familiar) welcome: for example,'prominent Irish families such as the Taafes, Butlers
and Wallis of Carighmain had records in the service of the Austrian
army'. As in France, the Irish in the Austrian service could maintain a
coherent community until a late date: one Irish soldier, for example,
'took his nephew very severely to task for failing to address him in
Gaelic on his arrival in Austria'.[167]

Three regiments were eventually formed in Spain, the first in 1709.
Many Jacobite officers rose high in the ranks and confidence of their
adopted country: Lieutenant-General William de Lacy was from 1750
member of the Supreme Council of War in Spain, while Lieutenant-
General Richard Wall even became Prime Minister. Until 1815, the
Ultonia (Ulster) Regiment was always commanded by an Irishman: it
was uniformed in 'Jacobite red',[168] and Jacobite colours were used by
Irish troops in France also as a mark of their closeness to the Stuarts, and
role as a force in reserve for use in any invasion attempt intended to
restore the dynasty, which indeed sometimes fought alongside them,
James III and VIII commanding a brigade at Oudenarde in 1708.[169]

Irish exiles were also influential in the development of continental
navies in the eighteenth century. George Camocke, who was dismissed
from the Royal Navy due to his Jacobite sympathies, entered the Spanish fleet as Rear-Admiral, subsequently taking King James to Scotland
in 1715. Both Christopher O'Brien and John O'Dwyer rose to admiral's
rank in the Russian service, as did John MacNamara in that of France.
As their community tended (and tends) to do in exile, many of them
remained at heart Irishmen, as is borne witness to in the rather touch-
ing inscription on the 'silver chalice' presented to a chapel near his
birthplace by Admiral O'Kuoney: 'The most illustrious Lord Daniel
O'Kuony, now Governor of Ferrola under the Catholic King, and who
had the command of his navy elsewhere on many occasions, bestoweth
this chalice on his native parish of Killanaspughlenane in the year

1756.'[170] The sad consequences of such clinging to national and local identities could be seen when these soldiers fought each other. On 14 October 1758, General (later Field Marshal) Charles O'Donnell's Austrian troops faced Prussians under the command of Field Marshal James Francis Edward Keith. When Keith fell, and his body was brought among the Austrian command, the senior Irish officers lamented the death of one who was by coincidence an adversary, but in essence a fellow Jacobite exile.[171]

The Brigade's finest hour was its decisive contribution to the French victory at Fontenoy on 11 May 1745,[172] which must have seemed to some Jacobite observers to presage their future success as an invasion force. As the rest of the French army was falling back, six Irish battalions 'advanced with bayonets at the level. The bagpipes, fifes and drums of the Irish played the Stuart hymn, "The White Cockade", and the officers yelled "Cuimhnigidh ar Liumreck agus feall na Sassanach" ("Remember Limerick and Saxon perfidy").'[173] What followed was, in Voltaire's words, revenge for 'their kings betrayed, their country and their altars'. The recorded shouts of the officers at Fontenoy emphasize an important feature about the Brigade and indeed the Irish community in general in France: its social cohesion and clearly Irish identity, seen in the preservation of Irish Gaelic for exhortation. This was not to persist: although recruitment from Ireland continued to blossom for a short time after the '45, with the coming of the 1748 Peace of Aix-la-Chapelle, 'and the decline in Jacobite prospects, recruiting of other ranks fell off':[174]

> In a sense the Irish Brigades never fully recovered from the War of the Austrian Succession, for the losses at Fontenoy and Laffeldt, two years later, were not wholly replaced from Ireland, and in part at any rate the strength was brought up to establishment by the inclusion of men who were not of Irish origin.[175]

The Irish composition of the Brigades was thus declining when Brigadier Count Lally took them to India to attempt to drive out the British in the late 1750s (Lally was eventually defeated at Wandewash by another Irishmen, Eyre Coote, and subsequently most unjustly made a scapegoat by France for its military failure in the Seven Years War). By 1779, fewer than one-tenth of the private soldiers among Dillon's casualties at Savannah were Irish, although that was to remain the nationality of Brigade officers until the 1790s: no fewer than eight future generals fought in Dillon's in this campaign.[176] The use of pro-Stuart oaths and asseverations belonging to an earlier phase of the culture of the Brigades continued in Ireland itself up to the close of the eighteenth century.[177]

Recruiting for the Brigades not only in Ireland but in Scotland continued after 1745, notably on the east coast and in the Highlands, utilizing both former Jacobite officers and those who had served elsewhere (e.g. Loudon's).[178] This activity may have continued up to 1789, when the Brigades' career was effectively cut short by the French Revolution: many subsequently served George III against the deist republicans who had supplanted their Bourbon leader, and at least two Irish generals were guillotined for anti-revolutionary activity.[179] Although Napoleon, with his Ossianic emphasis on the Celtic, founded an 'Irish legion' in 1803, it was merged with other foreign units eight years later, though in both the French and Spanish armies, company units still exist which can trace their genesis to the Brigades.[180]

5

The Jacobite Diaspora

Famed in their Absence

The Royal Family themselves were the leading Jacobite exiles, and after 1746 Charles continued for many years to struggle to secure from Europe's courts the support required to mount another rising. The elevation of his brother to the Cardinalate in 1747 was a considerable blow to these hopes: not only was it a propaganda gift to anti-Catholic sentiment; it was also a sign that the Prince's father and brother had given up all realistic hope of a Restoration, for Charles did not then or ever have a legitimate heir. Nonetheless, he persevered. In 1750, when he had secured 25 000 stand of arms, Charles visited London, and met 50 English Jacobites including the Duke of Beaufort at a house in Pall Mall: they wanted foreign help, not weapons, and probably wished also for Charles to land in Scotland, or at least as far away from them as possible. The Prince's conversion to Anglicanism on this trip made few converts to Jacobitism: indeed, Episcopalians grieved when they heard he was visiting Lutheran churches on the Continent. The conspiratorial visit of 1750 was thus 'a wasted journey': but at least the Newcastle keelworkers at last justified fears of their Jacobitism by proclaiming 'James III' when they went on strike.[1] This piece of *épater le bourgeois* bore no further fruit, and the Elibank Plot of 1751–53, which had as its aim the kidnapping of George II as part of a *coup d'état*, was no more successful: betrayed by Young Glengarry ('Pickle the Spy'), all it achieved was the execution of Dr Archibald Cameron, Lochiel's brother and the last man to die for his Jacobitism.[2] It was no coincidence that these attempts were aimed directly at London and the English heartland. Although sympathetic to Scotland's plight, Charles was resistant to any French attempts to create a Scotland-only solution: in this he was perhaps wiser than some of his companions in exile, such

as Lochiel:[3] indeed, by 1753 the Prince was considering the merits of
Union for both Scotland and Ireland, not united to England until 1801.[4]
French priorities were different, and tended towards the use of
Jacobitism to split the British state – as early as 1747, the authorities were
considering the possibility of a a Scottish Republic.[5] Despite the continuation of Jacobite papers in England (there were Jacobite-leaning
organs in York, Oxford and Bristol, as well as the *True Briton* and the
London Evening Post (which had a circulation of 5000)) into the 1750s, the
cause was clearly in decline, accelerated by increasing unwillingness to
pay Charles more subventions in the light of his deteriorating behaviour.[6] In 1759, the last major Jacobite attempt (planned by the Duc de
Choiseul) was brought to nothing by the French naval defeat at Quib-
éron Bay, though as late as 1770, Choiseul was considering the possibility of yet another Rising.[7]

After his father's death on New Year's Day 1766, Charles's finances
improved, but the political outlook continued to deteriorate. An increasingly Anglophile papacy was not interested in recognizing his
claim, and his state reception by the rectors and students of the English,
Scottish and Irish colleges in Rome was looked on with strong disapproval.[8] At the beginning of the War of American Independence
(which Charles followed with avidity), an approach may have been
made by a deputation from one of the states (possibly Massachusetts) to
the Prince to help head the insurrection (according to one account, to
become king).[9] Certainly, Jacobitism was strong in some of what were
to become the United States: notably South Carolina.[10] Charles was by
this time in no condition to oblige, or to satisfy the Americans that he
was capable of obliging such a request: in any case, anti-Jacobitism had
already a long history in the North American colonies. In 1746, the
Virgina Gazette of Williamsburg had published forged Jacobite battle
orders from Culloden which suggested that Lord George had offered
the Hanoverians no quarter, and at the Boston Tea Party 30 years later,
anti-Jacobite imagery was also in evidence.[11] There were few other
flickers of Jacobite activity after 1770, leaving aside John Caryll's uto-
pian approach to the French government concerning 'plans for a
Jacobite attempt in Scotland' in 1779.[12] Disturbances in Ireland in the
1780s briefly raised the threat of the Jacobite menace, which the French
Republic was still brandishing as a paper tiger ten years later.[13] The
Jacobite afterblow on other fronts was yet more fantastical. The Scottish radical Thomas Muir attempted to convince the Directory that
thousands of Highlanders would rise to put George III off his throne
and establish a free Scotland (the direct contrary of what was in all

probability the case).[14] Admiral Nelson was supposed to have had some Jacobite sympathies, there even being a tradition that he entertained Henry, Cardinal Duke of York on his flagship,[15] while in 1819 Lord Liverpool decreed court mourning for the death of the King of Sardinia (then the Jacobite heir): but such stories are elusive and probably insignificant, the products of sentiment or incurable optimism. Cardinal York's own title as King Henry 'IX', *non desideriis hominum, sed voluntate Dei*' ('king not by the desires of men but the will of God') was a more dignified farewell to Stuart prospects: the Cardinal continued to use the Royal Touch.[16]

The most senior Jacobite exiles outwith the Stuart family probably found it much easier to reconcile themselves to their fate than did Prince Charles: indeed, they sometimes seem to have (at least latterly) had little incentive to leave their glittering careers for fresh Jacobite efforts. Men like the Duke of Berwick, Charles O'Brien, 6th Viscount Clare and the Duke of Ormond rose to the highest circles in France and Spain.[17] James Francis Edward Keith, the Earl Marischal's brother, pursued an exceptionally successful military career on the Continent after his exile following the failure of the '15, rising to be Governor of the Ukraine and Field Marshal in the Prussian service before dying a hero's death at the battle of Hochkirk in 1758 and passing into German folklore.[18] On being asked for his brother's papers in order to write an account of his life, the Earl Marischal simply replied 'he lived well; he died bravely'. James Keith's statue stands in the town square in Peterhead (in its day a notoriously Jacobite town) in his family's home region.[19]

His brother, George Keith, the Earl Marischal, followed a diplomatic career in between his involvement in subsequent Jacobite risings, culminating in the '45, serving as both Ambassador Extraordinary to France and Spain and also as the Governor of Neuchâtel, where he met Jean-Jacques Rousseau, to whom he 'revealed ... his essential republicanism'.[20] In his absence, Marischal continued to support Marischal College, Aberdeen's second university (united with King's in 1860), which had been founded by his family in 1593, and to dream of establishing a community of scholars (to include Hume and Rousseau) in the eyries of his north-east heartland. Yet when the Earl Marischal finally did return to Scotland in 1761, diehard Jacobite opinion in the north-east could still regard him as a traitor despite his 45 years of exile. It was said that the church bell at Langside split when it was supposed to ring for the Earl Marischal's birthday on 2 April 1761. 'Do you know what the bell says by that ? even, The deil a cheep mair sall I speak for you, Earl Marischal' was the Episcopalian priest (and well-known songwriter) John Skinner's gloss on this event (Skinner himself perhaps remembered the plundering of his own house at Langside by the government in 1749). Within a few months, the Earl was reported as 'much despised and neglected'. Whether because of his chilly welcome, or the chilly climate of a Scotland from which he had been absent so long, the Earl Marischal soon returned to the Continent.[21]

Jacobite exiles were responsible for building up the Russian armed forces in the eighteenth century, just as exiled Royalist commanders such as Sir Tam Dalyell had in the seventeenth. Thomas Gordon, dismissed from his Royal Navy captaincy in 1715 on the grounds of suspected Jacobitism, joined the Russian service, recruited disaffected British naval officers, and became Peter the Great's admiral. In France, where exiled Jacobite officers conducted recruiting missions in Scotland as well as Ireland to strengthen their forces, by the 1740s there were 5000 Scots in the Royal Scots in the French service.[22]

Not all Scots abroad turned to military or diplomatic careers. John Law the financier, among the most famous of all Jacobite or quasi-Jacobite exiles, and the subject of a poem by Allan Ramsay mourning the loss his absence represented to Scotland, became Comptroller-General of the French finances in 1720.[23] Law, born in 1671, was from a financial family: his father sat on the Royal Commission 'to enquire into the working of the Scottish mint' set up in 1674. His own career as a theorist began early: in 1705, Law published an essay on the revival of the Scottish economy, *Money and Trade considered with a proposal for supplying the Nation with Money*. Following his flight from England due to a murder charge in 1695 (he killed an adversary in a duel), Law spent some time at St-Germain before founding a major private bank in France in 1716, subsequently developing the Company of the West, which was due to take over the National Debt of France until a panicky flight to specie brought its advanced system of paper credit to collapse. The Scots economist had introduced paper money to France for the first time, as well as other instruments such as futures and margin trading: these concepts were brought in too clumsily and rapidly in a country unused to and suspicious of them, though Law's bank was to become 'the prototype of the Bank of France'. Subsequently he was invited by Peter the Great to take over Russian finances, but the penalties for failure were so unlovely under the Tsar's regime that Law wisely declined. In the 1720s, he was used by the British government as a foreign agent, ending his life in poverty in 1729, although the credit that he championed was by that time well on the way to winning Britain its superpower battle with France.[24]

Among other figures in the world of Jacobite business and finance, Colin Campbell served in Gothenburg as director of the Swedish East India Company, while there were also Jacobite 'business communities' at Bilbao, Cádiz, Seville and Málaga.[25] There was also, of course, a significant Jacobite presence in North America, due to the repeated transportations of the disaffected after the major risings, as well as to voluntary emigration from this same group. Many of these were luckier than the government intended them to be: after the '45, 150 prisoners on the *Veteran* were captured by a French ship and set free on Martinique; in Maryland in 1747, Jacobite gentlemen clubbed together to buy nearly all the arriving transportees, setting them free immediately.[26] Perhaps the most distinguished American Jacobite was the Revd John Witherspoon, active in the '45, who signed the Declaration of Independence.[27]

Lord Ogilvy of Airlie, who commanded the Forfarshire Regiment in 1745, rose in France to the rank of lieutenant-general, as did Lord John Drummond, from which it can be seen that the '45 Rising was led by men of no mean military ability.[28] Among other participants in the Rising who later found a successful career abroad were Lord Macleod, who became a Swedish colonel, and William Sharp, an Ensign in the Life Guards, who became a major-general in the Portuguese Army (Sharp was the great-grandson of Archbishop Sharp, murdered at Magus Muir near St Andrews by Covenanting extremists in 1679). Colonel Henry Ker of Graden, Lord George Murray's ADC, became a senior field officer in the Spanish service.[29] It is worth noting also that among Jacobite officers both the Master of Lovat, who commanded the Frasers on his father's behalf, and Captain Allan Maclean subsequently achieved the rank of general officer in the British Army (MacLean, however, had the irritating habit of leading his men into battle wearing the white cockade).[30] In 1762, the three Scottish regiments in the French service were incorporated into the Irish Brigades, but members of the Scots Jacobite diaspora continued to rise to positions of eminence in the French army, most notably Marshal MacDonald, Duke of Taranto, one of Napoleon's most senior commanders, and a folk hero in his native Highlands, which he visited in 1825, being amazed by the tactical incompetence implicit in what he saw of Culloden Battlefield, and learnt of the disposition of troops there.[31]

The last category of Jacobite exiles were those who were not Jacobites. The increasing use of Highland troops in the Seven Years

War and thereafter removed thousands of people far from their homes and the patrimony they had once defended to fight in Britain's imperial wars. As early as the time of Union it had been proposed that the Scots forces should be used in the most dangerous campaigns: 'as good they perish as better men' was the view,[32] an uncanny foreshadowing of General Wolfe's 'Tis no great matter if they fall', an outlook which continued to affect the military use of Scots troops. The army was the last place where the wearing of tartan was legal, but those who wore it there often paid as high a price as if they had still been donning it for the Prince: at Fort Duquesne, Montgomery's Highlanders lost 231 from their roll of 400; at Ticonderoga, the Black Watch 650 from 1300 engaged; and at the Plains of Abraham and St Foy combined, the Frasers lost 380 from an establishment never exceeding 700. Although many non-Scottish units suffered heavily on an individual basis, the overall casualty rate in five major engagements is striking: 32 per cent for the Highlanders as against 9 per cent for English and American troops.[33] In the front line at Culloden, the Frasers had lost up to 250 from 400 (in a neat piece of reconciliatory symbolism, Wolfe, who had fought with Cumberland, was said to have died in the arms of a Fraser on the Plains of Abraham).[34] Whether fighting for Stuart or Hanover, the result for the rank and file was the same, and the Master of Lovat, commander of the Frasers for both dynasties, was in this light as much a fox as his father, albeit, in the end, more fortunate: though the rank of lieutenant-general in the British army could not compare with the dukedom under the restored Stuarts that Simon Fraser had once sought. No Jacobite commander suffered as few penalties as did the Master; and hardly any clan suffered more casualties than the Frasers.

Internal Exile

In *The Lyon in Mourning*, his celebrated account of the context and aftermath of the '45, Robert Forbes, Bishop of Caithness, left an invaluable source of anecdote and reportage concerning the fate of that highly significant body of internal exiles, the Scottish Episcopalians. A concatenation of poems, prolonged hopes and reported or doctored heroic scaffold defiances, *The Lyon* (the heraldic insignia of the King of Scots) illustrates the mentality of an underground community, driven in the aftermath of the '45 away from even the few refuges it had possessed. The despairing reports of 1746 that even meeting-houses at Tain and Fortrose in the Episcopal heartland were being burnt are the unmistakable cries of a community being forced even further to the margins (as far as Catholicism: the loss of the Roman Catholic library at Presshome in the Enzie due to government action was also deprecated in *The Lyon*). Although ritualistically decrying the 'corruptions of the Church of Rome', the Nonjurors who were executed or martyred in 1746 were equally antipathetic to 'the followers of Luther and Calvin', enthusiastic for the title of 'Catholic', and described the bogeyman status of Popery as a 'specious bugbear'. It was little wonder that the Anglican government was on the whole harder on them than on the Catholics, who were a known quantity, tended to be localized in the Highlands, could more readily be alienized and in any case were noticeably less unconditionally enthusiastic in their support for the Stuarts in Scotland.[35]

Despite the banning of Episcopal orders granted in Scotland from 1747 (it was not until 1867 that the Scottish Episcopal Church entered the Anglican Communion), the clergy still managed to maintain sizeable numbers of adherents in their heartlands. As late as 1774, single congregations in Edinburgh could rise as high as 200, and in Aberdeenshire up to four times as many as this.[36] In Moray in 1770, 500 were confirmed, and both the Scriptures and consecrations were available in Gaelic where required.[37] The continuing nationalism of the Episcopalian/Jacobite community is borne witness to in a number of sources: the writer of one letter reproduced in the *Lyon* proudly advertises the fact that 'this is written on paper manufactured in Scotland'.[38] On Prince Charles's death in 1788 the Episcopal Church as a whole accepted the claim of George III, but at least one bishop continued to hold out in favour of the Jacobites (thus the remaining Nonjurors supported the claim to the throne of a Catholic Cardinal!). Both in Scotland and England, the Nonjuring schism drew to a close at the beginning of the nineteenth century, though the last Nonjuror is reputed to have survived until the 1870s.[39]

In the Highlands and Lowland periphery meanwhile, things were more desperate. Towards the Highlands the government followed a policy in three stages: first, the wholesale slaughter under Cumberland immediately following the battle; secondly, 'selective terrorism' under the Earl of Albemarle; and thirdly, the starvation of Jacobite districts 'through the wilful destruction of crops, livestock and property with the stated intention to effect either clearance or death'. As Allan Macinnes argues:

The immediate aftermath of the Forty-Five was marked by systematic state terrorism, characterised by a genocidal intent that verged on ethnic cleansing; by banditry as a form of social protest; and by cultural alienation as chiefs and leading gentry abandoned their traditional obligations as protectors and patrons in pursuit of their commercial aspirations as proprietors.[40]

Yet despite the ferocity of official action, the continuing presence of armed Jacobite units in the field ensured 'the growth of banditry, not only in such traditional haunts as Lochaber and Rannoch Moor, but in most mountainous districts of the southern and central Highlands'.[41] Ten years after Culloden, there were no fewer than 60 British Army patrols and outposts in Scotland.[42] The tendency to ethnicize the '45 by blaming it on the Highlanders (later to have its equal and opposite reaction in an inaccurate romanticization of their role) increased as Lowland efforts at self-exculpation intensified: the appeal for a Scottish militia during the Seven Years War could emphasize Lowland trustworthiness and further alienize the '45 as an intrusion 'from the most remote parts of the Kingdom'.[43] It is instructive to note that the Revd Alexander Carlyle, one who publicly argued for the Militia in these terms, could privately note with satisfaction that even as early as 1750, his friend the Revd John Home and the Jacobite James Hepburn of Keith were in perfect amity, despite the fact that the latter 'had been in both the rebellions of 1715 and 1745, and had there been a 3rd . . . would have join'd it also'. Lowland trustworthiness was a matter of public relations rather than fact.[44]

Jacobite clubs continued to flourish in Scottish society. The Royal Oak Club, active in Edinburgh from the late 1760s, had definite Jacobite connotations: 'they have a sovereign whose head is adorned with a blue bonnet', as one sympathizer remarked. The Duke of Cumberland in particular was an object of hatred throughout Scotland (for example, in the Edinburgh Jacobite riots on Prince Charles's birthday in 1748, when a company of men openly marched down 'the Canongate to the Abbay [Holyrood] gate' in Jacobite uniform. His death in 1765 was commemorated in a poem later adapted by Robert Burns:

> He burnt and rob't, undeemus skaith !
> And starved the saikless unto death.
> He levied them o' baith meat and claith
>   The bony Duik,
> For which he sits now scarce o' breath
>   In a heat nook.[45]

The white rose and tartan were used in English and Welsh society, too, as symbols of Jacobite sympathy in the aftermath of the '45;[46] but the government appeared sated with its brutal treatment of the Manchester Regiment (the colonel, five of the six captains, five of the eleven subalterns, the chaplain and seven of the eight sergeants taken and tried were hanged, drawn and quartered), and was disposed to view such displays as tokenism, which indeed they perhaps were.[47] Nonetheless, six troops of horse were required to quell the last serious outbreak of plebeian Jacobitism at Walsall (again in the West Midland heartland) in 1750. There were riots in Exeter in 1752, possibly in connection with the Elibank plot, while as late as 1768 there were Jacobite candidates elected at Preston. The last prosecutions for Jacobite 'seditious words' in England took place in the north during the Seven Years War, with one in Hexham as late as 1761, while the last Jacobite riot in England was at Nottingham on 10 June 1779.[48]

Despite a general tendency to benevolent oversight (George III sent 'the Elector of Hanover's compliments to Oliphant of Gask, on hearing that the redoubtable laird remained irreconcilable), the authorities continued to be fearful of Jacobitism for longer than is sometimes admitted. Although 'seditious words' prosecutions petered out in the 1760s, Jacobite songs were still radical enough to be utilized by radical mobs in Scotland in the 1790s, being also present in Irish Defenderism.[49] Jacobite songs and symbolism thus clearly intrude into the Jacobin period: indeed, it has been said that 'a Jacobite is just a frustrated Jacobin'.[50] As late as 1808, Charles Kemble's translation of a French play, *Edouard en Ecosse* ('Charles Edward in Scotland'), was regarded as offensive by the Lord Chamberlain's office (it was not played until 1829),[51] and in 1817 the protest route of the Manchester Blanketeers followed in Charles Edward's footsteps to Derby.[52] It was the death of George III, rather than the French Revolution, which finally brought about a sea-change. In 1822, George IV (who had first worn tartan at a ball in 1789) became the first Hanoverian monarch to visit Scotland, and was greeted in Edinburgh not only by a tartan extravaganza, but also with a Jacobite concert, which included some songs of Carolina Nairne's own composing (Carolina, née Oliphant, was the daughter and granddaughter of Jacobite commanders; she married the heir to the attainted title of Lord Nairne: in 1824 this title, along with those of Mar, Kenmure, Perth and Strathallan, was restored).[53] The King also had an audience with the last survivor of the '45, Sergeant-Major Grant, who introduced himself as 'Your Majesty's oldest enemy'. When Grant died two years later, 'Wha Wadna fecht for Charlie's richt' was played at his funeral. The rehabilitation of Jacobitism under the distancing eye of romance had begun.[54]

The Jacobite Critique

The main reason for the underestimation of Jacobitism's importance in British history is also the reason for its marginalization in the first place: the fact that it was, in Jeremy Black's words, 'the greatest military challenge faced by the British state in the eighteenth century'. The key words here are those of 'British state'. It is no accident that those (either contemporary politicians or subsequent historians) who have sought and celebrated the coalescence of that state have also been responsible for the multiple misrepresentations of Jacobitism which have endured to our own day, some of which I analysed in *The Myth of the Jacobite Clans* (1995). Jacobitism was far more than the recidivist attempt to sustain the hereditary right of an unpopular dynasty, or the outdated lifestyle of marginal groups, though it may have comprehended these motives. It was rather a movement whose activists and supporters, while differing in their ultimate aims, tended to coalesce around a few key issues. Of these, nationalism was perhaps the most important, but in the case of English and Welsh Jacobitism scarcely relevant: indeed, the difference between the priorities of Anglo-Welsh and Scots-Irish Jacobites was arguably one of the most significant faultlines in Jacobite support (that there were also problems between the Scots and Irish, a cursory examination of the '45 makes clear). Historic English suspicion of the Scots no doubt played its part in the inactivity of English Jacobites: indeed the question of to what extent the very Scottishness of the Jacobite armies of 1715 and 1745 inhibited recruitment is an important one. In 1715, when there were a significant number of English troops, disagreement between English and Scots Jacobite commanders was frequent to the point of being endemic.

To turn to shared priorities, for Jacobites the deposition of King James in 1688–91 was not only the replacement of a rightful king with a usurper, but also arguably the end of a whole system of caesaropapist sacramental monarchy, the cessation of which rendered the Anglican and Episcopalian churches vulnerable to mainstream Protestantism, and, beyond that, Latitudinarianism and deism. Hence the large scale of the Nonjuring schism; hence the strong pro-Stuart streak in juring High Anglicanism as late as 1720; hence, too, the continuation by the Stuarts in exile of practices such as the Royal Touch, associated with their particular brand of caesaropapist Anglicanism. Before 1688, England's Anglican monarchs were (with the exception of Edward VI) High Church to the point of equivocating with Catholic doctrine, if not with the papacy itself; afterwards they became mainstream Protestants in general without sacramental pretensions. High Anglicanism thus became homeless in the state until the advent of the Oxford Movement, many of whose members took a dim view of the so-called 'Glorious' Revolution. The view of eighteenth-century juring Anglicanism as riddled with torpor, lassitude and Latitudinarianism was one not merely held by Dissenters, deists and Methodists, but also by the Nonjurors, who clung to a more stubbornly caesaropapist and caesaro-sacramentalist vision of Church and State. This was a great divide, especially after the state effectively politicized the bench of Bishops through a stream of Whig appointments after 1715.

The patriot or native qualities of the Stuarts were also important (one reason why Hanoverian propaganda often tried to alienize them or their support, particularly after High Anglicanism's pro-Stuart edge was blunted after 1715–22). The string of foreigners who had been apparently (and to some extent really) preferred in the entourage and service of William II and III or George I was a powerful motive for pro-Stuart feeling, representational as it was of an envisioned settled order from the past, linked to a pre party-political world when 'loyalty no harm meant'. On the other hand, Queen Anne's 'entirely English heart' and the native qualities so assiduously associated by some among the Patriots with Prince Frederick in the 1730s served to quieten Jacobite xenophobia: by the time of the '45, it had almost spent its force: indeed, the government and its supporters had more success in depicting Charles Edward as foreign than their opponents effected with regard to George II.

Allied with the confessional/sacramental and native qualities of the dynasty was the importance of its hereditary claim, the first to be undisputed in English history since the Conquest: hence the importance for his opponents of claiming James Francis Edward's illegitimacy. The pageantry of hereditary right which had been celebrated by James VI and I, heir to the houses of Tudor, Plantagenet and Wessex (by the marriage of St Margaret of Scotland to Malcolm III), was the representation of a reality which was still intact. George was fifty-eighth in line to the throne: it was a matter not of setting aside one heir or two, but a whole company of them, and on the grounds of their religion alone. This was a major innovation: attempted by Northumberland in 1553, it had failed resoundingly. In contemporary Europe, it was also avant-garde. The Orthodox Peter the Great (a bloody enough tyrant) maintained Lutheranism in his Baltic provinces, even guaranteeing religious toleration from 1702, while Catholic German princely families did not lack the opportunity to rule Protestant subjects. So ferocious indeed was British anti-Catholicism (matched only in part by French anti-Protestantism, though Huguenots tended to be tolerated after 1715), that religious toleration reached most of the European powers before finally making landfall on these shores.[55] If such a challenge to legitimacy was unusual on religious grounds, there were other points of concern. Such a development was seen by some as a metaphor for the undercutting of all property rights, since primogeniture had been so completely laid aside: the perceived rise of a new class of moneyed men, themselves the beneficiaries of new financial instruments introduced by the post-1688 regime, intensified this feeling, as did the overt suspension of rights of primogeniture in the case of Catholics under the penal laws passed by the new state. The bias to the poor and support for traditional gentry duties which the Stuart regimes had evinced, or were thought to have evinced, served in certain areas of England to coalesce the political interests of Tory gentlemen and the 'lower orders': the social spectrum involved in the Windsor Black activities is one sign of this, as is the protective gentry attitude towards smugglers in some areas.

Ideologically speaking, Stuart rule and power had been associated with the rural imagery of an idealized countryside at least since the War of the Three Kingdoms in the 1640s, and possibly as far back as the Book of Sports in the 1620s. Stuart links with the oak, memorably and providentially exemplified in Charles II's escape at Boscobel, were part of a presentation of the dynasty's rule as a function of idealized ruralism, fertility and renewal: a role which could easily be merged with that of their sacramental authority in a discourse of messianized fertility. In the end, this ruralism was to be refashioned in the nineteenth and twentieth centuries as an expression of ideal Englishness, much as the oak detached itself from the Stuart dynasty to become an icon of English identity by the 1730s. Although this particular Jacobite discourse had better results in art than action, being of its very nature nostalgic and/or idealistic in tone, it was still instrumental in intensifying levels of sympathy and support for the exiled dynasty, as were other cultural discourses such as (particularly in its Scoto-Latin formation) classicism, discussed in Chapter 3. The image of the Stuart heir as fertility king was a particularly potent one, frequently used.

All these motives for Jacobitism might have counted for nothing after the mid-1720s in England, if it had not been for George II's unwise policy of continuing to keep the Tories out of office, which led at least a rump, probably a sizeable rump and possibly a majority of that party, to agitate or consent to agitation for a Stuart restoration as the only reliable means of gaining political advancement. But for the Jacobite cause to have to depend on dissident and splintered factions within Parliament (which, in its post-1688 phase, there is little evidence that many Jacobite exiles understood, as was seen in James's rather supine negotiations with the wiley Harley), was itself a shifting and unstable basis of support: it was also one which by its nature was less adept at action than intrigue.

Things were otherwise in Ireland and Scotland, where national and religious issues placed practical support for the Jacobites in an entirely different perspective. In Ireland, the claims for national autonomy made by James's Dublin Parliament of 1689 were to remain a focus of nationalist nostalgia for centuries; following its failure, the Restoration revision of the Cromwellian land settlement was overturned, and the last case for Catholics was worse than the first; the Penal Laws were extended and intensified (this was a motive for Jacobite Catholicism on mainland Britain too, but not nearly to the same extent); the Treaty of Limerick was breached in the spirit if not the letter, and tens of thousands went into exile on the Continent (here there is a similarity with the 150 000–200 000 Huguenots driven from France in the aftermath of the revocation of the Edict of Nantes).[56] Moreover, the Stuarts alone (through their descent from the Scottish royal house's Irish roots) were regarded as rightful monarchs of Ireland, whose return would expel the Saxon and restore Catholicism and righteousness: in this context the continental outlook of Irish Jacobitism and its sympathy with Catholic France and Spain is worth noting.

Lying at the core of Jacobite ideology in Scotland were three key issues: Scottish nationalism, the restoration of the Episcopal Church to its established position, the indefeasible hereditary right of the exiled dynasty (in practice, given the deep Scottish roots of the Stuarts, this was conflated with the nationalist issue) and a desire to maintain the social *status quo ante*. Episcopalian Lowland Scots were in general the deepest-dyed ideologues of the Jacobite movement in Scotland, partly because in the period before 1746 they had most to lose.[57] Despite atrocities like Glencoe, the Jacobite clans had suffered relatively little, and by and large relied on their remoteness to secure their position in the event of any reverse, while Episcopalian society in the Lowlands had already been extensively purged in repeated visitations by the authorities. The situation after Culloden was to reverse this position, and break the military threat of the clans. Meanwhile, declining Episcopalianism undermined the particular nature of culture and society in east coast Scotland north of the Forth, while the depredations of the authorities in the Highlands and the passing of legislation to end heritable jurisdictions also had a marked effect. Opposition to the Union remained a feature of Scottish life right into the 1820s, but its militancy was increasingly subdued, and thereafter was largely (though not completely) transformed into romantic nostalgia.[58]

Yet Jacobitism has an enduring legacy which surpasses the misrepresentational sentiment under the guise of which it is so often presented to the world. Jacobite nationalism, ecumenism, defence of minorities and opposition to the structural modernizing of an agricultural economy through which many (lastly and most markedly in the Highland Clearances) suffered, were all features of the outlook of pro-Stuart activism. Under the Hanoverians, the British Isles consolidated as a state, a tendency also found at this time in Central and Eastern Europe, where major warfare led to the eradication of local autonomy. Just as Russia's absorption of its Baltic and Ukrainian neighbours pushed back the Swedish, Polish and Turkish threat, so England's Irish garrison and Scottish Union closed the door to French aggression.[59] The Stuarts continued to offer, or appear to offer, something different: and this was what many of their supporters wanted. The Jacobite critique of a centralized and centralizing state and its thirst for war and Empire has its echoes both in its own time and today, as does its emphasis on and suspicion of Parliamentary corruption. Jacobitism was the first fruit and for a long time the sole means of opposition to the British state as it developed in its modern guise after 1688: in this sense the adoption of Jacobite writers by twentieth-century Irish nationalist figures like W. B. Yeats and Daniel Corkery is part of a continuing process, just as no one who lives in or knows Ulster today can avoid the symbolism of the Jacobite war of 1689–91, the ultimate source of Unionist triumphalism. Meanwhile in Scotland, 5000 gathered at Culloden on the anniversary of the battle in 1996, many in Jacobite uniform: reenactments are forbidden, and this was an act of tribute and mourning. Scottish middlebrow and highbrow society remain fascinated by the Jacobite myth, the subject of endless articles in the Sunday papers, and the source of many of the metaphors which stalk Scotland's history today, as I argued in *The Invention of Scotland* (1991). And if England, the core of the imperial state which succeeded the Stuarts, has less reason to be fascinated by their passing, the presence of their imagery still lingers in the idealization of rural England as the 'true' *locus amoenus* of nationality and worth. When, in Jane Austen's *Mansfield Park*, the improving Rushworths cut down the oaks on their estate at Sotherton and close its chapel they are violating England and the organic heart of Englishness: but the symbolism their actions inherits is that of Stuart iconography, as

Jane Austen, who came from a Jacobite family, may well have known. Her idealized country gentleman, her Darcy or Knightley, is the Tory counterblast to Fielding's and Macaulay's caricatures of booby Jacobite squires. The symbols of Jacobitism as a cultural, military, national, social and religious movement always reverberated from greater depths than those of an opinion which arbitarily favoured Stuart Tweedledum over Hanoverian Tweedledee. The Jacobite cause maintains the power to mythologize the past, but the study of its reality is even more interesting.

NOTES

Introduction

1. Cf. Daniel Szechi and David Hayton's essay, 'John Bull's Other Kingdoms', in Clyve Jones (ed.), *Britain in the First Age of Party 1680–1750* (London and Ronceverte, 1987).
2. For an examination of Jacobitism in these terms, see Paul Monod, *Jacobitism and the English People* (Cambridge, 1989) and Daniel Szechi, *The Jacobites* (Manchester, 1994).
3. Murray G. H. Pittock, *The Myth of the Jacobite Clans* (Edinburgh, 1995), p. 25.
4. John Kenyon, *The History Men* (London, 1983), p. 155 and *passim.*
5. Cited in Pittock, *Myth*, p. 10.
6. Paul Langford, *A Polite and Commercial People* (Oxford, 1989), p. 197; the phrase is Jeremy Black's.
7. A. D. Innes, *A History of the British Nation From the Earliest Times to the Present Day* (London and Edinburgh, 1912), p. 601.
8. Cf. Murray G. H. Pittock, *The Invention of Scotland* (London and New York, 1991), pp. 120 ff.
9. For a recent discussion of Episcopalian Nonjurors and their impact on Tractarianism, see Peter Nockles, '"Our Brethren of the North": The Scottish Episcopal Church and the Oxford Movement', *Journal of Ecclesiastical History* (1996), 655–82.
10. Cf. Sir Charles Petrie, 'If: a Jacobite Fantasy', which first appeared in *The Weekly Westminster* for 30 January 1926, and thereafter in *The Jacobite Movement: the Last Phase*, revised edn (London, 1950).
11. Eveline Cruickshanks, writing in Romney Sedgwick (ed.), *The History of Parliament: the House of Commons 1715–1754*, 2 vols. (London, 1970), I: 62–78.
12. Cf. Ian Christie, 'The Tory Party, Jacobitism and the 'Forty-Five: A Note', *Historical Journal*, 30:4 (1987), 921–31.
13. Cf. E. P. Thompson, *Whigs and Hunters* (Harmondsworth, 1975).
14. J. G. A. Pocock, 'British History: A Plea for a New Subject', *Journal of Modern History*, 47:4 (1975), 601–21; 'The Limits and Divisions of British History: In Search of an Unknown Subject', *American Historical Review*, 87 (1982), 311–36.
15. Further details of Monod's work are to be found in his 1985 Yale Ph.D. thesis, 'For the King to Enjoy his Own Again'.
16. Cf. also Clark's essay, 'On Moving the Middle Ground: the Significance of Jacobitism in Historical Studies' in Eveline Cruickshanks and Jeremy Black (eds.), *The Jacobite Challenge* (Edinburgh, 1988).
17. Among them *The Invention of Scotland* (1991), by the present author.
18. Cf. Elizabeth Carmichael, 'Jacobitism in the Scottish Commission of the Peace, 1707–1760', *Scottish Historical Review*, 58 (1979), 58–69.
19. Daniel Szechi, 'Mythhistory versus History: the Fading of the Revolution of 1688', *Historical Journal*, 33:1 (1990), 143–54 (143).
20. Cf. in particular Bob Woosnam-Savage's 1995 Glasgow Museums exhibition.

1 A Foreign King and a Patriot Queen

1. Keith Brown, *Kingdom or Province? Scotland and the Regal Union, 1603–1715* (Basingstoke, 1992), p. 80; Keith Brown, 'The vanishing emperor: British kingship and its decline, 1603–1707', in Roger A. Mason (ed.), *Scots and Britons* (Cambridge, 1994), pp. 58–87 (87).
2. Brown in Mason, *Scots and Britons*, p. 86.
3. Michael Lynch, *Scotland: A New History* (London, 1991), p. 288.
4. Sir Charles Petrie, *The Jacobite Movement: the First Phase*, revised edn (London, 1948), p. 226.
5. Brown, 'Vanishing emperor', in Mason, *Scots and Britons*, p. 87.
6. J. G. A. Pocock, 'Two kingdoms and three histories? Political thought in British contexts', in Mason, *Scots and Britons*, pp. 293–312 (307).
7. Allan Macinnes, *Clanship, Commerce and the House of Stuart 1603–1788* (East Linton, 1996), pp. 79, 139, 140.
8. Ibid., pp. 139, 191.
9. A. H. Dodd, *Studies in Stuart Wales*, 2nd edn (Cardiff, 1971 (1952)), pp. 1, 19, 33–4.
10. Cf. ibid., and Murray G. H. Pittock, *Inventing and Resisting Britain* (London: Macmillan, 1997), p. 15.
11. Cf. Pittock, *Inventing*, pp. 10–11.
12. J. G. Simms, *Jacobite Ireland* (London, 1969), pp. 1, 3, 8; S. J. Connolly, *Religion, Law and Power: The Making of Protestant Ireland 1660–1760* (Oxford, 1992), pp. 14–15, 19, 21, 23, 32.
13. Simms, *Jacobite Ireland*, pp. 25, 32.
14. J. Kenyon and J. Miller in Eveline Cruickshanks (ed.), *By Force or by Default?* (Edinburgh, 1989), pp. 1–27; cf. Petrie, *Jacobite Movement*, p. 73.
15. W. H. Murray, *Rob Roy* (Edinburgh, 1993) (1982)), p. 84; John Miller, *James II*, 2nd edn (London, 1989), pp. 190ff.
16. Philip Aubrey, *The Defeat of James Stuart's Armada 1692* (Leicester, 1979), p. 22; Magnus Linklater and Christian Hesketh, *For King and Conscience: James Graham of Claverhouse, Viscount Dundee* (London, 1989), p. 144; Cruickshanks, *By Force*, pp. 28–43.
17. Cruickshanks, *By Force*, p. 32.
18. Aubrey, *Defeat*, p. 23.
19. Linklater and Hesketh, *For King*, pp. 147–9.
20. Cruickshanks, *By Force*, p. ii.
21. Murray G. H. Pittock, *Poetry and Jacobite Politics in Eighteenth-Century Britain and Ireland* (Cambridge, 1994), Ch. 1.
22. Eveline Cruickshanks, 'Attempts to Restore the Stuarts, 1689–96', in Eveline Cruickshanks and Edward Corp (eds.), *The Stuart Court in Exile and the Jacobites* (London and Rio Grande, 1995), pp. 1–13 (1–2); cf. *Letters of George Lockhart of Carnwath*, ed. Daniel Szechi (Edinburgh: Scottish History Society, 1989).
23. Pittock, *Poetry*, Ch. 5.
24. Tim Harris, 'London Crowds and the Revolution of 1688', in Cruickshanks, *By Force*, pp. 44–64 (58).
25. Daniel Szechi, 'Mythhistory versus History: The Fading of the Revolution of 1688', *Historical Journal*, 33:1 (1990), 143–54 (150).
26. Cf. Chris Fitter, 'Henry Vaughan's Landscapes of Military Occupation', in *Essays in Criticism* (1992), pp. 123–47 and James Turner, *The Politics of Landscape* (Oxford, 1979).
27. Paul Monod, 'Pierre's White Hat', in Cruickshanks, *By Force*, pp. 159–89 (160).
28. Charles Dalton, *The Scots Army 1661–1688 With Memoirs of the Commanders in Chief*, 2 parts (London and Edinburgh, 1909), p. xxvii.

29. Linklater and Hesketh, *For King*, pp. 148–51; Cruickshanks, *By Force*, pp. 28–43 (32).
30. Aubrey, *Defeat*, pp. 33–4; Anon., *An Account of the Proceedings of the Meeting of the Estates in Scotland* (London, 1689), p. 1.
31. Anon., *A Letter to a Member of The Convention of States in Scotland* (Edinburgh, 1689), pp. 6–7.
32. Bruce Lenman, 'The Scottish Nobility and the Revolution of 1688–1690', in Robert Beddard (ed.), *The Revolutions of 1688: The Andrew Browning Lectures 1988* (Oxford, 1991), pp. 137–61 (143, 153, 156).
33. Linklater and Hesketh, *For King*, pp. 152–65. For a discussion of Philp's poem, see Pittock, *Poetry*, Ch. 1.
34. Aubrey, *Defeat*, pp. 33–4; Daniel Szechi, *The Jacobites* (Manchester, 1994), p. 43.
35. Francis Godwin James, *Ireland in the Empire 1688–1770* (Cambridge, MA, 1983), p. 15.
36. Simms, *Jacobite Ireland*, p. 80.
37. Raymond Gillespie, 'The Irish Protestants and James II', *Irish Historical Studies*, XXVIII:10 (1992), 124–33 (131).
38. *Letters of John Grahame of Claverhouse Viscount of Dundee with Illustrative Documents*, ed. George Smythe (Edinburgh: Bannatyne Club, 1843), pp. 35–7.
39. Szechi, *Jacobites*, p. 43.
40. *Letters . . . Dundee*, pp. 38–41; Macinnes, *Clanship*, pp. 182n, 190.
41. Linklater and Hesketh, *For King*, pp. 178–9, 190.
42. *Letters . . . Dundee*, p. 48.
43. Ibid., p. 79.
44. Bruce Lenman, *The Jacobite Cause* (Glasgow, 1986), p. 24; *Letters . . . Dundee*, pp. 67, 70, 78.
45. Lenman, *Jacobite Cause*, p. 27.
46. Cf. Aubrey, *Defeat*, p. 46.
47. *Memoirs of Sir Ewan Cameron of Locheill*, ed. Bindon Blood and James MacKnight (Edinburgh: Abbotsford Club, 1842), pp. 294 ff.
48. Petrie *Jacobite Movement*, p. 84.
49. Aubrey, *Defeat*, p. 57.
50. Szechi, *Jacobites*, p. 49; Simms, *Jacobite Ireland*, p. 242; Frank McLynn, *The Jacobites* (London, 1985), pp. 15–18.
51. Szechi, *Jacobites*, p. 50.
52. Connolly, *Religion*, pp. 147 ff.
53. Simms, *Jacobite Ireland*, pp. 242, 252–3, 258, 260–2, 263–4, 267.
54. John Childs, 'The Abortive Invasion of 1692', in Cruickshanks and Corp, *Stuart Court*, pp. 61–72 (68–9).
55. Aubrey, *Defeat*, p. 78.
56. Childs, 'Abortive Invasion', p. 66.
57. Szechi, *Jacobites*, p. 55.
58. Aubrey, *Defeat*, pp. 116, 128.
59. Cruickshanks, 'Attempts', in Cruickshanks and Corp, *Stuart Court*, pp. 1–13 (4).
60. Aubrey, *Defeat*, pp. 74, 87.
61. Petrie, *Jacobite Movement*, p. 74.
62. Edward Corp, 'Introduction', in Cruickshanks and Corp, *Stuart Court*, pp. ix–xxiv (xiv–xv).
63. Nathalie Genet-Rouffiac, 'Jacobites in Paris and Saint-Germain-en-Laye', in Cruickshanks and Corp, *Stuart Court*, pp. 15–38 (18).
64. Corp, 'Introduction', in Cruickshanks and Corp, *Stuart Court*, pp. xvii, xx.
65. Ibid., pp. xx, xxi.
66. Rouffiac, in Cruickshanks and Corp, *Stuart Court*, p. 27.
67. Ibid., pp. 34–5, 38.
68. Ibid., p. 33.

69. Eveline Cruickshanks, 'Introduction', in Cruickshanks (ed.), *Ideology and Conspiracy: Aspects of Jacobitism, 1689–1759* (Edinburgh, 1982), pp. 1–14 (5–6).
70. Daniel Szechi, 'The Jacobite Revolution Settlement', *English Historical Review* (1993), 610–28 (624).
71. Paul Hopkins, 'Sham Plots and Real Plots in the 1690s', in Cruickshanks, *Ideology*, pp. 89–110 (89).
72. Cf. Szechi *Jacobites*, p. xiv.
73. Ibid., p. 56.
74. Cruickshanks, 'Introduction', in Cruickshanks and Corp, *Stuart Court*, pp. 1–13 (7–10).
75. Petrie *Jacobite Movement*, p. 112.
76. Szechi , *Jacobites*, p. xv.
77. H. T. Dickinson, 'The Jacobite Challenge', in Michael Lynch (ed.), *Jacobitism and the '45* (London, 1995), pp. 7–22 (11–13).
78. Anon., 'How the Risings of 1715 and 1745 affected Kincardineshire', *Aberdeen Journal: Notes and Queries*, I (1908), 83–4 (84).
79. Murray G. H. Pittock, *The Myth of the Jacobite Clans* (Edinburgh, 1995), p. 47; also see Jean McCann, 'The Organisation of the Jacobite Army, 1745–46', unpublished Ph.D. thesis (University of Edinburgh, 1963), pp. 137, 146, 147.
80. *Aberdeen Journal: Notes and Queries*, II (1909), p. 146.
81. Szechi, *Jacobites*, p. 67; Macinnes, *Clanship*, pp. 174, 176.
82. Macinnes, *Clanship*, p. 176.
83. *Aberdeen Journal: Notes and Queries*, I (1908), p. 126; Peter F. Anson, *Underground Catholicism in Scotland 1622–1878* (Montrose, 1970), p. 102.
84. Anson, *Underground*, pp. 93, 95, 102, 107, 111.
85. Bernard and Monique Cottret, 'La sainteté de Jacques II, ou les miracles d'un roi défunt (vers 1702)', in Edward Corp (ed.), *L'Autre exil: les Jacobites en France au début du XVIIIe siècle* (Les Presses du Languedoc, 1993), p. 79–106; Szechi, *Jacobites*, p. xv.
86. Pittock, *Poetry*, pp. 49–50.
87. Edward Gregg, *Queen Anne* (London, 1980), pp. 26–7, 53, 130, 131.
88. Szechi, *Jacobites*, pp. 70–1.
89. George Mackenzie, Viscount Tarbat et al., *The Laws and Acts made by the First Parliament of Our Most High and Dread Sovereign James VII* (Edinburgh, 1731), p. 723.
90. Patricia Dickson, *Red John of the Battles* (London, 1973), pp. 34, 39–40.
91. P. W. J. Riley, *The Union of England and Scotland* (Manchester, 1978), pp. 204–5; Szechi, *Jacobites*, p. 71.
92. Riley, *Union*, pp. 57, 198; Dickson, *Red John*, pp. 43, 50–1.
93. Szechi, *Jacobites*, p. 71; Lenman, *Jacobite Cause*, p. 40.
94. Gregg, *Queen Anne*, p. 148.
95. Riley, *Union*, p. 283.
96. Dickson, *Red John*, p. 102.
97. John Gibson, *Playing the Scottish Card: The Franco-Jacobite Invasion of 1708* (Edinburgh, 1988) pp. 75–8, 81–90; Szechi, *Jacobites*, p. xv.
98. Gibson *Playing the Scottish Card*, pp. 78, 81.
99. Frank T. Galter, 'On the literary value of some Scottish Presbyterian writings in the context of the Scottish Enlightenment', in Dietrich Strauss and Horst W. Drescher (eds.), *Scottish Language and Literature, Medieval and Renaissance* (Frankfurt, 1986), pp. 175–92 (181–2).
100. 'A speech without doors upon the present State of the Nation' [June 1718], National Library of Scotland MS 17498 ff. 134–44, 146:2v; Szechi, *Jacobites*, p. xiv.
101. Gibson *Playing the Scottish Card*, pp. 94–7.
102. Ibid., pp. 10, 19.
103. Ibid., p. 103.
104. Ibid., p. 46.

105. Ibid., p. 101.
106. Ibid., p. 99.
107. Lenman, *Jacobite Cause*, p. 41.
108. Ibid., pp. 41–2; Szechi, *Jacobites*, pp. 56–7.
109. Cf. Frank McLynn, 'An Eighteenth-Century Scots Republic ? – An Unlikely Project from Absolutist France', *Scottish Historical Review*, 59 (1980), 177–81.
110. Geoffrey Holmes, 'The Sacheverell Riots', *Past and Present*, 72 (1976), 55–85 (69).
111. Geoffrey Holmes, *The Trial of Doctor Sacheverell* (London, 1973), pp. 74, 230.
112. Szechi, *Jacobites*, p. xvi.
113. Holmes, *Doctor Sacheverell*, p. 265.
114. Nicholas Phillipson, 'Politics and Politeness in the reigns of Anne and the early Hanoverians', in J. G. A. Pocock, Gordon Schochet and Lois Schwoerer (eds.), *The Varieties of British Political Thought 1500–1800* (Cambridge, 1993) pp. 211–45 (213).
115. Daniel Szechi, *Jacobitism and Tory Politics, 1710–14* (Edinburgh, 1984), p. 86; Macinnes, *Clanship*, p. 176.
116. Holmes *Doctor Sacheverell*, pp. 263, 274.
117. Lenman, *Jacobite Cause*, p. 44.
118. Szechi, *Jacobites*, pp. xvii, 74; Dickson, *Red John*, p. 161.
119. Dickson, *Red John*, pp. 157–9.
120. Alistair and Henrietta Tayler, *1715: the Story of the Rising* (Edinburgh and London, 1936), pp. 311, 313.

2 Military Goals and Other Means

1. Daniel Szechi, *The Jacobites* (Manchester, 1994), p. 65.
2. Ibid., pp. 74–5.
3. Ibid., p. xvii; Richard Sharp, *The Engraved Record of the Jacobite Movement* (Aldershot, 1996), p. 203.
4. Leo Gooch, *The Desperate Faction? The Jacobites of North-East England 1688–1745* (Hull, 1995), p. 41; Murray G. H. Pittock, 'The Culture of Jacobitism', in Jeremy Black (ed.), *Culture and Society in Britain 1660–1800* (Manchester, 1997), pp. 124–45 (127); see also H. T. Dickinson, 'The Jacobite Challenge', in Michael Lynch (ed.), *Jacobitism and the '45* (London, 1995), pp. 7–22 (12).
5. Paul Monod, *Jacobitism and the English People* (Cambridge, 1989), p. 174.
6. Alistair and Henrietta Tayler, *1715: The Story of the Rising* (London and Edinburgh, 1936), p. xiii.
7. Monod, *Jacobitism*, p. 168.
8. Nicholas Rogers, *Whigs and Cities* (Oxford, 1989), p. 26.
9. Monod, *Jacobitism*, p. 181.
10. Ibid., p. 187; Pittock, 'Culture', in Black, *Culture*, p. 127.
11. Gooch, *Desperate Faction?*, p. 41.
12. Monod, *Jacobitism*, p. 222.
13. Rogers, *Whigs*, p. 366.
14. Monod, *Jacobitism*, pp. 220 ff.
15. David Hayton, 'Traces of Party Politics in Early Eighteenth-Century Scottish Elections', in Clyve Jones (ed.), *Parliamentary History: The Scots and Parliament* (Edinburgh, 1996), pp. 74–99 (76, 83, 88).
16. For discussion of Ramsay, cf. Murray G. H. Pittock, *Poetry and Jacobite Politics in Eighteenth-Century Britain and Ireland* (Cambridge, 1994), pp. 149–60 and 'Were the Easy Club Jacobites', *Scottish Literary Journal*, 17:1 (1990), 91–4.
17. Szechi, *Jacobites*, p. 22.
18. Taylers, *1715*, pp. 311, 313.

19. Anon., *A Discourse of the Necessity and Seasonableness of an unanimous Address for Dissolving the UNION* (n.p., 1715), 5.
20. Daniel Szechi, *Jacobitism and Tory Politics, 1710–14* (Edinburgh, 1984), p. 67; *Letters of George Lockhart of Carnwath*, ed. Daniel Szechi (Edinburgh: Scottish History Society, 1989), pp. 5n, 53n, 58n, 75n, 76n, 85n, 95n.
21. Szechi, *Jacobitism*, p. 19.
22. Taylers, *1715*, p. xix.
23. Gooch, *Desperate Faction?*, p. 34; Sir Charles Petrie, *The Jacobite Movement: the First Phase*, revised edn (London, 1948), p. 163.
24. Gooch, *Desperate Faction?*, pp. 36–7; Geoffrey Holmes and Daniel Szechi, *The Age of Oligarchy: Pre-industrial Britain 1722–1783* (London and New York, 1993), p. 98.
25. Petrie, *Jacobite Movement*, pp. 165–8.
26. Edward Gregg, 'The Jacobite Career of John, Earl of Mar', in Eveline Cruickshanks (ed.), *Ideology and Conspiracy: Aspects of Jacobitism, 1689–1759* (Edinburgh, 1982), pp. 179–200 (183); also L. B. Smith, 'Spain and the Jacobites, 1715–16', in the same volume, pp. 159–78 (168); Szechi, *Jacobites*, p. xviiii.
27. Petrie, *Jacobite Movement*, pp. 191–3.
28. *Letters of George Lockhart of Carnwath* (1989), pp. 118–19.
29. Taylers, *1715*, pp. 29–30.
30. Ibid., p. 31.
31. Ibid., pp. 36–7, 41.
32. Colonel Sir John Baynes, Bart., *The Jacobite Rising of 1715* (London, 1970), p. 29.
33. Patricia Dickson, *Red John of the Battles* (London, 1973), p. 182.
34. *A Fragment of a Memoir of Field-Marshal James Keith, Written by Himself 1714–1734* (Edinburgh: Spalding Club, 1843), p. 11.
35. Taylers, *1715*, p. 39.
36. Alistair and Henrietta Tayler, *Jacobites of Aberdeenshire and Banffshire in the Rising of 1715* (Edinburgh and London, 1934), p. xx; Szechi, *Jacobites*, p. xvii.
37. John, Master of Sinclair, *Memoirs of the Insurrection in Scotland in 1715*, ed. Messrs. MacKnight and Lang, with notes by Sir Walter Scott, Bart (Edinburgh: Abbotsford Club, 1858), p. 107.
38. Taylers, *1715*, p. 52.
39. Taylers, *Jacobites*, pp. xxviii ff.
40. Taylers, *1715*, p. 94.
41. Ibid., pp. 46, 48, 60; Dickson, *Red John*, pp. 184–5.
42. Taylers, *1715*, pp. 46, 48, 60.
43. Szechi, *Jacobites*, p. 77.
44. Taylers, *1715*, p. 72; Allan Macinnes, *Clanship, Commerce and the House of Stuart 1603–1788* (East Linton, 1996), p. 182n; Murray G. H. Pittock, *The Myth of the Jacobite Clans* (Edinburgh, 1995), pp. 50–1.
45. Bruce Lenman, *The Jacobite Cause* (Glasgow, 1986), pp. 51, 53.
46. National Library of Scotland MS 874 f. 2; Pittock, *Myth*, pp. 50–1.
47. Baynes, *Jacobite Rising*, pp. 100, 133; Sinclair, *Memoirs*, pp. 74, 178, 179, 180; Taylers, *1715*, p. 330.
48. Sinclair, *Memoirs*, pp. 77, 179; Baynes, *Jacobite Rising*, p. 91.
49. Gooch, *Desperate Faction?*, p. 43.
50. Bruce Lenman, *The Jacobite Risings in Britain 1689–1746* (London, 1980), p. 120.
51. Gooch, *Desperate Faction?*, p. 12; Baynes, *Jacobite Rising*, p. 91.
52. Gooch, *Desperate Faction?*, pp. 73–6.
53. Ibid., p. 76; Taylers, *1715*, p. 81.
54. Lenman, *Jacobite Cause*, p. 55.
55. Taylers, *Jacobites*, p. xiv; James Michael Hill, *Celtic Warfare 1595–1763* (Edinburgh, 1986), pp. 82–3.
56. Gooch, *Desperate Faction?*, pp. 77, 78, 79.

57. Monod, *Jacobitism*, pp. 321–2.
58. Geoffrey Holmes, *Augustan England* (London, 1982), p. 269.
59. Gooch, *Desperate Faction?*, pp. 80–2; Taylers, *1715*, p. 255; Frank McLynn, *The Jacobites* (London, 1985), p. 100.
60. Sinclair, *Memoirs*, p. xxiv.
61. Hill, *Celtic Warfare*, pp. 89–90.
62. W. H. Murray, *Rob Roy MacGregor* (Edinburgh, 1993 (1982)), pp. 184–5.
63. Taylers, *1715*, pp. 96, 98.
64. Murray, *Rob Roy*, pp. 184–5.
65. Ibid., pp. 184–5; Hill, *Celtic Warfare*, p. 90.
66. Hill, *Celtic Warfare*, pp. 90–2.
67. Christopher Sinclair-Stevenson, *Inglorious Rebellion: The Jacobite Risings of 1708, 1715 and 1719* (London, 1971), p. 121; Baynes, *Jacobite Rising*, p. 225.
68. Sinclair, *Memoirs*; Gordon Donaldson, *Scotland James V to James VII*, Edinburgh History of Scotland, 3 (Edinburgh and London, 1965), pp. 333–4.
69. Taylers, *1715*, p. 116.
70. Taylers, *Jacobites*, p. xvi.
71. Lenman, *Jacobite Cause*, pp. 57–8.
72. Taylers, *1715*, pp. 128–30.
73. James Thomson, *The History of Dundee* (Dundee, 1874), p. 114; Taylers, *Jacobites*, p. xvi; Szechi *Jacobites*, p. xviii.
74. Lenman, *Jacobite Cause*, p. 57.
75. Petrie, *Jacobite Movement*, p. 198.
76. Taylers, *1715*, pp. 137–8, 143; Lenman, *Jacobite Cause*, p. 58; Petrie, *Jacobite Movement*, p. 197.
77. Taylers, *1715*, pp. 173–4.
78. Ibid., p. 176.
79. Petrie, *Jacobite Movement*, pp. 200, 212.
80. Taylers, *1715*, p. 328.
81. Petrie, *Jacobite Movement*, pp. 200, 213.
82. Gooch, *Desperate Faction?*, p. 93.
83. Sharp, *Engraved Record*, p. 21.
84. Ibid., p. 31; Pittock, *Poetry*, pp. 67–8.
85. Cf. Sharp, *Engraved Record*.
86. Taylers, *Jacobite Rising*, pp. 218 ff.
87. David Dobson, *Jacobites of the '15* (Aberdeen, 1993); Taylers, *Jacobite Rising*.
88. Murray, *Rob Roy*, p. 172.
89. Jean McCann, 'The Organisation of the Jacobite Army, 1745–46', unpublished Ph.D. thesis (Edinburgh, 1963), pp. 138–9.
90. Michael Lynch, *Scotland: A New History* (London, 1991), p. 327.
91. Gooch, *Desperate Faction?*, pp. 98, 100 ff.
92. Ibid., p. 139.
93. L. B. Smith, 'Spain and the Jacobites, 1715–16', in Cruickshanks, *Ideology*, pp. 159–78 (161–3, 168).
94. Ibid., pp. 168–70; Szechi, *Jacobites*, p. 109.
95. Lenman, *Jacobite Cause*, pp. 60–1.
96. Cf. Szechi, *Jacobites*, pp. 105–7.
97. Lenman, *Jacobite Cause*, pp. 60–4; Peter Simpson, *The Independent Highland Companies 1603–1760* (Edinburgh, 1996), p. 102.
98. Lenman, *Jacobite Cause*, pp. 65–7.
99. Szechi, *Jacobites*, p. 110; Lenman, *Jacobite Cause*, pp. 64–7.
100. Lenman, *Jacobite Cause*, pp. 69–70; C. Sanford Terry, 'The Battle of Glenshiel', *Scottish Historical Review*, 2 (1905), 412–23 (414–15, 423).
101. Smith, 'Spain', in Cruickshanks, *Ideology*, p. 171.

102. Szechi, *Jacobites*, pp. xviii–xix; Eveline Cruickshanks, 'Lord North, Christopher Layer and the Atterbury Plot: 1720–23', in Eveline Cruickshanks and Jeremy Black (eds.), *The Jacobite Challenge* (Edinburgh, 1988), pp. 92–106 (93–4).

103. Cruickshanks, 'Lord North', in Cruickshanks and Black, *Jacobite Challenge*, p. 103.

104. Szechi, *Jacobites*, p. 92.

105. Clyve Jones, 'Whigs, Jacobites and Charles Spencer, Third Earl of Sunderland', *English Historical Review* (1994), 52–73 (62–3, 70, 71, 72, 73).

106. Cruickshanks, 'Lord North', in Cruickshanks and Black, *Jacobite Challenge*, pp. 92–106; Rogers, *Whigs*, p. 315.

107. Cruickshanks, 'Lord North', in Cruickshanks and Black, *Jacobite Challenge*, pp. 92–106.

108. Ibid., pp. 96–9, 103, 104.

109. For Burlington's possible involvement, see Lawrence Smith, 'The Life of Robert Boyle, Earl of Orrery', unpublished Ph.D. thesis (University of Edinburgh, 1994) and Jane Clark, ' "Lord Burlington is Here" ', in Toby Barnard and Jane Clark (eds.), *Lord Burlington: Architecture, Art and Life* (London and Rio Grande, 1995), pp. 251–310.

110. E. P. Thompson, *Whigs and Hunters* (Harmondsworth, 1975), p. 23.

111. Jeremy Black, 'Jacobitism and British Foreign Policy, 1731–5', in Cruickshanks and Black, *Jacobite Challenge*, pp. 142–60 (156).

112. Szechi, *Jacobites*, pp. 93–4, 104–7, 111–13.

113. Valerie Rumbold, *Women in Pope's World* (Cambridge, 1989), p. 187.

114. Gregg, 'Jacobite Career', in Cruickshanks, *Ideology*, p. 189.

115. Ibid., p. 191.

116. W. H. Langhorne, *Reminiscences* (Edinburgh, 1893), p. 9.

117. *Lockhart of Carnwath*, p. 221.

118. Lesley Lewis, *Connoisseurs and Secret Agents in Eighteenth-Century Rome* (London, 1961), pp. 25, 101.

119. Ibid., pp. 23–4, 101.

120. Edward Gregg, 'The Politics of Paranoia', in Cruickshanks and Black, *Jacobite Challenge*, pp. 42–56 (43).

121. Monod, *Jacobitism*, p. 289.

122. Paul Langford, *Walpole and the Robinocracy* (Cambridge, 1986), pp. 16–17.

123. Paul Monod, 'For the King to Enjoy His Own Again', unpublished Ph.D. thesis (Yale University, 1985), p. 51; Monod, *Jacobitism*, p. 30.

124. *A Collection of Miscellany Letters Selected Out of Mist's Weekly Journal*, 2 vols. (London, 1722), I:30.

125. Monod, *Jacobitism*, p. 78.

126. Pittock, *Poetry*, Chs. 1 and 2; Monod 'For the King', pp. 133–5.

127. James Turner, *The Politics of Landscape* (Oxford, 1979); Katherine Gibson, *The Cult of Charles II*, Royal Stuart Papers no. XLVII (London, 1996).

128. Monod, 'For the King', p. 260; *Jacobitism*, p. 35.

129. Monod, *Jacobitism*, p. 71.

130. Christine Gerrard, *The Patriot Opposition to Walpole* (Oxford, 1994).

131. Monod, 'For the King', pp. 58 ff.

132. James Hogg, *The Jacobite Relics of Scotland* (Paisley, 1874), p. 85.

133. Lenman, *Jacobite Cause*, p. 68; *Lockhart of Carnwath*, p. 140.

134. Lenman, *Jacobite Cause*, p. 83.

135. *Lockhart of Carnwath*.

136. Bruce Lenman, *The Jacobite Clans of the Great Glen, 1650–1784* (London, 1984), p. 19.

137. Holmes and Szechi, *Age of Oligarchy*, p. 95.

138. J. Cornelius O'Callaghan, *History of the Irish Brigades in the Service of France* (Glasgow, 1870), p. 269.

139. Austin Clarke, 'The Poetry of Swift', in Roger McHugh and Philip Edwards (eds.), *Jonathan Swift 1667-1967: A Dublin Tercentenary Tribute* (Dublin, 1967), pp. 94–115 (109); also J.G. Simms, 'Ireland in the Age of Swift', pp. 157–75 (166) in the same volume.
140. Cf. Ian Higgins, *Swift's Politics: A Study in Disaffection* (Cambridge, 1995) and F. P. Lock, *Swift's Tory Politics* (London, 1980).
141. O'Callaghan, *History*, pp. 193, 634.
142. Monod, *Jacobitism*, p. 274.
143. Ibid., p. 270.
144. Gooch, *Desperate Faction?*, pp. 124, 131–2.
145. Edward Hughes, *North Country Life in the Eighteenth Century*, 2 vols. (Oxford, 1952, 1965), I: 6, 20, 23, 414.
146. Sharp, *Engraved Record*, pp. ix, 19, 57, 68, 134.
147. Ibid., pp. 19, 57–61, 68.
148. G. D. Henderson, *Chevalier Ramsay* (Aberdeen, 1952), pp. 140–1.
149. Ibid., p. 58.
150. F. P. Lole, 'The Scottish Jacobite Clubs', *The Jacobite*, 81 (1993), 11–16 (11).
151. T. L. Kington Oliphant, *The Jacobite Lairds of Gask* (London: The Grampian Club, 1870), pp. 101–2.
152. Duncan Fraser, *The Smugglers* (Montrose, 1971), pp. 164, 178–9.
153. Macinnes, *Clanship*, pp. 5, 24, 176.
154. *Lockhart of Carnwath*, p. xxxiv.
155. Gooch, *Desperate Faction?*, p. 112.
156. J. H. Overton, *The Nonjurors* (London, 1902), pp. 87, 89, 119, 325 ff.; Henry Broxap, *The Later Non-Jurors* (Cambridge, 1924), pp. xvii, 5, 35, 66, 302n, 335; Monod, *Jacobitism*, p. 273; Peter Nockles, '"Our Brethren of the North": The Scottish Episcopal Church and the Oxford Movement', *Journal of Ecclesiastical History* (1996), 655–82 (656).
157. Monod, *Jacobitism*, p. 287.
158. Sharp, *Engraved Record*, pp. 68, 195.
159. Lewis, *Connoisseurs*, p. 12.
160. Pittock, *Poetry*, Ch. 6.
161. Frank McLynn, *Crime and Punishment in Eighteenth-Century England* (Oxford, 1991 (1989)), p. 73; Pat Rogers, 'The Waltham Blacks and the Black Act', *Historical Journal*, 17 (1974), 465–86 (466–7, 472).
162. John Broad, 'Whigs and Deer-Stealers in Other Guises: A Return to the Origins of the Black Act', *Past and Present*, 119 (1988), 56–72 (70); Eveline Cruickshanks and Howard Erskine-Hill, 'The Waltham Black Act and Jacobitism', *Journal of British Studies*, 24 (1984), 358–65.
163. McLynn, *Crime and Punishment*, p. 57.
164. Szechi, *Jacobites*, p. 24; McLynn, *Crime and Punishment*, p. 73.
165. Szechi, *Jacobites*, p. 26.
166. Ibid.
167. Malvin Zirker, *Fielding's Social Pamphlets* (Berkeley, California, 1966), pp. 47–8.
168. Paul Hopkins, cited in Paul Monod, 'Dangerous Merchandise: Smuggling, Jacobitism and Commercial Culture in Southeast England', *Journal of British Studies*, 30:2 (1991), 150–82 (153).
169. Monod, 'Dangerous Merchandise', 161, 177.
170. McLynn, *Crime and Punishment*, p. 176.
171. This event is of course the subject of Sir Walter Scott's *Heart of Midlothian*.
172. G. M. Trevelyan, *English Social History* (London, New York and Toronto, 1945 (1942)), p. 349n; cf also Petrie, *Jacobite Movement*, pp. 201–2.
173. Monod, 'For the King', p. 428.

3 Jacobite Culture

1. John Cannon, 'Historians and the '45: "Listening to Silence"', in Michael Lynch (ed.), *Jacobitism and the '45* (London, 1995), pp. 23–31; Murray G. H. Pittock, *The Myth of the Jacobite Clans* (Edinburgh, 1995), p. 32.
2. H. T. Dickinson, 'The Jacobite Challenge', in Lynch, *Jacobitism*, pp. 7–22 pp. (11); Geoffrey Holmes, *The Trial of Doctor Sacheverell* (London, 1973); Leo Gooch, *The Desperate Faction? The Jacobites of North-East England 1688–1745* (Hull, 1995), p. 61; Murray G. H. Pittock, *Poetry and Jacobite Politics in Eighteenth-Century Britain and Ireland* (Cambridge, 1994), pp. 60–1; PRO SP 35/41/86; Joseph Leersen, *Mere Irish and Fior-Ghael* (Amsterdam and Philadelphia, 1986), pp. 254, 260.
3. Cf. Pittock, *Poetry*, Chs 1, 2, 4.
4. James S. Donnelly, Jr., 'The Whiteboy Movement, 1761–5', *Irish Historical Studies*, XXI (1977–8), 20–54 (22–3, 29).
5. Pittock, *Poetry*, Ch. 4; Paul Monod, 'Pierre's White Hat', in Eveline Cruickshanks (ed.), *By Force or By Default? The Revolution of 1688–89* (Edinburgh, 1989), 159–89 (166); John Macinnes, 'Gaelic Poetry and Historical Tradition', in Loraine MacLean of Dochgarroch (ed.), *The Middle Ages in the Highlands* (Inverness, 1981), pp. 142–63 (150).
6. Leersen, *Mere Irish*, p. 277.
7. Ibid., p. 282.
8. Donnelly, 'Whiteboy Movement', pp. 27, 30.
9. Pittock, *Poetry*, Introduction, pp. 146, 187–201; J. Cornelius O'Callaghan, *The Irish Brigades in the Service of France* (Glasgow, 1870), p. 634; Leersen, *Mere Irish*, pp. 284, 286.
10. Paul Korshin, *Typologies in England 1650–1720* (Princeton, 1982), p. 119; Murray G. H. Pittock, 'The Culture of Jacobitism', in Jeremy Black (ed.), *Culture and Society in Britain 1660–1800* (Manchester, 1997), pp. 124–45 (133).
11. Pittock, *Poetry*, pp. 11–14; for Davidic reinterpretations of kingship, see Diarmaid MacCulloch, *Thomas Cranmer* (New Haven and London, 1996).
12. Murray G. H. Pittock, 'Jacobite Culture', in Robert C. Woosnam-Savage (ed.), *1745: Charles Edward Stuart and the Jacobites* (Edinburgh, 1995), pp. 72–86 (77 ff.).
13. Annabel Paterson, *Pastoral and Ideology* (Oxford, 1988), pp. 169 ff; Steven N. Zwicker, 'The Paradoxes of Tender Conscience', *English Literary History* (1996), 851–69.
14. Paterson, *Pastoral*, p. 225; Pittock, *Poetry*, pp. 27–8, 38 ff. and Ch. 3; also in Woosnam-Savage, *1745*, 78.
15. Pittock in Woosnam-Savage, *1745*, pp. 78–9.
16. Brian J. R. Blench, 'Symbols and Sentiment: Jacobite Glass', in ibid., pp. 87–102 (93); Pittock, *Poetry*, Ch. 1; Claire Lamont, unpublished paper on the White Rose delivered at the Eighteenth-Century Scottish Studies Society/Association for Scottish Literary Studies Jacobitism, Scotland and Enlightenment Conference, Aberdeen, 1995; Paul Monod, *Jacobitism and the English People* (Cambridge, 1989), p. 210; Bishop Robert Forbes, *The Lyon in Mourning*, 3 vols., ed. Henry Paton (Edinburgh: Scottish History Society, 1895), II:254, for white rose usage in England after 1745.
17. John Broad, 'Whigs and Deer-Stealers in Other Guises: A Return to the Origins of the Black Act', *Past and Present*, 119 (1988), 56–72 (69, 70).
18. Hugh Trevor-Roper, 'The Invention of Tradition: the Highland Tradition of Scotland', in Eric Hobsbawm and Terence Ranger (eds.), *The Invention of Tradition* (Cambridge, 1983), pp. 15–41: Pittock, *Myth*, pp. 55–7, 111 ff.
19. Cf. *House of Dun* (National Trust for Scotland Guidebook), pp. 8–10.

20. *John Byrom and the Manchester Jacobites* (City of Manchester Art Gallery, 1951), pp. 9, 15–16; Roger Turner, *Manchester in 1745*, Royal Stuart Paper XLIX (London: Royal Stuart Society, 1996), pp. 16–17.

21. *Byrom*, pp. 9, 15–16; Hugh Cheape, 'The Culture and Material Culture of Jacobitism', in Lynch, *Jacobitism*, pp. 32–48 (36–7, 41).

22. Blench, 'Symbols', in Woosnam-Savage, *1745*, pp. 94–8.

23. Ibid., p. 97.

24. 'The Agreable Contrast' forms the dustjacket of Monod, *Jacobitism*; *The Highlander's RIDDLE, Or Who's in the Right: Tell if you can* is at National Library of Scotland FB.1.162.

25. David Greenwood, *William King: Tory and Jacobite* (Oxford, 1969), p. 278.

26. Rosalind K. Marshall, *Women in Scotland 1660–1780* (Edinburgh, 1979), pp. 49 ff.; Patricia Kneas Hill, *The Oglethorpe Ladies* (Atlanta, 1977), p. ix; Valerie Rumbold, *Women's Place in Pope's World* (Cambridge, 1989), pp. 2, 234. Research on the role of women in Scottish nationalism is currently being undertaken by Catriona Burness at Dundee University.

27. *Anne Finch, Countess of Winchilsea: Selected Poems*, ed. Denys Thompson (Manchester, 1987), p. 7; Richard Sharp, *The Engraved Record of the Jacobite Movement* (Aldershot, 1996), p. 139.

28. Mary Mahl and Helene Keon (eds.), *The Female Spectator: English Women Writers Before 1800* (Bloomington, London and Old Westbury, 1977), p. 179.

29. Barbara McGovern, *Anne Finch and her Poetry* (Athens, GA and London, 1992), pp. 2, 24, 58, 65, 87, 93, 95, 182, 184–5; *Anne Finch*, p. 80.

30. Monod, *Jacobitism*, p. 274.

31. Ruth Perry, *The Celebrated Mary Astell* (Chicago and London, 1986), pp. 33, 41, 172.

32. Edward Gregg, 'The Jacobite Career of John, Earl of Mar', in Eveline Cruickshanks (ed.), *Ideology and Conspiracy: Aspects of Jacobitism 1689–1759* (Edinburgh, 1982) pp. 179–200 (194); Mahl and Keon, *Female Spectator*, pp. 7–8.

33. Sharp, *Engraved Record*, pp. 143–4; Agnes Muir Mackenzie, *Scottish Pageant 1707–1802* (Edinburgh and London, 1950), pp. 246, 250–1.

34. *The Miscellany of the Spalding Club*, 1 (Aberdeen, 1841): Order Book of the Forfarshires.

35. Sir Bruce Seton of Ancrum, Bart and Jean Gordon Arnot, *The Prisoners of the '45*, 3 vols. (Edinburgh: Scottish History Society, 1928/9), III:238–9, 250–1, 354–5; Mackenzie, *Scottish Pageant*, p. 247.

36. Dianne Dugaw, *Warrior Women and Popular Balladry 1650–1850* (Cambridge, 1989), pp. 47, 52; *Miscellany of the Spalding Club*, IV (Aberdeen, 1849), pp. 324–5.

37. National Library of Scotland MS 293.

38. Nathalie Genet-Rouffiac, 'Jacobites in Paris and Saint-Germain-en-Laye', in Eveline Cruickshanks and Edward Corp (eds.), *The Stuart Court in Exile and the Jacobites* (London and Rio Grande, 1995), pp. 15–38 (27, 33, 38).

39. John Childs, 'The Abortive Invasion of 1692', in Cruickshanks and Corp, *Stuart Court*, pp. 61–72 (64).

40. L.B. Smith, 'Spain and the Jacobites, 1715–16', in Cruickshanks, *Ideology and Conspiracy*, pp. 159–78 (161, 162, 167, 168, 170–1).

41. Jane Clark, '"Lord Burlington is Here"' in Toby Barnard and Jane Clark (eds.), *Lord Burlington: Architecture, Art and Life* (London and Rio Grande, 1995), pp. 251–310 (254); Monod *Jacobitism*, p. 286.

42. Gooch, *Desperate Faction?*, p. 38.

43. Monod *Jacobitism*, p. 270.

44. Eveline Cruickshanks, 'The Political Career of the Third Earl of Burlington', in Barnard and Clark, *Lord Burlington*, pp. 201–15 (209).

45. Smith, 'Spain' in Cruickshanks, *Ideology and Conspiracy*, p. 170.
46. Gooch *Desperate Faction?*, pp. 131, 136–7, 150.
47. A.H. Millar (ed.), *Scottish Forfeited Estates Papers* (Edinburgh: Scottish History Society LVII, 1909), pp. xv ff.; Geoffrey Holmes, *Augustan England* (London, 1982), pp. 67, 93, 99.
48. Eveline Cruickshanks, 'Lord North, Christopher Layer and the Atterbury Plot: 1720–23', in Eveline Cruickshanks and Jeremy Black (eds.), *The Jacobite Challenge* (Edinburgh, 1988), pp. 92–106 (96).
49. Clark, '"Lord Burlington"', in Barnard and Clark, *Lord Burlington*, p. 284.
50. Ibid., p. 273; Cruickshanks, 'Political', in Barnard and Clark, *Lord Burlington*, pp. 213, 273.
51. Clark, '"Lord Burlington"', in Barnard and Clark, *Lord Burlington*, pp. 277, 278.
52. Frank McLynn, *Charles Edward Stuart* (London, 1988), p. 141.
53. Frank McLynn, *France and the Jacobite Rising of 1745* (Edinburgh, 1981), pp. 14, 17, 18, 26, 29, 66.
54. Ibid., pp. 30–2, 186–7; Michael Hook and Walter Ross, *The 'Forty-Five* (Edinburgh, 1995), p. 10.
55. Eveline Cruickshanks, *Political Untouchables* (London, 1979), p. 82.
56. P. D. G. Thomas, 'Jacobitism in Wales', *Welsh Historical Review*, 1:3 (1962), 279–300 (296); McLynn, *Charles Edward Stuart*, p. 189.
57. Hook and Ross, *'Forty-Five*, p. 59; John Gibson, *The Diary of John Campbell: A Scottish Banker and the 'Forty-Five* (Eastbourne, 1995), pp. 15, 22, 25, 27, 51.
58. Hook and Ross, *'Forty-Five*, p. 59; Stuart Reid, *1745: A Military History of the Last Jacobite Rising* (Staplehurst, 1996), p. 200.
59. Frank McLynn, *The Jacobite Army in England 1745* (Edinburgh, 1983), p. 29; National Library of Scotland MS 3787 (Order Book of the Appin Regiment), 48.
60. Hook and Ross, *'Forty-Five*, p. 101.
61. McLynn, *France*, pp. 188, 199, 200, 234.
62. Ibid., pp. 3, 235.
63. Ibid., pp. 99–100; (1988), 123; Hook and Ross, *'Forty-Five*.
64. McLynn, *Charles Edward Stuart*, pp. 333, 539 ff.
65. H. Montgomery Hyde, *John Law* (Amsterdam, 1948), p. 79.
66. Gordon Donaldson, *Scottish Church History* (Edinburgh, 1985), pp. 191–203; Jonathan Clark, *Samuel Johnson* (Oxford, 1994).
67. *Musae Latinae Aberdoniensis*, ed. Sir William Duguid Geddes (Aberdeen: New Spalding, 1892), p. xxiii; G. D. Henderson (ed.), *Mystics of the North East* (Aberdeen: Third Spalding Club, 1934), p. 11.
68. Cf. Pittock, *Myth*, pp. 71–2; Edward Furgol, *A Regimental History of the Covenanting Armies, 1639–1651*, (Edinburgh, 1990), pp. 61, 133, 165, 195, 220, 296 ff., 378.
69. Donaldson, *Scottish Church History*, p. 191.
70. Peter F. Anson, *Underground Catholicism in Scotland 1622–1878* (Montrose, 1970), p. 107.
71. Henderson, *Mystics*, pp. 13, 14, 15, 18, 20, 44.
72. G. D. Henderson, *Chevalier Ramsay* (Aberdeen, 1952), pp. 18, 28.
73. Murray G.H. Pittock, 'The Political Thought of Lord Forbes of Pitsligo', *Northern Scotland* (1996), 73–86.
74. Henderson, *Chevalier Ramsay*, pp. 19, 23, 31, 87, 93–100, 109, 118, 135, 155, 156, 182, 199, 207, 213, 237.
75. Ibid., p. 234.
76. Cf. Peter Nockles, '"Our Brethren of the North": The Scottish Episcopal Church and the Oxford movement', *Journal of Ecclesiastical History* (1996), 655–682 (663).
77. Sharp, *Engraved Record*, pp. 167, 184.
78. Bruce Lenman, *The Jacobite Risings in Britain 1689–1746* (London, 1980), p. 58.

4 Bonnie Prince Charlie

1. Bruce Lenman, *The Jacobite Cause* (Glasgow, 1986), pp. 78–83.
2. Colonel James Allardyce (ed.), *Historical Papers relating to the Jacobite Period 1699–1750*, 2 vols (Aberdeen: New Spalding Club, 1895/6), I:131 ff.
3. Murray G. H. Pittock, *The Myth of the Jacobite Clans* (Edinburgh, 1995), p. 80.
4. Lenman, *Jacobite Cause*, p. 84.
5. Michael Hook and Walter Ross, *The 'Forty-Five* (Edinburgh, 1995), p. 6.
6. Lenman, *Jacobite Cause*, pp. 88–9.
7. Cf. Hook and Ross, *'Forty-Five*, p. 112.
8. David Greenwood, *William King: Tory and Jacobite* (Oxford, 1969), pp. 198 ff.
9. Frank McLynn, *Charles Edward Stuart* (London, 1988), pp. 17, 37; John Stevenson, *Popular Disturbances in England 1700–1832*, 2nd edn (London and New York, 1992), p. 328.
10. Lenman, *Jacobite Cause*, p. 93.
11. McLynn, *Charles Edward Stuart*, p. 77.
12. Frank McLynn, *France and the Jacobite Rising of 1745* (Edinburgh, 1981), p. 14.
13. Eveline Cruickshanks, *Political Untouchables: The Tories and the '45* (London, 1979), pp. 33–4.
14. McLynn, *Charles Edward Stuart*, p. 71.
15. McLynn *France*, p. 18; Hook and Ross, *'Forty-Five*, p. 5.
16. Cruickshanks, *Political Untouchables*, p. 54.
17. Allardyce, *Historical Papers*, p. 177.
18. Cruickshanks, *Political Untouchables*, p. 49.
19. McLynn, *Charles Edward Stuart*, p. 106.
20. McLynn, *France*, p. 29.
21. Hook and Ross, *'Forty-Five*, p. 8.
22. Lenman, *Jacobite Cause*, p. 95.
23. Hook and Ross, *'Forty-Five*, pp. 8–10.
24. Lenman, *Jacobite Cause*, p. 96.
25. McLynn, *France*, pp. 30–3.
26. Hook and Ross *'Forty-Five*, pp. 18–19; Lenman, *Jacobite Cause*, p. 96.
27. McLynn *France*, p. 62.
28. For Lochiel's views, cf. John Gibson, *Lochiel of the '45* (Edinburgh, 1994).
29. Lenman, *Jacobite Cause*, p. 97.
30. Hook and Ross, *'Forty-Five*, p. 26.
31. Lenman, *Jacobite Cause*, p. 99.
32. McLynn, *Charles Edward Stuart*, pp. 135, 136, 137, 140–1.
33. Alexander Keith, *A Thousand Years of Aberdeen* (Aberdeen, 1972), p. 277.
34. Alistair and Henrietta Tayler, *Jacobites of Aberdeenshire and Banffshire in the Forty-Five* (Aberdeen, 1928), p. 357.
35. The Miscellany of the Spalding Club, Vol. 4 (Aberdeen: Spalding Club, 1849), p. 322.
36. Walter Biggar Blaikie, *Origins of the 'Forty-Five: And Other Papers Relating to that Rising* (Edinburgh, 1916), p. 122.
37. Donald Nicholson (ed.), *Intercepted Post* (London, 1956), p. 65.
38. *Jacobite Correspondence of the Atholl Family*, ed. Burton and Laing (Edinburgh: Abbotsford Club, 1840), p. 24.
39. Sir Bruce Seton of Ancrum, Bart and Jean Gordon Arnot, *The Prisoners of the '45*, 3 vols. (Edinburgh: Scottish History Society, 1928/9), III: 338–9.
40. *Jacobite Correspondence*, p. 25.
41. Hook and Ross, *'Forty-Five*, pp. 50–1.
42. Ibid., p. 54; W. Forbes Gray and John H. Jamieson, *A Short History of Haddington* (Edinburgh, 1944), p. 58; Pittock, *Myth*.

43. Hook and Ross, *'Forty-Five*, pp. 33 ff.; *Extracts from the Council Register of the Burgh of Aberdeen 1643–1747* (Edinburgh: Scottish Burgh Records Society, 1872), pp. 375–6.
44. Nicholson, *Intercepted Post*, p. 10.
45. Allan Macinnes, *Clanship, Commerce and the House of Stuart 1603–1788* (East Linton, 1996), pp. 167–8; Hook and Ross, *'Forty-Five*, pp. 63–6.
46. Allardyce, *Historical Papers*, I: 188-9; Hook and Ross, *'Forty-Five*, p. 14.
47. John Gibson, *Edinburgh in the '45* (Edinburgh, 1995), p. 34.
48. Seton and Arnot, *Prisoners*, III: 292–3.
49. McLynn, *Charles Edward Stuart*, p. 149.
50. Hugh Cheape, 'The Culture and Material Culture of Jacobitism', in Michael Lynch (ed.), *Jacobitism and the '45* (London, 1995), pp. 32–49 (38, 39, 41).
51. Alistair and Henrietta Tayler, *Jacobites of Aberdeenshire and Banffshire in the Rising of 1715* (Edinburgh and London, 1934); Seton and Arnot, *Prisoners*, III: 316–17.
52. Frank McLynn, *The Jacobite Army in England* (Edinburgh, 1983), p. 102.
53. Ibid., p. 10.
54. Hook and Ross, *'Forty-Five*, p. 62.
55. McLynn, *Jacobite Army*, pp. 24–5; McLynn, *Charles Edward Stuart*, pp. 168, 175.
56. Ibid., pp. 43–4, 66, 76, 77, 89.
57. Hook and Ross, *'Forty-Five*, p. 73.
58. McLynn, *Jacobite Army*, pp. 118–20.
59. McLynn, *Charles Edward Stuart*, pp. 172, 185.
60. Lenman, *Jacobite Cause*, pp. 101, 107.
61. McLynn, *Jacobite Army*, pp. 125–31; Rupert C. Jarvis, *Collected Papers on the Jacobite Risings*, 2 vols. (Manchester, 1972), II: ix–x.
62. Jarvis, *Collected Papers*, II: 100, 221–32.
63. McLynn, *Jacobite Army*, pp. 79, 125–31.
64. Cf. Stuart Reid, *1745: A Military History of the Last Jacobite Rising* (Staplehurst, 1996).
65. Cf. McLynn, *Jacobite Army*, pp. 125 ff.
66. Cf. Diarmaid McCulloch, *Thomas Cranmer* (New Haven and London, 1996).
67. Murray G. H. Pittock, *The Invention of Scotland* (London and New York, 1991), p. 143.
68. Hook and Ross, *'Forty-Five*, p. 79.
69. Ibid., p. 79.
70. National Library of Scotland MS 17514 f. 127.
71. Richard Sharp, *The Engraved Record of the Jacobite Movement* (Aldershot, 1996), p. 186; Eveline Cruickshanks, *The Oglethorpes: A Jacobite Family 1688–1760*, Royal Stuart Paper XLV (London: Royal Stuart Society, 1995), p. 6.
72. Hook and Ross, *'Forty-Five*, pp. 81, 87.
73. McLynn, *Jacobite Army*, pp. 62–3.
74. Allardyce, *Historical Papers*, II:xx.
75. McLynn, *Jacobite Army*, p. 63.
76. McLynn, *France*, p. 111.
77. Jeremy Black, *An Illustrated History of Eighteenth-century Britain* (Manchester, 1996), p. 22.
78. *Jacobite Correspondence*, p. 116.
79. Seton and Arnot, *Prisoners*, II: 160–1; III: 386–7, 395.
80. Reid, *Military History*, pp. 84, 86–8.
81. McLynn, *France*, pp. 108, 115; McLynn, *Charles Edward Stuart*, p. 165.
82. Jarvis, *Collected Papers*, pp. 224–5; Hook and Ross, *'Forty-Five*, pp. 87 ff.
83. McLynn, *France*, pp. 134, 138, 141, 172.
84. Daniel Szechi, *The Jacobites* (Manchester, 1994), p. 102.
85. Reid, *Military History*, pp. 91n, 116.
86. Ibid., pp. 200–1.
87. McLynn, *Charles Edward Stuart*, p. 161.
88. *Jacobite Correspondence*, p. 187.

89. Jeremy Black, 'Military Aspects of the '45', in Lynch, *Jacobitism*, pp. 49–57 (55).
90. Reid, *Military History*, p. 116.
91. McLynn, *Charles Edward Stuart*, pp. 225–30.
92. Nicholson, *Intercepted Post*, p. 13.
93. McLynn, *Charles Edward Stuart*, pp. 235–6.
94. Gibson, *Lochiel*, for Lochiel's stand.
95. McLynn, *Charles Edward Stuart*, p. 251.
96. Lenman, *Jacobite Cause*, p. 109.
97. Reid, *Military History*, p. 117; McLynn, *Charles Edward Stuart*, p. 234.
98. Hook and Ross, *'Forty-Five*, p. 108.
99. Reid, *Military History*, pp. 156, 160.
100. Hook and Ross, *'Forty-Five*, p. 109.
101. Taylers, *Jacobites . . . in the Forty-Five*, pp. 186, 285.
102. Ibid., pp. 418 ff.
103. Hook and Ross, *'Forty-Five*, pp. 109, 112.
104. Reid, *Military History*, pp. 201–2.
105. Iain Gordon Brown and Hugh Cheape (eds.), *Witness to Rebellion: John Maclean's Journal of the 'Forty-Five and the Penicuik Drawings* (East Linton, 1996); *The Miscellany of the Spalding Club*, Vol. 1 (Aberdeen, 1841), Order Book of the Forfarshires; Allan Carswell, '"The Most Despicable Enemy that Are" – the Jacobite Army of the '45', in Robert C. Woosnam-Savage (ed.), *1745: Charles Edward Stuart and the Jacobites* (Edinburgh, 1995), pp. 29–40 (36).
106. Seton and Arnot, *Prisoners*, II: 228–9.
107. Reid, *Military History*, pp. 99, 205–7, 210n.
108. Seton and Arnot, *Prisoners*, III: 302–3.
109. National Library of Scotland MS 17514 ff. 55–6; Nicholson, *Intercepted Post*, p. 142.
110. Reid, *Military History*, pp. 205–7.
111. *Jacobite Correspondence*, pp. 96–7, 101.
112. *Miscellany of the Spalding Club*, Vol. 1 (1841), 291 (Day Book of Captain James Stuart).
113. McLynn, *Jacobite Army*, p. 97.
114. Jean McCann, 'The Organisation of the Jacobite Army, 1745–46', unpublished Ph.D. thesis (University of Edinburgh, 1963), pp. 135, 137, 141, 148.
115. Blaikie, *Origins*, p. 126.
116. Reid, *Military History*, p. 5.
117. National Library of Scotland MS 17514 f. 244.
118. Gibson, *Lochiel*; Cruickshanks, *Political Untouchables*, p. 100.
119. Katherine Tomasson and Francis Buist, *Battles of the '45* (London, 1962), p. 205.
120. Frank McLynn, 'Ireland and the Jacobite Rising of 1745', *Irish Sword*, 13 (1979), 339–52.
121. McLynn, *France*, pp. 184, 194.
122. Bruce Lenman, *The Jacobite Clans of the Great Glen 1650–1784* (London, 1984), p. 163.
123. S. J. Connolly, *Religion, Law and Power: The Making of Protestant Ireland 1660–1760* (Oxford, 1992), p. 246; Frank McLynn, 'Ireland and the Jacobite Rising', 339–52 (340, 342, 348).
124. Frank McLynn, '"Good Behaviour": Irish Catholics and the Jacobite Rising of 1745', *Eire-Ireland*, XVI:2 (1981), 43–58 (50, 53); McLynn, 'Ireland and the Jacobite Rising', 343.
125. Hook and Ross, *'Forty-Five*, p. 120.
126. McLynn, *Charles Edward Stuart*, pp. 275, 304.
127. Seton and Arnot, *Prisoners*, I: 8, 94.
128. Ibid., I: 294; Hook and Ross, *'Forty-Five*, p. 119.
129. Hook and Ross, *'Forty-Five*, p. 127.

130. Seton and Arnot, *Prisoners*, I: 224; Blaikie, *Origins of the 'Forty-Five*, pp. 111–64 (156).
131. Hook and Ross, *'Forty-Five*, p. 128.
132. Black, 'Military Aspects', in Lynch, *Jacobitism*, p. 53.
133. Cruickshanks, *Political Untouchables*, p. 80.
134. McLynn, *Charles Edward Stuart*, p. 195.
135. *Jacobite Correspondence*, p. 80.
136. McLynn, *Charles Edward Stuart*, p. 195.
137. Hook and Ross, *'Forty-Five*, p. 75; McLynn, *Jacobite Army*, p. 92.
138. Black, 'Military Aspects', in Lynch, *Jacobitism*, p. 53; McLynn, *Jacobite Army*, p. 77.
139. McLynn, *Jacobite Army*, p. 74.
140. National Library of Scotland MS 17514 f. 144.
141. Szechi, *Jacobites*, p. xxiii.
142. Stevenson, *Popular Disturbances*, p. 78.
143. Cruickshanks, *Political Untouchables*, pp. 88, 101.
144. Jarvis, *Collected Papers*, II:85; Stevenson, *Popular Disturbances*, p. 31.
145. McLynn, *France*, pp. 81, 106.
146. McLynn, *Charles Edward Stuart*, p. 170.
147. McLynn, *Jacobite Army*, pp. 14–15.
148. Lenman, *Jacobite Cause*, p. 113.
149. McLynn, *France*, pp. 196–7.
150. Ian Christie, 'The Tory Party, Jacobitism and the 'Forty-Five: A Note', *Historical Journal*, 30:4 (1987), 921–31 (923n, 930–1).
151. Nicholas Rogers, *Whigs and Cities* (Oxford, 1989), pp. 379–80.
152. Jarvis, *Collected Papers*, II:28.
153. McLynn, *Jacobite Army*, p. 107.
154. Bob Harris, 'England's Provincial Newspapers and the Jacobite Rebellion of 1745–46', *History*, 80 (1995), 5–21 (14, 15, 19, 20).
155. Keith Feiling, *The Second Tory Party* (London, 1938), p. 10.
156. McLynn, *Jacobite Army*, pp. 66, 70, 105, 115, 131.
157. Connolly, *Religion*, p. 158; Gerard O'Brien, *Catholic Ireland in the Eighteenth Century: Collected Essays of Maureen Wall* (Dublin, 1989), p. 58.
158. Connolly, *Religion*, p. 228.
159. J. Cornelius O'Callaghan, *History of the Irish Brigades in the Service of France* (Glasgow, 1870), p. vii.
160. Ibid., p. 33.
161. T. W. Moody and W. E. Vaughan, *A New History of Ireland 4: Eighteenth-Century Ireland 1691–1800* (Oxford, 1986), p. 637n; Richard Hayes, 'Irish Casualties in the French Military Service', *Irish Sword*, 1 (1949–53), 198–201 (198, 199).
162. Connolly, *Religion*, pp. 236–9.
163. Moody and Vaughan, *New History*, p. 636.
164. McLynn, 'Good Behaviour', 49.
165. Christopher Duffy, *The Wild Goose and the Eagle: A Life of Marshal von Browne 1707–1757* (London, 1964), pp. 2–3.
166. Hayes, 'Irish Casualties', 198; Duffy, *Wild Goose*, p. 3.
167. Duffy, *Wild Goose*, pp. 7, 15.
168. Micheline Walsh, 'Lieutenant-General Ricardo Wall (1694–1778)', *Irish Sword*, 2 (1954–6), 88–94 (93); Frank McLynn, *The Jacobites* (London, 1985), pp. 130 ff.; Frank Forde, 'The Ultonia Regiment of the Spanish Army', *Irish Sword*, 12, 36–41 (36).
169. Mark McLaughlin, *The Wild Geese* (London, 1980), pp. 9, 28.
170. Richard Hayes, 'Irishmen in the Naval Services of Continental Europe', *Irish Sword*, 1 (1949–53), 304–15.
171. Christopher Duffy, 'The Irish at Hochkirch, 14 October 1758', *Irish Sword*, 12, 212–20 (212, 218).
172. McLynn, *Charles Edward Stuart*, p. 121.

173. McLaughlin, *Wild Geese*, p. 14.
174. Moody and Vaughan, *New History*, pp. 635, 637.
175. Sir Charles Petrie, Bart, 'The Irish Brigade at Fontenoy', *Irish Sword*, 1 (1949–53), 166–72 (171).
176. Sir Patrick Cadell, 'Irish Soldiers in India', *Irish Sword*, 1 (1949–53), 75–9 (75); W. S. Murphy, 'The Irish Brigade of France at the Siege of Savannah, 1779', *Irish Sword*, 2 (1954–56), 95–102 (100); Moody and Vaughan, *New History*, p. 637.
177. Szechi, *Jacobites*, p. 133.
178. National Library of Scotland MS 98 f. 39.
179. Murphy, 'Irish Brigade', p. 100.
180. McLaughlin, *Wild Geese*, pp. 24, 33.

5 The Jacobite Diaspora

1. Frank McLynn, *Charles Edward Stuart* (London, 1988), pp. 396–8.
2. Ibid., p. 406.
3. John Gibson, *Lochiel of the '45* (Edinburgh, 1994), pp. 157, 163 ff.
4. Daniel Szechi, *The Jacobites* (Manchester, 1994), pp. 150–1.
5. Frank McLynn, 'An Eighteenth-Century Scots Republic ? – An Unlikely Project from Absolutist France', *Scottish Historical Review*, 59 (1980), 177–81.
6. James J. Sack, *From Jacobite to Conservative* (Cambridge, 1993), p. 8.
7. Sir Charles Petrie, *The Jacobite Movement: The Last Phase*, revised edn (London, 1950), p. 171; for the 1759 attempt, see Claude Nordmann, 'Choiseul and The Last Jacobite Attempt of 1759', in Eveline Cruickshanks (ed.), *Ideology and Conspiracy: Aspects of Jacobitism, 1689–1759* (Edinburgh, 1982), pp. 201–17.
8. Lesley Lewis, *Connoisseurs and Secret Agents in Eighteenth-Century Rome* (London, 1961), pp. 217, 234.
9. McLynn, *Charles Edward Stuart*, p. 519.
10. Sir Charles Petrie, *The Jacobite Movement: The First Phase*, revised edn, 2 vols. (London, 1948, 1950), p. 73; Petrie, *Last Phase*, pp. 173–5.
11. Allan Macinnes, *Clanship, Commerce and the House of Stuart 1603–1788* (East Linton, 1996), pp. 204.
12. Paul Monod, *Jacobitism and the English People* (Cambridge, 1989), p. 219.
13. McLynn, *Charles Edward Stuart*, p. 531.
14. National Library of Scotland Deposit 344/1 (Transcript of 'Thomas Muir of Huntershill' by George Pratt Insh).
15. Petrie, *Last Phase*, p. 182.
16. Cf. Noel Woolf, *The Medallic Record of the Jacobite Movement* (London, 1988), p. 132–6.
17. Frank McLynn, *The Jacobites* (London, 1985), pp. 130 ff. ; Richard Sharp, *The Engraved Record of the Jacobite Movement* (Aldershot, 1996), p. 163.
18. McLynn, *Jacobites*, p. 130; in 1989 I rather touchingly heard an Israeli professor sing of Keith in a song he remembered from his 1930s German childhood.
19. For Keith's own memoir, see *A Fragment of a Memoir of Field-Marshal James Keith, Written by Himself 1714–1734* (Edinburgh: Spalding Club, 1843).
20. McLynn, *Jacobites*, pp. 77, 135–6.
21. Bishop Robert Forbes, *The Lyon in Mourning*, ed. Henry Paton, 3 vols. (Edinburgh: Scottish History Society, 1895), II, pp. 259–60; III, pp. 198–9.
22. McLynn, *Jacobites*, pp. 135–6.
23. Ibid., p. 138.
24. H. Montgomery Hyde, *John Law* (Amsterdam, 1948), pp. 10, 15, 40, 47, 146–7, 178, 196; Fiona Robertson, 'Of Speculation and Return: Scott's Jacobites, John Law, and the Company of the West', in *Scottish Literary Journal* (forthcoming 1997).

25. McLynn, *Jacobites*, p. 138.
26. A. E. Smith, *Colonists in Bondage* (University of North Carolina at Chapel Hill, 1947), pp. 201–2.
27. Alistair and Henrietta Tayler, *Jacobites of Aberdeenshire and Banffshire in the Forty-Five* (Aberdeen, 1928), p. 416.
28. McLynn, *Jacobites*, p. 130.
29. Sir Bruce Seton of Ancrum, Bart and Jean Gordon Arnot, *The Prisoners of the '45*, 3 vols. (Edinburgh: Scottish History Society, 1928/9), II: 142–3, 318–19.
30. Mary Beacock Fryer, *Allan Maclean: Jacobite General* (Toronto, 1987).
31. Stephen Wood, *The Auld Alliance* (Edinburgh, 1989), p. 90.
32. John Gibson, *Playing the Scottish Card: The Franco-Jacobite Invasion of 1708* (Edinburgh, 1988), p. 105.
33. James Michael Hill, *Celtic Warfare 1595–1763* (Edinburgh, 1986), p. 168.
34. Alastair Livingstone of Bachuil *et al.* (eds.), *Muster Roll of Prince Charles Edward Stuart's Army 1745–46* (Aberdeen, 1984), p. 114.
35. *Lyon*, I: 13, 47; III: 163-5.
36. *Lyon*, III: 305–7; Murray G. H. Pittock, *The Myth of the Jacobite Clans* (Edinburgh, 1995), p. 105.
37. Revd J. B. Craven, *History of the Episcopal Church in the Diocese of Moray* (London, 1889), pp. 121–2.
38. *Lyon*, III: 327.
39. John Doran, *London in the Jacobite Times*, 2 vols. (London, 1877), II: 354.
40. Macinnes, *Clanship*, pp. 211–12.
41. Allan Macinnes, 'The Aftermath of the '45', in Robert C. Woosnam-Savage (ed.), *1745: Charles Edward Stuart and the Jacobites* (Edinburgh, 1995), pp. 103–13 (109).
42. National Library of Scotland MS 17505 f. 65.
43. John Robertson, *The Scottish Enlightenment and the Militia Issue* (Edinburgh, 1985), p. 99; Murray G. H. Pittock, 'Forging North Britain in the Age of Macpherson', *Edinburgh Review*, 93(1995), 125–39.
44. John Gibson, *Edinburgh in the '45*, (Edinburgh, 1995), p. 60.
45. *Lyon*, II: 218, 221–2; III:309.
46. *Lyon*, II: 254.
47. Livingstone of Bachuil, *Muster Roll*, pp. 195–6.
48. Monod, *Jacobitism*, pp. 217, 219, 229, 263.
49. Cf. T. L. Kingston Oliphant, *The Jacobite Lairds of Gask* (London: Grampian Club, 1870).
50. Gerard J. Cairns, 'Bonnie Prince Charlie and a 'That', in *Jacobite or Covenanter: Which Tradition? A Scottish Republican Debate* (n.p., Scottish Republican Forum, 1994), pp. 37–44 (37).
51. Doran, *London*, II:376.
52. Monod, *Jacobitism*, p. 341.
53. Doran, *London*, II:379.
54. David Greward, 'Auld Dubrach', *Aberdeen Journal: Notes and Queries*, III (1910), 134-6.
55. Jeremy Black, *Eighteenth-Century Europe 1700–1789* (Basingstoke: Macmillan, 1990), pp. 171, 174, 175–6, 179, 181, 182.
56. Ibid., p. 178.
57. McLynn, *Jacobites*, pp. 80, 86–7.
58. Cf. Murray G. H. Pittock, *The Invention of Scotland* (London and New York, 1991), Chs. 3 and 4.
59. Black, *Eighteenth-Century Europe*, pp. xiv, 283, 363.

FURTHER READING

Black, Jeremy, *Culloden and the '45* (Stroud, 1990).
Clark, J. C. D., *English Society 1688–1832* (Cambridge, 1985).
Cruickshanks, Eveline, *Political Untouchables* (London, 1979).
Cruickshanks, Eveline (ed.), *By Force or By Default ?* (Edinburgh, 1989).
Cruickshanks, Eveline (ed.), *Ideology and Conspiracy* (Edinburgh, 1982).
Cruickshanks, Eveline, and J. Black (eds.), *The Jacobite Challenge* (Edinburgh, 1988).
Cruickshanks, Eveline, and E. Corp (eds.), *The Stuart Court in Exile and the Jacobites* (London and Rio Grande, 1995).
Donaldson, William, *The Jacobite Song* (Aberdeen, 1988).
Gibson, John, *Playing the Scottish Card: The Franco-Jacobite Invasion of 1708* (Edinburgh, 1988).
Gibson, John, and B. Lenman (eds.), *The Jacobite Threat – England, Scotland, Ireland, France: A Sourcebook* (Edinburgh, 1990).
Gooch, Leo, *The Desperate Faction ? The Jacobites of North-East England 1688–1745* (Hull, 1995).
Gregg, Edward, *Queen Anne* (London, 1980).
Hopkins, Paul, *Glencoe and the End of the Highland War* (Edinburgh, 1986).
Jarvis, Rupert C. (ed.), *Collected Papers on the Jacobite Risings*, 2 vols. (Manchester, 1972).
Lenman, Bruce, *The Jacobite Risings in Britain, 1689–1746* (London, 1980).
Linklater, Magnus and Hesketh, Christian, *For King and Conscience: John Graham of Claverhouse, Viscount Dundee* (London, 1989).
Lynch, Michael (ed.), *Jacobitism and the '45* (London, 1995).
Macinnes, Allan, *Clanship, Commerce and the House of Stuart 1603–1788* (East Linton, 1996).
McLynn, Frank, *France and the Jacobite Rising of 1745* (Edinburgh, 1981).
McLynn, Frank, *The Jacobite Army in England 1745* (Edinburgh, 1983).
McLynn, Frank, *Charles Edward Stuart* (London, 1988).
Monod, Paul, *Jacobitism and the English People* (Cambridge, 1989).
O'Callaghan, John Cornelius, *History of the Irish Brigades in the Service of France* (Glasgow, 1870).
Pittock, Murray G. H., *The Invention of Scotland:The Stuart Myth and the Scottish Identity, 1638 to the Present* (London and New York, 1991).
Pittock, Murray G. H., *The Myth of the Jacobite Clans* (Edinburgh, 1995).
Reid, Stuart, *1745: A Military History* (Staplehurst, 1996).
Rogers, Nicholas, *Whigs and Cities* (Oxford, 1989).
Simms, J. G., *Jacobite Ireland* (London, 1969).
Smith, Annette M., *Jacobite Estates of the Forty-Five* (Edinburgh, 1982).
Szechi, Daniel, *Jacobitism and Tory Politics 1710–14* (Edinburgh, 1984).
Szechi, Daniel (ed.), *'Scotland's Ruine!' George Lockhart of Carnwath's Memoirs of the Union* (Aberdeen, 1995).
Tayler, Alistair and H. Tayler, *1715: The Story of the Rising* (London and Edinburgh, 1936).
Woolf, Noel, *The Medallic Record of the Jacobite Movement* (London, 1988).
Woosnam-Savage, Robert C. (ed.), *1745: Charles Edward Stuart and the Jacobites* (Edinburgh, 1995).

INDEX